Market Analysis
for Valuation Appraisals

Readers of this text may be interested in the following related texts:
The Appraisal of Real Estate, tenth edition
The Dictionary of Real Estate Appraisal, third edition
Hotels and Motels: A Guide to Market Analysis, Investment Analysis, and Valuations
The Office Building From Concept to Investment Reality
Shopping Center Appraisal and Analysis
Subdivision Analysis

For a catalog of Appraisal Institute publications, contact the PR/Marketing Department of the Appraisal Institute, 875 North Michigan Avenue, Chicago, Illinois 60611-1980.

Market Analysis
for Valuation Appraisals

Stephen F. Fanning, MAI
Terry V. Grissom, MAI, PhD
Thomas D. Pearson, MAI, PhD

Appraisal Institute
875 North Michigan Avenue
Chicago, Illinois 60611-1980

Reviewers: Howard C. Gelbtuch, MAI
                 Hugh F. Kelley
                 Richard Marchitelli, MAI
                 Robert S. Martin, MAI, SRA
                 Thomas A. Motta, MAI, SRA
                 Gary P. Taylor, MAI, SRA
                 Paula O. Thoreen, MAI

Vice President, Publications: Christopher Bettin
Manager, Book Development: Michael R. Milgrim, PhD
Editor: Stephanie Shea-Joyce
Manager, Design/Production: Julie B. Beich

For Educational Purposes Only
The material presented in this text has been reviewed by members of the Appraisal Institute, but the opinions and procedures set forth by the authors are not necessarily endorsed as the only methodology consistent with proper appraisal practice. While a great deal of care has been taken to provide accurate and current information, neither the Appraisal Institute nor its editors and staff assume responsibility for the accuracy of the data contained herein. Further, the general principles and conclusions presented in this text are subject to local, state, and federal laws and regulations, court cases, and any revisions of the same. This publication is sold for educational purposes with the understanding that the publisher is not engaged in rendering legal, accounting, or any other professional service.

Nondiscrimination Policy
The Appraisal Institute advocates equal employment and nondiscrimination in the appraisal profession and conducts its activities without regard to race, color, sex, religion, national origin, or handicap status.

Library of Congress Cataloging-in-Publication Data
Fanning, Stephen F.
        Market analysis for valuation appraisals/by Stephen F. Fanning, Terry Grissom,
    Thomas D. Pearson.
            p.   cm.
        Includes bibliographical references and index.
        ISBN 0-922154-18-X
        1. Real property—Valuation. 2. Real estate business.
    I. Grissom, Terry V. (Terry Vaughn) II. Pearson, Thomas D. III. Title.
    HD1387.F33 1994
    333.33'2—dc20

C O N T E N T S

PART I

Concepts and Techniques of Market Analysis

PART II

Market Analysis Applications

v

TABLE OF CONTENTS

PART III

Highest and Best Use Applications

FOREWORD

———————

Over the past decade, the appraisal community and other real estate-related professions have come to place increased emphasis on real estate market analysis. This new emphasis underscores the urgent need for a text that directly relates market analysis to real estate appraising. Although there is a substantial amount of technical literature available on the analysis of real estate markets, the existing literature does not generally address the specific concerns and questions of appraisers. I believe *Market Analysis for Valuation Appraisals* will meet the needs of appraisers in the field, and I take considerable pleasure in introducing this very timely text.

Market Analysis for Valuation Appraisals reflects the combined efforts of three appraisal specialists, and five years were devoted to its development. The authors of this text helped develop the Appraisal Institute course on highest and best use and market analysis. Feedback from students, instructors, and practitioners has contributed much to the elaboration and refinement of the market analysis process presented. Tempered by ever-changing market conditions over the past five years, the methodology that the book prescribes has already stood the test of time. The scope of coverage, the wealth of detailed explanation, and the step-by-step development of the applications all recommend this work as an especially welcome addition to any appraiser's library.

Douglas C. Brown, MAI

1994 President
Appraisal Institute

ABOUT THE AUTHORS

S teve Fanning, MAI, AICP, CRE, is the owner of a consulting firm which specializes in market analysis, highest and best use studies, and valuation. Fanning also has considerable experience in urban planning and community development, directing several planning agencies in northern Texas. He holds a bachelor's degree and a master's degree and has been an adjunct professor in real estate at the University of North Texas. Fanning has contributed to *The Appraisal Journal* and been active in the development and teaching of Appraisal Institute courses.

Terry Grissom , MAI, CRE, is national research director of real estate valuation services at Price Waterhouse. He has more than 20 years of experience in valuation, market and economic analysis, and real estate counseling. Grissom holds a bachelor's degree, two master's degrees, and a doctorate in business, real estate, and urban land economics. He has been affiliated with Texas A&M University and the University of Texas, and has lectured and written extensively.

Thomas D. Pearson, MAI, AICP, is the principal of a real estate consulting firm in Denton, Texas, which specializes in environmental and condemnation valuation and litigation support. He has a PhD in economics and has taught at several universities, including Georgia State University and the University of North Texas. Pearson is a regular contributor to academic and scholarly journals and has authored or co-authored three books. He has served on committees of the Appraisal Institute and The Appraisal Foundation.

PART I

Concepts and Techniques
of Market Analysis

INTRODUCTION

While market analysis is fundamental to real estate valuation, the tools and techniques of market analysis are often discussed in a highly technical and recondite manner. Practitioners have long needed a text that presents market analysis as an integrated, "hands-on" process. It is the authors' hope that this book will fill the current void in practical literature dealing with real estate market analysis. Market analysis is essentially a multistep study process analogous to the problem-solving approaches employed in other areas of economic and scientific investigation. In real estate market analysis, the productive attributes of a parcel of real estate are examined vis-a-vis the demand for the particular category of real estate and the supply of competitive properties within the defined real estate market.

This book focuses on the role of market analysis in real estate valuation. By identifying the components of value in a real estate parcel, market analysis provides critical support for the value estimate in two ways. First, the findings of real estate market analysis provide data required in the application of the three approaches to value. Second, the market forecast developed in market analysis is essential to estimating the capture rate and timing of prospective uses. This book introduces a six-step process for market analysis. The six steps include analysis of property productivity, market definition, demand analysis, supply analysis, comparison of supply and demand, and development of a subject capture estimate.

This book is divided into three parts plus an epilogue. The chapters in the first part provide an overview of the concepts and techniques of real estate market analysis. The six-step process is conceptually developed in this first part of the book. In the second and third parts of the book, case studies illustrating the market analysis process are presented. More specifically, the three chapters in Part II demonstrate how the conclusions of the market analyses of three existing, income-producing properties are used to support market value estimates. In Part III the conclusions of the market analyses of three more case study properties are applied to make highest and best use decisions. The concluding chapter, or epilogue, addresses the application of market analysis concepts in the three approaches to value.

The 11 chapters in Part I introduce concepts and techniques that will be encountered in the subsequent case studies. Special attention has been given to practical concerns. Chapter 1 examines the role of market analysis in an appraisal and identifies the three general problem types or scenarios that market analysis investigates. The extent of the market study process and the level of detail appropriate to a given appraisal assignment are addressed in Chapter 2. A significant distinction is made between techniques based on inferred or trend analysis and those that involve fundamental analysis or forecasting. Chapter 2 describes four levels of market analysis and provides a checklist to evaluate the level required, given the nature of the appraisal assignment.

Chapters 3, 4, and 5 discuss the productive attributes of real estate, which include physical, legal/regulatory, locational, and amenity characteristics. Understanding a property's productive attributes helps the appraiser identify the property's market, specifically the demand for the property type and the supply of competitive properties. Chapter 4 develops the concept of situs and Chapter 5 discusses the models of urban growth advanced by the social ecologists and rent theorists.

Chapter 6 introduces economic base analysis and offers useful techniques for estimating the population and employment of a community. The chapter demonstrates the various ways in which employment multipliers are estimated and applied. Chapter 7 focuses on the definition and segmentation of real estate markets, while Chapter 8 explores the techniques used to forecast market demand for retail space, office space, and housing. In Chapter 9 the components in the inventory of the competition are examined, and techniques for calculating the projected competitive supply are explained. Chapter 10 discusses types and sources of data, provides models that can be used to refine and test data, and analyzes problem situations that the appraiser may encounter in compiling data. The final chapter in Part I, Chapter 11, considers the effect of market cycles and changing market conditions on property value.

Market analysis is an eclectic field of study that draws on a number of other disciplines. These related fields include economics, statistical analysis, demographics, city planning, and location theory. Each field employs its own technical terms and usage, which may seem rather esoteric to a novice. The terminology employed in this book necessarily reflects the hybrid nature of market analysis. To assist the reader, terms such as *secular trend*, *frictional vacancy*, *centroid*, *gravity model*, and *location quotient* are defined where they first appear in the text. The topical bibliography at the back of the book will prove useful to readers who want to consult key surveys and anthologies on market analysis, technical literature from ancillary disciplines, or monographs on the market analysis of specific property types.

CHAPTER OBJECTIVES

⟫-0-⟪

- To explain how market analysis relates to value theory, valuation theory, and appraisal theory
- To identify the role of market analysis in the appraisal process
- To compare the scientific method to the appraisal process, and thereby clarify the role of market analysis in appraisal
- To characterize three general scenarios for market analysis—i.e., a site in search of a use or market, a use or market in search of a site, and the consideration of real property as an alternative investment instrument

CHAPTER ONE

---•◦•---

Market Research in
Real Estate Appraisal

arket analysis is a basic component of the appraisal process, yet it has received scant attention in existing appraisal literature.[1] This book will examine market analysis concepts and provide specific examples of how market analysis can be directly integrated into the appraisal process.

APPRAISAL THEORY AND MARKET ANALYSIS

Market analysis is essential to appraisals because it is the foundation for economic decision making. Economics is concerned with choices made in a competitive environment under the constraint of limited resources. In a real estate context, market analysis examines the productive attributes of a property vis-a-vis the relationship of supply and demand, delineating the market in which the property competes. Appraisal is concerned with the estimation of value, which may be approached on three distinct theoretical levels: value theory, valuation theory, and appraisal theory.[2]

Value theory and valuation theory are traditionally defined by economics. Value theory is concerned with establishing the basis of an asset's worth. It iden-

---

1. General appraisal books and articles include little treatment of market analysis in the alternative appraisal processes presented. Market concerns are implicitly addressed in the data collection steps, but data collection alone does not imply market analysis. Market issues are identified in these texts: *The Appraisal of Real Estate*, 10th ed. (Chicago: Appraisal Institute, 1992); "Valuation" by Fred Case in *Perspectives in Urban Land Economics* (Vancouver: The University of British Columbia Press, 1974); and *The Appraisal of 25 N. Pinckney* by James A. Graaskamp (Madison, Wis.: Landmark Inc., 1977).

2. Terry V. Grissom, "Value Definition: Its Place in the Appraisal Process," *The Appraisal Journal* (April 1985), 217-225.

tifies why real estate has worth. Valuation theory focuses on the techniques or methods through which value is measured, estimated, or forecast. Elaboration of the three approaches to estimating value has been the principal domain of valuation theory. Appraisal theory is the logical process linking valuation theory to value theory, as applied to a land parcel put to a specific use.[3] Appraisal theory refers to a procedure in which an individual identifies a problem, formulates a hypothesis, collects and classifies data, applies a methodology, and develops a conclusion.

Appraisal theory has evolved with the appraisal profession and been influenced by ongoing regulation, including the R-41 Memoranda Series of the Federal Home Loan Bank Board, the mandates of the Comptroller of the Currency, and the Competitive Equality Banking Act of 1987 (CEBA). The culminating package of regulatory legislation was the Financial Institutions Reform, Recovery and Enforcement Act of 1989 (FIRREA).

These regulations have fostered a growing interest in appraisal theory, which stresses the relationship between value factors and valuation techniques. Nevertheless, most current appraisal literature deals with valuation techniques.[4]

Utility and Scarcity—Value Components of Supply

In value theory *utility* refers to the function or use of a parcel of land. Market analysis considers the alternative uses of a property and the market analysis component of an appraisal investigates the support for a use or range of uses of a particular site. Determining whether or not there is market support for a probable use, i.e., if the use is financially feasible, is a function of market analysis.[5]

In value theory, *scarcity* increases the value of a commodity, asset, or resource in limited supply. Real estate may be described by all three terms, depending on the property type and the problem situation.[6]

As analysis of market absorption reveals, a large quantity of properties available in a market characterized by relatively stable demand generally tends to reduce the probable selling price of a typical property. Alternatively, a limited quantity of competitive properties can cause real estate prices to rise.

Desire and Effective Purchasing Power—Value Components of Demand

In value theory, *effective demand* refers to the ability of people who desire a good or commodity to act upon their desire. Consumers' ability to spend is con-

---

3. Ibid.
4. An investigation of the topics identified in *Bibliography of Appraisal Literature (1981-1986)* and updates to this publication for 1987, 1988, and 1989, performed by the Appraisal Institute's Research Department revealed that only approximately 40 articles out of 3000, or 1.3%, were concerned with value theory and only 8 or .26% addressed appraisal theory issues.
5. John B. Bailey, Peter F. Spies, and Marilyn Kramer Weitzman, "Market Study + Financial Analysis = Feasibility Report," *The Appraisal Journal* (October 1977), 550-577.
6. Stephen F. Fanning and Jody Winslow, "Guidelines for Defining the Scope of Market Analysis in Appraisal Assignments," *The Appraisal Journal* (October 1988), 466-476.

tingent upon their purchasing power or disposable income. Demand analysis identifies market segments. The demand for specific property uses must be understood to consider alternative uses, select appropriate comparables, identify the financial return or value range for various property types, and time when a property should be developed for a particular use and when its value should increase.

The balance of supply and demand at any given time is the key to estimating value. In a growth market characterized by increasing demand, the supply of all types of real estate may be relatively limited or inelastic and this scarcity will lead to higher prices in the short run. Supply may change over the long term, however, bringing about a decline in prices. Demand generally has a more immediate impact on value or probable selling price than supply. In an overbuilt market where supply exceeds demand, the quantity of existing and proposed supply will have a more immediate impact on value.

MARKET ANALYSIS IN THE APPRAISAL PROCESS

A major function of market analysis in the appraisal process is to identify key factors of value. Market analysis seeks to identify the highest and best use of a property in terms of market support (demand), timing (absorption rates), and market participants (probable users and buyers).

Supply and demand considerations direct the collection of data required to develop a perspective on the economic environment that affects the property. Such an economic overview includes a description of the general economy and analysis of economic patterns, trends, and cycles. Economic research provides the data and support to apply the three approaches to value. Market analysis facilitates the selection of comparables, the calculation of adjustments, and the forecasting of income streams. Market analysis makes it possible to identify the effective demand for and competitive supply of a particular property type in a specific location at a specific time.

A fundamental component of an appraisal is documented evidence that there is an appropriate level of market support for the existing use of the site or for alternative uses. Through supply and demand analysis, the appraiser can identify and test the level of market support, which is critical in the analysis of highest and best use.

Highest and best use links the physical, legal, design, and locational attributes of a property to market demand and financial feasibility. This linkage is essential to the appraisal process. Unlike many other products and commodities, real estate may have alternative uses; demand for a property with certain attributes may be expressed by different groups of users at different prices. In his classic text, *The Valuation of Real Estate*, Frederick Morrison Babcock described a two-tiered market composed of the competitive uses of a site and the competitive users (buyers) associated with these alternative uses.[7]

---

7. Frederick Babcock, *The Valuation of Real Estate* (McGraw-Hill: New York, 1932).

The two-tiered market that Babcock identified must be clearly delineated. One approach is to identify how desirable the attributes of the property are to alternative market segments. This approach is especially appropriate in real estate appraisal because a site's address is often the only information an appraiser has to begin his or her investigation. To define the market for the real estate, the attributes of the property are identified and analyzed in a process called *productivity analysis*. Productivity analysis examines a property's attributes to determine the marketability of the property in terms of the specific services it provides and the specific needs it satisfies. (An in-depth discussion of productivity analysis is found in Chapter 3.)

In productivity analysis the appraiser considers the attributes of the site and the improvement, concentrating on how these physical, legal, design, and locational attributes are combined to meet the needs of competitive users. Productivity analysis facilitates the determination of highest and best use by identifying a range of possible uses and thus linking the real estate product to specific markets. For example, productivity analysis could be used to delineate a market segment in the clothing industry. In the general market for men's clothing, a specific segment of this market can be identified as the market of consumers who prefer wool suits. Knowing the typical styles of suits that appeal to various groups of buyers allows for further market segmentation among probable consumers.

Productivity analysis is particularly important in the valuation of a complex product like real estate. Real property is an extremely heterogeneous product that is differentiated qualitatively and many real estate markets are characterized by a poverty of data. By concentrating on the site's attributes, productivity analysis can enhance the appraiser's understanding of the limited data available and help reduce the complexity of the valuation assignment. In *scoping*, the preliminary analysis of alternative uses for a given site, the analyst considers the combination of physical, legal, and locational property characteristics as a market package (see top box in Figure 1.2). By considering these attributes collectively, the analyst can assess the marketability of the property and its resulting value.

Because market analysis links the property's attributes to market preferences, it is indispensable to the highest and best use determination. Supply analysis not only identifies competitive properties, but also compares specific competitive attributes. The desirability of a property's attributes forms the basis for identifying the market segment that constitutes the demand for the property. By linking competitive supply to effective demand, productivity analysis helps the appraiser identify the marketability of a given parcel.

Although real estate is physically fixed, the attributes of a property can support a variety of uses. Therefore, real estate is said to be economically flexible. To address the complex physical and economic characteristics of a property, extensive data must be compiled. These data are used not only to fix the parameters of the market, but also to identify possible alternative real estate products. Because a broad range of issues influences real estate markets, a systematic approach to research is required.

THE SCIENTIFIC METHOD AND THE APPRAISAL PROCESS

The appraisal process is one approach to real estate decision making. It is an organized method for solving a problem. Another approach to problem solving is the scientific method. The scientific method can be applied to investigate economic problems[8] and to document value estimates empirically.

The five-step process described below compares the scientific method and the appraisal process.

Step 1

The scientific method begins with identification of the problem. Sometimes identifying the problem correctly can be 90% of the solution. The appraisal process also begins with the identification of a problem, but the range of problem situations is generally more limited. The problem to be solved in an appraisal is indicated by the use of the appraisal—i.e., the reason the client needs the property appraised. Problem identification directs the collection of information, documentation, and analysis.[9] Appraisals may be undertaken for various purposes, including

- Transactions—the acquisition or disposition of property
- The extension of credit—the estimation of collateral value
- Indemnification—compensation for property loss
- Taxation
- The development or redevelopment of real estate
- Alternative use considerations[10]
- Real estate portfolio analysis and management

This book focuses on the estimation of market value. As illustrated in Figure 1.1, the appraisal process begins with identification of the property, the property rights to be valued, the use of the appraisal, and the date of the value estimate.

Depending on the problem, a different starting point for the research process or a shift in emphasis may be required. Figures 1.2, 1.3, and 1.4 illustrate scenarios that may call for alternative starting points and emphases in the research process. These scenarios will be discussed later in the chapter. As mentioned previously, this book will examine the appraisal process as it is applied to estimate the market value of a specific site.

---

8. R. J. Johnston, *Philosophy and Human Geography: An Introduction to Contemporary Approaches* (London: Edward Arnold Publishers, 1983).
9. Grissom.
10. Richard U. Ratcliff, *Valuation for Real Estate Decisions* (Santa Cruz, Calif.: Democrat Press, 1972), 2-9.

Figure 1.1
The Valuation Process

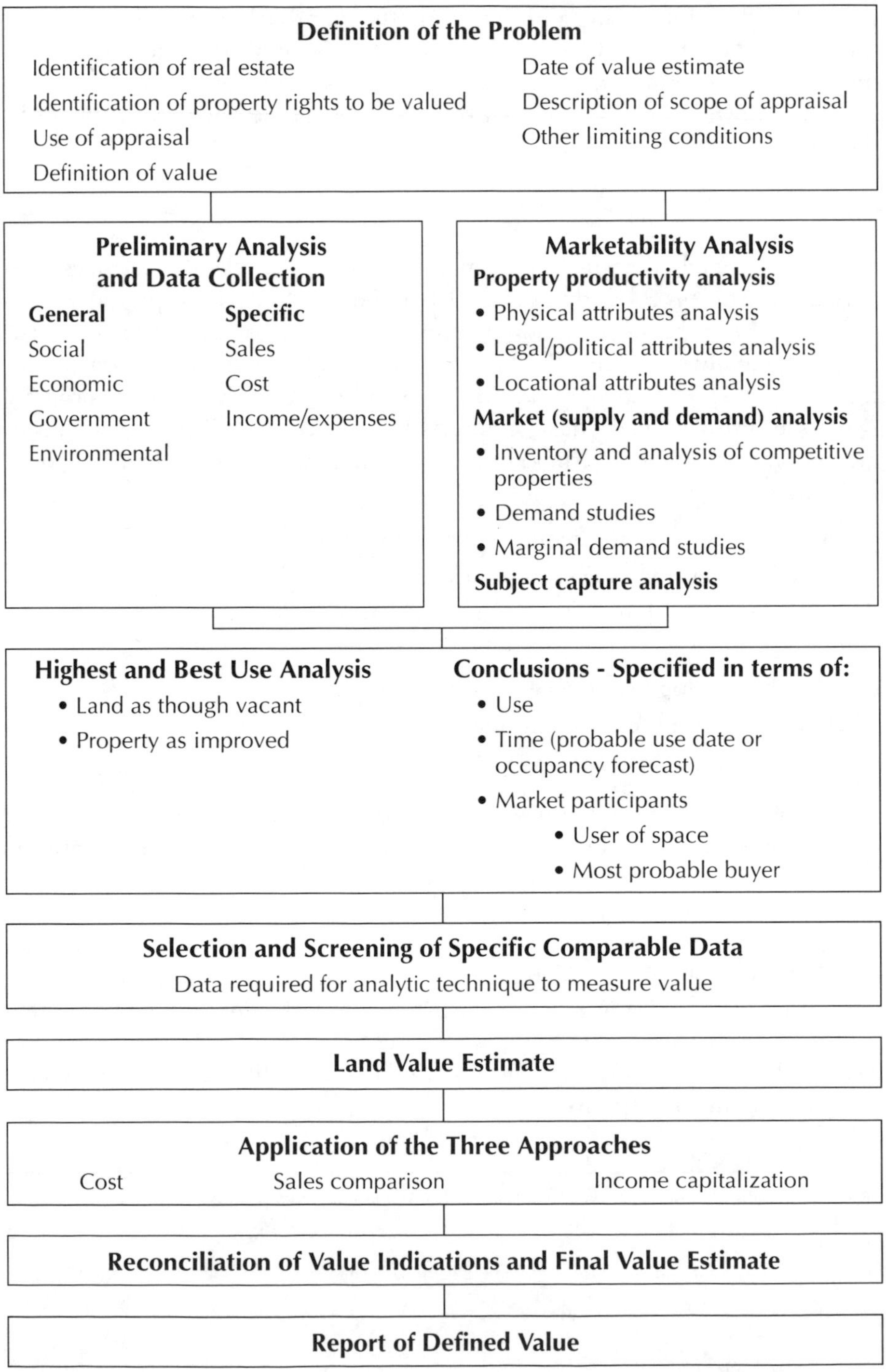

Definition of the Problem	
Identification of real estate	Date of value estimate
Identification of property rights to be valued	Description of scope of appraisal
Use of appraisal	Other limiting conditions
Definition of value	

Preliminary Analysis and Data Collection		**Marketability Analysis**
General	**Specific**	**Property productivity analysis**
Social	Sales	• Physical attributes analysis
Economic	Cost	• Legal/political attributes analysis
Government	Income/expenses	• Locational attributes analysis
Environmental		**Market (supply and demand) analysis**
		• Inventory and analysis of competitive properties
		• Demand studies
		• Marginal demand studies
		Subject capture analysis

Highest and Best Use Analysis	**Conclusions - Specified in terms of:**
• Land as though vacant	• Use
• Property as improved	• Time (probable use date or occupancy forecast)
	• Market participants
	• User of space
	• Most probable buyer

Selection and Screening of Specific Comparable Data
Data required for analytic technique to measure value

Land Value Estimate

Application of the Three Approaches
Cost   Sales comparison   Income capitalization

Reconciliation of Value Indications and Final Value Estimate

Report of Defined Value

Step 2

The second step in the scientific method is the formulation of a hypothesis. A hypothesis is a tentative assumption about the relationship between one situation and another. In an appraisal the hypothesis is stated in the purpose of the assignment, which is to estimate a defined value, generally market value. The defined value can vary with the appraisal problem. For example, the purpose of an appraisal required in an indemnification conflict may be the estimation of insurable value. The hypotheses offered in the alternative problem situations depicted in Figures 1.3 and 1.4 are more flexible than those established in traditional site- or property-specific appraisals. Generally, the hypothesis set forth in a real estate market analysis concerns supply and demand relationships with respect to a given product. Such a hypothesis is founded upon the productivity analysis of the property and the identified supply and demand relationships that characterize the market.

Step 3

The problem situation and the hypothesis set forth establish the data requirements for the research process. The availability and accessibility of data are major problems in conducting real estate research. Although the data available may not meet the needs of the research assignment, the best information available will have to be used. The data available often determine which valuation techniques are used in appraisal and market analysis. For example, the units of comparison selected in the sales comparison approach and the capitalization technique employed in the income approach may depend on the market data that can be collected. In market analysis, an employment forecast may be used to estimate demand when population forecasts are not available or do not appear to be realistic. The nature of the problem, the formulation of the hypothesis, and the availability of data help the analyst decide what research methodology should be employed.

Step 4

The fourth step in the scientific method is the application of an appropriate methodology. Once the problem is identified and a hypothesis is proposed, specific relationships can be tested. These relationships can be investigated by inductive and deductive means, using analogy, descriptive analysis, statistical analysis, observation, laboratory testing, and cause and effect analysis.

Most valuation techniques and methods of market analysis fall under the categories of analogy, descriptive analysis, and cause and effect analysis.

Step 5

The final step in the scientific method is the reconciliation of the findings to arrive at a solution that fits the problem. This is the concluding step in the appraisal and market research processes.

THE MARKET RESEARCH PROCESS

Market analysis for real estate is typified by three general scenarios: a site in search of a use or market, a use or market in search of a site, and real property as an alternative investment instrument.

In the first scenario, problems that concern a site in search of a use or market, the analyst must determine whether there is appropriate support for a use and, if so, delineate the market that supports that use.

In this case the analytic process begins by identifying the productive attributes of the site to delineate the market to be investigated. *Productivity analysis identifies the productive capacity of a property to determine the real estate services it can supply.* Thus, the analysis of a site in search of a use or market begins with the site attributes, which help delineate the market of potential users for the property.

The process followed in analyzing a site in search of a use is shown in Figure 1.2. Often any number of uses may be suitable for a given parcel of real estate. As a factor of production, land is an essential component of most economic ventures and a given parcel of land may be an appropriate site for residential, retail, office, industrial, or institutional use. The physical, legal, and locational attributes of the site determine its productive capacity and its use.

After completing the productivity analysis, the appraiser begins the second step in the process—identifying the competitive supply and effective demand that exist for the site. Supply and demand analysis is the essence of market research; real estate market research defines the market in a spatial or geographic context.

The patterns of market activity identified in the supply and demand analysis suggest the appropriate decision model. In analyzing a site in search of a use or market, the productive capacity of the property is related to market activity. This analysis sets the stage for the application of appropriate valuation techniques.

The second scenario concerns a use or market in search of a site. This scenario, which is shown in Figure 1.3, begins with the investigation of the broader market to identify the types of services or facilities the market is seeking. If the inquiry is focused on use, the analysis begins by addressing demand, e.g., basic and general demographics. If finding an appropriate site is the objective of the analysis, a particular use is identified, market preferences are studied, and the competitive supply is investigated.

As Figure 1.3 shows, this type of assignment begins with supply and demand analysis and then proceeds to productivity analysis, which addresses the physical, legal, and locational attributes of the site. The market analysis and productivity analysis are then incorporated into the appraisal process.

In comparing the two scenarios described, appraisers will recognize that the first scenario, a site in search of a use or market, is the basis of most appraisal assignments. Appraisers are asked to value a specific site. Although the appraisal process includes the analysis of general data on the city or region, the process focuses on the site. Analyzing the *situs,* or relationship of a property's location to the urban structure, is difficult if the assignment is not site- or use-specific. The second scenario, a market or use in search of a site, is often the task of a specialist in market analysis. Such an assignment is an extension of the traditional appraisal process, with a different emphasis and different applications of traditional analytical tools.

Figure 1.2
Market Research Scenario 1
A Site in Search of a Use or Market

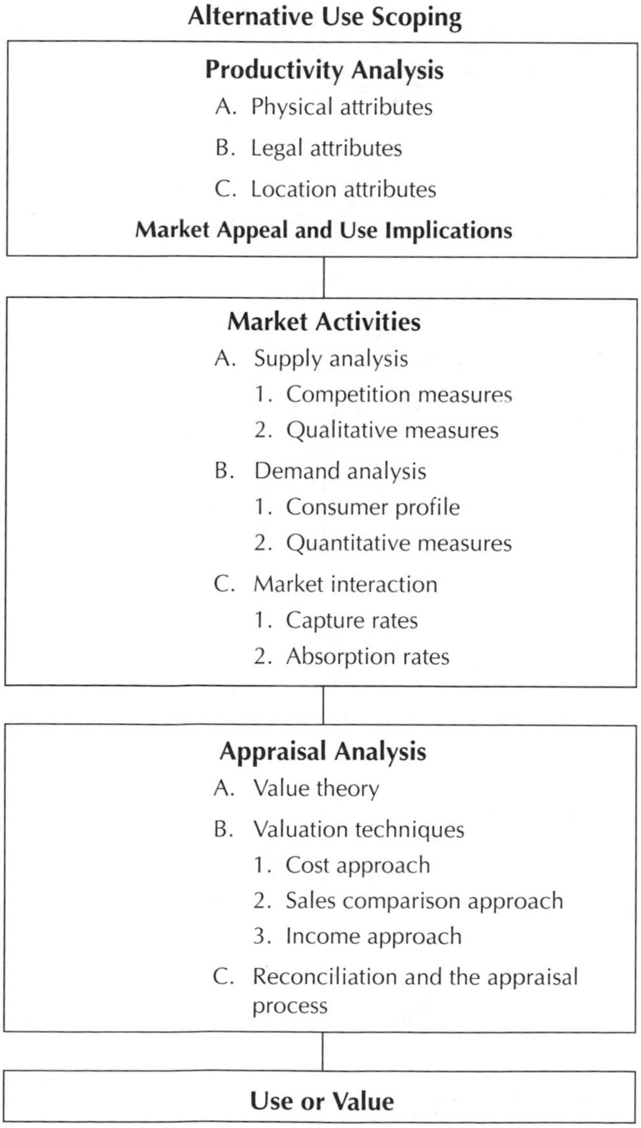

Alternative Use Scoping

Productivity Analysis
A. Physical attributes

B. Legal attributes

C. Location attributes

Market Appeal and Use Implications

Market Activities
A. Supply analysis

    1. Competition measures

    2. Qualitative measures

B. Demand analysis

    1. Consumer profile

    2. Quantitative measures

C. Market interaction

    1. Capture rates

    2. Absorption rates

Appraisal Analysis
A. Value theory

B. Valuation techniques

    1. Cost approach

    2. Sales comparison approach

    3. Income approach

C. Reconciliation and the appraisal process

Use or Value

Figure 1.3
Market Research Scenario 2
A Use or Market in Search of a Site

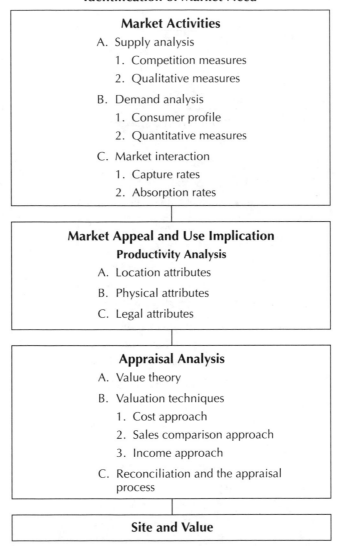

Identification of Market Need

Market Activities

A. Supply analysis
    1. Competition measures
    2. Qualitative measures
B. Demand analysis
    1. Consumer profile
    2. Quantitative measures
C. Market interaction
    1. Capture rates
    2. Absorption rates

Market Appeal and Use Implication
Productivity Analysis

A. Location attributes
B. Physical attributes
C. Legal attributes

Appraisal Analysis

A. Value theory
B. Valuation techniques
    1. Cost approach
    2. Sales comparison approach
    3. Income approach
C. Reconciliation and the appraisal process

Site and Value

The third scenario, which has received little attention in appraisal literature, involves the consideration of real estate as an alternative investment instrument. Again, this scenario has a different emphasis. To investigate market support for a real estate investment, the analyst may study an individual parcel of real estate or multiple parcels within a portfolio. Portfolio analysis is growing in importance due to the increased influence of institutional investors in both national and local real estate markets.

Figure 1.4
Market Research Scenario 3
Real Estate as an Investment Alternative

Risk and Return Objectives

Investment/Appraisal Analysis

A. Decision models and valuation
   techniques

   1. Return measures

   2. Risk measures

   3. Discounted cash flow analysis

B. Identification of rates in
   alternative markets

Market Activities

Market Risk and Return Analysis

A. Supply analysis

   1. Competition measures

   2. Qualitative measures

B. Demand analysis

   1. Investor profile

   2. Quantitative measures

C. Market interaction

   1. Capture rates

   2. Absorption rates

Market Appeal and Use Implication

Productivity Analysis

A. Location attributes

B. Physical attributes

C. Legal attributes

Figure 1.4 illustrates the analysis of real estate as an alternative investment. The focus of the analysis is to identify whether the levels of return and risk associated with the real estate are appropriate given the requirements of the investors. The decision-making models used by the investors are identified to establish the parameters of the problem. Measures of return and risk are linked to standards of market performance and opportunity cost.

Analyzing real estate as an investment includes the investigation of alternative investments as well as the decision-making models used by investors. Subsequent market analysis addresses competitive supply and effective demand. Because the location of a real estate investment significantly affects its profitability, the final stage of the analysis considers spatial concerns, exploring whether the macro-location of the property will allow it to achieve the desired returns.

The three scenarios described represent general problem situations in the market research process; each addresses the particular needs of different decision makers. This book is concerned with the first scenario, which most closely replicates the variety of problem situations appraisers face. The appraisal process is flexible enough to accommodate all three scenarios discussed here. The specific issues to be addressed are treated in different sections of the appraisal report, e.g., site and improvement analyses, neighborhood analysis, city/regional analysis, and highest and best use analysis.

Under the impetus of FIRREA, many appraisers have begun to provide separate market analysis sections in their reports. It is logical to link market analysis to highest and best use analysis, which explicitly addresses the components of value—i.e., utility, scarcity, desire, and effective purchasing power. Market analysis supports the conclusion of highest and best use by assessing the productivity of the property and documenting the level of market support and financial feasibility of the property use.

SUMMARY

The treatment of market analysis in an appraisal is determined by the nature of the assignment and the specific problem confronting the decision maker. Once the purpose and function of the appraisal are identified, the appraiser will select a level of analysis appropriate to the problem. An appraisal that gives ample attention to value theory and valuation methods will include a market analysis component that not only fulfills regulatory requirements, but also complements the steps in the appraisal process.

It is impossible to estimate the market value of a property without considering the supply of and demand for the property within a specific time frame. Market analysis links value theory and valuation techniques and documents the supply and demand relationship on which the value estimate is based. Moreover, market analysis identifies which use among alternative uses the market supports, and thus helps determine the highest and best use of a property.

The steps in the scientific method are analogous to the steps in the appraisal process. Three general scenarios for real estate market analysis can be identified: a site in search of a use or market, a use or market in search of a site, and real property as an alternative investment instrument. The appraisal process is flexible enough to accommodate all three scenarios.

In each market analysis scenario, a general overview of the economic base and a survey of growth patterns in the community are linked to the property's attributes. The economic overview is tied to specific data on the attributes of the subject and comparable properties. The dynamics of metropolitan growth are also related to the subject and comparable properties. These linkages, which are identified in market analysis, are examined to determine the highest and best use of a property. The relationship between the economic base, market activity, and property productivity provides the foundation for the three approaches to value.

CHAPTER OBJECTIVES

———⊸•⊷———

- To explain the concept of *levels* of market analysis
- To identify the criteria for determining the appropriate level of market analysis in a given assignment
- To describe each of the four levels as they apply to the following components of market analysis:
  — productivity (property location) analysis
  — demand analysis (inferred demand or fundamental demand)
  — competitive supply analysis
  — highest and best use conclusion and marketability analysis
- To identify key items to check in evaluating the adequacy of the market analysis in an appraisal.

CHAPTER TWO

———⟫•⟪———

Levels of Market Analysis

Appraisers need to identify the amount of market research and documentation required in appraisal analyses and appraisal reports. The various levels of analysis that may be appropriate range from the application of relatively general techniques to increasingly complex ones. Two broad categories may be distinguished: *inferred analysis* and *fundamental analysis*.

INFERRED ANALYSIS VERSUS FUNDAMENTAL ANALYSIS

Inferred analysis, which is sometimes called *trend analysis*, is similar to the technical analysis practiced by stock market analysts. This type of technical analysis is an attempt to estimate future changes in value by investigating past market behavior. Technical analysis identifies trends and patterns and infers expected market behavior. In a similar manner, real estate analysts frequently use statistics to draw inferences about a general class of phenomena, studying data from the recent past to predict future occurrences.[1]

It may be inferred, for example, that the future performance of the subject property will follow the past performance of other properties in its class. If the office occupancy rate in City X has increased from 80% two years ago to 90% today, it might be inferred from the macro data for a broad real estate sector that the subject will follow this trend, achieving 95% occupancy next year and

---

1. Gaylon E. Greer and Michael D. Farrell, *Investment Analysis for Real Estate Decisions*, 2d ed. (New York: The Dryden Press, 1988), 520 and 81.

full occupancy the following year. The stabilized occupancy inferred from this analysis might be used in the 10-year discounted cash flow (DCF) analysis required in most appraisals.

Fundamental analysis goes beyond trend analysis, forecasting demand based on segmentation of broad demographic and economic data to reflect the subject's specific market. To estimate the future capture rate of a retail property, for example, the subject is compared with specific properties that compete with the subject for the same market. Fundamental analysis of real estate markets is based on the principle that real estate value is tied to the services the real estate provides. As applied to the stock market, fundamental analysis may be defined as "an investment analysis technique that emphasizes investigation of the underlying business activity of the firm whose securities are being considered."[2] Fundamental analysis of stock or real estate is based on the theory that worth of an asset is "anchored in something called intrinsic value, which can be determined by careful (fundamental) analysis of present conditions and future prospects."[3]

A comparison can be drawn between inferred analysis and fundamental analysis using an example from the stock market. An investor who is considering the purchase of IBM stock may infer how IBM stock will perform by examining the daily report of Standard & Poor's 500. If the stock average is trending up, the investor might infer that IBM stock will also rise. Making use of fundamental analysis, the investor can take the study a step further and analyze underlying market demand for IBM products. Such an analysis might segment specific demand for IBM products to determine IBM's market share within the computer industry. The investor might also look into the management and tooling of IBM industrial plants to determine whether they are efficiently run and equipped to produce the products desired by today's computer market. Finally, rival computer manufacturers might be studied to assess the competitive potential of IBM. With an informed market outlook, the investor could reach a decision as to whether or not the purchase of IBM stock at today's price seems like a profitable investment.

In a real estate context, the performance of a property may either be inferred on the basis of macro trends or forecast through fundamental analysis of the specific property market. The anticipated level of occupancy for an office building provides an example. If the market has been steadily improving and the subject has a good location and a modern design, it can be inferred that the building will maintain a high level of occupancy for the typical 10-year discounted cash flow period considered in the appraisal. If, on the other hand, forecast white-collar employment is lower than current white-collar employment and new competition is likely to emerge over the next few years, then an inferred analysis of occupancy trends might be misleading. An analysis of occupancy trends might produce entirely different expectations than a fundamental analysis of the office building market.

---

2. Ibid., 81, 5, and 506.
3. Burton G. Malkiel, *A Random Walk Down Wall Street* (New York: W.W. Norton & Sons, Inc., 1990), 28.

In summary, inferred analysis may be described as a projection of historical trends focusing on macro data. Inferred analysis is not subject-specific. Fundamental analysis, on the other hand, is based on micro data for a specific real estate submarket and oriented toward future developments. Fundamental analysis is specifically focused on the subject real estate.

The two broad categories of inferred and fundamental analysis may be further broken down into sublevels. It is possible to identify many different sublevels, or strata, of analyses because there is considerable variation in assignments. This text will examine four general strata that can be identified as Levels A, B, C, and D. Level A represents the least in-depth analysis and Level D the most elaborate analysis. Market analysis at the A and B levels is generally interspersed throughout an appraisal report, in the sections on area or regional analysis, highest and best use, and the specific approaches to value. Level A and B market analyses reflect inferred analysis. The two more in-depth levels, Levels C and D, are most often presented in a discrete section of the appraisal report devoted solely to market analysis. Levels C and D represent applications of fundamental analysis. A comparison of the major characteristics of inferred and fundamental analyses appears in Figure 2.1.

Figure 2.1
Levels of Market Study in Appraisal

Level of Study	Inferred Demand Studies		Fundamental Demand Studies	
	A	B	C	D
Inferred subject attributes			Quantified subject attributes	
Inferred locational determinants of use & marketability by macro analysis			Quantitative and graphic analysis of location determinants of use & marketability by macro and micro analysis	
Inferred demand from general economic base analysis conducted by others			Demand derived by original economic base analysis	
Inferred demand by selected comparables			Forecast demand by subject-specific market segment & demographic data	
Inferred supply by selected comparables			Quantified supply by inventorying existing & forecasting planned competition	
Inferred equilibrium/highest and best use and capture conclusions			Quantified equilibrium • Highest and best use - concept plan • Timing - quantified capture forecast	
Emphasis is on: • Instinctive knowledge • Historical data • Judgment			Emphasis is on: • Quantifiable data • Forecast • Judgment	

Note. An appraisal without a fundamental demand study—i.e., Level C or D market analysis—is designed to estimate value only in a certain and stable market.

DESCRIPTION OF LEVELS

Although market analysis cannot be standardized, clients expect and reliable value estimates require some level of market analysis in an appraisal. Naturally, the level of study will vary with the client's needs, market conditions, and the property type. The general categories or levels of market study are described below.

Level A

Level A market analysis is general and descriptive, not subject-specific. This level of analysis relies on historical data rather than future projections. General data and selected comparables are presumed to reflect the market. The conclusions based on such a study might apply to most similar properties in the city. For example, a Level A location analysis provides only a general description of the area or neighborhood. The analysis usually relies on generic data that are updated annually. If general growth trends for the city and region are positive, future demand is assumed to exist. The treatment of the data does not usually relate area-wide demand to the subject, but rather leaves it to the reader to *infer* the level of demand that exists for the subject.

Typically, Level A analyses only indirectly address the supply side of the market by reference to vacancy rates for selected rent or sale comparables. These vacancy rates serve as indicators of oversupply or undersupply. Vacancy projections are based on the assumption that these rates will remain stable.

Figure 2.2 is an example of Level A analysis. The graph provides data on the residential building permits issued by the city over the past eight years. An appraiser could use these data to infer demand for all types of real estate. In the example, the trend seems to be a steady decline. Based on a "feel for the market," the appraiser might make judgments about the duration of this downward cycle and its impact on the subject property.

Level B

Level B analyses employ areawide market data on a general property class. The projected use conclusions are more subject-specific, and the timing projections depend on interpretation of marketwide data on the property type. For example, a Level B analysis typically employs data from regularly published, areawide market surveys prepared by proprietary firms or public agencies. These surveys are usually conducted for each class of property—i.e., retail, apartment, office building. The data are updated at regular intervals, either quarterly or semi-annually, but even periodic updates may lag behind changes in a dynamic market in which data become obsolete all too soon. These public and proprietary surveys cover broad areas in an urban setting. The geographic boundaries of the survey rarely conform to the submarket for the subject property.

In Level B studies, secondary data are used extensively and must be scrutinized to determine how well they fit the problem. It is usually inferred that the

Figure 2.2
Building Permits/Residential—Level A Analysis

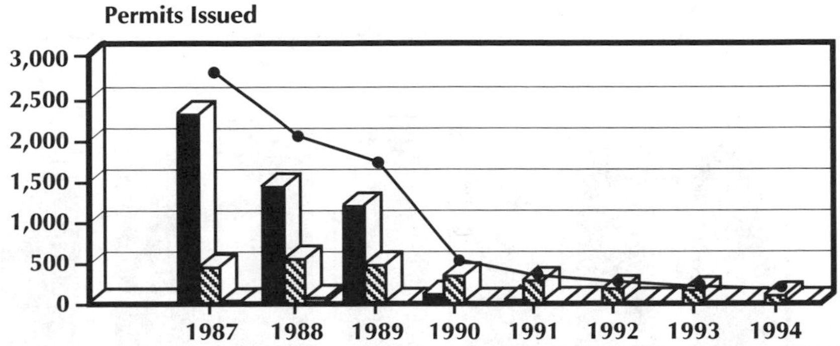

Permits Issued

	1987	1988	1989	1990	1991	1992	1993	1994
Apartment	2,277	1,398	1,173	120	23	10	0	17
Single Family	431	541	474	353	272	180	160	104
Duplex	11	22	4	7	1	14	0	0
Total	2,719	1,961	1,651	480	296	204	160	121

Property Type

■ Apartment   ▧ Single Family   ▨ Duplex   —●— Total

subject's submarket will perform in a manner similar to the historical performance of the broad class of property to which it belongs. The use of broad-based market survey data increases the reliability of the analysis, but reliance upon such data has its limitations. Level B analyses may cover many projects that are not competitive with the subject. Moreover, the historical pattern of the broader market may not reflect the future prospects of the property. The appraiser must carefully evaluate the data used to determine how well they fit the actual assignment.

A graphic analysis of Level B data is presented in Figure 2.3. The data show a decline in office occupancy over the past four years. The appraiser might infer that this indicates either a downward trend for the future or the bottoming out of a market that will be improving shortly.

Level C

Level C analysis goes further. Whereas Level A and B analyses use historical absorption rates as indicators of future absorption, a major shift occurs in Level C analyses, which incorporate future-oriented forecasting techniques. Future demand and absorption are forecast by first projecting the growth of population, income, and employment. A Level C study provides detailed submarket data on which to base absorption and *NOI* projections as well as a competitive ranking

Figure 2.3
Composite Occupancy Rate—Level B Analysis

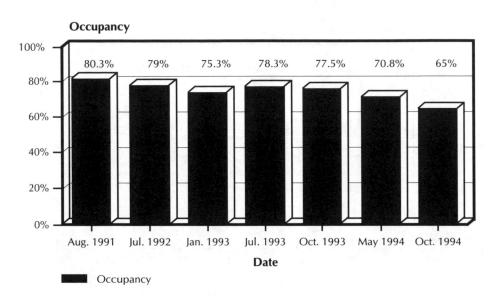

of the subject property. A Level C study for an appraisal of vacant land will include a proposed land use plan which specifies the probable property use, or most appropriate mix of uses, and the timing of development.

Level C analyses make extensive use of primary data, which are compiled by conducting field work and direct surveys. A Level C inventory includes all properties that currently exist in the defined market as well as all planned properties. (A more complete discussion of primary and secondary data is provided in Chapter 10.)

Figure 2.4 depicts a Level C study of *marginal demand*, i.e., any additional demand that exists (based on an inventory of current supply) or that is forecast to develop (based on an inventory of anticipated supply). The Level C study forecasts specific submarket demand for housing units similar to the subject property. In the example, an oversupply is forecast for Years 5, 6, and 7. These supply and demand data could be presented in an appraisal to support future rent and occupancy projections for the subject under the proposed use, the probable timing of the uses of vacant land, and other similar judgments made by the appraiser.

Level D

A Level D analysis provides the most detailed level of market study available. While the number of applications for Level D analyses is unlimited, only a few will be mentioned here.

Figure 2.4
Housing Unit Forecast—Level C Analysis

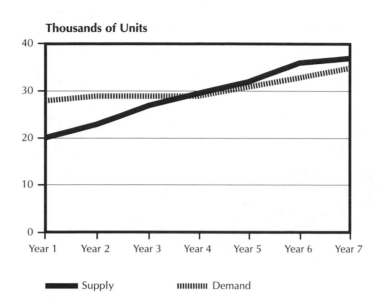

A Level D study might include an analysis of urban planning and land use policy, public and private fiscal capabilities, probability weighting of use projections, and risk ratings. Original economic base analysis is typical of Level D studies. Forecast demand based on employment projections is segmented in great detail, e.g., according to the categories specified in the SIC (Standard Industrial Classification) code. The demand forecast for a shopping center may be broken down into the demand for each retail product line.

Level D analyses may also call for attitudinal surveys and direct interviews with the market segment identified for the subject property. These techniques are applied in a structured manner that conforms to accepted standards of statistical analysis. For example, a market survey aimed at prospective apartment tenants might quantify the level of demand for fireplaces or other specific amenities that tenants would require as an inducement to relocate to the subject property. Probability weighting and risk analysis characterize the marketability conclusions.

Figure 2.5 indicates the level or levels of analysis appropriate to typical studies found in appraisal reports.[4]

---

4. Stephen F. Fanning and Jody Winslow, "Guidelines for Defining the Scope of Market Analysis in Appraisal Assignments," *The Appraisal Journal* (October 1988).

Figure 2.5
Levels of Market Analysis

WORK ITEM	LEVEL OF STUDY			
	A	B	C	D
LOCATION				
General description—city and neighborhood	x	x	x	x
Specific analysis of site linkages		x	x	x
Specific analysis of urban growth determinants		x	x	x
Detailed competitive location rating			x	x
Detailed probable future land use analysis				x
DEMAND ANALYSIS				
General evidence of sales/leasing activity	x	x	x	x
General city growth trends	x	x	x	x
Analysis of overall market absorption from secondary data		x	x	x
Demand forecast by specific projections of population, employment, and income			x	x
Demand forecast for subject market segment			x	x
Direct attitudinal survey of target market				x
COMPETITIVE SUPPLY ANALYSIS				
Vacancy rates for selected comparables		x	x	x
Vacancy rate from secondary data—broad market surveys			x	x
Field research on all competitive properties			x	x
Research on proposed properties—field inspection, building permit analysis, identification of potential sites			x	x
Detailed competitive amenities rating			x	x
Direct interviews with developers				x
HIGHEST AND BEST USE CONCLUSION AND MARKETABILITY OR TIMING				
Vacant Land				
Probable use and timing, but no specific timetable for development	x			
Generalized land use plan				
Probable use supported by present value analysis		x		
Timing supported by secondary data		x	x	x
Specific land use plan				
Probable use supported by present value analysis		x	x	x
Land plan drawn to site			x	x
Timing based on marginal demand and competitive rating analysis			x	x
Cost estimate for subject development				x
Value impact analysis of alternative marketing/ development strategies				x
Improved Properties				
General *ad hoc* judgments	x			
NOI projection supported by performance of selected comparables	x	x	x	x
Use, timing, *NOI* projection supported by analysis of secondary data		x	x	x
Capture rate/*NOI* projection supported by marginal demand of market segment and competitive ratings			x	x
Risk analysis of *NOI* forecast				x
Value impact analysis of alternative marketing/ development strategies				x

CRITERIA FOR DETERMINING THE LEVEL OF MARKET ANALYSIS

Appraisers use specific criteria to determine which level of market analysis is appropriate to a particular appraisal assignment. The appraiser might use the following guidelines in deciding which level of analysis to apply

- The regulatory requirements incumbent upon appraisers, e.g., the Uniform Standards of Professional Appraisal Practice, specific legislation, the memoranda or circulars of government agencies
- The needs of the client or user of the appraisal
- The market conditions prevailing at the time of the appraisal
- The complexity of the property being appraised

Regulatory Requirements

The need for market analysis is emphasized throughout the Uniform Standards of Professional Appraisal Practice (USPAP).[5] For example,

- Standards Rule 1-3(a) specifies the need for market analysis in all appraisals to support the use determination and estimate of value. The typical elements to be considered are "existing land use regulations, reasonably probable modifications of such land use regulations, economic demand, the physical adaptability of the real estate, neighborhood trends, and the highest and best use of the real estate."
- Standards Rule 1-4(g) states that an appraiser "must identify and consider...all physical, functional, and external market factors as they may affect the appraisal."
- Statement on Appraisal Standards No. 2 (SMT-2), which is concerned with discounted cash flow analysis, specifies "Revenue growth rate or decline rate assumptions are premised upon analysis of supply/demand factors and other economic conditions and trends within the market area of the subject."

Other standards also address the need for market analysis in all appraisals. The final guidelines to implement the Financial Institutions Reform, Recovery and Enforcement Act (FIRREA) require that the defined market value be "designed to provide an accurate and reliable measure of the economic potential of property involved in federally related transactions."[6]

Although these standards confirm the need for market analysis in an appraisal, they do not specify the extent to which any given component of market analysis should be developed. The comment to Standards Rule 1-4(g) suggests

---

5. The Appraisal Foundation, *Uniform Standards of Professional Appraisal Practice*, 1994 ed. (Washington, D.C.: The Appraisal Foundation, 1994).
6. *Federal Register*, August 22, 1990, Section C, 1608.2.

there are different levels of study and that some appraisals may require a more detailed study as specified in Standards Rule 4-4. (A detailed study would be equivalent to a Level C analysis as described in this text.)

Standard 4 of the Uniform Standards pertains to the appraiser's awareness, understanding, and employment of recognized methods and techniques in producing a creditable market analysis. The standard does not, however, indicate specific levels of analysis for particular appraisal assignments. The general comment to Standard 4 states "An appraiser must have the ability to develop an analysis/research program that is responsive to the client's objective; to perform primary research; to gather and present secondary and tertiary data; and to prepare a documented written report."

Because current requirements are confusing, the appraiser must remain cognizant of new interpretations of existing standards and of standards promulgated in the future. While a Level A analysis might be acceptable in some cases, Standard 4 implies that a Level B or possibly a Level C analysis would be the minimum requirement for the majority of commercial appraisals.

Client Needs

An appraisal serves the needs of the client, who is typically engaged in decision making for lending or underwriting purposes. The basis for property profitability and value is marketability. The level of market analysis performed should match the level of reliability a client requires to reach a decision. The appraisal may be viewed as a service to help reduce (but not eliminate) risk for the client and the public. The greater the potential risk, the more intensive the level of analysis required. The tolerance the client and regulatory agency have for risk will determine the level of study needed. The appraisal can impart confidence to the client's decision by providing the highest and best use conclusion, projections of *NOI*, the estimated timing of the project, and documentation for the demand forecast.

Prevailing Market Conditions

In a market characterized by stability or equilibrium, a less intensive analysis may meet the needs of the client. A stable or balanced market usually exhibits three features: a steady number of sales in the recent past, the absence of either overbuilding or an undersupply, and available public studies documenting market equilibrium. If these conditions exist, a Level A or Level B analysis may be acceptable.

An unbalanced market is characterized by few recent sales, much construction activity or an expected surge in such activity, and public studies reporting or forecasting market disequilibrium. Level C would most likely be the minimal level of analysis required to satisfy the exigencies of this kind of market.

Complexity of the Property

The level of market analysis varies with the type and size of the property. Property type refers to the use to which an existing improved property is put, the use proposed for a property that is to be developed, or the absence of any use designation, as in the case of raw land. Size is generally a function of property type. For a limited project such as a small, income-producing residential property, a Level A analysis might be adequate. For most income-producing properties, however, a Level B analysis would be the likely minimum. For moderate-sized commercial properties, a Level C analysis would seem to be the minimum, especially if the existence of sufficient demand to support the property is at all questionable. (Recent federal regulations imply that a property with a value in excess of $1,000,000 would be considered of moderate size.) The most complex properties, e.g., mixed-use properties, generally require a Level D analysis.

Existing improvements usually have some income history and the use determination is likely to be straightforward. *NOI*, however, is not always certain and it is here that market analysis becomes most significant. Raw land presents problems as to alternative uses and their timing. A Level B study is generally the appropriate minimum for a parcel of raw land in a fairly stable market with limited alternative use potential. As the size of the vacant tract and the number of alternative uses increase, the level of analysis required will become more in-depth. Whenever market conditions are unstable, Level C analysis is considered the minimum regardless of the size of the land parcel. Proposed improvements normally entail a degree of uncertainty and necessitate more in-depth study. Here Level C would appear to be the appropriate minimum for all but very small projects.

Property size is typically related to risk. Small properties usually have shorter marketing periods, more potential buyers, and, consequently, smaller financial outlays and lower risks. Large properties require longer marketing periods and, thus, entail higher risks. Property value must be considered in light of a reasonable marketing time. The bigger the property, the longer the projection period. A more detailed analysis will be required to enhance the reliability of the appraisal. If the market projection for a project is faulty, the error will be compounded as the size of the property increases. The appraiser must recognize the direct correspondence between project risk and the required level of market analysis.

Figure 2.6 outlines guidelines for determining the level of market analysis appropriate to a given appraisal assignment. Figure 2.7 presents a checklist which might be used in an appraisal review to identify inadequate market analyses.

Figure 2.6
Guidelines for Selecting the Appropriate Level
of Market Analysis in Commercial Appraisals

Criterion	Inferred	Fundamental
Market Conditions		
Stable market		
Steady number of sales		
Absence of overbuilding or undersupply		
Market balance reported in public studies		
Stable prices	x	
Unstable market		
Sharp increase or decrease in number of sales		
Evidence of overbuilding or undersupply		
Market imbalance reported in public studies		
Unstable prices		x

Note. If the subject is in a stable market, the lowest level of the given range should be selected; if the market is unstable, the highest level should be selected.

Criterion	Inferred	Fundamental
Property Complexity by Type and Size		
Vacant land		
Simple situation involving single use; clear timing for that use	x	
Complex situation involving multiple use potential; questionable timing for those uses		x
Proposed project		
Less than 50 lots/25,000 sq. ft.	x	
More than 50 lots/25,000 sq. ft.		x
Improved property		
Relatively simple assignment		
Less than 5 tenants		
Less than 25,000 sq. ft.	x	
Complex properties		
More than 5 tenants		
More than 25,000 sq. ft. or greater than $1 million value		x
Highly complex properties		
Hotels, resorts, mixed-use developments, or retail-office space over 25,000 sq. ft.		x
Properties whose future *NOI* is very uncertain		x

Note. If the subject is a small property in a big market, a lower level may be selected; if the subject is a big property in a small market, a higher level should be selected.

Figure 2.7

A Checklist for Determining the Adequacy of Market Analysis in Real Estate Appraisals

Key parts of the appraisal to check:

Identification of the Assignment, Assumptions, and Disclosures

☐ Is the market that is forecast consistent with the market for the subject property—i.e., are there any inconsistencies such as the presentation of "filler data" on retail buying power or office vacancy rates in a report on a residential apartment complex?

☐ Are there any special assumptions that make the market forecast untenable—i.e., an assumption that the population will grow by 10%, but no evidence presented to support it?

☐ Are the assumptions underlying the market capture rate estimated for the subject the same as those in the definition of market value?
  - Is there any special lender financing?
  - Does the marginal demand estimate support the timing?
  - Is either party operating under duress?

☐ Is the level of analysis appropriate for the property type and current market conditions?

☐ Who commissioned the appraisal? (Appraisals commissioned by third parties are less likely to be biased.)

☐ Does the analyst have a vested interest in the property? (Appraisers are required to disclose any personal interest in the certification statement.)

Market Analysis Component and Specific Approaches to Value

☐ Typical weaknesses of the market analysis (demand and competitive supply analyses)
  - Failure to show ranges
  - Overstatement of population forecast
  - Inadequate knowledge or information about the timing of public infrastructure development
  - No support for subject capture estimate, i.e., the capture rate given involves a "leap of faith" from the general data
  - Lack of analysis of different population forecasts
  - Overuse of macro data
  - Overly positive analysis of the subject or subject location
  - Only a general area description for the location analysis, without any focus on the subject or competitive properties

☐ Typical weakness of the cost approach
  - Estimates of economic obsolescence not consistent with market analysis

☐ Typical weaknesses of the sales comparison approach
  - Use of comparables that do not have the same locational and timing characteristics as competitive properties inventoried in the market analysis or lack of adjustments for such differences
  - Lack of analysis of competitive properties
  - Adjustment for changing market conditions (time) not consistent with the findings of the market analysis

☐ Typical weaknesses of the income capitalization approach
  - Forecast of increasing subject rent/sale price or of subject capture not consistent with market analysis
  - Forecast of subject rent/sale price or of subject capture not based on comparison with specific competition
  - Application of a discount rate not consistent with the findings of the market analysis; i.e., a low discount rate suggests lower risk, but the forecast and subject capture may be highly optimistic which suggests high risk.

SUMMARY

The four levels of market analysis are distinguished by their relative degree of complexity and manner of presentation. Level A analyses are the most general; Level D, the most in-depth. To determine which level is appropriate to the assignment, an appraiser considers four criteria: regulatory requirements, the needs of the client, prevailing market conditions, and the complexity of the subject property.

Each of the four levels may be described for the components in the market analysis, i.e., property location analysis, demand analysis, competitive supply analysis, and highest and best use conclusion/marketability conclusion.

Level A analyses are general and descriptive, not subject-specific. Anticipated market conditions are inferred from historical data rather than forecast. Level B analyses expand upon Level A analyses by examining site linkages and determinants of urban growth. Judgments about the use of the subject and the timing for that use are based on data from broad-based market surveys.

Level C analyses, which are based on data generated by the appraiser, include the development of a quantifiable location rating, a demand forecast, a survey of existing and planned competition, and an amenities rating. These facets of the analysis support conclusions about use and timing. Level D analyses examine the policy and budget of a municipality to determine the likelihood of new infrastructure development. Original economic base analysis and direct surveys characterize Level D demand and competitive supply analyses. Detailed development cost estimates, alternative marketing strategies, value impact studies, and risk analyses are associated with Level D procedures.

CHAPTER OBJECTIVES

- To introduce the concept of productivity analysis and relate property attributes to market activity and market identification

- To examine the physical features of real property, the first set of attributes studied in productivity analysis

- To discuss the dual nature of real estate, i.e., land vs. capital, commodity vs. resource

- To examine property improvements in terms of their quality, attractiveness, and functional utility and to link these attributes to market activity and property value

- To further define the realty product and its market by relating the legal dimension of real estate to property productivity

- To explore the quantitative and qualitative aspects of real property rights in defining a real estate product and its market

- To discuss the four powers of government, which affect the use and acquisition of private property and alter the market structure, and to examine how a community's regulatory environment is linked to market delineation

CHAPTER THREE

Productivity Analysis

Productivity analysis may be defined as analysis of the capacity of a property to house economic activities, supply services, and provide amenities to meet human needs. A property's productive capacity depends on the manner in which the factors of production are combined in the property and the way potential consumers react to the mix of property attributes. The need for productivity analysis arises from several factors, which include the heterogeneous nature of individual properties, the potential for any site to be put to more than one use, and the appraisal practice of analyzing data on comparable properties to arrive at a value estimate for the subject property. Productivity analysis focuses on the characteristics of a property to establish its competitive position in the market.

Productivity analysis is the concept that links Lancaster's consumer theory to real estate.[1] Lancaster's theory is based on the premise that the attributes of a product are priced in the market. Productivity analysis relates the value of a product to the marketability of its attributes. The concept is founded on the economic theory of distribution, which allocates the returns to a product among the factors of production. By identifying the value of a property's attributes and their pricing in the market, an appraiser can compare unlike, but similar, real estate products over time.

The comparison of two car models, a 1957 and a 1991 Thunderbird, illustrates the concept of productivity analysis. Both vehicles have the same basic

---

1. John C. Lancaster, "New Consumer Theory," *Journal of Political Economy* (April 1966), 132-157.

function as a means of transportation, but the cars differ in their capabilities and amenities. The 1957 model was a sports car, a two-seater, with the best technology of the period. The 1991 model seats five people and is fuel-efficient, computerized, and environmentally safe. By current standards, the 1957 model is functionally obsolete. Demand for the higher-priced, older model is inelastic. Thus, analysis of the fundamental attributes of the 1957 model helps delineate the car's primary market (the probable buyers), the depth of the market (market structure), and the competition.

Productivity analysis applies to real estate, as this chapter will illustrate. Property attributes delineate the highest and best use of similar properties. This is true not only when the similar properties are direct competitors based on their use, but also in limited cases where properties may compete even though other attributes make them more suitable for different uses and direct them to different markets.

The potential for attributes to direct land and property use, and thus delineate the market, is relevant in most market situations. In active markets, the analysis of a property's physical, legal, and locational characteristics helps define the specific product and the services it offers, thus facilitating a direct comparison of the subject to the most similar properties. In depressed markets, productivity analysis focuses on the potential use of an existing property based on its attributes, allowing it to be compared with properties that might have had very divergent uses as originally developed.

Productivity analysis enables us to compare and contrast similar and dissimilar attributes of competing assets, especially durable goods and real property. The analysis of attributes helps appraisers identify appropriate competitive properties, but competitive supply is more than just comparable properties. For example, an analysis of the supply of competitive housing must consider whether or not single-family residences or condominiums are viable alternatives to apartments. In the student housing market, dormitories represent another possible alternative. Assuming that apartment space has a 95% occupancy rate in a medium-sized market, what are the implications if the university, with an enrollment of 40,000 students, decides to build a dormitory to house 5,000?

Two of the functions of productivity analysis are

1. To identify the extent of the market and the possibility of further market segmentation. For durable goods and real property, productivity analysis reflects the operation of the principle of substitution.
2. To identify the attributes desired in the market, enabling the analyst to compare and contrast competitive properties to establish their differences and the market's pricing of those differences.

While productivity analysis emphasizes the specifics of particular properties, it also deals with general property attributes. The general categories of attributes studied in productivity analysis for real estate are physical attributes, legal attributes, and locational attributes.

Productivity analysis does not merely describe the site and improvements, nor is it simply a listing of property rights or a recording of the physical location. Productivity analysis examines how the market perceives the physical, legal, and locational dimensions of a property. It addresses the capacity of a property or numerous properties to accommodate specific activities and to satisfy market needs. The relationship between productivity analysis and market structure is addressed in the market analysis section of an appraisal.

In real estate, the value of a property is determined by the economic function that the property serves and the psychological satisfactions it offers. The attributes of a property account for its marketability and form the basis of its value. The value of a property is influenced not only by tangible attributes such as the soil, size, frontage, or construction quality of the improvements; value is also affected by abstract factors such as a scenic view, a babbling brook, or other natural amenities. Beyond the property's physical features, value is affected by the psychology of the people involved in the transaction. Therefore, behavior and psychological factors are a central concern of market research.

Market research is a recursive process with many interrelated parts. The concern at the initial phase of the process is the fundamental characteristics of a particular site. The physical attributes of a specific parcel of real estate include features such as its size, location, and amenities as well as other characteristics to be identified in the appraisal process. The pricing of the property's attributes is reflected in the adjustments made to comparables based on market analysis. The major purposes of site analysis are:

- To identify those attributes that motivate people to pay for the right to occupy and use a property.
- To provide insight into the components of a real estate product that galvanize market activity as measured in demand, transaction prices, and competition for that product.
- To provide a basis for comparing and contrasting properties and identifying their unique or distinct attributes.
- To directly relate the attributes supporting the specific property use to the valuation techniques employed.

PHYSICAL ATTRIBUTES AND PRODUCTIVITY ANALYSIS

Real estate is a real asset that is immobile, but can have many uses. The appraiser addresses the flexibility of real estate use in the highest and best use section of the appraisal report.

Highest and best use analysis begins with an investigation of the physical constraints on the possible use of the property. Physical attributes can influence use, development plans, location relationships, and value.

In analyzing productivity, the appraiser investigates the physical attributes of the subject property, identifies any limitations on its use, and considers the possibility that physical alterations will occur over the proposed holding period. Physical conditions can either create a comparative advantage for the property or reduce its market potential. A site's productive potential is analyzed to identify sites with the same or similar attributes, which represent potential competition.

Physical attributes can be divided into natural and man-made features. Natural features, which include geological features, place major constraints on the use potential of a site. Site terrain is a primary physical characteristic considered in the productivity analysis. To develop a site, the terrain may have to be graded or otherwise modified. The terrain may include natural amenities such as scenic views, creeks, and brooks, which can be important to both residential and commercial uses.

Some natural physical attributes that can influence property use and market potential are:

- Terrain or topography
- Soil composition and capacity
- Ground cover
- Site orientation (to sun, wind, infrastructure, and transportation)

Natural physical attributes often impact land use and market potential. For example, in high-tech industries campus-like sites are preferred for new facilities. Many industrial parks try to provide pleasant environments that foster worker productivity and new product development. The terrain and the elevation may determine the mix and layout of uses and recreational amenities. These real estate products attempt to replicate the facilities provided by large research universities, which are often centered around natural attributes.

Soil composition can be important to any development. Topsoils and subsoils that are especially prone to expansion and contraction may be unsuitable for building. Shifting soils and subsoils are not fit for bearing construction. The city planners of Austin, Texas, for example, had to take into account the limestone under sites to the west of the city and the impervious clay underlying land to the east. They drew up a city plan that allowed for growth, but preserved sensitive environmental areas. The result was a physically restrained, politically acceptable growth corridor running north and south through the city.

Knowledge of soil conditions and legal inducements, however, do not always redirect market preferences. Despite the preferential treatment given development within the growth corridor, building in the Austin market has tended to be more active in the southwest and northwest. The preferred direction of growth has been towards the hill and lake country to the west. Despite the high cost of development, the demand for the hill country terrain, which offers views and natural amenities in an otherwise level state, has placed market premiums on available land.

A site's orientation to sun and wind can also influence value. Site orientation can impact use, desirability, and occupancy. The downtown area of one Georgia community provides a good illustration. In the late 1960s and early

1970s, the community's major downtown retail area ran along a north-south axis. The stores on the east side of the street were exposed to the afternoon sun. The buildings on the west side were shaded, so most of the pedestrian traffic passed along the stores on that side of the street. The stores on the east side had more sun-faded inventory and incurred higher utility costs. In fact, operating expenses were generally much greater for stores on the east side. Vacancy in the downtown area at that time was 50%, almost all of which occurred on the east side of the street. Property values, returns, and rents were all based on these unique physical and locational circumstances. The marketability and worth of a building in this community was directly dependent on its location on the east or west side of the street.

The importance of the physical dimensions and other locational and legal attributes of a property to its value is addressed in the highest and best use section of an appraisal. The role of these attributes is often reflected in statements documenting the highest and best use conclusion, such as

- "The parcel is too small for a large, high-rise office facility."
- "The property shape is inappropriate for a retail enterprise, limiting visibility and access."
- "The topography is too steep for commercial use, but desirable for residential development."

Recognition of the physical constraints on a given site and an understanding of the legal attributes of the site are basic to a determination of site value. In site valuation, the analyst identifies the capacity of a site to capture a certain market share or to even monopolize demand in the given market. Many sites are endowed with unique characteristics. Critics of the appraisal process must recognize that appraisers have to deal with individual situations ad hoc.

Man-Made Features

Real estate is chiefly identified by man-made structures. Real capital improvements are added to a land resource, so real estate has a dual nature that comprises both land and capital assets. In an urban context, capital is the dominant concern because economic feasibility is a major criterion of the highest and best use of a land parcel.

Capital additions to land can be divided into two general groupings: site improvements and building structure(s).

Site Improvements

Site improvements are classified as on-site improvements and off-site improvements. On-site improvements, which are the most familiar capital additions to land, directly alter the site. Examples of on-site improvements are grading and leveling, terraced slopes, retaining walls, and drainage systems. Other on-site improvements include site and yard improvements such as landscaping, shrubbery, and surfaced areas (e.g., driveways, walks, parking areas). An amazing array of underground improvements are also necessary, including utility connections for sewers, water laterals, gas lines, and electrical wires. Expenditures for site improvements must be accounted for in the cost analysis of a specific property and tested for feasibility. The basis of feasibility must be market economics.

Off-site improvements also contribute to the value of an urban site. Off-site improvements, which are often held in common by the community, are considered in the analysis of the physical and locational attributes of the site. Examples of off-site improvements are the street and road system, the public sewage system, the water system, the disposal plant, the pumping station, sidewalks, and other infrastructure. Any of these improvements may afford competitive advantages to a given parcel and can explain differences in the incomes of competitive or substitutable properties.

Off-site improvements are installed by developers, governmental departments, or quasi-public agencies such as utility companies and can be paid for by various means. The capital outlay for off-site developments can be covered by incorporating the costs incurred by the developer into the lot prices or by levying a general property tax on the community. Other means of payment include specific user fees such as utility charges and special assessments to recover public expenditures for off-site improvements that may only benefit specific sites. Commercial lot development also requires additional capital expenditures to build streets, curbs, gutters, and sidewalks. These expenditures must be recaptured in some manner; the means of capital recovery may be reflected in price differentials.

Both on- and off-site improvements influence the cost and, hence, the supply of properties comparable to any given subject site or property group. Property attributes influence the nature of a product and thus define its competitiveness in the market.

The Building Structure

Analysis of the physical dimensions of real estate is important in market analysis for valuation. Productivity analysis investigates the physical attributes of a building improvement in terms of:

- The quality of the facilities
- The attractiveness of the structure
- The functional efficiency of the property

A principal concern of the analysis is understanding market preferences.[2] In other words, why are some projects more desirable than others? The quality of the facilities and their perceived attractiveness are dependent on demand, taste, and preferences.

Quality is often linked to the cost of construction, but is identified in a market context by structural standards and by alternative development in the market.

---

2. D. E. Hough and C.G. Kratz, "Can 'Good' Architecture Meet the Market Test?" *Journal of Urban Economics* (August 1983), 40-54.

The standards define the marketability attributes of a property or property type. Marketability attributes help the appraiser identify the real estate product, its use and market competition, and its potential capture and absorption rates.

Attractiveness is subjective and is not easily separated from the quality of a product. Quality appeals to different market segments, but attractiveness must be considered from the perspective of the market segment that defines the market standard. To do this the market analyst must identify the probable user group.

Functional efficiency describes the capacity of the property to satisfy contemporary tastes and preferences. The relationship between the property's internal design and current market standards as reflected in comparable properties is the test of functional efficiency.

LEGAL ATTRIBUTES AND PRODUCTIVITY ANALYSIS

The physical attributes of a realty product are part and parcel of the spatial nature of real estate. To understand property productivity, however, the legal dimensions of the realty must also be investigated because legal concerns as well as physical attributes set real estate apart from other types of assets. Legal vehicles are used to transfer and control the physical attributes of property. The right to use realty may be transferred on a temporary basis by means of a leasehold estate, or on a permanent basis by the passing of title to the fee simple estate. Different legal estates exist within a temporal framework. The combination of locational, physical, and legal dimensions forms the essence of the real estate product, i.e., the use of space over a defined period of time. Thus, real estate is a space-time product representing the combination of locational, physical, and legal attributes. An understanding of real estate's temporal dimension allows alternative products to be identified and further markets to be segmented.

Legal Concept of Real Estate

The legal status of real estate significantly affects its economic potential. The spatial dimensions of a parcel of real estate are generally defined in a legal description. The fourth dimension, time, is also fundamental to the creation of real estate value. The use and control of space occur within a temporal framework.

Legal concepts of real estate specify the interests of owners, users, and investors in a property. The legal transfer of property rights results in the assignation of surface rights, air rights, mineral rights, and subsurface tunnel rights. It forms the basis for investment strategies as complex as the "Hawaiian technique," a theory put forth by real estate developer William Zeckendorf that demonstrates that the sum of various leasehold interests can exceed the value of the fee simple estate.

The temporal dimension of real estate allows for the creation of alternative property products. The establishment of legal estates makes it possible to create financial interests such as mortgages and investment contracts. A special type of fee simple estate created by law is the fee simple condominium; another is the timeshare interest. A condominium owner holds rights to a three-dimensional space, usually an apartment unit, within a larger real estate entity. In a timeshare arrangement, an additional legal provision is introduced. The appraiser must estimate the value of the right to use the unit for a stipulated period of time.

Property Rights as the Basis of Productivity and Value

Legal arrangements can create new and alternative products which contribute to market segmentation. Market segments may also result from the different ways in which rights to property are assigned. Space may be transferred in perpetuity, i.e., for an indefinite period, by means of a fee simple estate or for a stated period through a leasehold. The various rights transferred by these legal arrangements are subject to certain constraints. The rights and limitations pertaining to the ownership, transfer, and use of a property can be separated into two general categories—private and public.

The ability to identify the level of supply and demand characterizing a market depends on an understanding of the specified number of rights describing the legal estate in the property. Property rights may also be legally transferred. The rights to most properties fall under the categories of fee simple and leasehold estates.

Property leases are classified according to the type of deed. Warranty deeds pass with the title to a parcel of realty. There are three types of warranty deeds: the general warranty deed, the special warranty deed, and the quitclaim deed.

The categories of warranty deeds and the title protection they afford are linked to corresponding levels of risk. Market analysis must address the levels of risk associated with the market and with the real estate venture. The potential for liability, loss, and additional expense is of primary concern in the valuation of property.

If the risk of a venture stems from a lack of title security, the property may be expected to sell for less and have a lower value. The value diminution attributable to this risk reflects the behavior of the market. In real estate, the market for a product must be clearly delineated to explain the prices actually paid and those offered or sought by market participants. Identification of the legal estates that define real property is essential to valuation.

The valuation process must focus on market activity. To estimate the market value of a specified legal interest, an appraiser must find a sale of a similar interest that is a reliable indicator of what the market is willing to pay. The appraiser investigates the supply of competitive alternatives and the effective demand for such an interest.

The markets for fee simple estates and for partial interests do not exist in a vacuum. Regardless of the degree of title security associated with a property transfer, each property and each transaction is subject to external forces. The real estate market is a regulated market. Even an estate held in fee simple absolute is, at the best, only exclusionary. (Exclusionary refers to the right of the property owner to exclude others from his or her property.) An estate held in fee simple absolute remains subject to the four powers of government.

The productivity of private property is constrained by certain public rights — i.e., the powers of government. The powers of government refer to the rights of federal, state, local, and quasi-public agencies to control, use, and acquire private property. The state and its numerous public agencies retain the rights of eminent domain, police power, taxation, and escheat.

Public Policy and Market Delineation

The attitudes and policies of a community can delineate a market. In major metropolitan areas, jurisdictions can change within a short distance. The Atlanta metropolitan area, for example, extends over several counties. Fulton and DeKalb are two of its primary counties. In the not too distant past, DeKalb County prohibited the sale of liquor while Fulton County did not. Land use along the major thoroughfares in east Fulton County was influenced by the demand for alcohol in DeKalb County. Accessibility to this demand was especially important. Thus, jurisdictional boundaries help to delineate markets.

Different jurisdictions hold distinct attitudes toward regulatory enforcement. These also must be considered in market delineation. The policy of a community can bring a windfall to individual property owners or wipe out their economic strength.

The state of Texas provides two examples of very different jurisdictions within 170 miles of each other. At one extreme is the city of Houston, which has resisted the adoption of a zoning code. In 1993 the city voted down proposed zoning restrictions. Control over land use is a judicial matter handled by the courts through the interpretation of restrictive covenants. The lack of zoning reflects the city's traditional laissez faire attitude toward property rights. The requirements that the city imposes on development fill less than two pages of its municipal ordinance book.

At the other extreme is Austin, which is located in an especially attractive setting, a much better environment than many other communities in Texas. Much of the citizenry and city leadership favor regulating land use to prevent the uncontrolled degradation of the surrounding countryside. Existing legal controls include zoning, watershed ordinances, hill country ordinances, roadway ordinances, extensive extraterritorial controls, and exactions and dedications. Whereas land use in Houston has long remained a private contractual matter subject to the judicial process, Austin has regulated land use with legislative and executive action. An encyclopedic knowledge of development regulations and ancillary literature is required before a developer can build in Austin. Local experts make themselves available as consultants just to get outside developers through the legal and regulatory dimensions of the development process.

Despite the differences in regulation and land markets, Austin and Houston have both experienced cyclical expansion, though the phases have occurred at different times. The level of regulation in a community affects the cost of producing a real estate product. Compared to Houston, Austin has markedly higher development costs. These costs impact the quantity of supply available over time. Community policy also influences the demand for different real estate products. As a general observation, recreational property now accounts for a larger share of Austin's real estate market.

The purpose of comparing these two cities is to illustrate the importance of regulatory requirements in delineating the market for a property. Failure to identify this factor will result in a flawed understanding of the market for the realty product.

Evaluating Preferences and Market Structure

Attitudes toward the regulation of real estate are not static features of isolated communities. Attitudes change and policies evolve. To identify the changes in a community's orientation, one must investigate recent legislation and litigation concerning land use. A community's inclination to control private real property use changes over time, often in a cyclical pattern. A period characterized by strong emphasis on the rights of government may be followed by a period of weak enforcement of public restrictions. A community may change its attitudes toward property rights or reconsider its position and go in an opposite direction. Many of the decisions involving the enforcement of rights have been ad hoc in nature.

The cyclical pattern of land use regulation can be traced to the changing attitudes and policies of our national government. Thomas Jefferson and the Founding Fathers believed that it was beneficial for the country to vest individuals with the right to property. This was the prevailing attitude for decades. The government promoted property ownership with land grants and land rushes. A vision of manifest destiny spurred the settlement of the American West. This attitude predominated as long as the country was basically rural. With urbanization, however, the potential for conflict over property rights increased. As people began to live in greater proximity to one another, conflicts arose involving not only land rights but also civil rights, e.g., racially restrictive covenants once prevented minorities from purchasing property in certain neighborhoods.

The government retained certain powers to deal with potential conflicts between the public interest and the rights of property owners. Over time, the courts have revised their position on the extent to which the state may enforce its regulatory powers. Appraisers must understand current attitudes toward the exercise of private property rights and public controls to evaluate the risk, returns, and expectations associated with property ownership and investment. Often the state's current enforcement of its regulatory powers can only be understood in light of past perceptions. These perceptions may explain in part the changes observed in price and yield data over time. The impact of changes in zoning and permitted density may also be related to historical change in the attitudes of a community or the residents of a jurisdiction. Legal or societal values can give rise to different economic values for parcels in the same tract. The following example illustrates how governmental rulings imposing different legally permissible uses may result in different estimates of a property's value.

Consider a vacant parcel of land of three acres that is to be appraised. Comparable sales data for vacant tracts that are similar in size, location, and other characteristics indicate a value of $60,000 per acre. Thus analysis of comparable sales data suggests that the parcel has a total value of $180,000.

Assume that the owner of the parcel has approved plans to develop a 150-unit hotel on the three-acre site and has filed for a development permit. For some reason the state government decides to block the development of the site as planned. In this case, the value estimate cannot be decided without determining why the state has refused to issue the development permit. The range of value would be between the $180,000 estimated above and the $8,262,000 estimate of prospective value that is developed below. It is not clear whether the state's ruling merely restricts the legal use of the property or represents an actual taking.

Because the owner will probably initiate proceedings to reverse the state's action, the following prospective value can be estimated based on the proposed plan of use.

150 units with 360 beds per night = 54,000 revenue units (beds per night)
54,000 revenue units @ $30.00 per unit = $1,620,000

The $1,620,000 figure represents the total potential revenue that could be generated by the development of the proposed facilities. Based on this income projection and supplementary information on vacancies, expenses, and market capitalization rates, the prospective value of the property may be estimated as follows:

Potential gross income (*PGI*)	$1,620,000
Less vacancy at 15%	243,000
Effective gross income (*EGI*)	$1,377,000
Less expenses @ 40% (of *EGI*)	550,800
Net operating income (*NOI*)	$ 826,200

$$NOI \text{ capitalized at a 10\% rate} = \frac{NOI}{R_O} = \frac{826,200}{.10} = \$8,262,000$$

The estimated prospective value based on the capitalization of *NOI* is $8,262,000.

Since the 1970s there have been many cases relating to the use of private property and a state's right to take private land or control its use. Much of this litigation arises from conflicts between a developer who wants to develop a property and a city that seeks to regulate growth, impose limits on development, and protect the environment. Because value is defined as the present worth of future benefits, these issues are important. The relationship between private property rights and public regulations determines the expected benefits accruing from property ownership, the limitations on these benefits, and the associated risks. As illustrated, different use scenarios result in different values. In the example presented above, the action of the state will decide the highest and best use of the property.

Legal trends influence society's attitude toward property rights. The legal environment affects both individual real estate products and the structure of the market.

PRODUCTIVITY AND LOCATION— THE SPACE-TIME PRODUCT

Physical and legal attributes combine to create real estate, which is essentially space used to house alternative uses over time. Physical and legal attributes and constraints determine the suitability of a piece of real estate for a particular use. The appropriate use of a site depends on the urban structure and the linkage of the site to the market. The following example illustrates how the combination of legal and physical attributes results in a space-time product. In the example, the use capacity of the property is determined through an analysis of both situs (the specific location) and urban structure. (These concepts will be covered in greater depth in Chapters 4 and 5.)

The Building Envelope: An Example

Characterizing a real estate product by its spatial and temporal dimensions may be alien to many real estate professionals. Viewing real estate as space used over time to house economic activities or satisfy human needs focuses attention on the behavioral foundation of value. This perception invalidates the notion that value is inherent in physical objects.

The interaction of legal and physical attributes to create real estate is illustrated by the development of the "building envelope" for a specific property, i.e., the area of the property reserved for setbacks, parking, or open space.

Consider a 150-ft.-by-100-ft. (15,000 sq. ft.) lot situated on the corner of two major streets. One interior property line abuts a residential neighborhood while the other abuts a commercially zoned lot. The zoning classification suggests that a one-story retail structure could be developed. Several other uses are possible, but the retail facility would generate the greatest potential return to the site.

The zoning of the site requires a 5-ft. setback on the side abutting the residential land. A 10-ft. building line is required at the rear of the property. This line prevents building within 10 feet of the rear property line, but this area can be used for parking. The 5-ft. area abutting the residential property cannot be used for parking because, by law, no improvements can be made on the setback that abuts a different property use. (See the plot plan in Figure 3.1.) Based on the zoning restrictions, the usable square footage is calculated as follows:

Basic land (150 x 100)	15,000 sq. ft.
Less setbacks (150 x 5)	750 sq. ft.
Land available for use	14,250 sq. ft.

Figure 3.1
Plot Plan for Proposed Retail Site

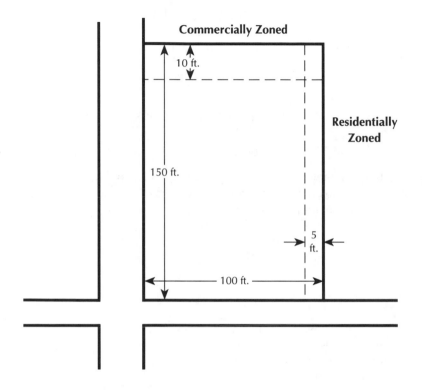

The development regulations and local zoning require that 300 square feet of parking be allotted for each 300 square feet of net building area planned. The estimated building efficiency ratio (i.e., the ratio of rentable area to gross building area) based on market trends and the ratios found in comparable structures is 90%. Thus 300 square feet of net building area translates into 333.33 square feet of gross building area.

300 sq. ft./0.90 = 333.33 sq. ft. of gross building

The allocation of land use for the one-story retail facility is set forth below. If 333.33 square feet of gross building area, "the building footprint," requires 300 square feet of ground parking (including parking stalls and access area), the basic land area equation is

Building footprint	333.33
Surface parking	300.00
Total land required per unit	633.33

Then land allocation units can be calculated.

$$\frac{14{,}250 \text{ sq. ft. of land available}}{633.33 \text{ sq. ft. required per unit}} = 22.50$$

The total land use allocation is calculated as follows:

Building area per floor
333.33 sq. ft. x 22.50 = 7,500 sq. ft. gross
Parking area
300 sq. ft. x 22.50 = 6,750 sq. ft.

Total land available for use   14,250 sq. ft.

The above example demonstrates how the physical and legal components of real estate interact to establish the space that will be developed. A general formula for calculating the building envelope is provided below.

$$\frac{A - Sb}{(Bu/Er) + Pu\,(S) + O} = LAU$$

Where: A is lot area
Sb is setback area
Bu is building area
Er is efficiency ratio
Pu is size of parking unit
S is number of stories
O is open space (if any)
LAU is land allocation unit

The data from the example can be substituted into the formula, as follows:

$$\frac{15{,}000 - 750}{(300/0.9) + 300\,(1) + 0} = 22.50$$

The land allocation unit (22.50) is then applied to the building and parking areas to check that the allocation for the adjusted lot size is correct.

The example illustrates that physical and legal constraints are important to product definition and estimates of projected income and value. In the example, the calculated building area is 7,500 sq. ft. At a development cost of $45 per square foot, the total building cost would come to $337,500. The land was purchased for $100,000, thus the total investment would be $437,500.

Net floor area can be used as the basis for estimating rental income. The net floor area of the proposed structure is 6,750 square feet. At an annual net rental of $8 per square foot (including an appropriate vacancy and collection loss), the property's probable net operating income would be $54,000. Applying a market-derived capitalization rate of 10%, the potential *NOI* can be capitalized into a value estimate of $540,000. This is $102,500 more than the cost of construction, which indicates that the market will support the retail facility and the project is economically feasible.

SUMMARY

In a real estate context, productivity analysis is the study of a property's capacity to house economic activities, supply services, and provide amenities to meet human needs. Productivity analysis relates the value of a product to the marketability of its attributes. The physical, legal, and locational attributes of real property are linked to market preferences.

The physical attributes of a property may make it appropriate for a specific use. Physical attributes may also act as constraints that limit the use of a property. Physical attributes include natural features and man-made site improvements and buildings.

The ownership, transfer, and use of property are subject to private entitlements and public controls. The rights to most properties fall under the categories of fee simple and leasehold estates. The type of deed further differentiates leasehold properties. Eminent domain, police power, taxation, and escheat constitute the four powers that government exercises over real property. The legal characteristics and physical dimensions of real estate are specified in a property's legal description.

The regulatory environment of a community is closely linked to market delineation within that community. Societal attitudes and judicial interpretation play a significant role in defining a realty product and delineating its market. Attitudes are continually evolving. Past, present, and future perceptions of the relationship between individual property rights and public regulation must be considered in the market research and valuation processes. The benefits that derive from real estate depend on how these rights are exercised. The character of a real property interest, the public constraints on its use, the timing of its development, and the risks associated with contractual agreements must be considered to derive a value estimate that accurately reflects market expectations.

CHAPTER OBJECTIVES

—⇒•⇐—

- To describe how the location of the site relates to its immediate surroundings
- To discuss the concept of situs
- To explain the relationship between the location of a site and its broader, urban surroundings
- To discuss the various land use environments that affect a location: the physical environment, the social and cultural environment, the psychological environment, and the institutional and political environment

CHAPTER FOUR

—▸•◂—

Introduction to Location

T he most important factor affecting real estate value is probably location. As the third aspect of property examined in productivity analysis, location is fundamental to an understanding of real estate and its value. Chapter 3 demonstrated that the physical and legal attributes of a property are important to its marketability. Any in-depth discussion of location must be presented in relation to the physical and legal aspects of property. Zoning, for example, has both legal and spatial, or locational, dimensions that influence property value and impact highest and best use.[1] Urban structure cannot be described without reference to the physical terrain, infrastructure, and skyline of the city.[2]

In this chapter the attributes of location are investigated on three levels. The first level of location covers the internal space planning of the site and its immediate surroundings. The second level studied is the relationship between the site and its surroundings. In land economics *situs* is the concept that addresses the relationship of the total urban environment to a specific use on a specific parcel of land functioning within a given time frame.[3]

---

1. Zoning is often plotted on city maps, which reflect the spatial nature of legal constraints and restrictions on land use.

2. The range of issues pertaining to urban structure is demonstrated by the research of urban and land economists, sociologists, geographers, and engineers. A series of monographs edited by Richard B. Andrews and titled *Urban Structure Theory*, Parts I - V, provides insight into the eclectic nature of the urban structure. The series is available through the Center for Urban Land Economics Research, Graduate School of Business, University of Wisconsin, Madison.

3. Richard B. Andrews, *Urban Land Economics and Public Policy* (New York: Free Press, 1971). Andrews thoroughly developed the concept of economic location within the framework of situs theory.

The third level of location analyzed is the overall urban structure and the interrelationships within a community's land use pattern. The study of location at this level is discussed in Chapter 5. As described in that chapter, urban structure is concerned with the community's economic base; its present, past, and future land use patterns; and the magnitude and direction of expected growth.

The interrelationship of the three levels of location is analogous to the biological interrelationship of a cell, an organ, and an organism (see Figure 4.1). As the figure illustrates, a site can be thought of as a cell. In a living organism, each individual cell has a specialized function in relation to the immediately surrounding cells and the overall organism. Despite the cell's unique features, it also has many attributes in common with other cells.

This relationship between the part and the whole applies to a site as well. Each parcel of land has characteristics that are similar, if not identical, to the attributes of other sites. The specific combination of property characteristics, however, limits the range of possible functions that can be conducted on any given site.

To carry the analogy further, a cell with specialized functions is interdependent on surrounding cells and relates to the organ of which it is a part. Similarly, a site is linked to the neighborhood, the land use district, or the trade area and to the total urban environment. The concept of situs analyzes the linkages of a site to the urban environment and can be used to explore the site's economic situation.

As the final step in the analogy, the cell, or site, is linked to the overall organism, which may be the city, community, metropolitan area, or metropolitan statistical area (MSA). An understanding of the development and economic base

Figure 4.1
Site as a Cell

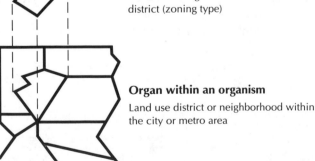

Site as a cell

Cell within an organ
Site within neighborhood or land use district (zoning type)

Organ within an organism
Land use district or neighborhood within the city or metro area

of the overall community provides insight into the spatial dimension and dynamics of the market. Urban economic analysis is the basis for the supply and demand relationship that defines real estate value.

The link between urban location and real estate value was first recognized by Alfred Marshall. In his *Principles of Economics*, published in 1890, Marshall established the foundation for the valuation approaches adopted by the Appraisal Institute in the 1930s and identified location as the essence of urban real estate. The term Marshall used was *urban situation value*.[4]

The biological analogy suggests a process for analyzing location by directly linking productivity analysis with the supply and demand relationship identified in the market. The supply of and demand for real estate must be considered within a spatial context. The projection of supply and demand must consider locational attributes to identify existing and proposed competition and to assess the magnitude of demand and the direction of development.

Market analysis may be seen as employing three filters or channeling agents. These filters are a location filter, which processes the locational attributes along with the other productivity attributes, a supply filter, and a demand filter. These filters are used to remove irrelevant data from the market analysis and to focus the analysis on the essential factors influencing the use and value of the site.

LOCATION: SITE AND SITUS

The study of location in productivity analysis corresponds to the typical appraisal problem, i.e., a site in search of a use or market. Generally, location analysis for an appraisal begins with a specific site. The appraiser inspects the site, investigating both the locational characteristics of the neighborhood and the locational attributes of the site. This is the stage of productivity analysis in which locational, physical, and legal attributes are interrelated and often cross-categorized.

Location analysis is concerned with the placement of spatial attributes and how these attributes relate to specific functions. It is difficult to analyze location without reference to a specific use. Just as the analysis of use requires an investigation of location, the analysis of location must be undertaken within the context of a specific use. Only the use type must be specified; the use need not exist at the time of the analysis. For example, in highest and best use analysis, various use scenarios are considered as though the site were vacant. One might begin by analyzing the property from the perspective of a potential office building use and then find that the site is inappropriate because the area lacks adequate support facilities. In this hypothetical case, a retail use might be considered next and subsequently be eliminated for the same reason. A residential use, however, might ultimately pass the locational scrutiny. Thus, the analytical process can be seen as a funnel or sieve in which various uses are sifted until one appropriate use is able to pass through all of the filters. An analyst could consider an office use, retail

---

4. Alfred Marshall, *Principles of Economics*, 18th ed. (London: Macmillan and Company, 1920).

use, residential use, and mixed use for a given property even though it is currently improved with a warehouse.

As these examples illustrate, even a generic location is considered in light of its suitability for a specific land use. Highest and best use is thereby tied to market analysis and valuation.

Site Location and the Immediate Area

The layout of a site and the location of various activities on the property must be related to the shape of the parcel. At this stage in the analysis, the physical and locational attributes of the site cannot be considered separately. The dimensions of the site determine the shape of the property and influence the placement of structures, the layout of yard improvements and parking facilities, and the general maintenance requirements. The shape of the site affects its adaptability to alternative uses and thus its market appeal over time. Some important spatial considerations are listed below.

- The number of sides a site has determines its degree of exposure or seclusion. For a retail use, exposure is desirable. Assuming that access is convenient and the flow of traffic is manageable, a multi-sided site is highly desirable for a retail use. For a residential site, however, privacy, not exposure, is usually desired.

- The functional layout of the facilities on a site are often the key to the site's marketability. The placement of structures and parking areas cannot be separated from the ease of ingress to and egress from the site.

- The degree of "friction" or inconvenience in accessing a site indicates how well the site is linked to its environment. In considering access, the appraiser should determine whether the traffic flow inward or outward is more significant and whether this flow involves goods, services, or people. If the site is primarily visited by consumers, its location should provide convenient access with a minimum of aggravation. The mode of transport for goods will vary with the weight and bulk of the material being conveyed. Service delivery requires reasonable access to the site.

- The flow of traffic within the site should also be considered. On-site "friction" can be reduced by the placement and design of facilities, which should ensure that the property has market appeal, both functional and aesthetic.[5]

The Concept of Situs

Situs theory rests on the belief that land uses are interdependent and economic activities are interrelated. It focuses on the movement between centers of activity, or

---

5. The relationship between traffic flow and site layout is discussed in Grady Clay's *Close-up: How to Read the American City* (Chicago: University of Chicago Press, 1973).

loci, and the accessibility of these loci. Situs has been defined as the relationship between the total urban environment and a specific land use on an individual land parcel at a specific time.[6] This definition encompasses several elements fundamental to appraisal and market analysis. One key idea is that the land use of a given parcel and the locus of the parcel are separate.

Any given site may have a range of possible uses that are suited to the site legally, physically, and locationally. Although the site is physically fixed, it is economically flexible in terms of use. *Economic location*, the concept that a site functions as a locus of economic activity in association with other loci within a dynamic urban structure, is a central concern in market delineation and valuation. In everyday practice, it may be difficult to separate the concepts of economic location and physical location. Physical location refers to the position of one site relative to that of another. The term *physical location* is often used interchangeably with *proximity* and *accessibility*. In this chapter, the concept of location is extended to include the economic concerns of appraisal and real estate market analysis. The general concepts of location, proximity, and accessibility will be examined from various technical perspectives to better understand the real estate product and market in a spatial context.

The definition of situs refers to the relationship of uses as a function of time as well as space. As forces outside the land parcel alter the relationships of uses, the activities conducted on the site and the economic nature of the site itself begin to change. From an appraisal standpoint, the location analysis of a site cannot be separated from the life cycle of the neighborhood. The concept of situs is the building block that undergirds all these economic issues and links highest and best use and market analysis to the valuation process.

SITUS PROCESS

Situs is not only a theory relating the individual site to its immediate neighborhood or overall urban environment, but also a practical analytical process. The situs process links the data and the concerns raised by the data into an overall study of location, land use, and market analysis. The situs process is applied in gathering, classifying, and analyzing information and comprises four steps. These steps are

1. Identification of the activities in the area
2. Study of the nature of the associations between these activities
3. Analysis of the accessibility of the site to the surrounding area
4. Evaluation of the impact of the total area on the site use

---

6. Andrews, *Urban Land Economics and Public Policy,* Chapter 2. Readers interested in situs topics may also wish to consult Robert H. Zerbst, "Locational Attributes of Property Values," *The Real Estate Appraiser* (May-June 1976), 19-21; R. James Claus and Walter G. Hardwick, *The Mobile Consumer* (Toronto: Collier-Macmillan, 1972), 8-10 and 143-144; and Grady Clay, *Close Up: How to Read the American City* (Chicago: University of Chicago Press, 1973).

To identify the activities in an area and analyze the associations between them, the appraiser must demarcate the spatial boundaries of the subject neighborhood. Understanding the spatial nature of real estate and real estate markets allows the analyst to define the physical limits of the real estate market. Boundaries identified with natural features can often be drawn for real estate markets, but such boundaries may not be appropriate for defining markets for consumer goods or commodities. The boundaries of non-real estate markets are often determined by the productive capacity of the manufacturer or the limitations of the distributor that markets or warehouses the product. For real estate, however, the locational or spatial dimension of the site is a key determinant of the product. While this fact complicates productivity analysis, it can facilitate delineation of the market.

Market Boundaries

The productivity of real estate is strongly influenced by its economic and physical location. The analysis of economic location goes beyond identification of the physical position of one property in relation to another.[7] Analysis of economic location begins with identification of the economic activities in the neighborhood or trade area, which is delineated by physical, political, and socioeconomic boundaries or by the time-distance relationships represented by travel times to and from common destinations.

A property can have an international or national market, a regional or statewide market, an urban or rural market, or a district or neighborhood market. In appraising a large industrial plant, for example, an appraiser might study the national or even the international market for the property. The geographic extent of the market for a property is determined by the real estate itself and by features such as the amount of space involved, the price level or price range of the property, and the current or intended use of the space. Therefore, the geographic extent of the market for office buildings in major commercial cities is generally broader than the market for single-family residences in rural communities.

Boundaries can be established using various criteria. The boundaries for neighborhoods and trade areas can be based on geographical features such as lakes, hills, and mountains. Markets can also be delineated by topographical features that prevent development or impede transportation between sections of a community. Man-made features such as expressways, divided highways, one-way streets, walls, building bulk lines (zoning mandates), bridges, infrastructure, and designed environments (e.g., landscaped lakes, parks) can create market boundaries, as can political or legal jurisdictions. Different incorporated communities within a metropolitan area may impose different legal restrictions on land use. A slight difference in location, e.g., a location within the limits of an incorporated community versus one outside the jurisdiction of the community, can alter the maintenance costs and lot prices prevailing in the market. Location can

---

7. Terry V. Grissom, "A Feasibility Process: The Benefits of Land Economics and Risk Management," *The Appraisal Journal* (July 1984).

also determine the services available to a real estate product. The combination of cost and available services can help delineate the competition and market for a particular facility.

The time/distance variable is a major economic determinant of a market trade area. The cost of transporting people or goods from a facility to other specific locales must be considered in relation to the cost to access competitive sites. The economic and psychological dimensions of a market area are often defined by the effort required to travel between one location and another. The distance workers are willing to commute often sets the boundaries of a neighborhood. This issue is further discussed under the analysis of accessibility in this chapter and in relation to the rent theorist school of urban structure in Chapter 5.

Neighborhoods are also defined by the homogeneity or compatibility of the land uses. The next step in location analysis, therefore, is to identify the major characteristics of a neighborhood.

Identification of Activities

The means of identifying the activities in an area range from a simple survey of existing land uses to a major economic base study. The key activities that characterize a neighborhood are those that attract people to the specific location. These activities, which function like economic magnets, may be represented by major employers, recreational facilities, institutions, services, or physical features such as rivers and roads. The activity of a shopping center, for example, generates further activity in the area.

Primary activities often define the character of a neighborhood and form the basis of the neighborhood's economy. For example, the central business district (CBD) of most communities is typified by high-rise office buildings. The activities of the office building tenants determine the overall character of the area. The office buildings along Madison Avenue and those along Wall Street in Manhattan are used by different tenant-occupants. The needs of these tenants and the character of surrounding land uses are different. The tenants on Madison Avenue are mostly marketing and advertising agencies, while Wall Street tenants provide financial services. Although both areas are dominated by business enterprises, the associated activities nearby vary.

The identification of primary activities in a city is the foundation for economic base analysis. These activities must also be identified for specifically defined trade areas and neighborhoods. A thorough understanding of a neighborhood is only gained through the identification of its key activities, which begins with a functional study of the general land uses in the area. After a drive through the area, the analyst can prepare a schematic drawing of immediate land uses, which can readily aid the decision maker. A simple land use survey such as this can be developed into a more sophisticated study. Rapid changes rarely affect an entire area within a short period of time. If changes are occurring in the neighborhood, the analysis should focus on identifying these changes.

The identification of primary activities and the related land uses that develop around them leads to our second concern—the association of land uses.

Identification of Associations

Associations characterize the relationship among the various activities in the subject neighborhood. Activities may be complementary, subservient, or competitive. They may even repell one another. Categories of land use associations are identified in Table 4.1. The nature of the relationship among any set of land uses is determined by their economic function.

Competitive automobile dealers, for example, generally locate next to one another. In most cases, a car is not bought on impulse. A car is a durable good purchased after one or more comparative shopping trips. Car dealers find it mutually advantageous to be close to their competitors and they often locate on cheaper, out-of-the-way land. The nature of activities and their associations influence the use of land in any particular area.

The first general category presented in Table 4.1 is a dominant use/subordinate use relationship in which the subordinate enterprises serve the operation of the dominant activity. For example, assume a major printing and publishing company locates in a community and hires 1,000 employees in various occupations. In due time, the analyst can expect supply and trucking companies to locate in the area to serve the large publishing company. These subservient activities may employ 100 more people. This same relationship can be seen in the proximity of machine shops to manufacturing plants, the location of food jobbers in areas with inexpensive access to fast-food restaurants and supermarkets, and the proximity of law offices to courthouses, public records offices, and law libraries.

In the dominant use/subordinate use relationship, the subordinate land use activity is directly involved in the dominant activity—e.g., a distributor supplies materials needed for manufacturing, a lawyer litigates cases at the courthouse.

The second type of land use association is a dominant use/ancillary use relationship in which the ancillary activity serves the clients or employees of the dominant use. Examples are cigar, gift, or florist shops located on the first floor of an office building. The ancillary character of the land use is emphasized when the shop has an internal orientation, with little or no external access or exposure to the outside of the building. If the shop fronts on the lobby, atrium, or foyer of the office building, it probably serves an ancillary function within the overall structure.

Other examples of ancillary uses are restaurants, bookshops, and computer stores located near a university. Bookshops and computer stores overlap

Table 4.1

General Categories of Land Use Associations

I. Dominant use/subordinate use

II. Dominant use/ancillary use

III. Codominant uses (or dominant use)/satellite uses

in the categories of goods sold. Books and computerware can be seen as direct inputs into the education of students, who represent the "product" of the university. Many items purchased at these ancillary facilities do not directly contribute to educational programs, but rather to the personal development of the students.

The third general category of land use associations concerns the relationship of codominant and dominant uses to satellite uses. This category is exemplified by the facilities at a shopping center or mall. The codominant uses are the large department stores, which draw consumers to the center. The codominant uses serve the same demand as the satellite uses, i.e., the customers who buy at the large department stores also patronize the adjacent shops where similar products are sold. In dominant/satellite relationships, the satellite facilities capitalize on the drawing power of the dominant anchors—e.g., a candy store in a shopping center or a cafeteria in a hospital. Often the satellite use in a dominant use/satellite use relationship takes on characteristics of an ancillary use, but the key to the satellite function is dependence on the drawing power of the dominant/codominant use.

Codominant or dominant use and satellite use relationships are not limited to shopping centers. They can be identified in a range of neighborhoods or trade areas. For example, the basic economic activities of Austin's central business district (i.e., the codominant uses) are governmental offices and financial institutions. The various state, federal, and local government offices often serve the same clientele as the financial service buinesses (banks and savings and loans). The law firms, lobbyists, and professional groups located near the courthouse and government offices can be considered satellite functions. Ancillary services in the CBD such as retail shops, restaurants, hotels, and recreational facilities are direct recipients of the business drawn to the dominant activities.

By understanding the quality and extent of land use associations, the analyst gains insight into the stability, durability, and development potential of a given property or neighborhood. Studying the associations among the land uses in an area over time will help the analyst forecast the direction of growth and future land use patterns.

Analysis of Accessibility

Accessibility, the third aspect of location analysis, addresses the degree of convenience or inconvenience involved in moving people, goods, and services between different loci of activity. The degree of friction, or inconvenience, is measured in terms of time, cost, and aggravation. Accessibility is akin to negative transportation cost. The greater the site's accessibility to major activities and complementary land uses, the lower the cost to get to the property and the higher the potential site return in income and market value. The importance of accessibility to a specific use is reflected in what one user (or buyer) will pay over another for any specific site.

The interrelationship of activities, associations, and accessibility affects the allocation of land uses. An understanding of these relationships facilitates the identification of the highest and best use or most probable use of a site.

The analyst should be concerned with accessibility on two levels. On one level, the flow of people between one area and another is considered. On another level, the analyst examines the subject site, ingress to and egress from the property, and the immediate area of the site. Various concepts have been developed by urban land economists, geographers, and landscape architects to facilitate this analysis.[8]

Macro-level Accessibility

Macro-level accessibility reflects the trade-off between the transportation cost to the site and the specific features and amenities the site offers. Macro-level accessibility is reflected in site rents or sale prices and can be linked directly to the drawing power of dominant or codominant land uses.

In gravity models of retail attraction, drawing power operates in inverse proportion to distance, like the relationship in Newton's law of gravity, which states that the force of gravity between two masses is inversely proportional to the square of the distance between them. The greater the number of competitors (dominant and codominant uses) in an area, the greater the total volume of potential consumers seeking access to the area.

Drawing power is contingent on specific land uses. As mentioned earlier, automobile dealerships cluster near their competitors. This clustering is called the *economics of agglomeration*. The economic advantage for automobile dealers is that many dealers offering only slightly differentiated products are found in proximity to one another. Since the purchase of an automobile requires premeditated travel and comparative shopping trips, a number of dealers located together creates a collectively dominant land use association and emits a gravitational pull. The accessibility of several alternative facilities in one location more than offsets any friction required to reach the location. Thus, even in regard to macro-level accessibility, the analysis must be use-specific to identify the relationships and linkages between activities. The analyst must develop an understanding of how the land uses operate.

The focus of analysis at the macro level is the competition of uses within the overall urban structure. This competition is based on the ability of a land user to pay a competitive price for a desirable location. If a land use is outbid by other land uses for a given site, and a less desirable site is obtained, then an additional transportation cost may be incurred because of the lack of accessibility. The economic trade-off between site rents and macro-level accessibility explains the economic structure of cities, which is addressed in Chapter 5.

---

8. Andrews, *Urban Structure Theory*, monograph series.

To investigate the importance of accessibility to a specific area, the analyst must describe or explain the character, direction, distance, and frequency of trips to and from a particular land use. On a macro level this can be done by focusing on the relationship between a neighborhood or trade area sector and the overall city. This relationship is important for two reasons:

1. The neighborhood is a focal point for inward and outward trips relating to specific land uses or aggregations of land uses.
2. The neighborhood monopolizes certain "packets" of movement and accounts for the majority of high-frequency, short trips.

Thus, while travel within a neighborhood defines the micro level of accessibility (down to site ingress and egress), travel between neighborhoods forms the basis of macro-level accessibility.

A neighborhood's drawing power and macro-accessibility can be determined by studying the size and traffic volume of connecting arterials, the nature of linkages outside the area, the number and types of establishments within the neighborhood, and the competition in other neighborhoods. Analysis of macro-level accessibility entails the identification of key roadways and public transportation lines, the study of traffic counts, and the measurement of travel time and distance to other centers of activity associated with the neighborhood.

The accessibility characteristics of a neighborhood will often determine the desirability of the neighborhood and its status within the overall community. The ease of access and desirability are indicators of the area's potential for growth and the future direction of that growth.

Movement patterns between neighborhoods are also useful for identifying areas of potential development. Urban geographers use the term *zones of conflux* for land segments where activities with considerable drawing power are located. In these areas arterials and other infrastructure have been developed to direct or pull vehicular traffic into the area. Most cities have zones of conflux where such characteristic economic activity and infrastructure combine. When these factors are present and identifiable in specific locales, the analyst can determine likely growth patterns and location rankings. The process for the real estate decision maker is to identify:

1. The major economic activities within the area
2. The associations between these activities and related activities
3. The relationship of the activity center to major or heavily traveled roadways

The zones of conflux will be found where the volume of activity exerts a strong pull and major roadways intersect or converge.

Micro-level Accessibility

After the drawing power and accessibility of the area are considered, the next objective of location analysis is to analyze micro-level accessibility. Micro-level accessibility is concerned with linkage relationships, i.e., the movement between, or proximity of, associated activities. (Linkage relationships were classified in Table 4.1.) A linkage relationship between activities is characterized by continuing or recurring interaction, which necessitates movement between the sites. Proximity may be a secondary component in the transportation of persons and goods.

Linkage relationships have various orientations.[9] Movements can have an inward or outward orientation—i.e., to or from a land use or establishment. It is possible to categorize movements more specifically as assembling movements, dispersive movements, and random movements.

An *assembling movement* is characterized by convergence on a focal point. This type of movement is illustrated by a commuter's journey to work in the CBD or the convergence of shoppers on a shopping center. In contrast, a *dispersive movement* spreads out from a focal point. On a micro level, dispersion is represented by outward movement from a given site, subdivision, or neighborhood. On a macro level, it is reflected in commuters leaving the aggregate of subdivisions and bedroom communities in the metropolitan area to journey to work. Often seen as assembling movements and dispersive movements are flip sides of the same movement. Commuting can be seen as an assembling movement from the perspective of employers in the labor market and as a dispersive movement from the perspective of residential neighborhoods.

A *trapping point* is a configuration of uses that is especially conducive to assembling movements. Trapping points are micro-level zones of conflux. A well-known site supported by good infrastructure and design features exerts a strong gravitational pull, creating an influx of people, goods, and activities to the area. Cincinnati's Fountain Square, Manhattan's Times Square, San Francisco's Fisherman's Wharf, and Boston's Faneuil Hall and Quincy Market are all trapping points.

In a *random movement* pattern, goods or persons are dispersed among various locations along the route. A random movement can occur at either end of the route—at its terminus or where it converges with another route.

Regardless of the pattern, it is difficult to analyze a movement without linking it to a specific use or activity. An understanding of existing activities and movement patterns helps identify the support network that surrounds a given site or will sustain a proposed use and market for that site. These factors must be considered to analyze a property's viability in terms of a highest and best use. The nature and orientation of the movement patterns must be identified along with the frequency and volume of trips. To measure specific activities on sites, trip patterns can be identified by survey or observation. For example, the number of trips made to a supermarket each week by its clientele and the typical dollar amount spent per trip indicate the nature and frequency of one movement pattern. Traffic volume counts may be used as a secondary data source.

---

9. Ibid., Part I.

The quantifiable measures of access are dollar costs, the time and distance traveled, the frequency of the trips, and the degree of irritation experienced. The importance of each of these factors varies with the mode of transportation involved.

The dollar costs of movement are either fixed or variable. For public transportation, these costs are measured in taxes and/or user fees. The former are fixed; the latter vary with the level of service provided. For private transportation, fixed costs include registration fees for the automobile license and title, the cost of insurance, and a personal property tax. Variable costs include expenses incurred for fuel, lubricants, maintenance, driving fines, and parking fees. Collectively, all the expenses incurred to access a site over and above the costs of accessing a more convenient location represent the opportunity cost of occupying that site. In effect, a higher cost of accessibility offsets the lower site rent. Accessibility on both a macro level and a micro level is a key attribute that strongly influences a property's use, marketability, and value. The land economist William Alonso propounded a theory of rent that segmented site value into two components—accessibility and location. In situs theory, however, accessibility is treated as a dimension of location. For purposes of analysis and decision making, the two attributes should be addressed as separate, but related, factors.

Impact of the Overall Environment on Site Use

The final element in the analysis of situs is the relationship between the total urban environment and the specific neighborhood. Like neighborhood analysis, the analysis of the urban environment considers social, physical, economic, and institutional features. These features are set, but the environment is also described in terms of access, specifically the surroundings through which goods and people must travel to reach a site. Certain amenities and noneconomic attributes are also classified as environmental components of situs. Thus, *environment* is a loosely defined term for the area surrounding a property. Although external to the site, the environment reflects certain spatial aspects of the site's physical and legal productivity attributes.

Environmental attributes are generally characterized as immobile externalities. Nevertheless, environmental attributes combine with accessibility in defining the gravitational draw of an area. Environmental attributes correspond to the measure of mass in the gravity models discussed in Chapter 7.

In general, environmental factors are often identified as area amenities. Investigation indicates that the environment encompasses many other spatial considerations—e.g., land use; physical, social, cultural, psychological, and economic factors; and institutional or political concerns.

The key to analyzing the environment is understanding that all the above-mentioned topics affect realty markets. Often the economic environment is said to be the focus of real estate decision makers. In a broad sense, the economic environment encompasses all the other dimensions. In fact, all these environmental attributes are interwoven so closely that any "true" breakdown for discussion purposes would be artificial. Most of the breakdowns available are the result of independent investigation into different real estate issues by various disciplines.

The following discussion should help real estate analysts and decision makers develop a systematic process for addressing this qualitative dimension of property. Such a process should include investigation of the:

- Land use environment. The land use pattern is usually based on function, the clustering of related land uses in a given area of the city.

- Physical environment. A description of the nature and extent of land use associations in an area is required to determine whether the land uses in the neighborhood or trade area are compatible, competitive, and/or supportive. Such associations influence the quality of land use and the exposure of the existing land use pattern to internal and/or external competition. The nature of the land use pattern also indicates the stage of the neighborhood in its life cycle.

- Highest and best use analysis. The nature of land use patterns accounts for the duration of existing uses and the spatial risks to which the specific market area is exposed. Identifying the land use pattern establishes a foundation for highest and best use analysis of the area.

Physical Environment

The physical environment is characterized by both natural and artificial features. Natural features include the topography (grade and elevation), vegetation and ground cover, the atmosphere (climate), the condition of the surface and subsurface soils, any bodies of water, and any natural phenomena in proximity to the neighborhood.

Most land uses adapt well to flat or gently rolling, well-drained land. Extreme grades are often an impediment to land use. Topography influences the potential for development and may often direct the nature of the land use pattern. For example, the development of El Paso, Texas, reflects the economic significance of the city's proximity to the Rio Grande and the Franklin Mountains. The extreme variation in terrain, from lush river valley to rugged mountains and desert, have strongly influenced the economic delineation of El Paso's neighborhoods.

The following features are considered in the analysis of the physical environment:

- Atmosphere and microclimate
- Surface infrastructure (street system and sidewalks)
- Topography
- Wind direction
- Soil composition and capacity to support structures
- Installation of subsurface utilities (water, sewer, gas, etc.)

- Vegetation (an aesthetic amenity that can enhance the area's competitiveness)

Of course, the natural physical environment must be linked to the artificial, or built, environment. The natural terrain directs the development, design, and cost of improvements in an area. Sometimes an artificial environment may be directly substituted for the natural environment. Where natural vegetation is lacking, for example, extensive landscaping may be required to make the subject area competitive.

The built environment is a major factor affecting the physical character of many neighborhoods. The environment can be described and analyzed based on the age and size of the structures in the area, the density of development and occupancy, and the degree of maintenance. The dominance of a specific architectural design and quality may reflect the age of neighborhood buildings. Analysis of the built environment can provide further insight into the impact of development on the area and indicate whether the development complies or conflicts with local building controls.

The physical environment influences and interacts with the land use pattern in an area and forms the basis for its future development potential. Both the existing pattern and future potential often may depend on the tastes and preferences of the resident population. These taste and preferences are linked to the social and cultural environment within the subject area.

Social and Cultural Environment

The social and cultural environment of an area is represented by the residents, clients, or employees that live in or frequent the area on an on-going basis. The interaction of these groups of individuals may be observed in the ancillary land use associations characteristic of the neighborhood. For example, a neighborhood bar situated across from a manufacturing plant can give a neighborhood a social dimension that would be absent in a new industrial park. A bar often extends the duration of activity in an area beyond the workday into the evening hours.

Studying the social and cultural environment provides information on the land use potential of an area that could not be gleaned from data on the quantity of land uses only. Investigation of the social dimension can indicate:

- The efficiency of the land use associations. An efficient land use pattern is one characterized by a high degree of compatibility and consistency.
- The lifestyle of the occupants or the clientele that frequents the neighborhood.
- The cultural environment, which is strongly influenced by the occupational and economic status of area households

Collectively, the lifestyles of the residents direct the quantity, quality, and efficiency of the potential land use associations in an area. The social and cultural environment is constantly changing. Shifts in behavior may be readily apparent and easy to detect; thus the pattern of change is usually linear and forecastable.[10]

Analysis of the social environment goes beyond investigation of the demographic variables typically studied in market analysis. The lifestyles and levels of communication among residents, neighborhood associations, and other political groups must also be addressed. Other concerns focus on the emphasis placed on tradition and custom and the fit between customers or clients and the products, services, and existing or proposed activities in the area. The degree of economic or political power in a neighborhood also depends on the social group or groups that are active there.

The social and cultural environment is reflected in the lifestyles and behavioral patterns observed in the neighborhood. These behavioral patterns are more thoroughly investigated in the context of the psychological environment.

Psychological Environment

The psychological environment focuses on how neighborhood behaviors are perceived. The social environment reflects the group's value system based on common heritage, experience, and culture. The psychological dimension pertains to how individuals or households respond to the group value system in effect and what prompts individuals or households to choose, safeguard, and promote a neighborhood. Often psychological promptings evolve into formalized traditions.[11]

A sense of prestige is one element of a psychological environment. To understand this attribute, *prestige* must be distinguished from *status*. Prestige is an ephemeral condition that describes the high regard which both direct users and third parties have for a specific area, district, or neighborhood. Status is a more general condition that can prevail over a range of urban areas. High-status areas are usually characterized by wealthy occupants or clients (e.g., Rodeo Drive in Los Angeles). Prestigious and high-status areas may overlap, but prestigious areas are not necessarily always wealthy neighborhoods; similarly, high-status neighborhoods may not have prestige.

The prestige associated with certain neighborhoods often has a rub-off effect. Many residential and retail facilities situate themselves as close as possible to traditionally prestigious districts. Because the rub-off effect skews the land use pattern, understanding prestige is useful in inferring or predicting the direction of growth.

The psychological environment is often considered only in connection with residential locations, but prestige and status are relevant to the location of of-

10. Richard B. Andrews, *Situs Theory*, Part III, *Situs: Its Relation to Environment*. Monograph published by the Center for Urban Land Economics Research, Graduate School of Business (Madison: University of Wisconsin, 1982), 33.
11. Ibid., 48.

fice and retail facilities as well. Certain types of businesses identify with specific office districts. The psychological environment of business activity is often defined by a street address. A location on Wall Street, for example, commands premium rent because it is advantageous for financial operations; advertising is linked to Madison Avenue. The locale must relate to the activity for which the neighborhood has drawing and holding power since the public's perception of the area affects business potential.

The prestige associated with retail or commercial areas is more fragile than the prestige attached to residential neighborhoods. In commercial areas additional factors are at work—competition from alternative sites, shifts in consumer and client preferences, the introduction of new retailing methods, changing perceptions of the area, and the relocation of anchor stores.

Other psychological factors that affect how an area is perceived include sentiment, heritage, and territoriality. Sentiment is reflected in the desire to preserve the old downtown areas of small rural communities despite competition from new shopping centers. Displacement can occur as a result of the functional and external obsolescence of the old downtown, but sentimental resistance by local residents may be sufficient to reverse the neighborhood's decline. Only a vibrant economy can ensure the area's survival, however.

A sense of heritage, which is often based on sentiment, may also prolong the stages of a neighborhood's life cycle. When several generations have lived in the same home or operated businesses in the same facilities, they have a vested interest in maintaining the area. In many American communities the sense of heritage has been eroded by increased mobility. Modern families often relocate to other parts of the country during economic downturns.

Territoriality is the psychological perception that specific individuals or activities belong in a particular area. If this perception is strong, it may lead to political action that contributes to the homogeneity of land uses, income groups, and demography in a specific area. The boundaries of a neighborhood are often established along distinct lines and become entrenched over time by tradition, custom, and sentiment.[12]

The psychological environment represents a mental map of the area, the "aura" associated with a neighborhood which forms the basis for its holding power and promise. Expectation is the key to potential growth. Psychological expectations underlie the subjective decision making that directs market expectations. Market expectations, in turn, set constraints on a neighborhood's economic environment.

Economic Environment—The Economics of Land Use

The economic environment of an area reflects the sale prices of properties, rental rates, land use patterns, and the mix of market participants in the neighborhood.

---

12. Ibid., 54.

Sale prices and rental rates, which are often stated in ranges, are tied to specific land uses and distinct property attributes. Market participants in an area are generally grouped into consumer, speculator, and investor categories. A descriptive analysis identifying each type of land use in the area and the market players involved is often sufficient to establish the economic status of the area as well as its potential for and direction of growth.

Price becomes a symbol for the expectations of an area—its capacity to absorb and support alternative land uses. But price is also an independent factor in real estate decision making. The analysis of prices in relation to land uses and the economic environment can become ensnared in a causal dilemma: Does use determine price or does price determine use?

Price and use are interwoven. The principles of competition and substitution affect land use patterns in a neighborhood as well as the uses of specific sites. On a micro level, a site's capacity to support a use indicates the return to the site or the price paid for the site. The use of a site is determined on a locational basis by its economic environment, other activities in the vicinity, and the associations between these activities.

On a macro level, the competition among uses is reflected in the prices paid for sites. These prices determine the sites' use potential. The economic topography of an area is the end result of the competition for uses. The economic topography may be depicted by means of the slopes or gradients of bid-rent curves plotted for different land uses. These conceptual tools, which are addressed in the discussion of urban structure in Chapter 5, are used to analyze the competition among uses within the overall urban structure.

A neighborhood functions like an organ within the overall organism of the city. Thus, the economic environment of a neighborhood is also shaped by city-wide competition. The relationship between micro-level and macro-level accessibility depends on linkages between activities outside the subject neighborhood and activities within it. Economic events in the metropolitan area can have a profound effect on price ranges in specific neighborhoods. Price or rent comparables found in alternative neighborhoods can sometimes be more appropriate than tracts of land within the subject neighborhood.[13]

The sale prices and rents in an area cannot be separated from the objectives of the market participants. Economics is concerned with choice; economic decision making is a process in which choices are made among limited options. The options in real estate are most often constrained by location. The spatial dimension of real estate limits its availability because there is only so much space available in a given area at a given time. If the needs of area users exceed the inventory available, i.e., if demand exceeds supply, then prices and/or rents will rise. If the available space greatly exceeds the amount of space required, i.e., if supply exceeds demand, then prices and rents should decline. Markets react or change di-

---

13. Kenneth M. Lusht and Frederick Pugh, "Appraising Houses: A Research Note on the Effects of Changing the Search Area for Comparable Sales" *The Real Estate Appraiser and Analyst* (Winter 1981), 34-36.

rection over time. The analyst must determine how long it will take buyers and sellers in the area to adjust.

The market participants that create demand in an area should be identified as consumers (direct users), speculators, or investors. Classifying potential buyers in this way helps focus on their objectives with regard to area properties. Further investigation may indicate the area's potential for change, the likely pace of growth, and the range of prices likely to be paid for neighborhood sites. Generally, an analyst expects direct users to offer less than speculators. However, financial analysis of a speculative purchase may indicate that favorable financing and tax deductions have influenced the price paid and effectively lowered the speculator's actual cost below what the agreed-upon price would suggest.

Investor objectives also influence the expectations for properties in a given location. This may be reflected by differentials in economic units—e.g., sale prices, adjustments for market conditions, cap rates and discount rates, and the rates of return characteristic of properties in the area. Another indication that change can be precipitated by investor activity is seen in the alternative forecasts of potential income developed for a given site. Speculation and investment generate growth and set the pattern of land use in an area. A fair level of investment activity and numerous property transactions generally indicate change in the economic environment of a neighborhood.

Financing terms and practices are keys to understanding an area's economic environment. The availability of mortgage funds is a portent of the development and maintenance of a neighborhood. The interest rates and terms available in the district indicate the neighborhood's development potential and the risk that financial institutions associate with the area. Studies show that debt costs vary among cities and among different neighborhoods in those cities.[14]

The availability of commercial credit in an area is an essential attribute of the economic environment. Commercial credit is a good indicator of financial support for the existing or proposed land uses in a neighborhood. The volume of capital available to businesses in a community reflects preceptions of the strength and durability of its economy. The terms of the loans offer further insight into the potential risk associated with specific economic environments.

Mortgage delinquency and foreclosures in a neighborhood are signs of an economic environment in transition. Such financial data must be segmented to pinpoint the areas of occurrence and the types of properties involved. In addition to the location and type of property, the analyst must consider the levels of debt incurred by the properties and the quality of their management. If a consistent pattern of mortgage delinquencies for specific property types in a given location is observed, this information can be used to project neighborhood trends.

---

14. Little research has been done on the spatial impact of financing and real estate markets. Two works addressing this issue are: Ted C. Jones, *Systematic Differences in Interest Rates for Conventional Fixed-Rate Residential Mortgage Loans Across Select U.S. Cities, 1980-83*, Ph.D. dissertation, Texas A&M University (Ann Arbor, Mich.: University Microfilms) and Alan R. Winger, "Regional Growth Disparities and the Mortgage Market," *Journal of Finance* (1969), 659-662.

Rental delinquencies and the availability of property insurance should also be investigated. Both are leading indicators of the economic environment of a property. Here too the analyst must check the pattern of delinquencies against the location, type, and management of the properties.

The availability of insurance depends on the ranking of the area, which determines the periodic insurance payment. The cost of insurance affects income projections for properties. The analyst must identify the levels and types of insurance available in an area; the relationship between insurance coverage, vacancy rates, and property uses; and institutional perceptions of risk in the area.

Property maintenance is a function of both the economic environment and the physical environment. Maintenance also has a psychological dimension. The level of stewardship in an area is often higher if properties are owned by user-occupants rather than absentee landlords. The form of tenancy in an area reflects the current and future status of the area's economy and potential for growth.[15] Maintenance requires the periodic investment of additional capital and labor. If expectations of future returns do not justify such an investment, expenditures are not made. Returns may come in monetary form (rent and capital gains) or in personal satisfaction (e.g., the pride of ownership, a better style of living, or a legacy bequeathed to future generations). In any case, the willingness to invest in existing structures indicates a positive perception of the economic environment. Rental or mortgage delinquencies, a high level of income loss, and lack of maintenance in an area all indicate diminished expectations. They also indicate economic or external obsolescence, which must be investigated as part of the valuation process.

Technology is the last major factor to be considered in relation to an area's economic environment. The economic potential of an area is often linked to its ability to adapt to changing market (demand) standards based on perceived needs. When business activities change, so do their space requirements; the changes they make will alter building structures in the neighborhood. The valuation process addresses such changes in response to economic environmental issues under the category of functional obsolescence.

The economic environment of a neighborhood overlaps all the other environmental dimensions—physical, social, psychological, institutional, and land use. The economic environment provides decision makers with important data that translate into units of comparison. With these units, decision making can be based on quantifiable rates of return, sale prices, and comparative costs.

Institutional and Political Environment

Like the economic environment, the institutional and political environment of a neighborhood has social, cultural, and psychological dimensions. The institutional environment comprises public laws and rules of behavior as well as city planning and services. Although many of the concerns of the institutional and

---

15. Terry V. Grissom, Ko Wang, and James Webb, "The Impact of Rental Properties on the Value of Single-Family Residences," *Journal of Urban Economics* (1991).

political environment are also considered facets of the social, economic, and psychological environments, the institutional environment may be distinguished by the level or degree of political organization.

The level of political organization is reflected in the size of the city's bureaucracy, the strength of district representation in elections, the area's contacts at city hall, neighborhood associations, and the power of city planners. Various organizations influence the availability of community services in a specific neighborhood, which must compete with other neighborhoods for limited services and benefits.

The public services a neighborhood receives depend on the institutional or political clout it wields. A neighborhood may be defined by the scale and cost of these services, which generally vary within a community. The availability of services is linked to their cost, which is represented by the taxes, special assessments, and user fees levied in the area. In fact, the nature of the public services desired can often be related to specific locations and specific uses within these locations. For example, police protection may be most important to residents, while street maintenance may be of prime concern to commercial users in the neighborhood.

Housing and building codes control the form and structure of cities. The implementation and enforcement of these codes and the link between code compliance and the provision of public services reinforce the city planning process. The perceptions and philosophies of the strategic planners in a community help determine the environment in which land use decisions are made.

It is important to realize that strategic planning is not limited to the public sector. Private developers and financial institutions help formulate land use policies and are integral to the decision-making process. Many municipal utility districts have been formed before individual property owners have had an opportunity to provide input and consider whether their properties should be included or excluded. The neighborhood environment must be analyzed with political awareness. The institutional and political environment of a neighborhood can only be understood within the context of the overall urban plan. Each site is linked to the neighborhood as the neighborhood is linked to the total urban structure.

SUMMARY

Location is a complex subject which has many dimensions. Although an understanding of location is essential to any analysis of property productivity, the locational attributes of property are often approached in a subjective manner. The linkages between a specific site and the overall city can be investigated in the contexts of situs and urban structure.

The concept of situs addresses the individual site within its environment. Situs theory separates the site into two components: the land use function and the land parcel. These two distinct property dimensions are then related to the overall urban environment within a specified time frame.

Based on this theoretical link between the site and the urban environment, the situs concept can be adapted and applied in a step-wise procedure. First, the subject area is delineated and the activities within the area are identified. Next, the association and accessibility of activities are examined. Finally, the activities are studied in terms of various components of the environment—the land use; social, cultural, psychological, and economic factors; and institutional and political dimensions. Although the environment is generally thought of as static, it is actually a dynamic force that shapes the potential of the site and the neighborhood.

Location analysis must also address the overall urban environment. The urban structure and land use patterns are tied to the economic base. Understanding the overall urban environment is the key to forecasting the potential of specific land parcels and neighborhoods. For purposes of real estate decision making, it is useful to consider the impact of individual land use decisions and property transactions in aggregate. Over time, urban land use patterns are directed by market trends, cultural preferences, institutional constraints, and technology. These key issues are identified in the environmental component of situs.

CHAPTER OBJECTIVES

⇒•◦•⇐

- To explain how social, physical, economic, and institutional support systems in urban areas ultimately determine land use and define highest and best use
- To examine the various theories or models of urban growth and how they relate to real estate appraisal
- To explore models of rent theory and how they help an appraiser understand land use patterns, land use succession, and property values
- To describe the relationship of real estate productivity to real estate market structure

CHAPTER FIVE

Urban Structure

Despite its fixed location, real estate is economically flexible. Although a parcel of real estate is physically tied to a particular place, location is an economic variable subject to change with the passage of time. Essentially, real estate is space used to house economic activities over discrete segments of time. As the surrounding neighborhood changes, the support system for the existing use may change. Change affects the use of the property, the market for the property, and the transfer price obtainable for the property at any given site. Therefore, the market for any given parcel of real estate cannot be analyzed without first considering the *use*. Consideration of use facilitates comparison of different sites to determine their substitutability.

To understand real estate markets, spatially defined land use patterns and associations must be examined. Situs theory addresses the relationship between a land use at a specific location and the urban structure. (Situs is discussed in Chapter 4.) The linkage between the land use on a given site and the broader urban structure further defines the product and its value. The geographical, or spatial, dimension is the key to urban structure.

The term *urban structure* refers to the social, physical, and economic aggregation of land uses in a community which serves as the support system for the land use on any given site. This support system directs the quantity, quality, and duration of returns to the site.

Urban structure connotes an orderly arrangement of discrete economic functions within an overall system. As economic interrelationships become more complex, functions tend to become more specialized and rational patterns of land use evolve. Urban activities such as retailing, manufacturing, and recreation tend to concentrate in specific areas.[1] This is how major land use clusters have formed in most cities.

As the urban network develops, site function becomes more specialized. Each individual parcel of land may be considered a "packet of functions,"[2] the locus of specific economic activities. A site can accommodate a variety of activities depending on surrounding land uses. Highest and best use analysis requires the identification of economic associations, the nature of which can vary. Associated activities can be complementary, competitive, or conflicting.

The urban structure reflects each community's cumulative land use needs over a number of years. For example, in some urban areas the skeleton of the street and utility systems may be a relic of the past,[3] while in other areas the street and utility plan may be current. Older buildings may be intermingled with modern facilities. To understand the current pattern of land uses and land prices, an analyst must identify the factors influencing the urban structure, its origins, and the changes it has undergone over time.

FORCES INFLUENCING URBAN STRUCTURE

Although similar forces may be at work in most cities, differences in topography and size can cause variation in urban structure. The original siting of a city is usually attributable to some primary activity or activities. These activities vary from commerce and manufacturing to political and social functions. Often cities were formed at shipment points or where transportation routes converged—e.g., where water routes met overland trails or railroads.

Economic activity draws people into an urban area, but topography often puts constraints on development. The direction of and potential for growth are forecast based on an understanding of both the urban economy and topography. Generally, the geographical features that most strongly influence the direction of urban growth are bodies of water and variations in terrain. Cities originate at the most convenient point of contact with the outer world and grow along lines of least resistance toward poles of greatest attraction.

Many land economists perceive that the prices paid for land are based on the ease of accessibility between the land and prominent areas of activity. Therefore, the price per square foot of site area is inversely related to the transportation cost or cost to access that site. High prices are paid for sites that provide the greatest number of people with the easiest access. A convenient location is highly desirable. Sites in the central business district (CBD) and other areas of great activity can command premium prices. The premium paid for convenience is

---

1. Richard U. Ratcliff, *Urban Land Economics* (New York: McGraw-Hill, 1948), 368.
2. Robert M. Haig, "Toward an Understanding of the Metropolis," *The Quarterly Journal of Economics* (February 1926), 414-20.
3. Ratcliff, 370-72.

related to the supply of land available in the city. Land in the center of the city is limited, so its price is driven up. Intensity of demand decreases along the urban periphery because the number of competing sites increases as a function of the square of the distance ($S_n \propto 1/D^2$) from the central point. Often land prices along the periphery of a city simply represent the cost of platting, opening streets, and/or discounting the returns expected from the projected development.

Proximity to the CBD or the core of economic activity is the strongest factor influencing land prices. One general pattern of growth is along transportation corridors (radii or axes); nearby sites become desirable because of their accessibility. Various models of urban growth will be discussed in this chapter. The two key ideas to remember are 1) the urban structure influences individual land use decisions and land values, and 2) the basic economic functions of a city influence the urban structure.

As demand pushes up the price of land in a desirable location, topography generally becomes less important. Nevertheless, certain amenities associated with the terrain may make particular locations especially attractive. For example, high-income residential users are able to outbid lower-income groups for land along high ground and near scenic riverfront locations. Thus, terrain also needs to be considered in delineating the competitive supply.

Other factors that impact the urban structure over time are[4]

- Government regulations and planning objectives
- Population changes
- Financing terms
- City size and age
- Tax rates
- Effective buying power (income levels)
- Supply of available land
- Transportation
- Expanded urban services
- Technology
- Employment centers
- Major groups of economic activities

These factors affect different cities in different ways. Their impact on particular neighborhoods or submarkets within a city may also vary. These factors can be grouped under the five principal forces discussed below.

Figure 5.1 illustrates how the forces that influence urban development and land markets affect the overall urban structure. The economic base, market forces, the institutional framework, technology, and cultural norms must all be

---

4. Paul F. Wendt, "Economic Growth and Urban Land Values," *The Appraisal Journal* (July 1958), 427-443.

considered in relation to physical topography. The physical attributes of property provide the foundation on which the other forces operate; the pattern of land prices is thereby linked to the physical terrain. As the forces interact within the physical terrain, they influence the development of a city and shape aggregate patterns of land prices. Each force is discussed below.

Figure 5.1
Forces Affecting Urban Structure

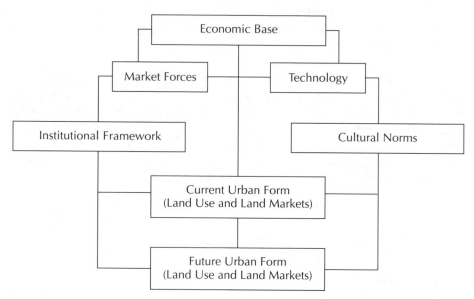

The economic base has a major influence on urban structure. To understand any real estate market fully, it is necessary to understand the economic base of the community. Before space set aside for a specific use can be absorbed, there must be demand for the activities, goods, or services associated with that use. The number of people employed in a given activity serves as evidence of the demand for that use. The activity is conducted because the output, be it a product or a service, is demanded by consumers.

The economic base of a community or neighborhood strongly influences the land use activities and land use patterns in the area. The local economy is the key to understanding real estate markets in the area and the source of the data on which supply and demand projections for property uses are based.

Market forces determine the supply of and demand for a property. Appropriate market support is needed if the property is to capture its market share and achieve the anticipated absorption rate for the specific use within a given time frame. Market forces also affect other economic variables such as land prices, returns (rents/incomes), and development costs.

The institutional framework consists of a mix of elements, including the procedures that govern property transactions; zoning, planning, and legislative controls; and regulations that impact land use decisions. Lending policies, insurance requirements, and public safety codes also fall within the institutional framework.

Technology refers to changing modes of manufacturing, communication, and transportation. The ongoing development of products and processes alters the way work is performed. New modes of communication enable, and sometimes even force, people to interact. Changes in technology impact land values because they affect accessibility and the aesthetic or functional desirability of existing real estate.

Cultural norms reflect the community's attitude toward property rights. A community's desire to protect the environment can alter the possible uses for a parcel of land. The level of political activity initiated by neighborhood associations varies, reflecting the environmental concern of area residents.

SOCIAL ECOLOGY MODELS

Various models can be used to describe the nature of urban land use and growth patterns. No single model adequately explains the full urban structure of most cities. Often a city's structure can best be represented by a combination of several models. Nevertheless, structural models provide useful insights into urban land use and growth patterns.

Four models are often grouped together and described as *social ecology models*. Many analysts consider the models of the social ecology school as a unified body of work on urban structure. Developed between the 1920s and 1940s, the models have undergone little change over the last 50 years.

The social ecologist sees a city as a system of interrelated land uses. The social ecology models include three discrete patterns—the concentric zone model, the sector (wedge) model, and the axial (radial corridor) model—as well as one hybrid, the multiple nuclei model. The models' names describe their formulation and point of origin. The models are used to predict where growth is likely to occur.

Understanding the direction of urban growth is a key element of market analysis. The social ecology models describe the physical and spatial dimensions of urban structure and may be used to segment markets because it is within this spatial context that the ever-changing relationship of supply and demand is forecast.

Represented graphically, three of the models are circular while one has an irregular center surrounded by disconnected points. The models originated with theorists in different disciplines and tend to emphasize different structural dynamics. The concentric zone model was developed by Ernest W. Burgess, a sociologist; the sector model, by Homer Hoyt, a land economist; the axial model, by Richard M. Hurd, a mortgage banker; and the multiple nuclei model, by Chauncy D. Harris and Edward L. Ullman, two geographers. Elements from each of the models appear in different combinations in most cities.

Concentric Zone Model

After studying several urban areas, Ernest W. Burgess concluded in 1923 that a city expands radially from its center to form a series of concentric zones.[5] Figure 5.2 illustrates the concentric zone model.

Figure 5.2
Concentric Zone Pattern of Land Use

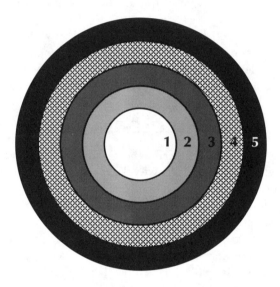

1	Central business district (CBD)	**4** Zone for middle- and high-income units
2	Zone of transition	
3	Zone for workers' homes	**5** Commuter zone

Source: T.V. Smith and L.D. White, eds., *Chicago: An Experiment in Social Science Research* (Chicago: University of Chicago Press, 1929), 114-123.

Zone 1 is the central business district, or CBD, where diverse economic activities take place. The CBD contains office buildings for financial and professional services, retail stores, theaters, museums, and warehouses. This area is the urban core, the heart of the major retail and service activities of the city. Growth from the city core encroaches upon Zone 2, which surrounds the CBD and tends to exhibit an unstable land use pattern. Zone 2 is a transitional zone with light manufacturing and substandard dwellings on its periphery; this may be an area of considerable poverty and crime.

5. E. W. Burgess, "The Growth of the City," *The City* (Chicago: University of Chicago Press, 1925).

Zone 3 is a relatively stable area because Zone 2 has absorbed most of the growth from the city core. Successful businessmen may have originally settled in Zone 3. When manufacturing was displaced from the city core and relocated to Zone 2, Zone 3 remained essentially untouched. As industry expanded, however, Zone 3 became populated mainly by blue-collar workers who preferred to live near their work. The middle-class population moved out to Zone 4, where lots and houses were larger than in Zone 3. Zone 4 is characterized as an area of middle-class homes. Better transportation systems allowed more prosperous households to move into Zone 5, an area surrounded by farms and recreational areas. Zone 5 is characterized as an area of nonurban land uses. Because many of the people who live in this area work in the city core, Zone 5 may be identified as the commuter zone.

Beyond the major built-up urban area lies the urban-rural fringe, a transitional zone between urban and rural uses. Although difficult to define, such an area outside a growing urban area often becomes a speculative land market. Analysis and valuation of properties in the urban-rural fringe can be difficult because a range of potential highest and best uses can be projected for any given lot. By comparing the range of unit prices for lots on the fringe with those in the other zones, it can be demonstrated that land use along the fringe is far more uncertain than in the central core.

Burgess put forth his theory as a very general model. As such it has been criticized for offering only limited insight into the analysis of cities. Critics contended that Chicago, the reference point for the model, had a more defined CBD than other American cities, even in the 1920s. The growth of Chicago's core was constrained by limited public transit (i.e., elevated trains and highways). In fact to this day the central business district of Chicago is a commercial anachronism, very different from most cities where CBD growth has sprawled in various directions.

Other critics faulted Burgess's model for neglecting to consider both topography and the impact of the automobile on land use. Burgess focused on residential land use rather than commercial and industrial uses, which has also been seen as a weakness of his model. Nevertheless, since residential use is the major land use in cities, the concentric zone model still offers useful insights into the patterns of urban growth and market delineation.

Burgess's zones impose an order on land use patterns, which facilitates the comparison of cities and submarkets within cities. The zones were an attempt to classify land use development patterns in *all* cities.[6] Focusing on residential markets, Burgess identified social status and income as key factors in land use development patterns. As a sociologist, Burgess studied the link between land use and social class or status.

---

6. Richard B. Andrews, "Urban Structure Theory, Part I." Discussion paper prepared for the Center for Urban Land Economics Research, Graduate School of Business (Madison: University of Wisconsin, 1984), 5.

The value of the zonal theory derives from its insight into the structural relationships between zones. The concentric zone model illustrates the tendency of each zone to expand outward until it spills over into the next zone. The outward movement from each zone is initiated by conditions in the previous zone. The dynamics of urban growth create an "overflow effect." As its density increases, the central city can no longer be contained within its former boundaries. Vacant land is quickly absorbed and any available space is priced at a premium. Population spills over into the suburbs and outlying areas. The overflow effect can produce exponential growth. Before internal growth reaches the city boundaries, the suburban ring is characterized by relatively light development and low density, generally scattered over satellite communities. As development expands beyond the city, the suburban population increases at a faster pace and eventually suburban growth outstrips growth in the central city.[7]

Research into how the overflow effect works has identified three distinct tendencies or patterns of growth for commercial and apartment districts.[8] In one pattern, these districts "slide" along an axis, outward from the core, in one or more directions. This sliding pattern may extend away from the original nucleus or from a point along the axis. The pattern may be distinctly elaborated or may be integrated into a second pattern.

The second pattern is "coalescence," the merging of two nuclei that have the same land use but originate in different locations. Sliding and coalescence help explain the dynamics of changing "highest and best use" patterns in transitional areas. The sliding pattern may be observed in commercial development along an arterial. Coalescence is illustrated by the growth corridors which bring cities or suburban communities toward one another, e.g., the development along I-35 between Austin and San Antonio, Texas. The growth of commercial activity along major arterials that carry a heavy flow of intercity traffic illustrates the integration of sliding and coalescence patterns.

The third pattern of movement is "jumping," which describes a situation in which commercial or apartment units in one area jump to disconnected points outside the zone. These outlying points may become new nuclei. "Jumping" also describes the movement of an entire original nucleus to an outlying location.

The concentric zone model delimits the urban area and its internal divisions. The boundaries of the zones may be determined by commuting patterns. The commuting distance from one land use area to another often sets the boundaries between different land use clusters. Because the model is plotted around a single center, it is useful for market definition. The overflow effect emanates from a hypothetical point of origin to expand the urban structure. The structure of Austin, Texas, for example, supports the notion of a hypothetical center—i.e., the economic base of the city is oriented around its dominant CBD.

---

7. James Heilbrun, *Urban Economics and Public Policy* (New York: St. Martin Press, 1974), 34-36.
8. Charles C. Colby, "Centrifugal and Centripetal Forces in Urban Geography," *Annals of the Association of American Geographers* (March 1933), 1-20.

The concentric zone theory offers both a general model of land use zones and the dynamic of the overflow effect to explain urban growth. Although it fails to consider the impact of topography, radial growth, and multiple clusters, the concentric zone model does provide a general framework within which these issues may be considered. The most important insight to be gleaned from Burgess's theory is that each inner zone tends to exert pressure on the next outer zone, thereby affecting the land use(s) and residential character of that zone. Thus, each ring builds on the previous ring.

Sector or Wedge Model

The sector, or wedge, model of urban growth was proposed in 1934 by Homer Hoyt, MAI, to describe more accurately how an urban area takes form.[9] The sector model was based on a study of 64 cities initially developed for the U.S. Federal Housing Administration (FHA). The study evolved into a theory of urban growth which recognizes the importance of transportation to a city's activities. In this regard, the sector theory is an improvement over the concentric zone theory. Industrial land use is also better addressed in the sector model.

The sector theory expands the concept of the overflow effect by considering the movement patterns of high-income residents and the effect of filtering. *Filtering* refers to the relationship between social and economic mobility and the quality of the housing stock. Generally, people are upwardly mobile, moving up to higher-priced housing in neighborhoods that confer status or prestige. As the high-quality housing stock ages, however, it declines in prestige and desirability. Older housing is purchased by members of a lower, upwardly mobile income stratum. Filtering suggests that urban growth is driven by high-income residential markets.

In the sector model, the overflow effect is observed as the tendency of sectors to expand along transportation routes. Retail businesses predominate along main thoroughfares that provide the most convenient access. The sector model also addresses the impact of topography—e.g., the elevation of terrain, the location of bodies of water—on the direction of growth and patterns of development.

Like the concentric zone model, the sector model has a single center. It traces a city's origins to an economic activity or siting factor such as the location of a transshipment point. (A transshipment point is where a change in the mode of transportation occurs: a change from ship to wagon or rail, as in early New York and Chicago; from cattle trail to railroad, as in Fort Worth; or from riverboat to ship, as in New Orleans.) Homer Hoyt found that within the core area different land uses often competed for location. He then hypothesized that once a land use had established itself in a sector of the core, that use would expand outward as the city grew.[10] Distinctive land use wedges were seen as growing out from the center core along major arterials.

---

9. Homer Hoyt, "Recent Distortions of the Classical Models of Urban Structure," *Land Economics* (May 1964), 199-211.
10. James H. Johnson, *Urban Geography* (Oxford: Pergamon Press, Ltd., 1967).

Hoyt's theories of growth centered on high-income housing. Once a high-income residential district was established, the most expensive sites for new homes would lie along the outer edge of this sector. If a sector of an urban area initially develops as a high-, medium-, or low-income residential district, it will tend to retain that character and growth of the city will cause the sector to expand outward. Figure 5.3 illustrates the sector theory.

Figure 5.3
Sector Pattern of Land Use

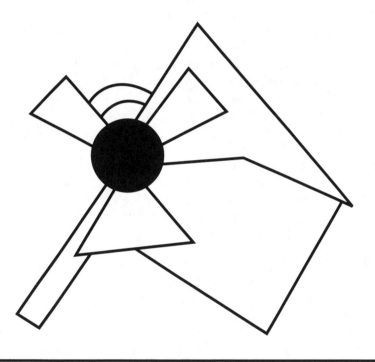

Source: Homer Hoyt, "The Structure and Growth of Residential Neighborhoods in American Cities," Federal Housing Administration (Washington D.C.: U.S. Government Printing Office, 1939).

According to the concept of filtering, groups of people tend to segregate themselves on the basis of income and social position. People form groups based on their work and residence. The tendency of different income groups to segregate is largely a function of economics. The wealthy can afford to live where they choose and make choices that may not always reflect rational economic motives. The low- and moderate-income residents of a city, however, are constrained by economics and concerned with accessibility and purchasing power (i.e., their ability to pay the rent). The sector theory holds that although the choices of high-income city residents may not always reflect economics, this group is the most influential in determining the direction of urban growth.

Several residential sectors usually develop within an urban area. As the population of a sector increases, pressure builds up and pushes the sector outward. Each residential group seeks to maximize the number of amenities and amount of space that it can afford. Residential groups generally socialize with those on a similar educational, cultural, or social level, but the overriding factor in differentiating residential groups is income.

Hoyt observed that low-income districts tend to be located farthest from high-income districts, and that low-income housing is usually found on the least desirable land, alongside railroads, commercial districts, or industrial areas. Eventually, as the perimeter of the urban area expands, the urban core may be occupied by the poor or abandoned altogether. The zone of high-income housing, on the other hand, becomes concentrated in one sector of the city rather than in a concentric ring as proposed by Burgess. High-income residential districts tend to be found upwind and upstream from concentrations of industry.

The sector model makes the following assumptions about high-income residential locations.

1. High-income residential growth proceeds from a given point of origin along established lines of travel or toward existing commercial or office building nuclei. This phenomenon, referred to as *scatteration*, is seen in the tendency of residential development to fill in vacant areas around a mall located at a major intersection on the urban-rural fringe. The mall developers considered the micro-location appropriate because they anticipated that residential growth would follow. Situs theory shows that land uses are interdependent—i.e., the presence of a mall will attract residential development.

   The concepts of scatteration and situs answer one of the criticisms of the sector model, namely that it does not deal with interstitial areas, the land lying between the transportation routes along which the high-rent commercial enterprises are situated.

2. Expensive homes are built on desirable high ground, which is free of flooding and offers panoramic views. As this sector grows, it spreads along scenic waterfronts (lakes, bays, rivers, or oceans) which do not have industrial uses.

3. Higher-income residents seek out sections of the city that are open to the country rather than dead-end areas where expansion is blocked by barriers.

4. Higher-priced residential neighborhoods grow toward the homes of prominent members of the community.

5. The development of office buildings, banks, and stores pulls the higher-priced residential neighborhoods along in the same general direction (scatteration).

6. High-priced residential areas develop along the most convenient lines of transportation.

7. High-income neighborhoods continue to grow in the same direction over long periods of time.

8. Deluxe, high-rent apartment areas tend to be established near the business center in old residential areas.

9. Real estate promoters can sometimes bend the direction of high-priced residential growth by means of advertising and marketing campaigns. Their efforts may counteract the tendency of residential development to direct overall urban growth toward desirable topography and along major arterials.

These nine observations can be used to help forecast the direction of growth and land use patterns in a given city or neighborhood.

Hoyt noted that the age and condition of structures in residential areas are important determinants of the prices and rents typical of the area. In fact, the housing policy that guided the FHA, which was founded in 1934, was based on the concept of filtering. The sector model influenced the urban land use pattern of many communities during the late 1940s and early 1950s.

Multiple Nuclei Model

In 1945 Chauncy Harris and Edward Ullman proposed the multiple nuclei model as a modification of the concentric zone and sector models.[11] The multiple nuclei theory holds that a city does not necessarily expand from a single central core; rather, urban areas develop from several nuclei created by governmental or economic activities. The multiple nuclei theory emphasizes the influence of the automobile on urban growth patterns, not the overflow effect. In this model, cities take on a cellular structure, with distinctive land uses grouped around nuclei or growth points.

The grouping of land uses is tied to the needs of specialized economic activities. On a micro level, the nature of these land group associations is explored through situs concepts identifying the four factors that influence the spatial distribution of activities within a city.

1. Certain activities require specific site characteristics, which may be natural or man-made. For example, a site may be desirable because it happens to have appropriate natural grading in relation to its frontage along an arterial. Man-made curb cuts can enhance a site's accessibility.

2. Cohesion often helps generate profits. The economic concept of agglomeration demonstrates that profits can be made by grouping land uses. The uses so grouped may be mutually supportive, complementary, ancillary, or competitive. Significant benefits can be gained from closely

11. Chauncy D. Harris and Edward L. Ullman, "The Nature of Cities," *The Annals of the American Academy of Political and Social Science* (November 1945).

observing major competitors, especially their turnover of durable goods and services.

3. The relationship between land uses can be either beneficial or detrimental. As Hoyt observed, high-income residential districts are rarely located next to heavy industry.

4. Not all economic land uses can meet the rents or prices paid for desirable sites within specific neighborhoods or within the overall community. The nature of an activity generally determines its ability to pay for a location. The principle of substitution explains the tendency of similar land uses to group together. Low-cost housing and bulk storage facilities are examples of lower-end groupings that result from price competition.

The principle of land use association and the economics of agglomeration determine the highest and best use of the sites within a district and the land use groupings of a city. The multiple nuclei model also identifies land use groupings linked to activities outside the city's core.

Figure 5.4 illustrates the multiple nuclei model. The number of nuclei tends to increase as the urban area grows. The multiple nuclei model recognizes that the internal geography of cities owes much to the relationship between the unique characteristics of sites and general social and economic factors. The history of a city is especially important to an understanding of its existing and future land

Figure 5.4
Multiple Nuclei Pattern of Land Use

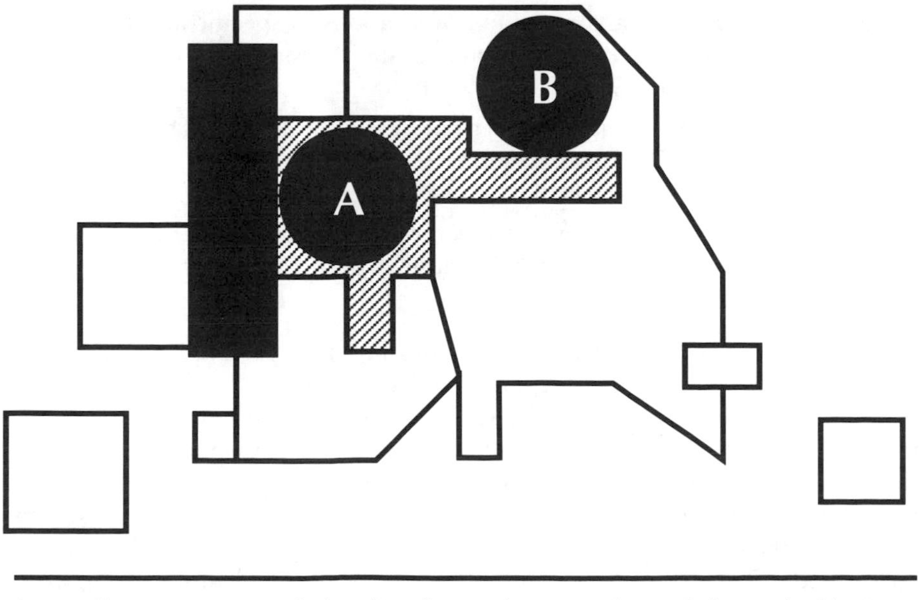

Source: Chauncy D. Harris and Edward L. Ullman, "The Nature of Cities," *The Annals of the American Academy of Political and Social Science* (November 1945), 7-17.

use patterns. The origin of a city and its economic base define the urban geography. As land use groupings become distinct, these nuclei articulate the existing urban structure and establish a basis for the pattern of its future development. The timing of a city's growth spurts, which are often cyclical, also influence the pattern of urban geography.

Houston, Texas, can be immediately identified as a multiple nuclei city. Evidence of concentric zones and sector patterns can also be observed in its structure. A specific illustration of the combination of these patterns can be found in the residential development that extends westward from the CBD towards Freeway 1960. A high-income residential area, River Oak, forms the third zone from the CBD. This zone forms a wedge that is pulled along into the interstitial areas between I-10 to the north, Richmond Road to the south, and other key thoroughfares that extend west from the CBD such as Memorial Drive and Westheimer Road. This high-income residential wedge is juxtaposed against an area of industrial development along the ship channel to the east of Houston's CBD. Houston's land use pattern conforms with Hoyt's hypothesis that high-income residential development occurs in a direction away from areas occupied by industry.

In Houston, the individual nuclei of development are influenced by the economic forces at the center of the city. The center is tied to the nuclei by major transportation arteries that may pass through areas of little or no development. Raw land located between the nuclei is held by speculators who anticipate that its value will increase as development accelerates.

Harris and Ullman based the multiple nuclei model on four assumptions:

1. Certain activities require specialized facilities—i.e., financial institutions need easy access to law offices.
2. Certain land uses are priced out of locations in specific areas. Low-income families who cannot afford desirable housing are seldom found in proximity to high-priced housing.
3. Dissimilar activities are often detrimental to one another. The odors from a petrochemical complex would be incompatible with high-class restaurants or retail stores which require a cleaner environment.
4. Similar activities often group together because they benefit from proximity. Automobile dealers tend to cluster together to facilitate comparison shopping.

The multiple nuclei model is broad enough to address unique urban situations and to incorporate the concept of situs. The model is premised on the competition of land uses for locations. The model attributes current changes in the urban structure to the effect of the automobile. The automobile and the overflow effect tend to promote decentralization. The greater mobility provided by automobiles helps explain land use activities in interstitial areas, and thus strengthens the multiple nuclei model against one of the principal criticisms of the sector model. The effect of the automobile is especially evident in the "newer" cities of the West and South, but can also be seen in suburban areas of older northern and midwestern cities. The multiple nuclei model recognizes accessibility as a key factor in urban development. Accessibility is also emphasized by the rent theorists in their analyses of urban structure. The importance of transportation to land use patterns is reiterated in the following discussion of the fourth social ecology model, the axial model.

Axial (Radial Corridor) Model

The axial, or radial corridor, model is often regarded as a subset of the concentric zone or sector models, even though it was advanced in 1903 and thus precedes the two other models.[12] The sector model owes much to the radial corridor model. Many attribute the radial corridor model to Richard Hurd and his classic text, *The Principles of City Land Values*. This model locates urban development along major transportation routes such as highways, railroads, and waterways.

Hurd devised the axial model to facilitate decision making for investment and mortgage underwriting. Approaching the study of cities historically, Hurd identified city origins and urban development patterns. His practical approach resulted in the following observations about urban land use patterns.

- Cities tend to be organic in their composition and growth. Hurd believed that cities grow in conformity with biological laws, in particular with the law of evolution. Increasing differentiation is accompanied by increasing integration.

- The organic view of urban growth applies to the origins of cities. According to Hurd, cities originate at points where contact with the outside world is most convenient. In other words, accessibility accounts for both the economic base and location of a transshipment point.

- The same factor—accessibility for economic activities—underlies the origins of all modern cities. Given their common origins, cities may grow from a central core via the overflow effect or in an axial pattern.

The axial theory lacks an explanation of interstitial development because Hurd advanced the theory before the advent of the automobile.

Like other social ecology models, the axial model characterizes urban development as centered upon a point of origin. Growth moves axially in various directions away from this point. The axial pattern is created by pressure at the center and the process of aggregation at the edges. The city grows outward in an organic, or cellular, manner from "center points" at which key activities are located. These points can be at the city center or at various subcenters.

Figure 5.5 illustrates the axial (radial corridor) model. In the figure, the central business and industrial districts are shown as Areas 1 and 2. Retail and service-oriented businesses are located along transportation routes from the central

---

12. Richard Hurd, *The Principles of City Land Values* (New York: The New York Times Press/Arlo Press, reprinted 1974).

Figure 5.5
Axial (Radial Corridor) Pattern of Land Use

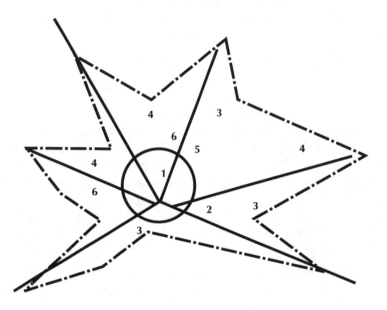

core. Area 3 usually is an apartment district inhabited by lower-income families who live there because of the low rent and availability of public transportation. The middle-class population is found in Area 4, far from the busy commercial and industrial areas, yet close to transportation corridors and public facilities such as hospitals and schools. Secluded higher-income residential areas are located in the open space beyond Area 4.

Urban growth causes each area to encroach on the adjacent area. As a result, industrial parks and commercial facilities may develop in Areas 5 and 6.

The Social Ecology Models Summarized

The social ecology models examine the relationship between socioeconomic factors and land use patterns. While these models are basically descriptive, they do consider the dynamics of growth and offer causal explanations for land use patterns. Understanding organic or cellular growth as originating from one center or from multiple centers is useful in the delineation of trade areas. Theories of central place (i.e., city centers where activities are concentrated command the highest rents) and efficient location (i.e., the loci of greatest activity command the highest rents) cannot be separated from the social ecology models. Moreover, demographic distribution cannot be considered apart from economic location.

The rationale for the social ecology models is economic activity. Thus, the analytical models formulated by the rent theorists are necessarily linked to the descriptive models of the social ecology school. The social ecology models also provide intuitive insights useful in decision making.

RENT THEORISTS' MODELS

Bid-Rent Curves

The rent theorists represent a second school of thought on urban structure. For the rent theorists, the city structure reflects a trade-off between rents and transportation costs. Rent is basically the payment for location, over and above compensation for use and occupancy of the land parcel. Thus, the return to a parcel of land involves two factors: the overall accessibility of the site and the competitive price that has to be paid to occupy a given locus in the urban terrain. In the calculation of rent, payment for the use and occupancy of the site is extracted to arrive at a measure of the price of location. The rent theorists view the entire city from the perspective of the economics of location; they identify the amount of income spent on location as an economic good in its own right. The basic model developed by William Alonso, a land economist, illustrates this concept of the city.

According to the basic model, the choice of location reflects an allocation of income dollars between rent and transportation costs at varying distances from the CBD. The vertical axis in Figure 5.6 represents the income to be spent on location. The selection of a site reflects a trade-off between the rent paid for the location and the transportation costs. The model suggests that the further one moves from the center of the city or focal point of the neighborhood, the lower the rent per unit of area (per square foot) and the higher the transportation costs.

Figure 5.6
Alonso Model of Urban Structure

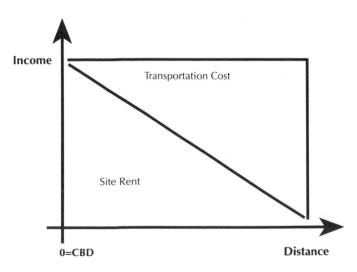

Note. The model illustrates the inverse relationship between site rent and transportation cost.

Alonso's analytical model of urban structure demonstrates that economics underlies the choice of location. Basically, Alonso's model is limited to a demand perspective, i.e., the trade-off between the advantages of location and the costs of transport to and from the urban center. Transportation costs may actually be viewed as negative accessibility. In the formation of a city, sites are chosen on the basis of trade-offs between location and accessibility. Thus, the economics of choice upon which the Alonso model is based elucidates real estate decision making. Study of the trade-off between location and accessibility within the overall city provides one approach to analyzing the competition among alternative land uses within a given area or neighborhood.

Trade-offs between location and accessibility are graphically illustrated by the slopes or gradients of the bid-rent curves plotted for different land uses. (Bid-rent curves plot the rents offered at different locations in a city.) For example, the trade-off between location and accessibility may produce a curve such as Bid-Rent Curve 1 in Figure 5.7, which depicts citywide office demand. Office demand in the area tends to be highest in the CBD. Five miles from the CBD of the city, the income spent on site rents for office use is zero dollars. A preference for office locations in the CBD is indicated by the relatively high site rent paid at point 0. This bid-rent curve illustrates the importance of a central location for office uses.

Bid-Rent Curve 2 in Figure 5.7 depicts the trade-off of location and accessibility for retail facilities in the city. This second curve illustrates that retail space users do not attach the same importance to central-city location as do office space users. Retail space users assign a higher premium to locations five miles away from the CBD; at a distance of 15 miles, however, the retail premium for

Figure 5.7
Bid-Rent Curves

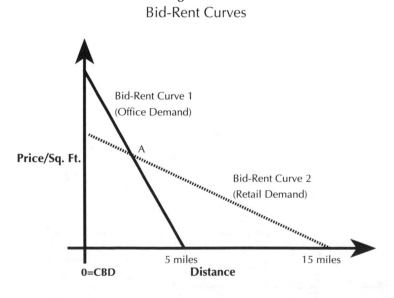

location is zero dollars. The competition between land uses is reflected at point A, where the dominant use shifts from office to retail activities in the overall land use pattern of the city.

The economics of location have been used to analyze the competition between commercial and residential land uses in Austin, Texas (see Figure 5.8). This study, which serves as an empirical test of a rent theorists' model, investigated the sale price per square foot of land under different uses. Figure 5.8 shows that the commercial market tends to predominate up to a distance of six miles on the south side of Austin. It is essential to note that a residential market does exist within this area, but in most situations commercial activities are able to outbid residential uses. It is important to keep in mind that any given site might prove an exception to the general pattern because of the specific attributes of the parcel.

Figure 5.8
Land Use Competition in Austin

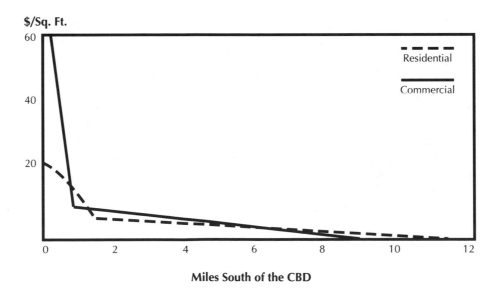

Miles South of the CBD

Empirical comparison of the commercial and residential land markets in Austin revealed that the trade-off between site location and accessibility is not the direct linear relationship illustrated in the Alonso model. The trade-off depicted by the Alonso model is based on a demand perspective, i.e., the allocation of income between two distinct goods. The curvilinear character of actual bid-rent curves reflects both supply and demand. Supply is represented in the limited availability of sites near the CBD and demand, in the allocation of income between two goods. The impact of available supply on bid-rent curves is addressed by Richard F. Muth in his economic model of the city. Muth plotted the physical limits of supply in a mononuclear city as asymptotic curves which show a rapid decline from the high site rents in the central city to the lower rents paid along the fringe of the city. This pattern is attributable in part to the potentially geometric increase in land available as the distance from the city core increases, assuming that there are no topographical barriers or transportation obstacles limiting the city's expansion.

Applicability and Theoretical Foundation

The rent theorists' approach has also been used to analyze the density of population settlement within the geographic limits of cities. Most studies of population gradients conform to the geometric pattern of Muth's bid-rent curves.

Although the rent theorists' models are based on valid assumptions, they lack the flexibility and descriptive insight of the social ecology models. The rent theorists do provide an analytical framework that is absent from the ecology models, however. The rent theorists' models represent aggregate or macro-level applications of gravity and central place theories, which are key to the delineation of retail trade areas. Moreover, the rent theorists provide alternative insights into the decision-making process applied to location. Whereas the social ecologists consider the overall urban environment, the rent theorists identify the economics of location as the key to urban land use patterns.

The urban structure establishes the context for real estate market analysis. Once the structure is understood, a process for analyzing markets can be developed. The theories of the social ecologists and rent theorists are useful in delineating retail markets. The works of modern theorists such as William Reilly, Walter Isard, and Brian Berry[13] can all be tied to Walter Christaller's work. Christaller put forth the theory of central place and the concept of a spatial hierarchy in which larger retail centers provide services not found in smaller centers.

Walter Christaller (1893-1969) was a German economic geographer who theorized that the siting of towns and urban growth were based on accessibility to demand rather than favorable topographic or historic circumstances. His work, *Central Places in Southern Germany*, which appeared in English translation in 1966, examined the role of the city as a trade center for its hinterland or tributary area. (Although Christaller developed elaborate overlapping hexagons and plotted rings along points equidistant from central place locations as models, critics do not feel he was entirely successful in mustering the empirical evidence to support his theory.) Christaller's work reflects a tradition of location theorists.

August Lösch (1906-1945), another German economic geographer, held that location explains the relationships of markets, production centers, transport lines, and population distributions. A member of the World Economics Institute in

---

13. See William J. Reilly, *Methods for the Study of Retail Relationships* (Austin, TX: Bureau of Business Research, University of Texas, 1929 and 1959); Walter Isard, *Methods of Regional Analysis* (Cambridge, Mass.: MIT Press, 1960); Brian L.J. Berry, "Spatial Theories of Marketing Systems, Abstract and Operational" in *Marketing and the New Science of Planning*, Robert L. King, ed. (Chicago: American Marketing Association, 1968); and Brian L.J. Berry and J.B. Parr, *Market Centers and Retail Location: Theory and Applications* (Englewood Cliffs, N.J.: Prentice-Hall, Inc., 1988).

Kiel, Lösch advanced location theory to clarify the relationship of units of production to units of consumption and to explain the locational linkage of markets, production centers, transport lines, and population distributions. An English translation of his text appeared in 1954 under the title, *Economics of Location*.

Location analysis can be traced back further to Johann Heinrich von Thünen (1783-1850), a German landowner and economic theorist. Von Thünen analyzed the unit cost to transport agricultural commodities to markets at city centers as a way of understanding agricultural land use patterns. He developed the theory that concentric zones around a city are differentiated according to the type and intensity of land use.

URBAN STRUCTURE AND REAL ESTATE MARKETS

Sample Application

Theories of urban structure demonstrate the impact of geography on real estate markets. These theories allow us to segment markets and to identify substitutable tracts and land use support systems.

Both the social ecology and rent theorists' models can be used to identify land use clusters and directions of urban growth. An analysis of Austin, Texas, is described on the following pages to illustrate how theories of urban structure can be applied to identify directions of growth and the impact on land values. One theory applied is the sector theory, which hypothesizes that growth is driven by high-income residential development along major arterials, extending from the central business district toward hills, bodies of water, and other natural attractions. A map of Austin shows that to the west of the city lies the Balcones Escarpment, which separates the flat to gently rolling plains of East Texas from the Central Texas hill country. Seven large, man-made lakes have been created in the hill country from the Colorado River. These topographical features guided the development and early growth of the city of Austin.

The analysis began by locating the homesteads of community leaders who were influential in the early 1900s.[14] Research showed that Austin initially grew in a northeasterly and then a northwesterly direction. With the creation of the lakes, most growth veered toward the nearby hills in the northwest. After the development of bridges and roadways, growth was redirected to the southwest. The area between the northwest and southwest wedges has begun to fill in.

Once the city development pattern is identified, another theory of urban structure can be applied to project future development. The bid-rent analysis illustrated in Figure 5.9 supports the model of Austin as a mononuclear city. The highest sales prices per unit are found in the CBD. Prices decline in all directions from point A (the intersection of 6th Street and Congress Avenue), which

---

14. Sharon Alexander, *An Assessment of the Applicability of the Sector Theory of Urban Growth to Austin, Texas.* Unpublished master's thesis, University of Texas Graduate School of Business, 1985.

Figure 5.9
Bid-Rent Analysis of Austin, Texas

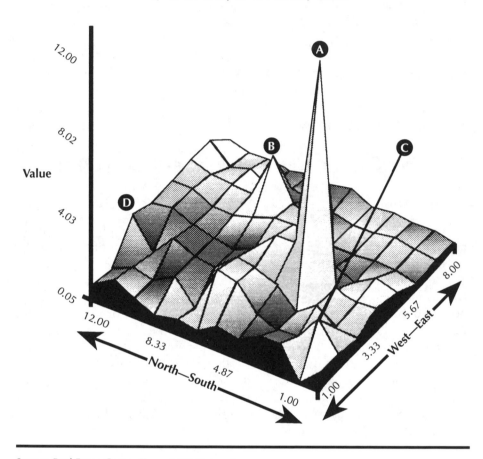

Source: Real Estate Center, Texas A&M University

indicates the center of the CBD. The potential for multiple nuclei development is evident. Land pricing peaks in the east-central region at point B (near I-35 and Highway 290) and to the northwest and southwest at points C and D, respectively. The northwest corridor along Highway 183, indicated by point D, is projected to be the first fully developed urban center outside of the CBD. A better understanding of the direction of growth for the land market is thus obtained from the use of several theories in combination.

Economic Location

The conceptual link between multiple nuclei models and rent theory is depicted in Figure 5.10. The figure shows the economic boundaries of specific retail nuclei. Using rent theory, the economic boundary between two competitive facilities is established where the combined costs of rent and travel for one site intersect with the combined costs for the other site. The two sites are identified as location A and B. The sites are depicted in both the multiple nuclei schematic at the top of the figure and the rent theory graph below.

The rent for location A is amount E. The rent for the location B is amount C. The transportation costs are represented by the lines radiating above the rents for locations A and B. The combined costs (vertical axis) are the sum of the location rents and the delivery costs. Delivery costs include both the cost of delivering a good to a customer and the cost of acquiring a good by a customer. For example, the cost of a can of peas is not just the retail cost of the can, but also the cost in time and travel to purchase the peas. Point X, where the costs intersect on the graph, is the point of indifference, i.e., at this point it costs a consumer located at point D the same amount to acquire goods from location A or B. To the left of point D, it is less costly to make purchases at location A. To the right of point D, it is less costly to acquire goods at location B.

Figure 5.10 illustrates the application of urban structure theory to market delineation. It shows how rent theory can be used to explain and document the impact of socioeconomic and physical factors in the ecology models. The ecology models may also be used to adjust a model that has been developed using rent theory.

Figure 5.10
Linkage of Multiple Nuclei Models and Rent Theory

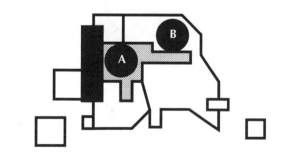

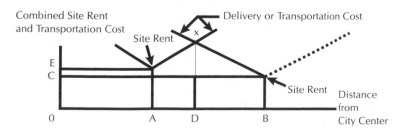

The analysis of economic location involves more than simply identifying the physical placement of one property in relation to another.[15] Economic location can only be understood by linking urban structure to market analysis. The productivity of real estate is greatly influenced by economic and physical location.

Both market analysis and location analysis begin with identification of the economic activities in a neighborhood or market area delineated by time-distance relationships and physical, political, and socioeconomic boundaries. The key activities to identify in any neighborhood are those that act as economic magnets attracting people into the area. Major employers, institutions, services, recreational activities, and shopping centers draw people from other neighborhoods to the subject area. Identifying key activities helps define the linkages and associations between land uses. The key components of location are analyzed at the micro level as well as the macro level. Thus, the analysis of location has been discussed both under situs theory in Chapter 4 and urban structure in this chapter.

The economic decision of where to locate an enterprise cannot be separated from the specific land use. Location theory covers the full range of relationships among situs, urban structure, and market analysis. Because it is fixed in location, real property is influenced by changes in its surroundings. The relationship between a specific neighborhood and the total urban environment accounts for the returns and risks associated with neighborhood properties and ultimately their value. Like neighborhood analysis, the analysis of the total urban environment includes consideration of social, physical, economic, and institutional features and their accessibility.

The urban setting is like an economic terrarium, the arena in which the real estate game is played. By studying macro data relating to the key features that influence the neighborhood and the subject parcel, the analyst clarifies the relationship between the urban setting and a specific site. Understanding a site's location in relation to the urban structure is the basis for real estate forecasting. Land use succession is an especially useful theory for developing such a forecast.

Land Use Succession

The theory of land use succession explores how time affects location decisions and the land market. Land use succession underlies the neighborhood life cycle, which identifies specific economic changes that impact the highest and best use of properties in the neighborhood.

While locational analysis links land use to surrounding activities in an ecological chain, land use succession identifies the breaks that occur in this chain over time. Observing changes in the economic activities and physical condition of properties in the area may help the analyst forecast possible changes in the subject property. The neighborhood surrounding a university provides a good example. Initially older single-family homes may be converted to boarding houses that rent to students. This conversion of space does not change the use or basic

---

15. Andrews, *Urban Land Economics and Public Policy*, Chapter 2 (New York: Free Press, 1971).

structure of properties, only the residential density. As the demand for residential space near the university increases, however, the boarding houses are razed and new apartment buildings are constructed. The use remains the same, but now the structures change. Over time, the apartment buildings deteriorate and incur obsolescence. They cannot readily compete with the newer facilities built to accommodate students in the expanding neighborhood. In the next phase of the neighborhood's life cycle, the existing structures are converted into condominiums. The residential use continues with only superficial changes in the structure of the buildings, but the economic and legal framework has changed significantly. The succession of land uses generally begins with a simple break in the ecological chain. At first the activities and associations vary only slightly. Once the system is altered, however, the potential for change increases exponentially.

Land use succession may follow different scenarios. Residential facilities may be converted into office space, changing the use while the structure stays intact. Over time market preferences might support the construction of new office facilities in a previously residential neighborhood.

Various factors can be studied to help document expected trends. Such indicators allow citywide forecast data to be broken down into useful information relating to the subject neighborhood and site. In his classic text on urban land economics, Richard Andrews identified 10 indicators of possible changes in land use.[16]

1. Investment return	6. Use controls
2. Market competition	7. Situs quality
3. Vacancies	8. Property turnover
4. Physical changes	9. Family cycle
5. Structure density	10. Structure value

Along with indicators of land use succession, analysts study two general economic factors that account for land use changes: the functional weaknesses evidenced in existing properties and external pressures that force a change in the existing land use pattern.

Identifying the pattern and extent of change enhances productivity analysis which, in turn, strengthens market analysis. By linking land use succession to the spatial concerns of situs and urban structure, the analyst ties the key components in an urban real estate product to supply and demand issues. These concerns are at the heart of market analysis, property valuation, and investment analysis.

THE RELATIONSHIP OF PRODUCTIVITY TO REAL ESTATE MARKET STRUCTURE

The primary focus of any market analysis is the supply of and demand for a product. Supply and demand analysis for real estate requires an understanding

---

16. Ibid., Chapter 5.

of the real estate product. Because real estate is physically fixed, market analysis must examine the spatial or geographical context in which the property is found. Real estate is an especially heterogeneous product because each parcel of land is unique in its location and physical characteristics. The uniqueness of real estate, however, is not limited to its physical attributes. In essence, real estate is space to be used for an economic activity *over time*. The economic activity established on a parcel of land interacts with other economic activities at other locations.

As stated at the beginning of this chapter, real estate is a space-time product which must be considered within locational and temporal contexts. This understanding sheds light on two important aspects of supply and demand analysis. First, even if real estate is perceived to be heterogeneous and unique, different sites can be compared or substituted for one another to some degree. For example, a site with certain physical attributes may be a viable alternative to a site with different attributes. A site with rolling terrain, a location near an intersection, and exposure to an interstate highway might be an alternative to another site with level topography, a location one mile away from an intersection, and indirect accessibility to the interstate.

Second, although real estate is physically fixed, it is economically flexible. Despite the fact that a parcel of real estate is immobile, its location is an economic variable that can change over time. Essentially, any piece of real estate is space used to house an economic activity for a time. As the surrounding neighborhood changes, the support system for the existing use may change. Change affects the use of the property, the market for the property, and hence the transfer price obtainable for the property. The market for a given parcel of real estate cannot be analyzed without first analyzing the use. When the value defined is market value, highest and best use becomes the standard for estimating the property's value. Highest and best use analysis considers the substitutability of heterogeneous sites.

To understand real estate markets, the concept of highest and best use must be thoroughly understood. Property use is linked to the real estate market structure and a key element in that structure is the geographical or spatial dimension. The aggregation of uses or activities in a community represents the support system for the use of the property being appraised. This support system determines the quantity, quality, and duration of returns to the property, and thus its value over time. The interrelationship between a site and its support system defines the demand for the property and the available supply of substitute properties in the market.

To understand a real estate market in depth, the economic base of the community must be examined. If the space for a certain use is to be absorbed, demand must exist for the activities, goods, or services characterizing that use. The number of people employed in a given activity provides evidence of the demand for that use. Furthermore, the product or service resulting from that activity is produced because demand is generated by consumers.

The economic base governs the land use activities and land use patterns in an urban environment and defines the geography of the real estate market. Supply and demand for any property use may be projected from economic base data.

CHARACTERISTICS OF REAL ESTATE MARKETS

The geographic characteristics of real estate markets differentiate them from more efficient financial markets.[17] The productivity attributes and fundamental nature of real estate belie the assumption of an open or pure competitive market, which is the traditional focus of the appraisal process.[18]

The concept of an efficient market is based on certain assumptions about the behavior of buyers and sellers and the characteristics of products. Market participants respond differently to real estate products; their motivations and criteria for making decisions vary whether they are end users, investors, or speculators. Market patterns for specific neighborhoods or even individual parcels may be extremely diverse. Real estate markets are not highly efficient, as the following comparison of market characteristics demonstrates.

The goods or services in an efficient market area are essentially homogeneous and readily fungible, or substitutable, for one another. Real estate is not homogeneous, but heterogeneous, since no two parcels are physically identical. Certain parcels may be economically similar and substitutable, but they differ in location. This fact underscores the importance of location analysis in delineating the market for real estate.

In an efficient market, a large number of buyers and sellers create a competitive market and no participant exerts a direct and measurable influence on price. In real estate, however, there are only a few buyers and sellers competing at one time, in one price range, and at one location for any type of property. The high value of real estate requires strong purchasing power, generally supported by debt. Therefore, real estate markets are highly sensitive to changes in wage levels, the stability of income, and the employment rate. Construction costs, housing costs, and rent levels are all affected by the ability of market participants to pay.

There are price-setters in real estate markets. Because there are usually a limited number of market participants, their decisions are important. With just a few property suppliers in any given market (an oligopoly), the actions of each seller, developer, and subdivider affect the market and impact the actions and decisions of every other player. The behavior of each buyer, investor, and speculator is important too. One major real estate developer can alter not only a given neighborhood, but an entire city. To understand the process by which value and returns are estimated, an analyst must understand the objectives, goals, and mindset of key players in the local market and link the urban structure to their decision-making criteria.

---

17. Appraisal Institute, *The Appraisal of Real Estate*, 10th ed. (Chicago: Appraisal Institute, 1992).
18. Byrl Boyce and William Kinnard, *Appraising Real Property* (Lexington, Mass.: D.C. Heath and Co., 1984).

Buyers and sellers in an efficient market are knowledgeable and well-informed about market conditions, past market activity, product quality, product substitutability, and the behavior of other market participants. In real estate markets, however, a premium is generally paid for real estate information in the form of appraisals and market analysis services. The information needed to make bids, offers, and sales is readily available in efficient markets, but often nonexistent in real estate markets.

Buyers and sellers of real estate are not always well-informed about the product. Most people do not buy and sell real estate frequently, so they are not familiar with what to look for in a property. Information on a particular property or property type is not readily available and once relevant real estate data are collected, thorough analysis is needed to determine how influential players in the specific market process this information. A key concern of real estate market analysis is identifying the decision-making criteria and objectives of the movers and shakers in the market.

The spatial dimension of real estate at both micro and macro levels affects market structure. Often the bargaining power of buyers and suppliers is unequal, which affects the transaction price. Spatial constraints that limit the number of real estate suppliers help determine the marketing and pricing of property.

In real estate markets, demand can be volatile due to sudden shifts in population. A sudden influx of population results in high prices because it can take years to increase supply to meet the new demand. A sudden migration caused by an economic downturn may result in an oversupply of real estate and lower prices. Real estate markets are risky and uncertain. Analytical models for decision making can address these concerns. The timing of decisions depends on an analysis of absorption and potential capture, the integration of key market concerns.

In the future, analytical models may replace the traditional tendency to weight the three approaches equally in the hierarchy of valuation techniques. New methodology may emphasize the application of income analysis, an "inferential" sales comparison approach, and cost analysis within the context of investor expectations. The income approach—i.e., discounted cash flow analysis and yield capitalization models—explicitly considers annual expectations over an intermediate length of time. The sales comparison approach reflects short-term market expectations. Theoretically the cost approach approximates value over the long run, but it is practical only for new buildings and provides limited analysis of market expectations.

CONCLUSIONS

The economic location of real estate is considered on three levels: the specific site and its internal layout, the situs or linkage between the specific site or land use and the urban environment, and the total urban structure in which neighborhoods and districts function as components of an aggregate market. These three levels can be seen as a continuum from the micro level of site analysis to the macro level of total urban structure. The locational or spatial dimension of real estate is basic to understanding this distinct product and its characteristic market. Within the market analysis process, the analyst proceeds from investigation of the city and region to the study of market structure and decision-making criteria.

Analysis of the total urban structure facilitates investigation of the broad market for real estate. An understanding of urban market structures and land price trends provides insights into levels of risk exposure and directions of growth and change that are not available by other means. Given the inefficiency of real estate markets, such knowledge is the key to successful decision making.

SUMMARY

Urban structure refers to the aggregation of land uses that act as a support system for the land use on any given site. The development of an urban structure is influenced by physical characteristics, the economic base, market forces, the institutional framework, technology, and cultural norms. Urban structure models fall into two broad categories: social ecology models and rent theorists' models. The social ecology models include the concentric zone, sector (or wedge), multiple nuclei, and axial (or radial corridor) models. Each model uses a different set of dynamics to explain urban development. The rent theorists' models focus on the trade-off between rent and transportation costs, or price of location and accessibility. The rent theorists' and social ecology models can be applied in combination to analyze urban growth patterns.

Real estate is essentially space used to house economic activities over discrete segments of time. Analysts study land use succession to understand the effect of time on real estate markets and to identify changes in the predominant land use patterns in neighborhoods. Real estate productivity must be analyzed in light of its unique characteristics. Real property is a space-time product that is physically fixed but economically flexible. Its value depends on the support system or aggregation of land uses represented by the urban structure. Because of the spatial or locational dimension of real estate markets, they are not efficient markets. An understanding of this spatial or locational dimension is essential to the analysis of real estate productivity.

CHAPTER OBJECTIVES

—————⇒»◦«⇐—————

- To compare and contrast economic base analysis with traditional analysis of the area, region, and city
- To demonstrate the fundamentals of economic base analysis
- To demonstrate how an economic base analysis is performed
- To explain the strengths and weaknesses of the various techniques employed in economic base analysis

CHAPTER SIX

———»·0·«———

The Economic Base

Economic base analysis is widely used to generate primary data for real estate market research. The economic base consists of the industries and economic activities that generate employment and income in the area. Generally, population growth and decline in an area may be considered functions of employment opportunities. As employment opportunities increase, people move to the area; when opportunities decline, they move away. A collapse of the economic base created the ghost towns of the Old West. When the gold ran out, the miners, saloon keepers, and dancehall girls left. In the mid-1980s, stories abounded of economic collapse in oil-producing areas around Houston, Oklahoma City, Tulsa, New Orleans, and Port Arthur/Beaumont. As the production cost of domestic oil increased relative to the significantly lower cost of oil from the Middle East, demand for domestic oil plummeted. The economic base of the Oil Belt collapsed and the cities suffered the effects. With ongoing diversification of its economic base, Houston is on the rebound, but other cities have been less fortunate.

When employment opportunities are growing, the economy of the area is healthy. A city can assume some measure of control over its economic destiny by attracting industries with long-term growth prospects and by diversifying its economic base.

A real estate appraiser examines an area's economic base to gain an understanding of the economic strengths and weaknesses of the community. In economic terms, this is called studying the city's *comparative advantage*. A comparative analysis is undertaken to identify the resources and productive capabilities of a city to determine what it can produce relative to other geographic areas. The appraiser then relates this information to local real estate and translates economic base data into a demand projection for the subject property. Knowledge of the economic base is used to project the demand for housing; office, retail, recreational, and industrial space; and other types of real estate.

The appraiser focuses on the generation of income that will be spent on real property. Ideally the analysis would trace all income flows for a city, but such an analysis would be expensive. Studying economic base concepts is more cost-effective.

Economic base analysis focuses on employment, which becomes a proxy for income. As people move into the area to find employment, they generate demand for housing, retail stores, office space, recreational facilities, and public services such as schools, fire stations, post offices, hospitals, and roadways. The infusion of people produces a multiplier effect and has a widespread impact on employment and income.

The types of employment available in an area indicate how much income prospective employees will earn. Income levels, in turn, influence market segmentation, economic stability, and the demand for real estate. For example, average monthly wages of $2,000 indicate one level of housing and retail demand, while incomes of $4,000 per month would identify a different market segment to be served by real estate developers and retailers. Similarly, job opportunities in the warehousing and distribution industries create a different type of local real estate demand than jobs in service industries such as banking, finance, and real estate consulting.

The economic base defines the linkages between the local economy and the broader state, national, and international economies. As these economies wax or wane, the demand for the goods and services exported by the local economy increases or decreases, depending on how closely the local economy is tied to these larger economies. Thus fluctuations in the state, national, and even international economies will affect the income generated in the local economy and the local demand for real estate.

How does an appraiser develop an economic base analysis, make a population or employment forecast, and use this information to estimate demand for the subject property? The process has five basic steps. The appraiser

1. Identifies the basic components of the economy that generate sales to areas outside the local community (These components are the basic sources of employment.)
2. Determines the prospects for growth (or decline) in basic employment
3. Estimates an employment multiplier
4. Develops a population or employment forecast
5. Develops a real estate demand forecast

This chapter will address the first four steps in the process, which are associated with economic base concepts. Demand estimation will be addressed in subsequent chapters.

BASIC AND NONBASIC SOURCES OF EMPLOYMENT

To understand economic base concepts, it is helpful to begin with some background information on the circular flow of the economy. For purposes of simplification, the local economy can be divided into two major components: households and businesses. Households account for the productive resources of land, labor, capital, and entrepreneurship, which are sold to the business community in return for money (incomes). The business sector employs these resources to produce goods and services, which may be categorized as either basic or nonbasic. Basic goods and services are exported to areas outside the local community—i.e., to other cities and communities in the state or to national or international markets. From the sale of basic goods, money flows into the local economy. Nonbasic goods and services are both sold and consumed by the local population.

Because the export industries cause money to flow into the local economy, they are called *basic*. They are the base, the foundation, on which the local economy is built. Nonbasic industries develop to provide goods and services for those employed in the basic economy.

Figure 6.1
Circular Flow of the Economy

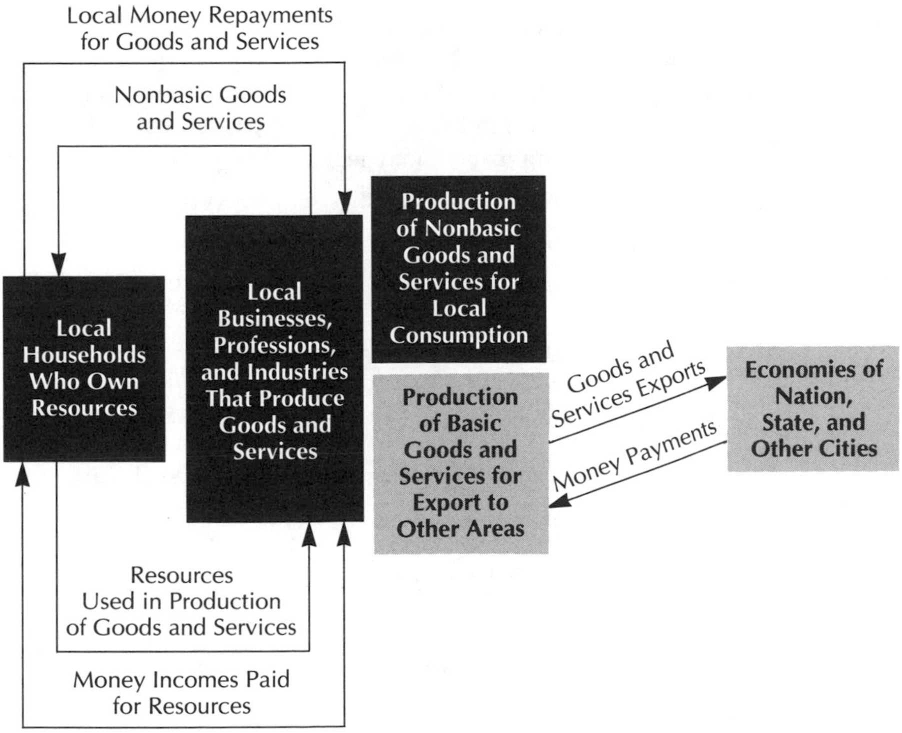

Thus, total employment can be divided into basic and nonbasic employment. *Basic employment* industries produce goods and services that cause money to flow into the local economy. Frequently these are called *export industries* on the assumption that the goods and services are exported to other areas in return for money that flows into the local economy. This description is not quite accurate, however. The tourism industry caters to people who visit an area. Tourists bring money from outside the area and spend it locally. The same type of economy exists in small college towns. Students from outside the area bring money with them and spend it locally. Degreed students, the "product," leave the area and the skills they acquire from their education are consumed elsewhere. The key to distinguishing basic employment is identifying activities that cause money or income to flow into the community. Some examples of basic employment follow.

- Mining and extractive industries (oil in Houston and Tulsa)
- Manufacturing (cars in Detroit and steel in Pittsburgh)
- Tourism (in Hawaii, Las Vegas, and New Orleans)
- Federal government (military bases in Norfolk and San Diego and government bureaucracy in Washington D.C.)
- State and local government (state-funded universities, state-supported hospitals, and state and local government offices).
- Retail and financial services that attract consumers to a particular city (the major business center of a predominantly rural area).

Nonbasic employment, which includes all industries that are not basic employment, is frequently referred to as the *service sector*. Again, this is an oversimplification because some segments of the service sector may be considered basic activities. Nevertheless, the service sector is usually associated with nonbasic employment. Nonbasic employment may include:

- Local professionals such as attorneys, physicians, real estate brokers, and appraisers
- Employees of service-oriented businesses such as gas stations, hardware suppliers, grocery stores, clothing stores, and other retailers
- Local construction workers
- Local government workers employed in sanitation departments, municipal offices, public schools, and city hospitals.

Together, basic and nonbasic employment constitute the work force in a community. This is stated in the equation:

$$B + NB = T$$

where

B = workers in basic employment
NB = workers in nonbasic employment
T = total employment

A simple employment multiplier reflects the relationship expressed below:

$$K = T/B$$

where

K = the employment multiplier
T/B = the relationship between total
employment and basic employment

For example, if $T = 140,000$ and $B = 51,700$, $K = 2.71$. The effect of the multiplier is such that any increase in basic employment has a multiple impact on the local economy. As new jobs in basic industry are created, additional jobs in nonbasic industry are generated to support and supply the new individuals employed in basic industry.

Another way of looking at the relationship between basic and nonbasic employment is to consider the number of nonbasic jobs that are generated by the creation of each new basic job. This relationship is represented by the following equation:

$$m = NB/B$$

where m = the simple multiplier effect of basic employment upon nonbasic employment

Using the data set forth earlier

$$m = 88,300/51,700 = 1.71$$

Thus for each new basic job created, 1.71 nonbasic jobs will be created indirectly.

Estimating Employment Multipliers from Basic Employment

To estimate the employment multiplier, basic employment must first be estimated by one of several methods. All the methods described here require the application of judgment. The only alternative to these methods is a detailed economic base study, which can be very expensive.

Method 1: Existing data

The appraiser may have access to planning agency data that are already disaggregated into basic and nonbasic employment data. Regional planning agencies such as regional councils of governments often conduct studies in which data are broken down into basic and nonbasic employment categories. These data are available at a modest cost.

Method 2: Whole industry

A second approach is to study industry-specific employment data. Certain industries can be identified as wholly export industries in the basic employment category. For example, employment in manufacturing, wholesaling, and the federal government is generally considered basic. By designating certain categories of industry as basic, a simple employment multiplier can be calculated. The inherently flawed assumption that a number of employment categories are wholly basic industries is offset by the countervailing assumption that the remaining industries are wholly nonbasic. To some extent these assumptions counteract one another and nullify any grievous error.

Method 3: Major employer

Another way to estimate basic employment is by compiling a list of the major employers in the area. Ordinarily a firm that is a major employer may be assumed to be a basic industry. Usually the chamber of commerce maintains a list of major employers which can be used as a starting point. An appraiser can generally compile a comprehensive list of the major employers in a city or region by conducting some research, contacting state commerce and labor departments, and checking the telephone book. Other possible data sources include *Forbes* and *Fortune* magazines and Dun & Bradstreet.

Method 4: Refined lists of major employers

Major employers may sell many of their goods and services to local consumers and therefore not represent wholly basic employment. To determine if this is the case, the appraiser may choose to refine the list of major employers by conducting telephone interviews. Through interviews appraisers can often get information about

1. The percentage of sales to buyers outside the defined market area
2. The firm's current total employment
3. The number of employees who are directly involved with production intended for sale outside the market area

Although gathering detailed information is time-consuming and expensive, this process produces more accurate results than the preceding methods. The primary shortcoming of this method is that the survey is limited to major employers. A comprehensive survey of all employers would be more desirable, but from a cost-benefit perspective, this approach may be appropriate.

Method 5: Location quotient

A final method that may be used to identify basic industries is a location quotient (*LQ*). A location quotient is a ratio of the percentage of local employment in a given industry to the percentage of national employment in the same industry. It is derived with the following equation.

$$\frac{LE_i \,/\, LE_t}{NE_i \,/\, NE_t} = LQ_i$$

where

LE_i = local employment in industry i
LE_t = total local employment in all industries
NE_i = national employment in industry i
NE_t = total national employment
LQ_i = location quotient for industry i

A numerical example appears below. Assume that

LE in manufacturing	42,700
LE_t	140,000
NE in manufacturing	20,017,000
NE_t	147,000,000

The location quotient for manufacturing is calculated as follows:

$$\frac{42{,}700/140{,}000}{20{,}017{,}000/147{,}000{,}000} = \frac{0.305}{.13617} = 2.24$$

A location quotient in excess of 1.00 suggests that the local industry is producing goods for export. In the example the LQ for manufacturing employment in the community was 2.24. Of this total, 1.24 points (2.24 - 1.00) may be interpreted to represent employment devoted to producing goods that are exported to consumers outside the local economy; the remainder represents employment that produces goods for local consumption. Conversely, an LQ below 1.00 suggests that the local economy probably imports goods that are produced outside the area, and that nonbasic employment accounts for more local jobs than basic employment. Lastly, an LQ of exactly 1.00 suggests the community produces an amount equal to what is locally consumed.

The location quotient technique is problematic.[1] It produces systematically biased results which derive from several implicit assumptions: 1) that consumption patterns are constant and do not vary from one geographic location to another; 2) that labor productivity is also constant in all parts of the country; and 3) that each industry produces a single, homogeneous good. Empirical research demonstrates that the LQ generally understates the amount of basic employment. Therefore, this technique must be used with utmost caution.

---

1. For further discussion of the weaknesses and shortcomings of the locational quotient technique, see Charles M. Tiebout, *The Community Economic Base Study*, Supplementary Paper No. 16 (New York: Committee for Economic Development, December 1962), 47-49, especially Table 10. See also R.W. Pfouts, ed., *The Techniques of Urban Economic Analysis* (West Trenton, N.J.: Chandler Davis Publishing Co., 1960). A textbook interpretation of basic and nonbasic employment, location quotients, and employment multipliers is provided in James Heilbrun, *Urban Economics and Public Policy*, 2d ed., (New York: St. Martin's Press, 1981), chapter 7, especially pp. 154-170.

Table 6.1 provides a sample of how some very simple methods may be applied to estimate basic employment in the area.

Table 6.1

Basic Employment Breakdown and Derivation of Multipliers

Industry Category	Total Employment 1994	Whole Industry Export Jobs	Major Employer Export Jobs	Refined Major Employer Export Jobs	Location Quotient	Location Quotient Export Jobs
Agriculture	4,500		3,400	1,200	1.82	3,690
Construction	5,400		00	00	0.79	
Manufacturing	32,700	32,700	20,200	18,300	1.71	23,217
Transportation	14,100		4,200	3,800	.26	
Wholesale	12,100	12,100	8,800	7,300	1.63	7,623
Retail	19,300		5,100	4,300	.59	
Finance	7,700		7,500	4,800	.94	
Service	14,900		3,100	1,500	.92	
Fed. government	6,900	6,900	6,900	6,900	1.88	6,072
Local government	10,300		00	00	.52	
Miscellaneous	12,100		00	00	1.06	726
Total employment	140,000	51,700	59,200	48,100		41,328
Employment multiplier		2.71	2.36	2.91		3.39
Total population	250,000					
Population multiplier		4.84	4.22	5.20		6.05

Using the whole industry, major employers, refined lists of major employers, and location quotient methods, various employment and population multipliers can be developed. Which multiplier is correct? Which one does the appraiser use? All four employment (and all four population) multipliers are conceptually correct, so the selection must be left to the appraiser's judgment. The situation is analogous to choosing a capitalization rate. A profusion of rates are available: the overall capitalization rate, the Ellwood rate, the Akerson rate, J and K factors, mortgage-equity rates, land and building residual capitalization rates, and, of course, discount rates. The circumstances and the data may indicate that one rate should be used under one set of circumstances and another rate under a different set of circumstances. Similarly, the choice of a multiplier may depend on a variety of factors, such as the availability and reliability of the data, the level of the study required, and the needs of the client.

From a conceptual standpoint, the multiplier derived from the refined list of major employers may be the most accurate. The whole industry multiplier or major industry multiplier will be the least expensive for the client. The whole industry multiplier may be adequate for a quick, rough estimate. Some students of the subject favor the location quotient multiplier, but in so doing, they frequently gloss over the weaknesses of this technique. Although it is conceptually correct and lends an air of technical sophistication to the study, its shortcomings must be recognized and considered in interpreting the results.[2]

Applying the Employment Multiplier

Once basic employment has been estimated, any expected change in basic employment can be translated into a corresponding change in total employment and population.[3] Employment and population serve as surrogates for the potential demand in the community. In the following example, the employment multiplier (K) and the expected change in basic employment (cB) are used to derive the change in total employment.

Assuming

$$K = 2.71$$
$$cB = 4,800$$

---

2. The authors feel compelled to emphasize the weaknesses of the location quotient because some real estate and market analysis textbooks have presented this technique without mentioning its shortcomings. As a result, appraisers may use the method, believing it conveys a greater degree of scientific certainty than is warranted. We are very apprehensive about the potential for misapplication and abuse of this technique.

3. At this point, a critical assumption comes into play — namely, that the average employment multiplier will reflect the pattern of change in employment, which economists refer to as *marginal change in employment*. This assumption may or may not be valid. It is expressed in the equation

$$T/B = cT/cB$$

where: T = total employment; B = basic employment; cT = expected change in total employment; and cB = expected change in basic employment.

Although it can result in biased projections, such an assumption is usually made for the sake of expediency and economy.

The expected change in total employment (cT) can be calculated with the following equation:

$$K = cT/cB$$
$$K \times cB = cT$$
$$2.71 \times 4,800 = cT$$
$$13,008 = cT$$

Thus the 4,800 jobs in basic employment anticipated for the local economy will likely generate a total of 13,008 new jobs. Of these, 8,208 (13,008 − 4,800) will be in nonbasic employment. Obviously, basic and nonbasic employment jobs will not come on line simultaneously. The creation of nonbasic jobs will lag behind the creation of basic employment jobs as the local economy will take some time to respond to the basic employment stimulus.

Assuming that the percentage of the population in the work force is 56%, the multiple of people per worker, or population multiplier (k), can also be calculated.

$$1.00/.56 = k$$
$$1.79 = k$$

The expected increase in total population resulting from the change in basic employment can be estimated by applying the population multiplier to the expected change in total employment ($k \times cT$).

$$1.79 \times 13,008 = 23,284$$

The total population at the beginning of the period was 250,000. The expected change in population will bring it to 273,284 (250,000 + 23,284).

Using another simple relationship, total anticipated population may be estimated with a different equation.

$$k = P/B$$

where

k = population multiplier
P = total population in the community
B = basic employment

Thus, when P = 250,000 and B = 51,700, k is calculated to be 4.84.

$$4.84 = 250,000/51,700$$

If the employment multiplier (K) is calculated with the equation, $K = T/B$

when

$$T = 140,000$$
$$B = 51,700$$

then

$$K = 2.71$$

The expected change in total employment can be estimated by applying the employment multiplier (K) to the expected change in basic employment (cB). In the previous example, the expected change in basic employment (cB) was 4,800. Thus,

$$K \times cB = cT$$
$$2.71 \times 4,800 = 13,008$$

The expected change in total population can be estimated by applying the population multiplier to the expected change in basic employment.

$$k \times cB = cP$$
$$4.84 \times 4,800 = 23,232$$

After the multiplier effect works its way through the economy, the total expected population will be:

$$250,000 + 23,232 = 273,232$$

The slight difference in the answers derived from these two methods (23,232 here versus 23,284 previously) is due to rounding.

REFINEMENTS TO THE ECONOMIC BASE CONCEPT

It has been demonstrated that the economic base concepts of basic and nonbasic employment and employment multipliers can be used to project changes in employment and population. The appraiser can refine such estimates by considering more than one period in the economic base analysis. By analyzing local trends and evaluating their likely duration, appraisers can develop more reliable population and employment projections. Table 6.2 shows such a projection for a city that had a population of 250,000 in 1994.

By examining data covering several periods, an appraiser can plot trends in employment growth or decline. In Table 6.2 absolute employment figures (i.e., the actual number of people employed) are presented along with figures for the individual employment categories as percentages of total employment and population. Absolute changes in employment (i.e., the actual numerical changes in employment) are also given. Extrapolating from these trends, an appraiser can project three, five, and 10 years into the future. Ordinarily, appraisers use knowledge about the local economy to interpret trends and make projections. For example, if a new major airport is planned, the appraiser may undertake primary research to obtain estimates of the number of people to be employed at the airport. Such estimates can be used to make adjustments to the general projection pattern. Similarly, if an employment category has experienced unusual growth in the recent past, the appraiser may deduce that this rate will be difficult to sustain and reduce the rate over the projection period. These types of adjustments call for appraisal judgment.

Table 6.2.

Projecting Population and Employment Using Economic Base and Trend Analysis

	1980	1988	1994	Percentage of Total						Change in Employment		Projected Employment			
				1980		1988		1994		1980-1988	1988-1994	1994-2000		2000-2006	
				Empl.	Pop.	Empl.	Pop.	Empl.	Pop.			%	Est.	%	Est.
Agriculture	8,100	6,000	4,500	8.4	3.9	5.2	2.5	3.2	1.7	-25.9	-25.0	-25.0	3,400	-25.0	2,600
Construction	4,200	5,200	5,400	4.4	2.0	4.5	2.2	3.9	2.2	23.8	3.8	4.0	5,600	4.0	5,800
Manufacturing	19,500	28,600	32,700	20.3	9.3	24.9	12.2	23.4	13.1	46.7	14.3	9.0	35,600	7.0	38,100
Transportation	10,300	12,700	14,100	10.7	4.9	11.0	5.4	10.1	5.6	23.3	11.0	10.0	15,500	10.0	17,000
Wholesale	9,600	10,100	12,100	10.0	4.5	8.8	4.3	8.6	4.7	5.2	19.8	12.0	13,600	8.0	14,700
Retail	10,600	15,400	19,300	11.0	8.8	13.4	6.5	13.8	7.7	45.3	25.3	20.0	23,200	15.0	26,700
Finance	3,500	4,200	7,700	3.6	1.7	3.6	1.8	5.5	3.1	20.0	66.6	30.0	10,000	10.0	11,000
Services	8,900	9,300	14,900	9.4	4.2	8.1	4.0	10.6	6.2	4.5	60.2	30.0	19,400	20.0	23,200
Fed./state gov't.	6,000	6,500	6,900	6.3	2.9	5.7	2.8	4.9	2.7	8.3	6.1	6.0	7,300	5.0	7,700
Local gov't.	4,900	6,500	10,300	5.1	2.3	4.8	2.3	7.4	4.1	12.2	87.3	15.0	11,800	5.0	12,400
Miscellaneous	10,400	5,500	12,100	10.0	4.9	10.0	4.9	8.6	4.8	10.6	5.2	5.1	12,100	5.0	12,700
Total employed	96,000	115,000	140,000	100.0		100.0		100.0							
Projected employment													157,500		171,900
Actual population	210,000	235,000	250,000												
Employment participation rate					45.8		48.7		56.0				.59		.62
Projected population													266,949		277,258

116

Employment (labor force) participation rates, which break down employment data by marital status, sex, age, and number of dependents, can be used to convert employment estimates into population projections. The analyst can use the completed projections along with other data to estimate demand for the subject property.

SUMMARY

Economic base analysis is an essential tool used by appraisers to examine employment as an indicator of demand for real estate. To perform an economic base analysis, the appraiser

1. Identifies the components of the economy that generate sales to areas outside the local community to determine basic employment
2. Investigates the prospects for growth in basic employment
3. Estimates the ratio of basic to nonbasic employment to derive an employment multiplier
4. Develops a population/employment forecast

Basic employment may be estimated using existing data for basic and nonbasic categories of employment, industry-specific employment data, surveys of major employers, or a location quotient. An employment multiplier, which represents the ratio of total employment to basic employment, may be used with current and projected data to estimate future employment and population.

CHAPTER OBJECTIVES

- To explain why a market must be defined
- To provide definitions of *real estate market* and *market area*
- To present techniques for identifying, segmenting, and delineating a market

CHAPTER SEVEN

———✦———

Defining the Subject's Market

A property is subject to the operation of the forces of supply and demand which shape the market environment. An appraiser is best prepared to define the market for a subject property if the reasons for defining it are clearly understood. An operational definition of *real estate market* is needed to distinguish between the market and the *market area*. The appraiser also needs a set of tools and techniques to define the market segment for the subject property.

REASONS FOR DEFINING THE MARKET

Real estate valuation is unique because it requires the appraiser to analyze two market segment simultaneously: the buyer/seller market and the user market. This discussion considers both.

Traditionally appraisers have not formally defined the markets for subject properties. After examining the subject, the appraiser generally proceeds to the selection of comparables, choosing properties that reflect the subject's prospective sale price or potential net operating income (productivity). The appraiser may also estimate the depreciated cost of constructing the subject improvements using data from comparable properties. In the process of selecting comparable properties and analyzing the data obtained from these comparables, the appraiser does, in effect, define and segment the subject's market. Although in many cases this approach is adequate, the appraiser may be better equipped to define the market if the reasons for so doing are clearly understood. These reasons may be identified with the four productivity attributes of the property, i.e., locational, physical, legal, and design attributes.

Market Segmentation by Area and Locational Attributes

The market area is the geographic area in which a property competes. An appraiser segments the market geographically to determine whether the property competes in an international, national, regional, or local real estate market. Most propeties compete in a local or regional market, but certain national and international markets are growing in prominence. Japanese, German, British, Dutch, and Canadian investors among others have acquired real estate in the United States. When a foreign acquisition company buys American real estate, it is likely that the scope of the competitive market for that real estate is national or, perhaps, even international. The market area must be defined accordingly. It may be appropriate to select properties in Chicago and Atlanta as comparables for a subject property in Dallas. Of course, the best comparables would be located in the same metropolitan area and have been acquired by investors willing to assume comparable levels of risk in anticipation of comparable rates of return.

Most appraisers are concerned with defining local or regional market areas because most properties to be appraised compete with other properties that are bought and sold in the same city. In metropolitan areas, further locational segmentation is needed to define urban, suburban, and specific neighborhood markets. Office buildings in a central business district do not typically compete with buildings in the suburbs of the metropolitan area. Similarly, a warehouse on the east side of a city may compete only with other warehouses in the same section or quadrant of town. Apartment units close to specific employment centers may compete only with other units that provide easy access to the same employment centers.

Once the geographic submarket has been defined, the analyst examines secondary locational features. For example, a beachfront cottage should be compared with other beachfront properties, not with properties that are a quarter mile from the beach. In some coastal areas of the United States, properties are classified by locational features such as waterfront, waterview (but not waterfront), and nonwaterfront/nonwaterview. Each property competes in a different market and definite price differentials exist. One reason for identifying the market segment is to determine adjustments for possible differences between the subject and a comparable property. Rent differentials may exist within a single large, downtown office building. Space in a corner that commands a breathtaking panoramic view will rent for a premium, while noncorner space that faces the windows of the building across the street will go for considerably less. Thus, on-site property characteristics also contribute to property productivity and help delineate the subject market.

Market Segmentation by Property Type and Physical Attributes

The market segment must be defined in terms of the property type, i.e., residential, office, retail, manufacturing, warehouse, or recreational. Each of these categories may be subdivided to define the market segment more precisely. Table

7.1 lists subcategories for four major property types. Similar breakdowns can be developed for manufacturing, warehouse, and recreational properties and for other property types.

Table 7.1

Residential, Office, Retail, and
Other Specialized Market Segments by Property Type

Residential	Office	Retail	Specialized Area
Single-family	Single-tenant	Shopping centers	Automobile showrooms
Detached	Multitenant	and retail	Print district
Attached		clusters	Entertainment area
Townhouse	Low-rise	(nucleations)	Medical district
Plex	Mid-rise	Convenience	Furniture stores
Duplex	High-rise	Neighborhood	
Triplex		Community	
Quadraplex	Class A, B, C	Regional	
Patio house	Prestige/image	CBD	
Multifamily		Strip commercial	
Garden apts.	CBD	(ribbons)	
Mid-rise	Suburban node	Shopping street	
High-rise	Freestanding	Urban/suburban	
		Arterial	
Areas		Highway	
Mobile home			
Manufactured			
home			

Besides property type, physical features such as the characteristics of the site and the quality of construction define the market segment. A land parcel is similar to other parcels in its market in terms of its topography, its size, and the soil's load-bearing capacity. A high-quality, steel-frame office building with expensive tenant improvements is obviously not comparable to a wooden structure with minimal tenant finish. Similarly, a single-family dwelling with a well-built foundation and roof and costly finish work is comparable only to properties of equal construction quality. Analysis of the physical attributes of the property and their contribution to the property's productivity helps the appraiser segment and delineate the market in which the property competes.

Market Segmentation by Legal/Regulatory Attributes

The legal and regulatory attributes of comparable properties must also be similar. The legal features of a property often inhibit and occasionally enhance its productivity. Hence, legal features influence the market in which the property competes.

The legal attributes of property may be divided into public regulations and private property rights. Zoning, subdivision regulations, and building codes are examples of public regulations that determine market segmentation. Other public regulations to be considered may include rent controls, any allocation for public housing, public funding for infrastructure, and community attitudes toward development (i.e., the number of building permits issued over the past five or 10 years or recent moratoriums). Private property rights differentiate "for sale" and "for lease" markets.

Additional legal considerations include cooperative and condominium ownership forms, deed restrictions, easements, and various types of liens. Appraisal theory and practice require that the appraiser clearly and definitively identify the legal attributes of the market segment being investigated. Comparable properties must have similar legal attributes or the appraiser may misidentify the market for the property under consideration.

Market Segmentation by Design/Amenity Attributes

A real estate product is often designed to appeal to a specific segment of the market. Thus to determine the market in which a property competes, its market appeal must be assessed. Typically, market appeal refers to consumers' response to amenity and design features. The amenity features of property must be linked to consumer needs or preferences.

For example, an apartment complex designed and marketed to appeal to young, single tenants may have a clubhouse, sauna, pool, and weight room. The management may even organize social gatherings. An office building with an exciting design may become a unique metropolitan landmark. As a showpiece, it will appeal to tenants who want a prestigious location and are willing to pay a premium for it. A subdivision designed to attract upper-income empty-nesters who frequently travel may offer secluded, fenced-in, low-maintenance homes equipped with security systems.

Further Market Segmentation

Real estate is a multifaceted product. Each parcel of real estate is a composite of various physical, locational, legal, and design attributes, which account for the productivity of the property and determine its market segment. The most direct way to define a subject property's market segment is by means of a thorough productivity analysis. The characteristics that account for property productivity will attract certain types of users. Thus one common way to segment a market is to examine demographic data which shed light on the most probable users of the property.

Demographic data provide a wealth of information about the prospective customer base in a geographic area. Information can be obtained on the size and growth rate of the population, the overall labor force and its growth rate, the employment breakdown by industry, and the number of households and the rate of household formation. A profile of the population can be compiled by age, sex, income distribution, social status, activity patterns, marital status, and tastes and preferences. With this information the real estate analyst can target a specific market for the property and precisely estimate the demand for the property in the defined market area. For example, a site in a residential neighborhood may appear to be ideal for a convenience store. If the retail facilities available in the neighborhood are already more than adequate given the population and income of residents, the highest and best use of the site may be for apartments. Thus demographic data become critical in identifying the appropriate market segment for a site.

MARKETS AND MARKET AREAS

Real Estate Markets

A market is formed by the interaction of the forces of supply and demand. The supply side is represented by sellers. Each property has a set of physical, locational, legal, and design attributes that makes it suitable for different uses. Sellers auction these attributes to the highest bidders. The demand side is represented by buyers, who bid for the attributes that the properties offer.

A working definition of a *real estate market* may be stated as follows:

> A real estate market is a group of individuals and firms that are in contact with one another for the purpose of conducting real estate transactions. Transaction participants may be buyers, sellers, renters, lessors, lessees, mortgagors, mortgagees, developers, builders, managers, owners, investors, or brokers. It is unneccessary for each transaction participant to be in contact with every other participant; a person or firm is part of the market if that person or firm is in contact with another subset of market participants.

Markets vary enormously in size and in the arrangements and procedures that govern their operation. Major office and retail buildings have long been part of a national market, which is increasingly becoming an international market. Transactions conducted in this market are complicated and may involve culturally divergent business practices, foreign legal systems, international currency markets, and other potential obstacles. Local markets, on the other hand, may be very limited in scope such as the owner/investor market for single-family residential property. Most buyers who purchase single-family homes as equity investments are concerned primarily with local properties. They are aware of the strengths, weaknesses, and idiosyncracies of the local market. Of course, there is also a major national market that deals in investments in single-family home mortgages.

Basically, real estate markets consist of the buyers, the sellers, and the brokers who bring the buyers and sellers together. The major variables characterizing real estate markets are outlined below. Included among these variables is the property's *market area*, which refers to the geographic parameters within which similar properties compete with the subject property.

1. Definition by property type
2. Definition by other property features such as
   a. Single-tenant or multitenant occupancy (residential, apartment, office, and retail)
   b. Customer base, i.e., the most probable users (demographic breakdown according to age, sex, employment, income level, social status, and activity patterns)
   c. Quality of construction
   d. Design and amenity features
3. Definition of the market area for the property by geography or location— e.g., an international, national, regional, or local market; an urban or suburban market; the quadrant of a city; the specific neighborhood; the trade area (e.g., a one-mile radius from a store); or the length of commute (e.g., a 30-minute drive to a place of work).
4. The availability of equally desirable, substitute properties competing with the subject in its market
5. The presence of complementary properties (Property users need to have access to complementary properties.)

Thus, real estate markets are formed by the interaction of market participants representing the forces of supply and demand. These participants conduct transactions which involve the purchase or sale of the physical, locational, legal, and design/amenity attributes of properties. Market analysts also consider a property in terms of its customer base, market location, substitutability, and complementarity. Defining the market carefully before undertaking an appraisal facilitates the collection and analysis of data. One component of the market definition that must be carefully identified is the market area in which the subject property competes.

TECHNIQUES FOR DEFINING THE SUBJECT'S MARKET AREA

Two types of techniques may be used to define a property's market area. General techniques can be adapted to a variety of real estate problems, whereas specific techniques are designed to define the market areas for particular types of property. The appraiser must use judgment to determine which techniques suit the problem.

General Techniques

There are three general techniques for defining market areas: 1) delineation of the market area according to appropriate tracts identified in population/employment censuses and projections; 2) identification of the market area by the location of substitute properties; and 3) specification of the market area based on analogs, or analogous situations.

In analyzing real estate problems, appraisers often make population or employment projections from which other demand data may be derived. The projection area is usually delimited by means of census tracts or subcensus tract areas for which data are available.[1] Figure 7.1 demonstrates how census tracts may be used to define a subject property's trade area. After careful analysis, the appraiser may conclude that all five tracts shown in the figure or only specific parts of these tracts represent the area within which the subject property will compete for buyers, renters, or customers. The appraiser may find it necessary to use other techniques in conjunction with census tract data to support the definition of the market area.

Figure 7.1
The Use of Census Tracts to Define a Market

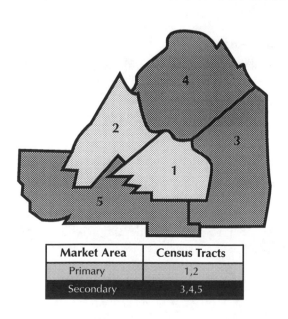

Market Area	Census Tracts
Primary	1,2
Secondary	3,4,5

---

1. In many communities, local urban or regional planning offices make population or employment forecasts for subcensus tract areas, i.e., areas that are smaller than census tracts. These data are updated more frequently than census data.

Market Definition by Census Tract

If the subject property is a subdivision or an apartment complex, the census tracts represent the area from which the subdivision or complex will draw prospective home buyers or renters, who are part of the population of the census tracts. If the subject is a neighborhood shopping center, the census tracts represent the area from which its retail customers will be drawn. Population and employment projections for census tracts that delineate the market area will constitute the population and employment base for that market area. The appraiser must then determine the segment of the market that the property will capture.

Market Definition by Substitute Properties

The principle of substitution is applied in defining market areas for subject properties. A residential buyer will purchase the least expensive unit from among equally desirable, substitutable units. The substitutable units may be taken to constitute the market in which the subject property will compete. The appraiser delineates the market area by identifying substitute properties and their geographic distribution in relation to complementary population areas and employment centers. If the subject property is a subdivision, the appraiser identifies competing subdivisions in the area. The geographic distribution of these subdivisions delimits the market area. Then the appraiser identifies the census tracts that correspond to the defined market area. By matching the census tracts with the distribution of substitute properties, an estimate of the population/employment in the market area can be derived. Figure 7.2 demonstrates how this method is applied.

Market Definition by Analogs

The third general method of market definition that can be readily adapted to various appraisal problems is use of an analog, i.e., a comparable setting or situation. The use of an analog is similar to the use of comparable properties in the sales comparison approach. First the appraiser finds a property in a setting analogous to that of the subject property. Assuming that the market area for the analog is known, the market area for the subject can be projected by extension. This technique is most frequently used to estimate the size of the market for retail centers. For example, consider a corner parcel of vacant land that has the potential to become a major retail node in the area. The appraiser researches similar retail nodes and identifies these with an analogous market area, which in this situation is a complementary residential neighborhood. Once the size of the analogous market area has been established, the analyst can estimate the subject's market area.

Specific Techniques

The specific techniques described below are useful in determining the market areas for retail and office properties.

Figure 7.2

Defining a Market Area Based on Substitute Properties

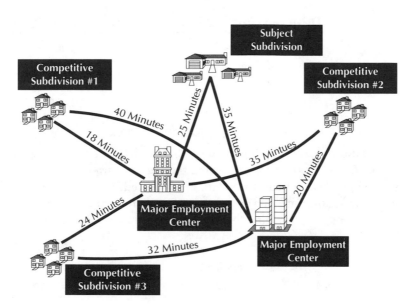

Defining a Retail Market Area

Reilly's law. One traditional technique for estimating a retail market area is Reilly's law of retail gravitation, which is used to delineate the boundaries between trade areas. This model is called a "gravity model" because it is based on Newton's law of gravity, which states that the attraction between two particles is in direct proportion to the product of their masses and in inverse proportion to the square of the distance between them. Simply stated, Reilly's law holds that the trade area boundary between two competing retail centers is a function of their sizes and the distance between them.[2] This relationship is expressed with the following equation.

$$\text{Breaking point time from B to A} = \frac{\text{Driving time from A to B}}{1 + \sqrt{\dfrac{\text{Center A Size}}{\text{Center B Size}}}} \qquad \text{where A > B}$$

Table 7.2 shows data on a subject shopping center and three competing centers. The drawing power of each center relative to the subject is calculated using the equation. Once the breaking point between the subject and each competing center has been calculated, the subject's market area can be delineated (see Figure 7.3).

---

2. William J. Reilly, *Methods for the Study of Retail Relationships*, Monograph No. 4, University of Texas Bulletin No. 2944 (Austin: University of Texas Press, 1929).

Table 7.2

Data on Four Shopping Centers

Center	Drive Time from Subject	Center Size in Sq. Ft.
1	42 minutes	350,000
2	34 minutes	180,000
3	28 minutes	210,000
Subject	0 minutes	560,000

Applebaum customer spotting technique. The Applebaum customer spotting technique is another method for measuring the size of a trade area.[3] The technique is so named because customer data are "spotted," or located on a map. The analyst may gather the data by interviewing customers or by examining a store's credit records and mailing lists. Alternatively, data may be obtained by

Figure 7.3

Application of Reilly's Law to Determine a Trade Area Boundary

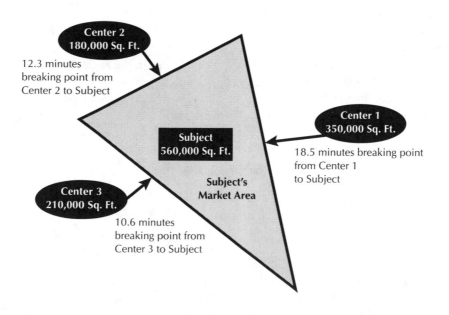

3. William Applebaum, "Method for Determining Store Trade Areas, Market Penetration, and Sales," *Journal of Marketing Research* (May 1966), 126-141.

taking a sample of the license plate numbers of the automobiles in the store's parking lot at different hours on different days. From the license plate numbers, the analyst can find the addresses of the vehicle owners and spot the customers' residences on a map. Once all the data are spotted, it is possible to identify the boundaries for the trade area. The area from which 70% to 80% of the store's customers are drawn is considered the primary trade area. Figure 7.4 demonstrates the Applebaum technique.

Figure 7.4

Application of the Applebaum Spotting Technique

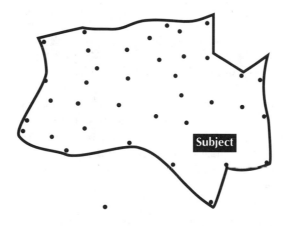

Note: Each dot represents three customers' addresses. Thus most of the customers live to the north and northwest of the store.

Nelson technique. Richard L. Nelson offers another technique for estimating the size of a retail trade area.[4] Nelson's technique is similar to Applebaum's, but Nelson relied on a set of *a priori* assumptions to develop his model. Nelson intended his model to be a means to an end, i.e., the basis for additional, in-depth research into store location. The appraiser, however, may use the model simply to estimate the size of a trade area. Nelson assumes that shoppers are drawn to a retail center for the following reasons

1. The availability of merchandise (The greater the variety of stores, the broader the selection.)

---

4. Richard L. Nelson, *The Selection of Retail Locations* (New York: F.W. Dodge Corporation, 1958), Chapter 17.

2. The competitive pricing of the center

3. Physical amenities such as air-conditioning, eating establishments, decor, and interstore circulation.

4. The degree of convenience, including factors such as accessibility, adequacy of parking, and favorable traffic conditions.

5. The dominance of the trading center in the area

6. The lack of intervening facilities (Shoppers will not go past one retail center with equivalent shopping facilities to get to another center.)

7. The proximity of the center (Shoppers will go to the closest center with adequate facilities.)

8. Force of habit (Shoppers tend to follow customary travel and circulation patterns.)

With these working assumptions, the analyst investigates the retail site, the population and income in the area, nearby competitive stores, traffic patterns, ingress to and egress from the site, and physical barriers that may impede accessibility.

The analyst should also be alert to other factors that can influence shoppers' habits. A variety of subjective features must be considered in defining a retail trade area. Such features may include the image of the shopping center, the type of customer to which it appeals, the income and socioeconomic status of potential shoppers, and possible social or psychological barriers. The "subjective distance" of the center is a factor. *Subjective distance* refers to the perceived convenience of access to a retail facility in terms of time and distance. By studying all these features, the analyst can plot the likely boundaries of the trade area. Ongoing analysis will delineate the trade area more precisely.

Defining an Office Market Area

Office projects do not have narrow, geographically defined trade or market areas like shopping centers or residential developments. The appraiser has to begin with an analysis of the entire metropolitan area.[5] It can be assumed, however, that the most comparable properties will be similar properties situated in the same geographic area as the subject.[6] Although the analysis must cover a city-wide market, that market can be segmented by focusing on the particular features of the site and the realty product. Significant categories for defining office building markets include:

1. General location—city core vs. surburban

2. Single-tenant vs. multitenant occupancy

---

5. *Office Development Handbook* (Washington, D.C.: Urban Land Institute, 1982), 16.

6. Edmond S. Gordon, *How To Market Space In An Office Building* (Boston: Warren, Gorham, and Lamont, Inc., 1976), 5.

3. Class or quality of office building—Class A, Class B, and Class C buildings
4. Specific location—i.e., the office node and the class of office building within the node

City core vs. surburban location. The central business district is the major office market area in most metropolitan areas of the United States. The CBD is easily identifiable. It has the highest single concentration of economic activity, is the principal focus of automobile and pedestrian traffic, and accommodates a burgeoning daytime population. Most CBDs are on an extended vertical, but limited horizontal, scale and are characterized by highly intensive land use. Because of these conditions, the highest land values in the city are usually found in the CBD.

The typical CBD has undergone a transformation over the past 25 years. Its character has changed from a diversified economic center replete with commercial, retail, and office space to a basic concentration of office buildings. Retail activity has been abandoning the CBD for the outlying suburbs, while an unprecedented office building boom has been taking place in both the CBD and suburbs. This transformation has had a major impact on American urban structure.

The suburban office market lies outside the central city in both incorporated and unincorporated areas with concentrations of population. Even while the office building boom in the CBD was underway, the suburban office market began to challenge it. Since 1960 the suburbs have captured an increasing share of the office market and office-based work force, especially in the smaller, newer metropolitan statistical areas. For example, in 1964 Atlanta had only one suburban office park; by 1974 the number had increased to 40. The suburbs have captured much of the office market for several reasons: cheap land, lower taxes, lower construction costs in office parks, and, perhaps most importantly, lower commuting costs for employees.

Single tenant vs. multitenant occupancy. A single-tenant office building is occupied by one and only one tenant, whereas a multitenant structure has multiple tenants. Usually a single-tenant office building serves as the headquarters of a company or the regional headquarters of a large coporation. Multitenant office buildings obviously represent a different market segment.

Class or quality of office space. Office buildings are rated as Class A, B, or C according to their construction quality, condition, and appeal.[7] Class A office space is most frequently located in the CBD. Construction materials, workmanship, and design are of the highest quality. Class A buildings are relatively new structures. The best Class A buildings command the highest rents and occupy the most desirable locations in the city. Occupancy of Class A office space enhances the prestige or image of a corporation.

---

7. See Chapter 2, "The Characteristics of Today's Office Buildings," in John R. White, ed., *The Office Building: From Concept to Investment Reality*, a joint publication of the Counselors of Real Estate, the Appraisal Institute, and the Society of Industrial and Office Realtors®, Chicago and Washington, D.C., 1993.

Class B buildings are also of high-quality construction and occupy good locations. Built within the past 10 to 15 years, their high level of maintenance ensures that physical depreciation has been kept to a minimum. Class B office buildings may incur some functional obsolescence. While rents for Class B space are below those for Class A space, tenant standards remain high.

Class C office buildings are older (up to 25 years old), but they are still able to maintain steady occupancy. Class C buildings will suffer both physical depreciation and functional obsolescence. Their rents are lower than rents for Class B space.

Office node and class of office buildings within the node. Office parks are, in effect, clusters of office buildings, or office nodes. The largest single node in a metropolitan area has traditionally been the CBD itself. Suburban office development is also centered on nodal points. Suburban office parks are situated at convenient locations adjacent to or near airports and regional shopping malls, and along freeways with easy access. Thus, the market area may be defined with respect to a specific node and to other competitive nodes.

Within an office node, the appraiser must identify the class of the buildings. Typically, a node will consist entirely of Class A, Class B, or Class C structures. Occasionally there may be a mix of space classifications.

SUMMARY

A real estate product provides or supplies a set of attributes that may be described as physical, locational, legal, and design characteristics. Many properties supply similar attributes which are placed on the market for a discrete period of time. An examination of the attributes provided by an individual property is absolutely essential. This examination is called productivity analysis because the attributes examined indicate the productive capabilities of the property. To reiterate, productivity analysis implies property use (supply) analysis.

To define the market for a property, the appraiser carefully analyzes its physical, locational, legal, and design attributes. The market represents the interaction of supply and demand, which establishes price. Supply and demand structure the market, interact to create a product, and establish its price.

Demand is also reflected in the attributes of a product. By examining a product's attributes, we gain an understanding of who is likely to purchase the product and can identify the market segment to which the product will appeal. The attributes supplied by the product have a pronounced influence on the market segment that generates demand for the product. Defining a market could just as easily be labelled *analyzing a market segment* because the analysis focuses on property features that will appeal to specific, segmented demand groups. To recap, market segment analysis implies property user (demand) analysis. Once the property features are identified, the various end users that make up the market segment can be identified.

Identifying the specific market segment helps the appraiser select appropriate comparables. Similarities among properties are the basis for their comparability, while differences necessitate adjustments. Market definition is, therefore, extremely important to ensure that the appraiser has identified the appropriate property attributes. A market is defined based on the analysis of several factors:

- Geographic area. Locational attributes define a market area.
- Property type (e.g., residential, retail, office, manufacturing, warehouse, recreational) and physical attributes. With regard to land, physical attributes include the load-bearing capacity of the soil, the topography, the site size, and the grade. For improved properties, the size of the structure(s), the construction materials, and the quality of workmanship are significant.
- Legal/regulatory attributes. Public regulations include zoning, building, and subdivision codes; rent controls; community provisions for public housing; the availability of public funding for infrastructure (e.g., sewer taps); and community attitudes toward development (e.g., the number of building permits issued). Private property rights identify "for sale" and "for rent" markets and address condominium/cooperative ownership, deed restrictions, easements, and various liens.
- Design/amenity attributes. Spectacular architectural design, a panoramic view, or special amenities can make a property more or less appealing than competitive properties.
- Other property attributes such as single-tenant or multitenant occupancy and the customer base. Those who will use the property can be segmented demographically according to age, sex, employment, income level, social status, and activity patterns.

CHAPTER OBJECTIVES

- To contrast general area analysis as currently practiced with demand forecasting for a segmented market
- To explain the importance of examining demand
- To provide definitions of *real estate demand* and *market segmentation* and to explain the role that property productivity analysis plays in defining the market segment
- To present a variety of techniques for examining demand in a market under investigation

CHAPTER EIGHT

—»•–0–»•‹—

Estimating Real Estate Demand

The price of a commodity, service, or product is created by the interaction of supply and demand. Market analysis investigates supply and
demand as economic forces that establish the price of a real estate
product. An estimate of price reflects the anticipated benefits to be
derived from the real estate product, so the appraiser must act as an economic
forecaster. Demand estimation and economic forecasting differ considerably from
general area analysis. To conduct a demand analysis, the appraiser needs working definitions of *demand* and *market segment* as well as a set of cost-effective
techniques for estimating demand. After constructing a model to analyze demand, the appraiser inputs primary or secondary data, tests the estimates produced by the model, and develops the demand forecast.

REASONS FOR EXAMINING DEMAND

The general area analysis undertaken in many appraisals has serious shortcomings. The appraiser may fail to focus on the relationship between area trends
and the value of the subject property. In many appraisals the area analysis section
begins with information on international and national economic developments
such as the recession, the savings and loan crisis, or downsizing in the real estate industry.

When information about local activity is presented, it often comes from prepared statements provided by the local chamber of commerce or a regional planning agency. Little, if any, analysis focuses on how area or citywide trends will

affect the value of the subject property. Typically appraisers describe area trends by citing volumes of data on area growth over the past 25 years. They reason that past development indicates that growth will likely continue in the future. While such a presumption may be justified, it is problematic. Growth may occur in the overall metropolitan area while the subject's submarket may register negative or limited growth. Conversely, although the metropolitan area may expect slow growth, the subject's submarket could anticipate a period of rapid growth for some explainable reason(s). Although area analysis is often based on the premise that general population and employment growth in the region will automatically result in growth in the submarket for the subject, this premise is a non sequitur—i.e., the effect does not necessarily follow the cause.

The neighborhood analysis section of an appraisal provides the last opportunity for the appraiser to examine demand. Unfortunately, like the area and city analysis sections, the neighborhood analysis often does not relate to the value of the subject property or to the discussion of the larger economic base and future land use patterns of the city. In many cases, the reader must make inferences from the discussion and the data to understand how the property's value may be affected by area, city, and neighborhood trends. In effect, the reader must draw his or her own conclusions; this is what the appraiser is supposed to be doing for the client.

Examining the demand for a real estate asset means that the appraiser must begin with the specific property and focus on how various economic and demographic trends in the area will affect its value. Thus in the area, city, and neighborhood analyses, the starting point should be the real estate; the pivotal question is: How do area, city, and neighborhood trends affect the anticipated benefits from, and value of, the subject property? These trends reflect the dynamics of the forces of supply and demand embodied in the physical, locational, legal, and market appeal attributes of the property. They have a decisive impact on the value of the subject property, which is fixed at a point in time and in space.

Typical area, city, and neighborhood analyses do not relate the impact of various trends to the subject's value. By beginning the analysis with the property, however, the appraiser can simultaneously identify the property's productive attributes and the market segment to be studied. Using this approach, the appraiser also establishes a tentative highest and best use for the property early on. If the market analysis determines that there is appropriate market support for this use, the tentative highest and best use becomes the highest and best use conclusion. Thus, to forecast the demand for the subject, the appraiser focuses the analysis on the specific property and seeks to answer the following questions:

- How strong is the current demand for the subject property?
- How will that demand change over the projection period?
- How will that demand be affected by the various physical, locational, legal/regulatory, and design/amenity attributes of the property?

DEFINING DEMAND

A practical, working definition of real estate demand follows.

Real estate demand. In a given market area, the quantity of a particular type of real estate product or service that will be purchased or leased. Demand is determined by the price of (or rent for) the real estate as shaped by several factors. These factors include the number of prospective purchasers and their incomes (economic forces), the price of related real estate goods and services (economic forces), the appeal of the real estate to the tastes and preferences of consumers (social and psychological forces), the role of the government in determining or influencing the availability of the product (legal and regulatory forces), and the expected rate of change in price (economic forces).

In an analysis of real estate market demand, the factors described above are the major variables to be investigated by the analyst.

Real estate demand is derived from the demand for the product or service that the real estate provides. Thus, the analysis is tailored to the property type. To estimate the demand for

- Retail property—An estimate is made of the demand for retail services by retail customers.
- Office space—An estimate is made of the demand for services provided by businesses housed in offices. The demand of these businesses for employees who will use the office space must also be estimated.
- Housing—An estimate is made of population, employment, and households in the area.
- Industrial space—The demand for industrial products that are produced in the area is estimated along with industry's corresponding demand for employees.
- Recreational space—The ability of the recreational use to attract vacationers and tourists is estimated.

Although this list could be expanded, it demonstrates that the demand for real estate must be estimated from the number of businesses, employees, and residents that use, or are housed in, the real estate facilities in the area.

An individual parcel of real estate is fixed in location and has certain attributes that generate demand. In most appraisal assignments, the real estate product already exists. The improvement is standing and occupies a specific number of square feet. Its building materials, quality of construction, and design are fixed. The services that the property provides its users are evident. The appraiser, therefore, is estimating the demand for an existing real estate product that usually can be modified only marginally.

DEMAND AND MARKET SEGMENTATION

Property productivity analysis and market segment analysis both identify the physical, locational, legal, and design/amenity attributes of the subject property. These qualities of the subject account for its utility and productivity. The analyst asks these questions:

- What demand is there for the attributes of the property? Who can use these attributes?
- How will the attributes of this particular property attract users to the real estate?
- How many people are willing to pay for the attributes of this particular property?
- How much are people willing to pay for these attributes?

By identifying the subject's attributes, the appraiser has also defined the market segment to which the property will appeal. Thus, *real estate market segmentation* means dividing market demand into meaningful buyer groups based on the property's attributes—i.e., identifying different buyer groups attracted to the physical, locational, legal/political, and design/amenity attributes of the real estate.

A spreadsheet can be constructed to analyze the productive attributes of a property. Often productivity analysis is conducted with a mental spreadsheet, but sometimes it may be helpful to construct a formal spreadsheet like the one shown in Table 8.1. Once the spreadsheet is constructed, the analyst can begin to identify the different buyer or user groups to which the property attributes appeal. Some of the variables used for market segmentation are listed below.

Socioeconomic variables:	Geographic variables (location and size of area):	Buyer behavior variables:
Age		End user
Sex	Nation	Speculator
Family size	State	Investor
Household size	Region	Image-sensitive, prestige seeker
Income	County	
Occupation	City size	Price-conscious economizer
Education	Sector of the city	
Stage in family/life cycle	Neighborhood	Convenience or quality seeker
Religion		
Race		
Ethnicity		
Social class		

Table 8.1
Spreadsheet Analysis of Productive Attributes
of Subject and Comparables

Item	Subject	Comparable 1	2	3
Physical attributes				
Size in sq. ft.	560,000	350,000	180,000	210,000
Construction— quality, maintenance	Excellent	Similar	Good	Good
Age	2 years	5 years	8 years	15 years
Conclusion		**Similar**	**Inferior**	**Inferior**
Locational attributes				
Access/linkages	Good	Superior	Similar	Inferior
Market area density	Fair	Superior	Similar	Inferior
Market area income	Excellent	Similar	Inferior	Similiar
Direction of urban growth	Fair	Superior	Similar	Inferior
Conclusion		**Superior**	**Similar**	**Inferior**
Legal attributes				
Zoning	Beer/wine sales (allowed)	Similar (Allowed)	Similiar (Allowed)	Inferior (Not allowed)
Conclusion		**Similar**	**Similiar**	**Inferior**
Design/amenity attributes				
Design	Good	Similar	Similar	Similar
Amenities	Excellent mix of shops	Inferior	Inferior	Inferior
Conclusion		**Inferior**	**Inferior**	**Inferior**

Different productivity characteristics will attract different types of users. Further market segmentation can be based on other property attributes such as:

- Single-tenant or multitenant occupancy, i.e., single-family or multifamily residential, single-tenant or multitenant office buildings/retail properties
- Customer base, i.e., the probable users of the property based on a demographic breakdown (age, sex, employment, income range, social status, and activity patterns)
- Quality of the construction

TECHNIQUES FOR EXAMINING DEMAND

A demand estimate may be based on secondary or primary data on population and employment. Frequently, a combination of the two types of data is used. Generally secondary data serve as the basis for certain assumptions underlying demand projections, while primary data are needed to refine the analysis. Before demand can be examined further, two relevant terms must be defined: estimate and forecast.

An *estimate* refers to the current population, employment, and demand. Estimates are used to update data from the last census. A *forecast* refers to the future population, employment, and demand. A forecast attempts to measure changes that may occur, given certain assumptions inherent in the methods and data employed to make the projection. Typically several projections are made, each based on a different set of assumptions. Often minimum, maximum, and midpoint projections are made and each is plausible to a degree. Forecasting requires the application of judgment. A forecast is the projection, or set of projections, deemed most likely to occur. It is based on the set of assumptions that the analyst considers most probable.

Types of Demand Estimates

As previously noted, the demand for a particular property type bears a specific relationship to population and employment. Understanding the relationship between data on population and employment and the particular type of real estate can be very useful in identifying demand. The number of methods that can be used to develop demand estimates is limited only by the availability of data and the resourcefulness of the analyst. The following techniques may be used to derive demand estimates for commonly appraised properties. The analyst should focus on demonstrating the existing relationships between population, employment, and income. Using primary data to refine the demand estimate will add greater precision to the results.

Retail Space Demand Estimates

Demand estimates for retail properties focus on the demand for retail services by retail customers. Two simple relationships can provide insight into the demand for a retail property. The ratio of retail space in the market area or city to the population of the market area or city is expressed by the following equation:

$$R_m/P_m = r_m \qquad R_c/P_c = r_c$$

The ratio of retail space in the market area or city to the number of households in the market area or city is expressed as

$$R_m/H_m = r_m' \qquad R_c/H_c = r_c'$$

The symbols used in these equations are explained below.

R_m and R_c = number of square feet of retail space in the market area and the city, respectively

P_m and P_c = population of the market area and the city, respectively

H_m and H_c = number of households in the market area and the city, respectively

r_m/r_m' and r_c/r_c' = the ratio of retail space in the market area/city to the population/households in the market area/city

Two other useful ratios are sales per capita in the market area or city

S_m/P_m = sales per capita in the market area

S_c/P_c = sales per capita in the city

and sales per household in the market area or the city

S_m/H_m = sales per household in the market area

S_c/H_c = sales per household in the city

where

S_m and S_c = volume of sales (in dollars) in the market area and in the city, respectively

P_m and P_c = population of the market area and the city, respectively

H_m and H_c = number of households in the market area and the city, respectively

If the sales ratio for the market area exceeds the sales ratio for the overall city, there may be strong demand for retail services in the market area; conversely, if the sales ratio for the city exceeds the sales ratio for the market area, the retail market may be saturated.

The market situation should be very carefully examined. If the market area has an average income level that is substantially higher than income levels for the overall city, the market may be able to support extra retail facilities. The next step is to determine the market share that the retail outlet is likely to capture. To project the demand for retail space in a market area, a ratio derived by the technique shown in Table 8.2 may be employed.

Another technique for projecting demand makes use of an existing and a projected population figure. To apply this technique, the appraiser also considers land use conversions to retail use in the market area and the development of new retail space in the market area.

Table 8.2

Projection of Supportable Retail Space in Square Feet

Year	Data Set	Space Requirement Per Capita in Sq. Ft.*	Population	Total Retail Space Requirement in Sq. Ft.
1994	1	3.06	9,774	29,908
1999	1	3.06	10,817	33,100
1994	2	3.06	20,798	63,642
1999	2	3.06	23,211	71,026

* The 3.06 ratio was derived by dividing the per capita demand in the subject county by retail sales per square foot in neighborhood shopping center retail space. The data employed in calculating this ratio came from the sources listed below.

Retail sales data were found in *Reported Gross Sales and Taxable Sales*, provided by the state comptroller of public accounts. These sales totaled $122,340,419. County population was estimated by the Council of Governments *1994 Current Population Estimates* to be 281,100. Thus, county per capita demand for neighborhood shopping center retail space is $122,340,419/281,100 = $435.22.

Retail sales of $142.33 per square foot were derived from the Urban Land Institute's *Dollars and Cents of Shopping Centers 1987*. Demand per capita divided by retail sales per square foot in neighborhood shopping center retail space ($435.22/$142.33) indicates 3.06 sq. ft. of retail space required per capita.

Note. A more detailed version of this table appears as Table 16.4 in Chapter 16.

The following formula is used to estimate the demand for retail space in a given year:

$$\frac{(cH \times AHi \times CRi)}{\text{Sales per sq.ft. per year}} = \text{Retail space demand in a given year}$$

where

cH = change in number of households in market area (i.e., anticipated growth over projection period divided by household size)

AHi = average household income

CRi = capture rate of household income by retail facilities

The application of this technique is demonstrated using a five-year projection period and the following data.

Given:

$$cH = 16,949/2.45 = 6,918$$
$$AHi = \$35,000$$
$$CRi = 34\%$$
$$\text{Sales per sq.ft. per year} = \$50$$

The demand for retail space can be calculated as follows:

$$(6,918 \times \$35,000 \times 0.34)/\$50 = 1,646,484 \text{ sq. ft. of retail space}$$
needed in 1994–1999 period,
or 329,297 sq. ft. per year

Office Space Demand Estimates

The demand for office space is generated by the services provided by businesses housed in offices and, in turn, the demand of these businesses for employees who use the office space. In the short run, the ratio between the general population and the number of people employed in offices remains relatively constant. Office space demand can be analyzed by means of the following relationships:

$$OS_m/P_m = (OS/P)m \qquad OS_c/P_c = (OS/P)c$$
$$OS_m/OE_m = (OS/E)m \quad \text{and} \quad OS_c/OE_c = (OS/E)c$$

where

OS_m and OS_c = square feet of office space in the market area and the city, respectively

P_m and P_c = population of the market area and the city, respectively

OE_m and OE_c = office employees in the market area and the city, respectively

$(OS/E)m$ and $(OS/E)c$ = office space per employee in the market area and the city, respectively

The demand for office space may be stated in the generalized equation

$$cOE \times SF,OS/E \times CR_m = \text{square footage of office space demand in the submarket}$$

where

$$
\begin{aligned}
cOE &= \text{change in the number of office employees} \\
&\quad \text{over a given period} \\
SF,OS/E &= \text{the number of square feet of office space} \\
&\quad \text{per employee} \\
CR_m &= \text{capture rate for the submarket}
\end{aligned}
$$

The key to applying this method is understanding the sources of office employment. The analyst must investigate the various employment categories because certain types of employment require more office space than others. Most of the workforce in service sector employment categories (finance, insurance, real estate, and government) uses office space.

In the following example, assume an increase of 8,700 in area employment over the five-year period between 1994 and 1999. From data on individual employment categories, the analyst discovers that 69% of these employees are likely to be housed in offices and that, on average, each office employee uses 235 square feet of space. The analyst then estimates that the expected capture rate in the submarket is 9.5% of the total office market. Thus, demand can be calculated as follows.

$$8{,}700 \times 0.69 \times 235 \times 0.095 = 134{,}017 \text{ square feet of office space demand}$$
in the submarket during 1994 and 1999 period, or an average of 26,803 sq. ft. per year

Equipped with this demand estimate, the appraiser can better understand the competitive position of the subject property. If the subject has 4,000 square feet of vacant space yet to be absorbed, the analyst can use the following equation to make an informed estimate of the required absorption period for the property.

$$\frac{4{,}000 \text{ sq. ft.}}{26{,}803 \text{ sq. ft. annual demand}} = 14.9\% \text{ capture if the property}$$
is to lease up in one year.

After thorough analysis, the appraiser may determine that the property is not advantageously located or is not competitive in other ways. It may be concluded that the property will require two or more years to be fully leased. In other words, the appraiser may decide that because the property is not highly competitive, it probably cannot capture 14.9% of the market in one year. It may have the capacity to capture 7% or 8% of the market given the competitive environment.

Housing Demand Estimates

Estimates of housing demand are based on population, employment, and income data and the number of households in the market area. The following generalized equation can be used to obtain an estimate of the demand for new housing units:

$$(cH + nR) - (V_a - V_n) - (UC_a - UC_n) = \text{demand for new housing units}$$

where

cH = change in the number of households in community or market area over a given period

nR = net removals of units (demolitions) from the housing inventory

V_a = actual vacancies

V_n = normal vacancies (*normal* meaning the average number of units vacant)

UC_a = actual housing units under construction

UC_n = the normal (average) number of units under construction

The following example demonstrates how the equation is used. Assume the following:

cH = 16,949/2.45 = 6,918 new households

(The 16,949 figure is taken from the population forecast and 2.45 is the number of persons per household in the market area.)

nR = 324 removals (demolitions)

V_a = 8,000 units actually vacant

V_n = 6,500 units normally vacant (i.e., 5% of total)

UC_a = 800 units actually under construction

UC_n = 1,200 units normally under construction

The demand for new housing units is estimated by inputting the data into the equation.

$$(6,918 + 324) - (8,000 - 6,500) - (800 - 1,200) = 6,142$$

Thus, 6,142 new housing units will be in demand over the 1994-1999 period.

This estimate can be allocated to single-family and multifamily units using the percentage breakdown for the community. If, for example, 72% of the households in the community live in single-family, detached dwellings and there are 2.59 persons per household, the above equation can be adjusted as follows:

$$(.72 \times 16,949)/2.59 + (.72 \times 324) - .72(8,000 - 6,500) - .72(800 - 1,200) = 4,153$$

Thus, over the 1994-1999 period, demand for 4,153 single-family dwelling units will come on line, averaging 831 units per year. With the additional information that 12% of the households have incomes of $50,000 or more, the analyst can further refine the estimate. According to the general rule of thumb, a household can meet payments on a mortgage amount equal to twice its annual household income. Thus, a household that can make a 20% down payment will be able to purchase a house in the $125,000 range. Of the 831 units demanded each year, approximately 100 units will be in the $125,000 range.

Two calculations were performed to reach this conclusion:

$$(\$50,000 \times 2)/0.80 = \$125,000 \text{ house price}$$

and

$$831 \times 0.12 = 99.7, \text{ or } 100 \text{ units demanded}$$

RELATIONSHIP OF DEMAND TO URBAN GROWTH

Two basic concepts characterize the relationship between demand and urban growth.

1. The rate of growth in the economic base determines the increase in demand for real estate and the rate at which land is absorbed for use.
2. The direction of growth determines where demand for real estate and land use will accelerate and where land will be absorbed. As a corollary, when growth moves in a direction away from the real estate, demand and absorption rates will fall off.

In estimating market value, an appraiser is making a prediction or forecast about the future net benefits accruing from a property and the anticipated supply and demand situation. Because appraisers are predictors or forecasters, they must understand the dynamics of urban land use. If the appraiser is developing a 10-year cash flow analysis for an income-producing property, for example, an understanding of how urban land use patterns may change will enhance the accuracy of the income forecast. If the value of a tract of vacant land is being estimated, an understanding of urban growth patterns will help determine when the parcel will likely be absorbed.

While employment and population are the forces that generate demand, it would be impossible to exclude locational considerations from demand analysis. In the world of real estate, demand shifts over time and space. Real estate products and services, however, are created at a specific point in space and the real estate remains bound to that location. The real estate supply is immovable, but demand consists of people and people are mobile. As people move into an area, they spread out in predictable directions and real estate development takes place. This is how urban land use patterns evolve over time: new neighborhoods grow as old ones decline. Chapter 5 of this text discusses urban land use patterns and the dynamics of real estate demand.

Demand estimates must also take into account macro demand concepts, which relate to the broader metropolitan area beyond the immediate neighborhood. Over time, real estate market demand moves in generally predictable directions within an urban area. As demand moves in one direction, the urban structure changes and property values are affected. The direction in which demand is moving will influence the subject's value. If demand is moving toward the subject property and population density is increasing in the vicinity, the subject's value will rise. As demand moves away from the subject, its value will decline.

To gain a better understanding of these dynamics, the appraiser should be familiar with urban growth patterns, which reflect the channeling of demand forces. The social ecology models discussed in Chapter 5—the concentric zone theory, the sector (wedge) theory, the multiple nuclei theory, and the axial (radial corridor) theory—are especially relevant in determining the direction of urban growth.

Predicting the Direction of Growth

Because an estimate of property value rests on the anticipated benefits to be derived from the property, the appraiser needs to predict the direction of urban growth and determine where population density and demand will increase.

The interaction of macro demand and micro demand determines the direction of urban growth. The critical features an appraiser should examine are proposed developments in the urban infrastructure, specifically transportation and utility linkages. The development of linkages integrates individual sites into the metropolitan matrix.

The social ecology theories of urban growth provide insight into the direction of urban growth. Briefly stated, the concentric zone theory suggests that an urban area usually expands outward from a principal node or nucleus. The sector theory indicates that upper-, middle-, and low-income residential development tends to occur in select sectors of the urban area. The axial (radial corridor) theory supports the sector theory and expands on it by suggesting that development will occur along major transportation arteries. Concentric zone and sector theories postulate that new urban development occurs at the urban periphery, while the radial corridor theory indicates that development tends to follow transportation corridors. The multiple nuclei theory explains why certain land uses attract or repel other land uses.

No one theory provides all of the answers, but considered together the models should help the appraiser interpret growth or decline in the demand for real estate. Given a specific set of circumstances, the appraiser should be able to observe the dynamics of one or more of these urban growth patterns at work.

Factors Influencing Growth Patterns

Because of the emphasis that appraisal literature places on the "four forces that influence demand," it is appropriate to relate these forces to this discussion of the social ecology theories of urban growth and macro demand. Although they have been classified in slightly different ways over the years, the four forces typically refer to

1. Social forces
2. Economic forces
3. Political (or governmental/legal/regulatory/institutional) forces
4. Physical (or natural/locational/environmental/external) forces

E.W. Burgess, who developed the concentric zone theory, was a sociologist interested in the social advancement of immigrant groups. Thus his model represents a sociological explanation of land use patterns. Homer Hoyt, who formulated the sector theory, was a land economist investigating economic variables. His theory reflects underlying economic relationships—primarily land values. Harris and Ullman, who proposed the multiple nuclei theory, were geographers analyzing spatial relationships in urban growth patterns, so their model tends to focus on locational or spatial considerations.

Hoyt and Burgess both acknowledged that physical elements play an important role in shaping urban development patterns. Hoyt argued that physical features influence the location and, ultimately, the direction of growth of upper-, middle-, and lower-income sectors. Upper-income groups seek the best, most expensive land; middle-income groups seek the next most desirable land; and lower-income groups must settle for the least desirable land. Burgess recognized that physical features influence urban land use patterns. He acknowledged that his model was an abstraction from reality since Chicago, the focus of his studies, extends along Lake Michigan and could not therefore grow in a circular pattern.

Growth and the Economic Base

The rate of growth in the economic base determines the demand for real estate and the rate at which land is absorbed for use. The economic base concept attributes a city's growth to the goods and services that it exports. The more goods and services that are sold outside a community's immediate environs, the more money is brought into the community. To produce more goods and services, the work force must expand and more people must move into the area. This growing population creates greater demand for real estate because more people need places to live, work, and play.

SUMMARY

The general area or city analysis found in many appraisals is often far too general to be of much assistance in real estate market analysis. Serious practitioners need to be more specific, more critical, and more precise in their analyses, focusing on the subject property and the factors that contribute to its value. The study of value-creating factors makes the appraiser an applied economist, studying and interpreting the forces of supply and demand.

To study the value-creating components of a property, the appraiser must analyze how the forces of supply and demand come to bear on the property in its fixed location. Through productivity analysis the appraiser focuses on the components of the property that make it productive and, in this way, identifies its prospective uses. Tentative property uses indicate the property's prospective users and the market segments that constitute demand for the property. Once these market segments have been identified, the appraiser can estimate the demand for the specific property.

This chapter has presented some general concepts and techniques employed in estimating demand. These tools reflect the fundamental relationships between the demand for real estate and employment and population in the market area and the overall city. The use of simple equations for estimating demand in retail, office, and housing markets has been demonstrated. Because real estate demand has a spatial dimension, urban growth patterns have been reviewed and related to real estate demand.

Finally, the chapter emphasizes an important relationship — i.e., the rate of growth in the economic base determines the increase in the demand for real estate. By coupling economic base analysis with an understanding of land use patterns, the appraiser will be able to identify the rate and direction of urban growth and, ultimately, the rate at which land is absorbed for use. Once the rate and direction of urban growth have been determined, the appraiser can make use of various models to estimate demand.

CHAPTER OBJECTIVES

———⟫•⟪———

- To contrast general area or regional analysis as currently conducted with competitive supply projections
- To explain the importance of examining competitive supply
- To provide a definition of projected competitive supply for the defined market segment
- To present a variety of techniques for projecting competitive supply in the market under investigation

CHAPTER NINE

Estimating Competitive Supply

Competitive supply is the other side of the demand-supply equation. Appraisal theory and practice have long called for examination of economic trends, including indicators such as population, employment, purchasing power, and interest rates. Unfortunately, many appraisers have interpreted this to mean that they should load the general area analysis or regional analysis section of the appraisal report with volumes of regional or city data.

The discussion of area trends in a report most often consists of boilerplate—i.e., standard data pertaining to the entire region or city. This information is taken from the appraiser's files, which are updated perhaps once or twice a year. Such material is rarely examined in connection with the market value of the subject property. Interpretation of the trends described and their impact on the subject is left to the reader. The following quotation, taken from the fifth edition of *The Appraisal of Real Estate*, which was published a quarter of a century ago, reminds us of what should be considered.

> The appraiser's knowledge should include some recent history of these [trends], their present status, and a logical idea of what to expect of them in the foreseeable future. However, the appraiser should reflect in his value estimate *only those trends which presently affect [the] market value [of the subject]*. (page 80, emphasis added)

Another problem with regional analysis, as it is typically performed, is that it often considers only demand-side factors, ignoring supply-side factors. For example, a report may include demand-side data such as the names of the major employers in the area, exhibits on population/employment trends, or graphs plotting the growth in demand deposits at local banks. These data demonstrate that demand is growing, but shed no light on the market supply. The unspoken assumption is that because there is growth in demand, demand must exist for the subject property in its submarket. This argument does not necessarily follow. Competitive supply must also be examined.

DEFINING COMPETITIVE SUPPLY

The real estate supply being examined consists of the competitive properties in the market area. The quantity of competitive supply is, in turn, a function of the prices being paid for properties and the costs of building new units. There are two components of supply to be considered: the *existing supply*—i.e., the stock or inventory of the specific type of real estate being studied—and the *new supply* that will enter the market during the projection period.

Competitive Supply in the Defined Market Segment

Property productivity analysis defines the physical, locational, legal, and market appeal attributes that the subject property can provide. These attributes are shared by competitive properties. When these attributes are examined, the productive capabilities of the property and the likely users of the property will come into focus. Thus, productivity analysis helps define the attributes that competitive properties must have and the market segment in which the subject property competes.

One way to identify competitive property attributes is to use a spreadsheet that lists the productive attributes of property. Tables 12.4 and 12.17 in Chapter 12 are examples of spreadsheets. The spreadsheet may also list financial attributes, which include the price or rent levels of the properties, any special financing (e.g., below-market financing or rent concessions), and any special assessments for public utilities. A property's productivity characteristics will attract certain types of users.

Further market segmentation can be conducted based on other property attributes such as:

- Single-tenant or multitenant occupancy, e.g., single-family or multifamily residential, single-tenant or multitenant office buildings/retail properties
- Customer base, i.e., the probable users of the property based on a demographic breakdown of their ages, sex, employment, income range, social status, and activity patterns
- Construction quality and property condition
- Financial attributes

Competitive Supply and the Level of Market Analysis[1]

Level A market analysis is the traditional level of market analysis employed by appraisers. Level A analysis draws on readily available regional and city data. A description of the general area is provided as a backdrop for the analysis of data on comparable properties, which are taken as representive of conditions in the market. The analysis focuses on the generators of real estate demand in the area. The appraiser does not usually relate areawide demand to the subject, but leaves it to the reader of the appraisal report to infer the level of demand that exists for the subject. Typically, Level A analyses refer to the supply side of the market only indirectly by citing vacancy rates for selected rent or sales comparables. The vacancy rates of these comparable properties serve as indicators of any oversupply or undersupply in the market. These rates are taken as representative of the market. Projected vacancies are based on the assumption that these rates will remain stable.

Level B market analysis incorporates and builds upon a Level A analysis. Level A is descriptive and historical in content, using past data on selected comparables to represent the market. Level B is more analytical. The appraiser studies broad-based surveys of the market to estimate supply and uses quantifiable data to make judgments about use and timing. In Level B supply analyses, regularly published market studies are examined to provide an idea of the number of similar-use properties in a designated geographic area. Thus, Level B analysis can be further contrasted with Level A analysis, in which conclusions about the entire market are based on the vacancy rates of selected comparables. Level C analyses are much more sophisticated and require more extensive data.

ESTIMATING SUPPLY WITH SECONDARY DATA

Secondary data consist of published information collected for purposes unrelated to the specific research at hand. Using such data saves time and expense. However, this advantage must be weighed against the potential inaccuracies that can arise from data that are not tailored to fit the market area defined in the problem.

Sources of Secondary Supply Data

A variety of secondary data is available in most major cities and can be used to estimate the supply of a given property type. An office brokerage or leasing company may conduct semiannual surveys of office buildings to determine the amount of space on the market, changes in the quantity of available space, and vacancy rates. Similarly, a retail brokerage may conduct surveys of retail space. In

---

1. Four levels of market analysis were described in Chapter 2. The three levels discussed here (Levels A, B, and C) represent the kinds of analyses typically undertaken for valuation appraisals.

some metropolitan areas, commercial market research firms collect real estate statistics on various types of real estate and sell these data to appraisers, brokers, leasing agents, developers, or others. City and regional planning agencies also collect and process data that may be of use to real estate appraisers. Level B analyses make extensive use of secondary data. With regard to such data, however, a few caveats are warranted. The appraiser must carefully consider the nature of the data—i.e., the purpose for which the data were collected and what the data do and do not address. The boundaries of any designated submarket must also be identified. The analyst must then consider the data in terms of what is needed to solve the appraisal problem at hand.

The analyst should assess whether or not the collector/disseminator of the data has biased the information or its interpretation to serve some special interest. For example, consider three office market reports published by three different brokerage firms in a major southwestern metropolis. As is typical, these reports contain divergent data on vacancy rates, absorption rates, and the amount of office space that is coming on line. When the nature of these data is carefully investigated, the appraiser discovers that the studies cover different, but overlapping, components of the office market. The first company tracks only Class A buildings that contain 100,000 or more square feet of space. The second company reports on the office space in the CBD found in both Class A buildings, containing 20,000 or more square feet of space, and Class B buildings. This second company openly acknowledges that its surveys cover only 50% to 60% of the markets it follows. The third company tracks all Class A buildings from which it can readily obtain data, but does not indicate what percentage of the market this group may represent! This third company's report subtly identifies the buildings the company has leased and notes that they have occupancy rates higher than the market average. The appraiser must take note of these qualitative differences in data and select the data that best address the problem.

ESTIMATING SUPPLY WITH PRIMARY DATA

Level C analyses make extensive use of primary data and employ secondary data much more sparingly. To estimate the supply of real estate in the market area, Level C analyses depend on fieldwork and direct surveys.

The supply of real estate includes all properties that currently exist in the given market because any available property may be bought, sold, or leased at any moment. In addition to existing units, supply includes new properties that may be developed or built within a given time frame. (A corollary to the quantity of units being developed is the number of units that may be demolished and permanently removed from the market.) Thus the first component of supply refers to the stock or inventory of existing units in the market, while the second component comprises the influx of properties into the market over the projection period. Both components must be investigated. A third component, competitive sites suitable for development, is also considered by the appraiser.

Existing Stock or Supply of Competitive Properties

To estimate the stock of competitive properties, the analyst delimits the market area and does field work to survey the competitive projects in the area defined. The analyst identifies units that may be considered competitive with the subject and personally inspects each property to collect the requisite data. Basic information may include the following:

- Name and address of the project
- Name and phone number of the contact person
- Project size
- Occupancy level
- Parking facilities
- Amenities

Of course, much more information may be gathered. The definition of the problem will suggest the quantity of information needed to solve it.

While conducting the field work, the analyst organizes the data in a worksheet format. After systematic collection and analysis, the data will indicate which properties are competitive with the subject.

Building permit data can also be used to estimate the existing supply of a given property type. These data, which are obtainable from city governments, may be used to track the number of new buildings being constructed in the market area. Permit data should be used with caution because not all permits are acted upon—i.e., some buildings for which permits are issued are never built. The best way to ascertain whether or not a building has been constructed is to personally inspect the area. Another method involves taking a sample of the permits issued over a given period, checking to see how many were acted upon, and developing an adjustment factor. For example, if 86% of the permits tracked have been put to use, an adjustment factor of 86% may be applied to the total number of building permits issued in the market area. As market conditions change, the sample survey will have to be periodically updated to ensure its reasonableness.

Competitive Supply Under Construction or Planned

The second component of supply is the number of new properties currently under construction or in planning. Projects currently under construction are identified by inspecting the market area and contacting knowledgeable people. To survey planned projects the analyst may conduct telephone interviews with developers, city planning officials, plat map compilers, and others who may be aware of planned construction projects.

Competitive Sites in the Market Area

The final step in the supply estimate is a comprehensive survey of prospective sites for competitive properties in the market area that may be developed in the near future.

DESIGN/AMENITIES RATING

In addition to quantitative analysis of the inventory of competitive properties, in-depth supply studies call for qualitative analysis to assess the relative competitiveness of the subject. This information is needed to estimate the subject's market capture rate. The analysis is conducted by assigning design/amenities ratings, which rank the subject and competitive properties according to features such as design, quality of construction, condition/maintenance, profile/visibility, access, proximity to support facilities, and the quality of the management and tenants. In this ranking, features that strongly influence a tenant's decision to lease space in a property may be accorded more weight.

SUMMARY

The price of property is determined by the interaction of supply and demand. Demand is a function of the size of the population and the income levels in a market area. Supply is developed to meet the population's demand for places to live, work, and play. Without supply, there can be no market; similarly, a market cannot exist without demand. It takes both supply and demand to create a market, a price, and a value.

The area or regional analyses conducted by appraisers often do not specifically address market conditions. Perhaps the most obvious shortcoming of area analyses is their failure to focus on the value of the subject property. Data may be incorporated into an appraisal report without any attempt to relate market conditions to the value of the subject property. The readers of the report are left on their own to interpret what the data mean with regard to the property's value.

Another problem arises when area analysis concentrates on the demand for the real estate, while ignoring the supply of competitive properties. Demand-side data on population, employment, and income are included in most area analyses. These data serve as indicators that demand is growing or declining, but they say nothing about supply.

The competitive supply of real estate is determined by the price of similar properties and the cost to build new units. As the price paid for a particular type of property increases, the number of properties of that type placed on the market also increases, all else being equal. As the price paid declines, the quantity of properties declines as well.

Competitive supply may be estimated by a variety of techniques. Secondary data generated by market research groups often provide excellent information. However, a more in-depth analysis may require primary data, which are only obtainable by conducting personal surveys and fieldwork.

CHAPTER OBJECTIVES

- To review the definitions of *primary* and *secondary data*
- To provide definitions of other essential terms employed in data analysis, i.e., *model, data, information*
- To provide a list of data sources for the appraiser
- To evaluate secondary data employed in Level A and B analyses
- To explore traditional methods for gathering primary data
- To examine innovative approaches for generating primary data
- To demonstrate the use of modeling to refine data

CHAPTER TEN

Data Sources

This chapter discusses the sources, uses, and evaluation of data for the supply and demand analyses within an appraisal. Appraisers make use of both primary and secondary data in the models they use to generate information essential to decision making. It is useful to define some key terms at the outset.

A *model* is an artificial representation of, or abstraction from, reality that describes a particular aspect of the world. Models are generally used for decision-making purposes. For example, a road map can be considered a model. A road map of the United States can show a driver how to get from New York City to San Francisco. It represents a high level of abstraction. As you travel through the various states, you may find you need a state map. And if you are to be in a particular city for a while, you might want a local city map. Each map reflects a different level of abstraction. None depicts the actual world as we see it when we drive down the road. Reality is far too complex for a map to reflect its totality.

Appraisers use models to understand the market. Examples of appraisal models include the sales comparison approach, the income capitalization approach, discounted cash flow analysis, the gross income multiplier, and the Akerson or Ellwood formula. Models do not replicate the complexity of the real world. In fact, if there are too many variables to incorporate into the model, the model becomes unmanageable.

In the sales comparison approach, the appraiser collects data on comparable sales which are adjusted for differences using a matched pairs model. Even when data on very comparable matched pairs are available, the adjustments are only approximations and the effect of the distinguishing feature cannot be totally isolated. Other differences can impinge on the final outcome. However, for a matched pairs model to be effective, only significant, critical variables need to be identified in the model. This point is important. Just as the road map forces the user to focus on the critical route, blocking out the scenery and detours, an appraisal model forces the appraiser to focus on *critical variables* while downplaying the role of other variables.

Data are observations and evidence that bear on some aspect of the appraisal problem. *Information* is produced through interpretation of data for purposes of decision making. The data the appraiser collects are incorporated into and filtered through various appraisal models, which generate information that can be used in solving the appraisal problem. *Primary data* are collected directly by the appraiser to solve the defined problem. The appraiser gathers primary data for use in the appraisal models that will be tested. *Secondary data*, which are generated for reasons other than the appraisal problem at hand, often must be adapted for use in the selected models. Appraisers must be adept at generating primary data such as comparable sales, rents, incomes, expenses, capitalization rates, and property specifications. Much of the market analysis within an appraisal, however, will utilize data that have been collected for purposes other than the appraiser's specific research problem. In other words, much of the data will be secondary data.

SECONDARY DATA

The following discussion will first focus on secondary data, which are published and readily available.

The use of secondary data, collected for purposes other than the needs of the specific research at hand, saves time and expense. Secondary data used for real estate analysis include statistics published by the Bureau of the Census (U.S. Department of Commerce) and the Bureau of Labor Statistics (U.S. Department of Labor) on population, birth rates, death rates, employment, retail sales, interest rates, housing starts, and building permits.

Guide Note 6 to the Appraisal Institute's Standards of Professional Appraisal Practice states that whenever an appraiser uses secondary data, he or she has a responsibility to investigate the sources and reliability of the data. One of the first duties of an appraiser, therefore, is to evaluate the secondary data to be used. Problems arise when the data do not fit the appraiser's problem. The accuracy of the data may be questionable because they were not collected firsthand by the appraiser. Furthermore, if the secondary data were compiled for market areas that do not conform to the market area under study, they may not be representative of the defined area. Just as adjustments are made to comparable sales data, the appraiser will frequently need to make adjustments to the secondary data used.

Sources of Secondary Data

A sampling of data sources is discussed here.[1] There are hundreds, perhaps thousands, of data sources available. The sources listed will give the reader some idea of the wide variety of data available to anyone willing to put forth some effort. The list describes only the more common sources and is not intended to be comprehensive. The analyst will recognize that many private sources of data are not cited. Such proprietary data may be obtained for a fee or by expending extra effort. The analyst tries to find data that meet the needs of the job at hand, given the time and budget constraints of the assignment. The list includes a brief evaluation of the data and the source; such an evaluation must be made for every data source employed by the appraiser.

Buying Power, Consumer Spending, Income and Earnings

1. *Survey of Buying Power*—Data Service
   Kind of data: buying power, retail sales, sales potential.
   Coverage: States, MSAs, counties.
   Frequency: Annually.
   Source: Sales and Marketing Management magazine, 633 Third Avenue, NY, 10017 (212/986-4800).
   Content: State and county outline maps, household income distribution, population, effective buying income, demographics, total retail sales, detailed characteristics, and buying power index. The data cover retail stores and the most recent economic census comparisons with growth rates by 10 merchandise categories and 12 individual store groups.
   Methodology: No information is provided. Readers may direct inquiries to (212/986-4800, ext. 361).

2. *Consumer Expenditure Survey*
   A. *Diary Survey* (Bulletin 2245)
   B. *Interview Survey* (Bulletin 2267)
   Kind of data: Consumer spending.
   Coverage: Regional.
   Frequency: Biennially.
   Source: Superintendent of Documents, Bureau of Labor Statistics, Department of Labor, U.S. Government Printing Office, Washington, DC 20402. (202/783-3238).
   Content: Expenditure categories are cross-tabulated by consumer characteristics; selected expenditure categories. (Bulletin 2245 contains 31 categories of goods and services; Bulletin 2267 covers 66 categories).

---

1. These data sources are taken from Waldo L. Born and Karl D. Svoboda, *Special Report: Real Estate Market Research Data Publications* (College Station: Real Estate Center, Texas A & M University, November 1987).

Methodology: Diary Survey—Consumer units complete a record of expenses for two, consecutive one-week periods. The sample is augmented during periods of increased buying activity such as the month of December; *Interview Survey*—An interviewer visits each of the consumer units in the sample every three months over a 12-month period. The expenditures are based on consumer recall for the period.

Validity: Standard errors of estimates are available on request.

3. Employment and Wages by Industry and County

Kind of data: Employment, income, earnings.

Coverage: States and counties.

Frequency: Quarterly, semiannually—varies from state to state.

Source: State Department of Labor or Employment Commission. Offices of these departments exist in each state. Statistics are compiled by at least one of these agencies, and sometimes by both.

Content: Varies from state to state, but generally the data will cover monthly employment and earnings for two-digit SIC codes. There are general employment categories for the following: agriculture; mining; construction; manufacturing; transportation, communications, and public utilities; wholesale and retail trade; finance; insurance and real estate; services and other; state government; and local government.

Methodology: Typically data are compiled from quarterly contribution and wage reports submitted by employers subject to the State Unemployment Compensation Act.

Validity: Data are not subject to sampling error.

4. *Money Income of Households, Families and Persons in the United States*

Kind of data: Income and earnings.

Coverage: United States, regions, and divisions.

Frequency: Annually.

Source: Superintendent of Documents, Bureau of the Census, U.S. Government Printing Office, Washington, DC 20402 (202/783-3238).

Content: Provides total income in current and constant dollars and median income for households, families, unrelated individuals, and persons.

Methodology: Most of the estimates are based on data obtained from the Current Population Survey (CPS). However, some of the estimates are based on decennial census data. The CPS sample covers 629 areas comprising 1,148 counties, independent cities, and minor civil divisions in the United States. In this sample, approximately 61,500 occupied households were eligible for interview. The estimation procedure involved inflating the weighted sample results to obtain independent estimates of the total civilian, noninstitutional population by age, race, and sex.

Construction/Space Inventory

1. *Building Stock Database and Forecast*

   Kind of data: Construction activity, real estate space inventory.

   Coverage: United States, states, counties.

   Frequency: Annually.

   Source: F.W. Dodge Data Resources, Inc., 235 Peachtree St., Atlanta, GA 30303 (404/661-1930).

   Content: Floor stock benchmarks and historical series for 35 structure types aggregated into 15 structure groups including retail, restaurants, offices, and manufacturing plants.

   Methodology: Benchmark year is 1977; developed by two separate methods employing a variety of data from public and private sources.

   Validity: Information is not available because the data are generated by means of a proprietary database and model.

2. *Dodge Local Construction Potentials*

   Kind of data: Construction cost and activity.

   Coverage: United States, states, counties.

   Frequency: Monthly with annual summary.

   Source: F.W. Dodge Division, McGraw-Hill Information Systems Company, 1221 Avenue of the Americas, New York, NY 10020 (212/512-6711).

   Content: Project data are classified by type of building or nonbuilding as residential and nonresidential with additional differentiation according to use. Nonresidential includes commercial, manufacturing, educational, hospital/health-related, public, and recreational.

   Methodology: Information on construction potentials is a by-product of the F.W. Dodge Report service to contractors who supply the requested bid information. The reports contain pertinent construction information once contracts have been issued. Data are complied from a 1,300-reporter/correspondent network covering every state. Items included are planned projects, projected costs per project, addresses of architects/engineers, proposed bidding dates, types of construction, and materials to be used.

   Validity: Visits are made to contractors and construction sites to verify information initially obtained by building permits and other sources. The data are more accurate and are available sooner than building permit data from the Bureau of the Census.

3. *Real Estate Analysis and Planning Service*

   Kind of data: Economic base, real estate space inventory.

   Coverage: Major U.S. cities.

   Frequency: Semiannually.

   Source: F.W. Dodge Data Resources Inc., Construction and Real Estate Information Service, 235 Peachtree St., Atlanta, GA 30303 (404/869-8260).

Content: In-depth coverage of 50 cities, providing economic, demographic, construction, and real estate activity data that include six years of historic data and five years projected data for four types of nonresidential real estate. The historic analysis focuses on supply, demand, market equilibrium, market size, and market potential. Data include square footage, dollar value, number of projects, story height, location (county), structure type (of 209 types), and whether the construction was new or consisted of additions and alterations.

Methodology: Combines files of Data Resources Inc., which contain extensive regional information and economic data, with the data files of F.W. Dodge on construction and real estate. The F.W. Dodge data are the only comprehensive and consistent source of construction square footage and dollar value data available.

Validity: Information is not available because the data are generated by means of a proprietary database and model.

Population, Demographics, Employment, Economic Base

1. *Census of Population, Census of Construction,* and *Annual Housing Survey*

   Kind of data: Demographics, housing, population.

   Coverage: States, MSAs, counties, census tracts.

   Frequency: Every 10 years.

   Source: Superintendent of Documents, Bureau of the Census, U.S. Government Printing Office, Washington, DC 20402 (202/783-3238).

   Content: Data are published in a variety of different reports that cover the following: general population characteristics, general social and economic characteristics, detailed population characteristics, and number of inhabitants. Includes 229 tables covering a wide range of population characteristics.

   Methodology: The methodology is described in the *Census of Construction* and *Annual Housing Survey*.

   Validity: The Bureau of the Census uses cross-checks with the postal service, available commercial mailing lists, records checks (drivers licenses, etc.), and rechecks of housing units as well as other cross-checking methods.

2. Demographics, Population, Employment, Economic Base, Housing: Proprietory Data Services

   Kind of data: Demographics, housing, economic base, sales potential, employment, incomes, lifestyles, etc.

   Coverage: The user is permitted to define the market area by a variety of means, e.g., census tract, circle, polygon.

   Frequency: By user request.

   Sources: There are numerous sources of proprietary data. Data services use an assortment of techniques and methodologies to update decennial census data.

Listed below are several of the more widely known companies that supply these data.

- CACI Marketing Systems
  9302 Lee Highway
  Fairfax, VA 22031
  Toll free: (800) 292-CAC1
- CLARITAS
  201 North Union Street
  Alexandria, VA 22314
  (703) 683-8300
- Donelly Marketing Information Services
  70 Seaview Avenue
  Stamford, CT 06904
  (800) 866-2255
- DRI/McGraw-Hill
  24 Hartwell Avenue
  Lexington, MA 02173
  (800) 541-9914
- National Planning Data Services
  P.O. Box 610
  Ithaca, NY 14851
  (607) 273-8208

Content: These companies prepare an assortment of studies that can be tailored to the user's needs. These include demographics, housing, income, age groups, sex, five-year forecasts, and other breakdowns of data. The studies are provided for the market area defined by the user. In addition, such firms provide market segmentation studies that further identify consumer characteristics on the basis of psychographic profile and other criteria.

Methodology: Varies from company to company. The analyst should discuss the methodology used with a demographer on staff. Essentially, these companies update data from the previous census and make forecasts. They determine the population distribution for small market areas by means of a smoothing technique using centroids. (A centroid, which represents the center of mass, is graphed as the point at which population is concentrated. A centroid is plotted by coordinates which are the averages of the coordinates for a given set of points.)

Validity: Typically the analyst will want to discuss the updating, forecasting, and smoothing techniques applied to disaggregate data for small areas with a demographer in the firm to decide which data set best suit the needs of the analyst. There are often significant variances between the results provided by different companies for the same defined market area. See John Chapman's article, "Cast a Critical Eye," in *American Demographics Magazine* (February 1987), pp. 31-33.

3. *County Business Patterns: Economic Base*

   Kind of data: Economic base, employment, income, labor force.

   Coverage: United States, states, counties

   Frequency: Annually.

   Source: Superintendent of Documents, Bureau of the Census, U.S. Government Printing Office, Washington, DC 20402 (202/783-3238).

   Content: Provides data by county on number of employees, payroll, number of establishments, and number of establishments by employment size. The data are cross-tabulated by two-, three-, and four-digit SIC codes. The data further describe the economy.

   Methodology: Data are extracted from the Standard Statistical Establishment List (SSEL) of the Bureau of the Census. SSEL covers all employers who have made social security payments for their employees under the FICA Act. Other details about the data should be investigated.

   Validity: Data are not subject to sampling error.

Real Estate Space Inventory and Operating Experience

1. *Building Stock Database and Forecast*

   Kind of data: Construction activity, real estate space inventory.

   Coverage: United States, states, counties.

   Frequency: Annually.

   Source: F.W. Dodge Data Resources, Inc. 235 Peachtree St., Atlanta, GA 30303 (404/661-1930).

   Content: Floor stock benchmarks and historical series for 35 structure types aggregated into 15 structure groups including retail centers, restaurants, office buildings, and manufacturing facilities.

   Methodology: Benchmark year is 1977. Inventory and forecast are developed by two separate methods that make use of various data from public and private sources.

   Validity: Information is not available because the data are generated by a proprietary database and model.

2. *Real Estate Analysis and Planning Service*

   Kind of data: Economic base, real estate space inventory.

   Coverage: Major U.S. cities.

   Frequency: Semiannually.

   Source: F.W. Dodge Data Resources, Inc., Construction and Real Estate Information Service, 235 Peachtree St., Atlanta, GA 30303 (404/869-8260).

   Content: In-depth coverage of 50 cities. Provides economic and demographic data as well as data on construction and other real estate activity. These include historical data for six years and projection data over five years for four types of nonresidential real estate. The historical analysis focuses on supply, demand, market balance, market size, and market potential. Data include square footage, dollar value, number of projects, story height, location (county), structure type (of 209 types), and the nature of the construction (whether it was a new building, an addition, or an alteration).

Methodology: Combines extensive regional economic data from Data Resources Inc. with the construction and real estate data from the F.W. Dodge files. F.W. Dodge is the only available source of comprehensive and consistent data on the square footage and dollar value of new construction.

Validity: Information is not available because the data are generated by a proprietary database and model.

3. *BOMA Experience Exchange Report*

Kind of data: Operating experience of real estate space.

Coverage: United States, Canada, major cities.

Frequency: Annually.

Source: Building Owners and Managers Association International (BOMA), 1250 Eye Street, N.W., Washington, DC 20005 (202/289-7000).

Content: Divided into sections: U.S. private, U.S. government, Canada private, and Canada government. Office building operating data are subdivided into downtown or suburban and categorized by square footage and special building type (i.e., medical, financial, single-purpose, etc.). Analysis includes national comparisons by age, size, and height of building every two and five years.

Methodology: Voluntary survey of office building investment/ownership and management by BOMA. Data are provided on a common form.

Validity: Data are probably biased towards the high-quality end of the building spectrum with higher rents and lower expenses. This reflects the nature of the types of buildings owned and managed by BOMA members and affiliates.

4. *Dollars and Cents of Shopping Centers*

Kind of data: Operating data for real estate space.

Coverage: United States and six regions.

Frequency: Every three years.

Source: Urban Land Institute (ULI), 1090 Vermont Avenue, N.W., Washington, DC 20005 (202/289-8500).

Content: Comparative income and expense data on shopping centers. Provides data under seven categories: gross leasable area, sales, rate of percentage rent, total charges, total rents, common area charges, and rent and common area charges as percentage of sales. Data are presented by center size and cross-classified by tenant type.

Methodology: Compiled by ULI in conjunction with the International Council of Shopping Centers (ICSC). Approximately 1,000 centers participated in the last survey.

Validity: Voluntary participation probably biases the data towards the higher-quality centers. Hence, data on operating revenues may be on the high side and data on expenses on the low side in comparison with a random sample of centers. Regional data are probably less reliable than national data because in some areas, where the number of centers is limited, data are withheld from disclosure.

Evaluating Secondary Data

Several rules should be followed in evaluating secondary data. First, the appraiser must determine who compiled the data and for what purposes. For example, the Texas Department of Water Resources makes 30-year forecasts of county populations. These forecasts are designed so that any error will be in overestimation because the department does not want Texans to run out of water! If an appraiser were to base population and absorption forecasts on these data, the results would be especially optimistic.

Second, the appraiser should examine the methods used to collect the data. Collection techniques and their reliability can vary immensely. For example, substantial differences may exist in the data compiled by two agencies that collect building permit data and forecast housing starts. One agency may make a mechanical, rule-of-thumb adjustment to update data, while the other sends its staff out to neighborhoods to count the actual number of units being constructed. Similarly, population forecasts may differ significantly. A data supplier may base a population forecast on the number of building permits issued, then adjust this figure for nonstarts, and check the result against data on water connections. The local chamber of commerce, on the other hand, may employ a straight-line projection technique based on the growth rate over the last two years. Both techniques are legitimate and can produce accurate results, given the assumptions and purposes of the analysis.

Third, the appraiser should examine the market area covered by the data and compare it with the market area defined in the analysis. When the market areas do not correspond, a bias is introduced into the analysis. The appraiser may need to adjust or modify the data so that the two market areas more closely correspond and the bias can be reduced.

Using Secondary Data to Estimate Demand

Demand forecasts are developed from projections of population, employment, and income. The kind of secondary data used by appraisers generally includes small area projections such as census tract figures or countywide data. Sometimes subcensus tract data may be available. In areas such as North Texas, councils of governments (COGs) generate data for small areas called *traffic survey zones* (TSZs). A single census tract may be divided into three, eight, or even 20 or more traffic survey zones. Obviously, such small areas can be tailored to fit a defined market area more easily than larger ones.

Projections are often made by city and regional planning offices as well as other public or private agencies. After examining the methodology used to develop the projections that are available and rejecting those based on methodologies unsuitable to the needs of the assignment, the appraiser may wish to take a simple average of the acceptable projections. Averaging may be appropriate because the strengths and weaknesses of each projection may cancel each other out to some extent. Any discrepancies between the projections should be offset by averaging them.

Once a preliminary estimate has been derived, the appraiser may wish to compare the projection with data from an analogous city. After such comparison, the appraiser may conclude that the estimate is too high or too low. Then, with a clear rationale, the appraiser may make adjustments upwards or downwards just as estimates derived from different valuation approaches are reconciled into a final value estimate. From small area population and employment estimates, the appraiser develops a demand estimate. The appraiser may then decide whether a Level A or Level B demand analysis is appropriate. Finally, the analyst refines the data so that they accurately represent the desired market segment. Techniques for refining data will be discussed later.

Level A Market Demand Analysis

Level A market analysis is the traditional, generally descriptive type of study undertaken by many appraisers. Based on readily available secondary data on the region and city, a general area description is provided as the backdrop for the analysis of data on comparable properties. Such data are used to represent market conditions. The level of current demand may be estimated based on evidence of sales and leasing activity involving similar properties over the past year. The existence of future demand is frequently assumed if growth trends in the general region and city have been positive.

Level B Market Demand Analysis

Level B market analysis incorporates and builds upon Level A analysis. Level A analyses are descriptive, drawing on selected comparables to represent the market. Level B analyses are more analytical, relying on broad-based surveys of the market to estimate demand. In Level B analyses, judgments about use and timing are based on quantifiable data. In these studies, secondary data are used extensively and they must be scrutinized to determine how well they fit the problem at hand.

In a Level B demand analysis, the analyst examines secondary data from regularly published, areawide market surveys. Using public and proprietary surveys saves time and expense. This type of data is readily available because data services or state agencies in most urban areas routinely survey real estate submarkets, gathering data on office, retail, and apartment space. Data of this nature are more specific than the general data typically included in a Level A analysis. These data are updated at regular intervals—i.e., quarterly or semiannually.

There are also disadvantages to using survey data. The surveys cover broad areas in an urban setting and the geographic boundaries designated for the survey rarely conform to the geographic submarket for the subject property. Therefore, survey data must be used with caution or else the appraiser could draw an inappropriate conclusion. Although proprietary and public survey data are updated more frequently than census data, the data may soon become obsolete. Semiannual or quarterly updates may lag behind change in a dynamic market. Demand is usually projected by estimating net lease-up (i.e., the difference between new leases and leases that are not renewed) or time on the market (the period it takes for new properties to sell). Thus, the current market leasing or sales pattern is projected as the level of marginal demand that might be expected over the next few years.

A further caveat is needed. Although the use of broad-based market survey data increases the reliability of the analysis, it also has its limitations. Data of this type may cover many projects that are not competitive with the subject. The appraiser must carefully evaluate the data being used to determine how well they fit the specific appraisal assignment.

An Example

An assignment to appraise a tract of land was undertaken in 1989. After analyzing the productivity attributes of the property, the appraiser concluded that the property was best suited for the development of a neighborhood supermarket, pending a supply and demand analysis. Two sets of population data were used in the supply and demand analysis: one was published by a local planning agency and covered a subcensus tract area identified as a traffic survey zone; the other was published by a private demographics firm. The former contained population projections for the entire city for 2000 and 2010. The latter included forecasts for the specific market area (the northeast quadrant of the city) for 1995 along with updates of income and age breakdowns and other standard demographic data. Figures 10.1 and 10.2 graph these data. (Note that Figure 10.1, Figure 10.2, and Table 10.1 also appear in Chapter 16, where they are discussed in connection with a case study application.)

After these forecasts have been studied, the next step for the analyst is to estimate the net demand in the trade area for supermarket space. Table 10.1 illustrates this process.

Figure 10.1
Population Projection for Subcensus Tract (TSZ)

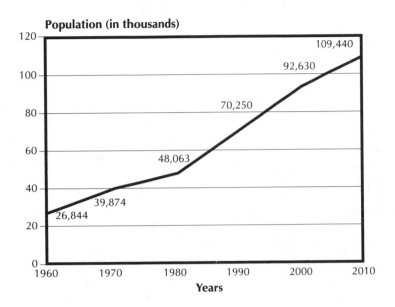

Figure 10.2
Population Forecast for Market Area

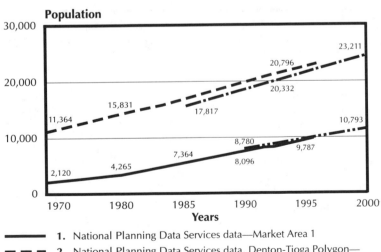

1. National Planning Data Services data—Market Area 1
2. National Planning Data Services data, Denton-Tioga Polygon—
   Market Areas 1 and 2
3. North Central Texas Council of Governments data—Census
   Tracts 1 and 2
4. North Central Texas Council of Governments data—Census
   Tracts 1, 2, 3, and 4

Table 10.1
Market Support for a Supermarket

	1994	1999
Demand Estimate		
Population in trade area*	9,774	10,812
Annual per capita food expenditure†	$1,516	$1,516
	$14,817,384	$16,390,992
Net leakage estimated @ 25%‡	−$3,704,346	−$4,097,748
Estimated demand	$11,113,038	$12,293,244
Supply Inventory		
Total competitive supermarket space in trade area	00	00
Net market support—excess demand (demand minus supply)	11,113,038	$12,293,244
Average sales/sq. ft.§	$312	$312
Supportable supermarket space in the trade area	35,619 sq. ft.	39,401 sq. ft.

---

* Primary trade area consists of Census Tracts 1 and 2. Data are taken from the North Central Texas Council of Governments (NCTCOG) *Dallas-Fort Worth Economic Outlook; Recent Trends and Long-Range Forecasts to the Year 2010, Traffic Survey Zone Level Forecasts* (Arlington, Texas: March 1989). The data for the primary trade area were adjusted to reflect only the portions of the traffic survey zones that are in the trade area.

† Annual per capita expenditures are based on Bureau of Labor Statistics, Department of Labor, *Consumer Expenditure Survey Results* (Washington, D.C.: U.S. Government Printing Office), Table 1. Because the market area has a high median income level, the fourth and fifth decile food expenditures were averaged.

‡ Net leakage is the estimated amount of food expenditures that will be lost to stores outside the trade area. Although 25% is a high leakage factor, it is considered reasonable because of the nature, extent, and size of the trade area.

§ A rough guide employed by supermarket site location specialists is $6/sq. ft. per week, or $312/sq. ft. per year. This will vary depending on a variety of factors.

PRIMARY DATA

Primary data are generated by the researcher for the specific study at hand. Primary data may be obtained in three ways: through respondents, analogs, and experimentation.

Respondents

An appraiser may either communicate with respondents or observe respondents. Commmunication with respondents simply means asking questions of people who may have the answers. Interviews may be informal or formal. Appraisers most often conduct informal interviews. They call real estate market participants for information on sale prices, rents, and occupancy rates. Appraisers also interview property managers, tenants, owners, investors, and developers in the field on topics such as investor motives, costs, vacancies, rents, and finishing expenses. Sometimes formal questionnaires are developed and administered to select individuals who constitute a statistical sample. The special research skills required to develop and administer questionnaires are not addressed here. Nevertheless, questionnaires are an important tool used by marketing researchers, especially for in-depth, Level D analyses.

Appraisers often obtain primary data through observation. An appraiser may count the number of competing properties in the area or drive around a neighborhood to determine its character. Similarly, the researcher may count the number of customers going into a store or the number of vehicles passing an intersection. Often an appraiser will pace off or measure the number of front feet occupied by a storefront or the square feet in a warehouse. All these techniques depend on observation.

Analogs

Studying an analogous or comparable situation can shed light on an appraisal problem. For example, an appraiser may use case histories of comparable areas to estimate the amount of land that is likely to be absorbed over a specified period given the projected population. The appraiser may also examine the amount of land that was put to various uses as the population of the comparable area increased. Thus, an appraiser who is estimating the demand and absorption rate for a large, single-family subdivision may examine a similar community which is currently the size that the subject community is expected to be by the end of a designated period. By examining the amount of land allocated to single-family residences in the comparable community, the appraiser may be able to estimate the amount of land that will be needed for single-family housing units in the subject community. The appraiser can then estimate the capture rate for the subject subdivision to determine how many units may be absorbed over a specified time.

Experimentation

Sometimes appraisers may derive data through experimentation with a model. Such a model can be developed based on information obtained from an analog, as discussed above. By changing the assumptions and corresponding variables entered into the model, the appraiser can simulate alternative scenarios. A simple example is illustrated in Table 10.2.

Table 10.2
Experimental Model Based on Land Uses in Analog City XYZ

Analog City XYZ	1980		1990	
Land uses	**Acres**	**% of Total**	**Acres**	**% of Total**
Total acres	16,000	100.0	20,000	100.0
Single-family	4,252	26.6	5,680	28.4
Multifamily	960	6.0	1,140	5.7
Retail	1,152	7.2	1,580	7.9

Subject City ABC	1990		Projected 2000	
Land uses	**Acres**	**% of Total**	**Acres**	**% of Total**
Total acres	13,500	100.0	17,000	100.0
Single-family	3,267	24.2	4,590	27.0
Multifamily	851	6.3	1,020	6.0
Retail	932	6.9		
Retail Scenarios				
#1			1,173	6.9
#2			1,224	7.2
#3			1,275	7.5

The assumption underlying this example is that the subject parcel of land will eventually be developed for a retail use. The appraiser's objective is to estimate how many additional acres of land under retail use can be absorbed during the coming years. Equipped with such information, the appraiser can determine the likelihood of the subject being developed as a retail use. By examining city planning data about land uses in Analog City XYZ, the analyst is able to estimate the land use breakdown in Subject City ABC. Stated differently, the appraiser finds that City XYZ is very similar to City ABC and realizes that the patterns of land absorption in City ABC will resemble those observed in the analog city.

If development proceeds according to the adage "retail follows rooftops," the appraiser should be able to estimate the number of residential acres that will be absorbed over a period of time by applying a rate comparable to the growth rate for the analog city. Assuming that the cities' land use patterns will be similar, the appraiser can then forecast the amount of retail land to be absorbed in the subject city. Based on the changes in land use in City XYZ, the appraiser estimates the percentage changes for City ABC and then estimates the number of acres for each type of land use. By changing the critical ratio between land uses, the appraiser can use the model to run experiments, each with different outcomes.

Using the figures shown for the three retail scenarios in Table 10.2, the appraiser may conclude that City ABC will bring between 241 (1,173 - 932) and 343 (1,275 - 932) additional acres under retail use. With these data the appraiser can now estimate the likely absorption for the subject property, whose highest and best use is for future retail development.

Sources of Primary Data

Primary data may be generated in any number of ways. The methods that can be applied are limited only by the imagination and initiative of the analyst and the constraints of time and expense. The traditional methods for generating primary data have already been discussed. These include telephone and field interviews with people directly or indirectly involved with the subject or the comparables as well as the use of analogs and experimentation. Using some common sense, however, the appraiser can come up with new and innovative ways to obtain more or better information. The following list presents approaches that have been used successfully at one time or another. First, a problem is set forth and then one possible solution is suggested. Only one possible solution is given for each problem, but there could easily be more than one solution.

1. *Problem:* To establish a vacancy rate for an apartment submarket within the city.

   One solution: The appraiser checks with the local post office or postmaster in the city. Post offices do weekly updates on all addresses to which mail is delivered. New construction addresses are added and address changes are noted. The data available may be used to establish the desired vacancy rate for the multifamily submarket under study.

2. *Problem:* To estimate vacancy rates for two apartment complexes. These rates are critical to the appraisal.

   One solution: If the units are individually metered, the appraiser should obtain a utility company's readouts from the past 12 months for the two complexes under investigation. The number of electrical hookups, for example, should be an excellent indicator of the number of vacancies in the past year.

3. *Problem:* To estimate the demand for elderly housing in a small suburban community. The estimate is needed for the appraisal of a proposed housing project for the elderly.

   One solution: The local property tax office can provide information about the number of houses in the area whose residents pay reduced taxes because they are over age 65. The number of these units is an indication of the number of households that may be seeking elderly housing units in the coming years.

4. *Problem:* To estimate the number of properties that compete with an old office warehouse building in an older part of the city. The appraiser also needs to estimate the square foot area of these competitve properties.

   One solution: The fire department catalogs the different buildings in the city and notes their condition for firefighting purposes. Therefore, the fire department may be able to provide the appraiser with a comprehensive list of older warehouse properties.

5. *Problem:* To assist a client in deciding where to make long-term land investments, the appraiser needs to know where city growth will likely occur over the next 10 to 20 years. In what direction will the city be growing, and when will specific parcels be ready for development?

   One solution: Utility companies, telephone companies, and school districts all make long-term projections about the direction and rate of urban growth. These companies have a vital interest in mapping the future growth of an area and are usually quite willing to share their forecast data.

6. *Problem:* To help the owner of a supermarket assess the impact of two proposed supermarkets, the appraiser has to define the client's trade area.

   One solution: Some fundamental market research is recommended. The analyst could hire a pollster to ask customers leaving the supermarket where they live. Their addresses can then be spotted on a map with different colored pins which represent the number of bags of groceries each customer purchased. (Each bag of groceries can be seen to represent a standardized dollar expenditure). Such a map will provide a picture of the spatial distribution of the supermarket's customers and an estimate of the dollar sales in the store's major market.

7. *Problem:* To estimate the market areas of the existing supermarkets that compete with the subject supermarket in Problem 6. The customers of these stores cannot be spotted.

   One Solution: On several randomly selected weekdays and weekends, the appraiser copies down the license plate numbers of cars parked in the competitors' parking lots. Municipal offices can provide a breakdown of the license plate numbers by geographic area and perhaps the addresses of the vehicle owners.

THE USE OF MODELING TO REFINE DATA

Another method for generating data is to use a model to refine secondary data into data that satisfy the analyst's specifications. However, an additional element of uncertainty is introduced in applying this method because the secondary data from which the refined data are extracted were not specifically compiled for the model, and faulty assumptions may have been built into the model itself. The analyst must be extremely careful in using this technique.

To conduct a Level C demand analysis, the appraiser must generate primary data. This level of analysis relies extensively on primary data; secondary data are also used, but somewhat more sparingly. Level C demand analysis requires the appraiser to become a data generator, which is usually accomplished by relying on some type of model. Levels A and B demand analyses are based on techniques involving simple assumptions about historical data; a Level A demand analysis relies on model-generated primary data to make forecasts. Forecasting demand allows the analyst to identify whether supply exceeds demand, demand exceeds supply, or the market is in equilibrium. Once market conditions are understood, the appraiser can form judgments about absorption rates, prices, rents, and leasing. The analytical techniques employed to generate primary data may also be applied to estimate the subject's market share and the competitive supply. For example, the subject's competitive position and capture potential may be analyzed by rating or weighting features such as location and design amenities.

Whereas Level A and B analyses extrapolate future absorption from historic absorption rates, Level C analysis makes a major shift to future-oriented forecasting techniques. The following equation, which is a model used for estimating marginal demand, provides an example of a Level C market forecasting method.

$$(D_{NG} + D_{MU} + V_N) - (CS_V + Sp_{PN}) = D_M$$

Where:

$$
\begin{aligned}
D_{NG} &= \text{demand from new growth} \\
D_{MU} &= \text{move-up demand} \\
V_N &= \text{normal vacancy} \\
CS_V &= \text{competitive vacant space} \\
Sp_{PN} &= \text{planned new supply}
\end{aligned}
$$

The result of the equation is marginal demand.

$$D_M = \text{marginal demand, or the net difference between projected growth in demand and supply}$$

The equation provides information about the relationship between demand and supply and enables the appraiser to make judgments about absorption, marketability, and timing. The appraiser is called upon to generate much, if not all, of the data needed to use the model. After they are calculated using information from secondary sources, the data are input into the model. The results can then be interpreted.

One (or more) of the input datum may vary in magnitude. In this situation, the appraiser can experiment with different scenarios based on assumptions about the variable data input. A range of possible outcomes, with a high end and a low end, will be the developed.

For example, given the marginal demand model, negative marginal demand (where $D_M \leq 0$) implies: 1) slow absorption or lengthy marketing time, 2) decreasing occupancy rates or increasing vacancy rates, 3) decreasing rents, and 4) decreasing prices. Alternatively, positive marginal demand (where $D_M \geq 0$) implies the opposite circumstances: 1) rapid absorption or short marketing time, 2) increasing occupancy rates or decreasing vacancy rates, 3) increasing rents, and 4) increasing prices.

SUMMARY

The analyst generates primary data though interviews with respondents, the use of analogs, or the creation of models with which the analyst runs experiments. Published secondary data are compiled for purposes other than the specific research problem and are readily available. The analyst should investigate why the secondary data were compiled, the methodology used to gather the data, and how well the area described by the data corresponds to the market area of the subject property.

Level A demand analyses rely entirely on general secondary data to describe the city or region. The difference between Levels B and C demand analyses depends on the extent to which the appraiser uses primary and secondary data. In Level B analysis, demand is estimated based on secondary data. The area for which the secondary data were compiled does not usually correspond to the specific market area of the subject property. For Level C analyses, the appraiser generates primary data for the defined market area, which are required to forecast subject-specific demand. Level C techniques that rate or weight the physical, legal, locational, and amenity features of the subject and its competitors can provide the appraiser with greater insight into the competitive position of the subject property. The appraiser can thereby form better judgments about absorption rates, prices, rents, and leasing.

CHAPTER OBJECTIVES

- To explain the cyclical patterns in the real estate market and the relationship between the national business cycle and the local real estate cycle
- To explain the underlying causes of long-term and short-term real estate cycles and their interaction
- To explain why it takes the market some time to adjust itself to shifts in supply and demand within real estate market cycles
- To define *market conditions*, explain why they are evaluated, and establish a systematic framework for identifying their direction and intensity.

CHAPTER ELEVEN

————◆◆◆————

Market Dynamics
and Market Conditions

Real estate analysts need to understand the dynamics of market cycles and how these cycles affect real estate values and value estimates. In this chapter the business cycle and real estate cycle are explained and the fundamental causes of the cycles are investigated. Also examined are the interaction of the national business cycle and local real estate cycles and the mechanisms by which the market adjusts to shifts in supply and demand. With an understanding of these processes, the analyst will be able to determine the impact of market cycles and market conditions on property values.

FORECASTING CYCLICAL MARKET PATTERNS

Real estate markets operate through the dynamic interaction of supply and demand, which can be perceived as cycles of activity. Because real estate values are likely to change during different phases of a cycle, analysts must understand and address the effects of these cycles. When supply and demand are out of balance, an excess of supply or demand creates market conditions that cause property values to change. Cyclical activity and market conditions must be examined in all appraisals; if they are not, the value estimate may be misstated. Specifically, market dynamics and market conditions exert major influence on the rate of absorption, the timing of lease-up and sales, and the establishment of sale prices. A forecast of the dynamics of the cycle affecting the subject property is absolutely essential to arrive at a reasonable value estimate.

BUSINESS CYCLES

The economy tends to move through predictable, recurring stages of business activity. Collectively, these stages constitute the business cycle. There are four stages in the business cycle:

1. Expansion: a period of economic upswing characterized by growing employment, production, and income and basically stable or moderately rising prices.

2. Slowdown, peak, and downturn: a period characterized by movement toward full employment and manufacturing capacity, positive but declining rates of economic growth, and a rising rate of inflation. Once the peak of the cycle is attained, the economy begins a moderate downturn, which accelerates and sets the stage for an economic contraction.[1]

3. Contraction: a period of economic downturn characterized by declining employment, production, and income accompanied by price stabilization and then price deflation.

4. Slowed contraction, trough, and upturn: a period characterized by a bottoming out of the economic downturn, stabilized rates of unemployment and unused manufacturing capacity, and a slowdown in deflation. Once the trough, or low point, of the cycle is reached, the economy begins a moderate upturn, which accelerates and sets the stage for the next economic expansion.

Shifts in supply and demand over time explain the dynamics of national business cycles. As a simple example, assume that the federal government decides to reduce taxes. The population has more money to spend and the demand for goods and services, relative to the supply, begins to increase. The market responds to the excess of demand over supply, and an expansionary stage in the business cycle occurs. A tax increase, on the other hand, would set into motion the opposite chain of events.

Relationship of National to Local Business Cycles

Reverberations from the national business cycle are transmitted to the local economy through the linkages that tie the local economic base to the national economy. Basic industries and employment in the community produce goods and services that are exported to the national market. Thus, as the national economy moves through the phases of a cycle, local employment and local demand are also affected.

During an economic expansion, for example, the demand for basic goods and services produced in the community grows. Stepped-up demand results in

---

1. Economic contraction reflects a composite index of leading and lagging economic indicators that track the number of bankruptcies, foreclosures, unemployed workers, etc.

expansion of basic employment, production, and income in the community. The expansion of employment in basic industries has a multiplier effect, bringing about an expansion in nonbasic employment as well. People seeking employment will move into the community. Conversely, when the national economy contracts, the demand for basic goods and services produced in the community declines. The falloff in demand results in a contraction of the local economy. Employment declines, and ultimately there may be an outward migration as people seek employment in other communities.

The strength of the relationship between the local economic base and the national economy is pivotal in this scenario. If the local economy is closely tied to the national economy, it will be especially responsive to phases in the national cycle. If, on the other hand, nonbasic employment constitutes the economic base of the community, the local economy will not be seriously affected by changes in the national economy. For example, employment in a small town with a major university depends mainly on the number of students that attend the university. The local economy is largely independent of the national business cycle.

REAL ESTATE CYCLES

Like the business cycle, the real estate cycle consists of four stages:

1. Expansion: a period characterized by rising occupancy and absorption rates, increasing prices, and ultimately greater construction and development activity.
2. Slowdown, peak, and downturn: a period characterized by positive, but declining, absorption rates and a slackening in construction and development activity. Prices, which are already high, are rising and occupancy rates remain high. Once the peak of the cycle is attained, absorption rates and construction and development activity begin to decline.
3. Contraction: a period characterized by declining occupancy and absorption rates, decreasing prices, and, ultimately, a falloff in construction and development activity.
4. Slowed contraction, trough, and upturn: a period characterized by a bottoming out of the construction downturn and stabilization of both absorption and occupancy rates. Once the trough, or low point, is reached, the real estate industry begins a moderate upturn, which sets the stage for the next expansion.

The analyst should look for indicators of long- and short-term real estate cycles and attempt to identify what stage the cycle is in.

Long-Term Real Estate Cycles

Long-term, or secular, real estate cycles are primarily a function of nationwide changes in population and income. If the birthrate and real income are rising nationally, demand for real estate will grow. The relationship is simple and direct: a growing population with higher income needs places to live, work and play. If the birthrate and real income are declining nationally, the demand for real estate will fall off. The most recent example of this phenomenon is the wave of demand unleashed by the post-World War II baby boomers, the generation of individuals born between 1946 and 1966.

A lack of real estate development during the 1930-1945 period had created great pent-up demand. As soldiers returned to civilian life after the war, the rate of household formation picked up. American industry, which had remained intact throughout the war, was converted to peacetime production. Birthrates and incomes both began to rise and real estate demand took off.

As the postwar years wore on, the baby boomers matured. They became a part of the workforce and began to seek housing. Again there was a tremendous surge in the demand for real estate. By the mid 1980s, most of the baby boomers had been absorbed into the workforce, and many had their own homes. The demographic blip began to recede and the unprecedented boom in real estate of the postwar period started to wane.

The relationship between the economic base of a community and a long-term real estate cycle at the local level becomes clearer if local growth in population and income is examined vis-a-vis activity in the local real estate market. If the local economy is able to generate new jobs, people seeking employment will move to the area. The types of employment determine the levels of income in the community, while the rate of job creation influences the size of the in-migration. Other factors may also have an impact on the rate of population growth. For example, the warm climate of Sun Belt states attracts many people.

Once real estate has been financed and developed, it becomes a long-term investment. A real estate analyst assesses the long-term health of the local economy by examining the components of the economic base upon which long-term growth depends. The analyst will seek answers to questions such as these: Which industries are likely to grow? Which are likely to stagnate? How will these industries influence the long-term, local demand for real estate?

Short-Term Real Estate Cycles

The primary determinants of the short-term demand for real estate are the availability of credit and the level of interest rates. In comparison to other types of business and corporate transactions,[2] purchases of real estate generally require a considerable amount of debt financing. Interest represents the price paid for credit. Interest charges, therefore, become a primary concern for real estate investors. The development and acquisition of real estate are extremely sensitive to changes in interest rates. As interest rates rise, the demand for real estate plummets; as rates decline, demand increases.

---

2. Leveraged buyouts are a notable exception.

Real estate activity, as measured by the number of housing starts, takes the lead in upturns and downturns of the national business cycle. This is so because interest rates are responsive to the phases of the business cycle. When the economy is in a trough, interest rates generally bottom out as a result of monetary and fiscal policies aimed at reviving the economy. Real estate is very sensitive to interest rates. Low interest rates, therefore, stimulate real estate activity, which helps lead the economy out of recession. A real estate expansion generally precedes an upturn in general business activity.

Similarly, once an expansionary phase of the business cycle is well underway, interest rates begin to rise, first slowly and then more rapidly. As the business cycle approaches its peak, interest rates rise sharply. The real estate industry, being especially sensitive to rising interest rates, responds ahead of the general economy. Even before business activity peaks, real estate may begin its downturn, leading the economy into a recession. The sequence is illustrated in Figure 11.1. This abstract relationship is valid in theory, but somewhat variable in practice.

Figure 11.1
Relationship Between the Business Cycle
and the Short-Term Real Estate Cycle

Economic Activity

Interaction of Long-Term and Short-Term Cycles

The long-term real estate cycle is a function of growth in population and income; the short-term cycle depends on the availability of mortgage credit and the level of interest rates. The short-term cycle, which has a narrower amplitude and a shorter duration, tends to oscillate over the long-term cycle.

CYCLES AND TIME LAGS

As short-term shifts in demand and supply give rise to the successive phases of a cycle, time lags will occur as the market attempts to adjust. Real estate markets do not transmit information instantaneously. When there is excess demand, prices and rents begin to rise before the need for new construction is perceived. Once new construction is initiated, another lag will occur because it takes time to complete the building process.

An excess in supply results in an alternative scenario. While prices and rents continue to rise, excess space is being built or coming onto the market. Even after the excess in supply becomes apparent, projects currently under construction have to be completed, adding still more stock to the existing surplus. Thus the real estate market's response to shifts in supply is delayed.

MARKET CONDITIONS

The term *market conditions*, which is commonly associated with one of the adjustments in the sales comparison approach, refers to the imbalance between supply and demand in the market. When the demand for a particular property type exceeds the available supply, real estate buyers will bid prices and rents upwards. When the supply of property exceeds the demand, downward pressure will be exerted on prices and rents. In either case, appraisers must consider market conditions in analyzing comparable sales, rents, and construction costs.

Identifying, evaluating, and forecasting market conditions are essential for the following reasons:

- Market conditions determine the period over which the appraisal may be valid. If market conditions are stable, the appraisal may be valid for an extended period of time. If conditions are changing rapidly, the appraisal will be reliable for a shorter period. When estimating property value, an appraiser should specify the period for which the estimated value is expected to be valid or the period within which the property is expected to sell.

- The rate of absorption for new properties is a function of market conditions. If demand exceeds supply, absorption should be rapid. When excess supply exists, absorption will be slow. The appraiser must also estimate the holding, marketing, and lease-up costs incurred over the anticipated absorption period. In oversupplied markets (e.g., markets in the "oil patch" states during the mid- and late-1980s), appraisers can adjust the property value estimates indicated by the cost approach to compensate for the reduction in value attributable to shifts in supply and demand.[3]

- The extent of excess demand or excess supply determines the direction and rate of change in prices, rents, and costs. An understanding of the demand and supply relationship helps the appraiser forecast cash flows and probable sale prices more accurately.

- Finally, market conditions must be identified to arrive at adjustments in the sales comparison approach. The sales data on which the appraiser relies all reflect previous transactions. If market conditions have changed, the appraiser must adjust the comparable sale prices to bring them into line with what the properties would sell for today.

Market conditions may be evaluated in three steps:

1. Identify the appropriate market segment by both property type and geographic area.
2. Identify the current stage of the real estate cycle and an appropriate time frame for the cycle. Typically the appraiser seeks to estimate a current sale price, so the short-term real estate cycle will usually be considered.
3. Identify the supply and demand conditions prevailing in the market—e.g., excess demand, excess supply, market balance.

Equipped with an understanding of market conditions, the appraiser is ready to apply the information in reconciling value indications and estimating a final value. Critical items for consideration include:

The time frame for the demand-supply forecast

- What is the relevant time frame for the demand-supply forecast and the value estimate?
- What is the current stage in the cycle?
- How will the cycle change within the time frame?

Current demand-supply conditions

- Does an excess in demand or supply exist? If so, how great is the excess?
- What are the short-term and long-term consequences of excess demand?
- What are the effects on prices, rents, absorption, and vacancies?

---

3. This is referred to as an adjustment for *external obsolescence*. The term *externality* is used by economists to refer to a cost or benefit that accrues to someone other than the person who created it when no contractual procedure exists to allow the one party to render the other compensation. An externality may also be caused by factors outside the market—e.g., the air pollution generated by automobiles.

- What are the short-term and the long-term consequences of excess supply?
- What are the effects on prices, rents, absorption, and vacancies?

Market conditions in relation to the value of the subject property

- How does the local real estate cycle affect the value of the subject property?

SUMMARY

Real estate market activity is cyclical and subject to the effects of both national business cycles and real estate cycles. As the market adjusts to changing conditions over the successive stages of a cycle, supply and demand shift. Business cycles are characterized by four stages: 1) expansion; 2) slowdown, peak, and downturn; 3) contraction; and 4) slowed contraction, trough, and upturn. The effects of a national business cycle are transmitted to the local economy through the linkages that tie the national economy to the basic industry and employment base of the community.

The real estate cycle passes through four comparable stages. The two types of real estate cycles are long-term, or secular, cycles which reflect long-term trends in population and income, and short-term cycles, which are generated by the availability of credit and the level of interest rates. Real estate activity generally responds to an increase or decline in interest rates before the overall economy. Thus real estate activity may be considered a leading indicator of economic trends. Generally the real estate market does not readily adjust to short-term shifts in supply and demand and construction activity lags.

An understanding of market conditions is essential to 1) determine the period for which an appraisal may be valid, 2) estimate the rate of absorption, 3) forecast the direction and rate of change in prices, rents, and costs, and 4) estimate the adjustment for market conditions in the sales comparison approach.

PART II

Market Analysis
Applications

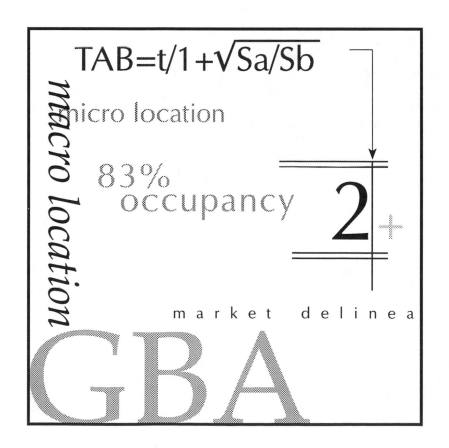

INTRODUCTION

In this second part of the book, the six-step market analysis process for valuation appraisals is demonstrated with three sample applications. Every appraisal typically includes an inferred market analysis or trend analysis. Many appraisal problems also require fundamental analysis. The examples provided here primarily illustrate fundamental analysis. Although only brief coverage is given inferred methods, inferred analysis is an integral part of any complete study.

The difference between fundamental and inferred analysis is discussed at length in Chapter 2. In preparing a fundamental, forecast-oriented market analysis, the analyst segments demand and supply in the subject submarket and ranks the marketability attributes of the subject against those of its competition. Fundamental, forecast-oriented studies emphasize micro-market analysis, while inferred studies rely on historical data and focus on macro-market analysis. All appraisal assignments differ. For some appraisals inferred market analysis is adequate, but many assignments require both inferred and fundamental analyses.

The three applications presented in the following chapters are concerned with existing properties. Case studies of market analyses for appraisals of a community shopping center, an office building, and a multitenanted apartment complex are presented. Each chapter begins with a discussion of concepts unique to the specific property type. Next, a step-by-step analysis of the market for the subject property is provided. Lastly, the findings of the market analysis are put to use in the appraisal.

The market or marketability analysis section of an appraisal is discussed here,[1] but a complete appraisal is not presented. Most appraisals include an eco-

---

1. The terms *market analysis* and *marketability analysis* are used in this book to describe the process of establishing a foundation for forecasting the revenues and expenses of a property as a part of estimating its market value. Other terms used to refer to this forecasting process are *feasibility* or *economic feasibility study, market* or *market demand study,* and *financial projection study.*

nomic overview of the broad market for the subject market and a description of the subject property, which precede the market and marketability analysis section of the report.

The basic market analysis process presented in the case study applications includes six steps:

1. Property productivity analysis. The analyst examines the productivity attributes of the subject property. These are the features that shape the productive capabilities and potential uses of the property, i.e., its physical, legal, locational, and amenity attributes. Identifying the potential uses of the property enables the analyst to target potential users or the specific market segment to which the property is most likely to appeal.

2. Specification of the market of most probable property users. The analyst pinpoints the precise market segment to establish the behavioral components of market demand.

3. Demand analysis and forecast. The analyst estimates existing and anticipated market demand by examining population and employment data based on economic base analysis.[2]

4. Competitive supply analysis and forecast. An inventory of existing and anticipated supply is developed to establish marginal demand.

5. Supply and demand study. Supply and demand are compared to determine whether marginal demand exists or to forecast when the market is expected to move out of equilibrium.

6. Capture estimation. The analyst ranks the productive attributes of the subject property against those of competitive properties considering market conditions, demand, and the competitive supply. This ranking is used to forecast the market share the subject is likely to capture.

The data studied and the conclusions reached in the analysis are used in the appraisal to test alternative highest and best use conclusions and to apply the three valuation approaches. The appraiser may also draw on components of the market analysis to develop a final value conclusion in reconciliation.

---

2. Time and budgetary constraints typically prevent the analyst from investigating all the demand-side variables in a market study. It is imperative that the analyst select the variables most relevant to the assignment.

THE MARKET ANALYSIS PROCESS FOR AN EXISTING SHOPPING CENTER

- Analyze property productivity.

- Delineate the market of property users.

- Forecast demand.

- Measure competitive supply.

- Analyze market equilibrium/disequilibrium.

- Forecast subject capture.

CHAPTER TWELVE

———▸•◂———

Existing Shopping Center

T his chapter presents a step-by-step procedure and sample techniques for performing a market analysis of an existing retail shopping center. First, concepts and terms unique to retail properties are discussed. Second, an overview of the analytical process is provided. Finally, the process is applied to the appraisal of a specific retail subject and each step is discussed in detail. The application presented is a Level C fundamental market analysis. Moreover, the procedure described is only one of the many variations that could be applied. The analytical techniques employed depend on the characteristics of the subject property, the market conditions on the date of the appraisal, the availability of data, the needs of the client, and the judgment and experience of the appraiser.

CONCEPTS AND TERMINOLOGY

A *shopping center* is a tract of land, under individual or joint real estate ownership or control, improved with a coordinated group of retail buildings that contain a variety of stores and offer free parking.[1] Shopping centers are planned and managed as units. The location, size, and retail mix of a center are determined by the trade area it serves. A shopping center must provide on-site parking; the amount of parking area relates to the type and size of the center's stores.[2]

---

1. Appraisal Institute, *The Dictionary of Real Estate Appraisal*, 3d ed. (Chicago: Appraisal Institute, 1993), 331.
2. Urban Land Institute, *Shopping Center Development Handbook*, 2d. ed., in the Community Builders handbook series (Washington, D.C.: ULI, 1985), 1.

Shopping centers are based on the *principle of cumulative attraction*[3] which recognizes that a location in a retail cluster brings a retailer more customer traffic than the retailer would have if it were located by itself. The benefits of increased customer traffic outweigh the negative effects of the store's proximity to competitors.

Until the mid-twentieth century, retail activity in the United States was concentrated in the downtown areas of cities and towns. Since that time, however, retail activity has been dispersed throughout metropolitan areas and into specialized areas and outlying centers.

The nature of retail activity continues to change. The overexpansion of shopping centers in the 1980s created a surplus of retail space. Operating expenses rose while profits declined. Retailers who did not deal successfully with market change floundered and many companies were taken over by outside investors. The leveraged buyouts popular in the mid-1980s forced many companies to focus on short-term profits and changed the identity of many established retailers. Developers introduced new types of centers (e.g., off-price centers, power centers) in an attempt to draw customers and increase revenues. Uncertainty will continue to plague retailers in the 1990s, but restructuring of the retail industry and the new focus on management and merchandising may lead to a more stable market in the future.[4]

At each step in the appraisal process, the appraiser must remember that retail centers have changed in the past and will continue to change. Their dynamics may depend on changes in linkages to demand and\or product distribution, changes in demographics, or changes in retail marketing techniques. As one observer has pointed out, the changing nature of retail centers forces analysts to reconsider their analytic criteria.

> Some directions already evident are the creation of new center types, an interest in middle market communities, the focus on in-fill locations previously bypassed or ignored, and the revitalization of downtown areas. However, if these directions are to succeed, and if the industry is to continue to grow, more sophisticated levels of site location and center planning, design, and operation are required. No longer is a location accessible to a large population the only criterion for success. Today a shopping center developer must have a clear and reliable understanding of all the dynamics of the marketplace before committing time and money to a project.[5]

The appraiser's challenge is to assess how the shopping center being valued compares with competitive properties, both existing and anticipated. Current

---

3. Richard L. Nelson, *The Selection of Retail Locations* (New York: F.W. Dodge, 1958), 59.

4. James D. Vernor, MAI, PhD, and Joseph Rabianski, PhD, *Shopping Center Appraisal and Analysis* (Chicago: Appraisal Institute, 1993), 35-36.

5. Ruben A. Rocca, ed., *Market Research for Shopping Centers* (New York: International Council of Shopping Centers, 1985), 2.

competition may be directly investigated; future competition, however, requires more study because of the ever-changing nature of shopping centers.

General concepts

The success of a shopping center depends on unique dynamics. Shopping centers have traditionally followed, rather than led, community growth. Shopping centers may locate at major intersections where new residences are expected to fill in interstitial areas, but a shopping center's prospects for high occupancy levels and rents generally improve in areas where growth is evident.

The market analyst must consider existing as well as planned and potential competition. The ability of a shopping center to capture a share of market demand depends on the size of its trade area and its major tenants. Finally, the drawing power of dominant centers is subject to the principle of interception, or the principle of intervening opportunities, which recognizes that most shoppers will not drive by a dominant center to get to a subordinate center.

These and other related concepts demonstrate how shopping centers differ from other types of real estate. Moreover, the principles and concepts underlying the operation of shopping centers are not static. Additional specialty stores and a broader product mix in community centers, for example, may counteract the effects of the principle of interception.[6] The anchor concept is also changing. At one time, a major anchor assured a center's success. Currently, the "anchorless" concept has begun to take hold. Anchorless centers of approximately 150,000 square feet are being developed to house specialty stores of 700 to 12,000 square feet. These centers require less land than large malls, produce less traffic congestion, and have lower occupancy costs. Anchorless centers are also less risky. The vulnerability of department stores to bankruptcy and downsizing may account in part for the success of the anchorless concept. Also, if one retailer moves out of an anchorless center, the loss in income is relatively small since the tenant occupied comparatively little of the center's overall space.

If change is constant, the appraiser's dilemma is apparent. In appraising a shopping center, the appraiser must consider whether or not the subject real estate is still competitive. If the subject is on the verge of becoming outdated, comparable sales that are two or three years old may be of little use. The subject's historic income may be misleading because future income may be declining. Major renovation or alternative uses may have to be considered. Thus, understanding the retail business and the real estate product (the shopping center) which houses it is the key to estimating the subject's value.

Types of shopping centers

Shopping centers are usually classified according to two criteria: their size in square feet of gross leasable area and their tenantry, i.e., the anchor or princi-

---

6. American Planning Association, "Changing Retail Trends," *Planning* (January 1981).

pal tenant and the tenant mix. The trade area of a shopping center is broken down into primary, secondary, and tertiary trade areas based on the population in the surrounding area, travel distances (time), and sales volume percentages. The traditional types of centers include convenience centers; neighborhood, community, regional, and superregional shopping centers; and specialty or theme centers. Variations and new types of centers are continually evolving. Some examples of new center types are off-price outlets and discount centers, festival shopping centers, hypermarts, supermalls, power centers and thoroughfare- or highway-related commercial developments. (See Table 12.1 Types of Shopping Centers.)

Building terms

Some important industry terms are defined below.

Gross leasable area (GLA). The total floor area rented to tenants, including basements and mezzanines. Gross leasable area is measured from the outside wall surface to the center of interior partitions.

Gross floor area (GFA). Gross leasable area plus all common areas.

Gross sales area (GSA). Gross leasable area minus storage and work areas.

Common area. The total area within a property that is not designed for sale or rent but is available for common use by all owners, tenants, or their customers, e.g., mallways, parking, restrooms; not included in gross leasable area.

Parking area. The area of a facility designated for the parking of employee and customer automobiles, including parking surface, aisles, stalls, islands, etc.

Parking ratio. The ratio of parking area to *GFA* or *GLA*. This figure is used only as a rough estimation of the parking area needed.

Parking index. The number of car parking spaces per 1,000 square feet of *GLA*.

Trade area

A *trade area* is delineated on the basis of area population, time-distance relationships, sales volume percentages, and/or the percentage breakdown of total customers drawn to the retail center. Different types of shopping centers have distinctly different tenant compositions and trade areas (see Table 12.1). A trade area is often broken down into the geographic core (primary trade area) and concentric zones (secondary and tertiary trade areas). The general guidelines for trade area delineation provided in Table 12.2 must be modified to fit the characteristics of the specific shopping center under consideration.[7]

---

7. Urban Land Institute, *Shopping Center Development Handbook*, 22.

Table 12.1
Types of Shopping Centers

Type	Tenantry	Size	Trade Area
Convenience center	Stores selling convenience goods, e.g., groceries, pharmaceuticals; not anchored by supermarket, but typically has a convenience market as its primary tenant.	Less than 30,000 sq. ft.	Under 5 minutes driving time
Neighborhood shopping center	Stores that sell convenience goods and stores that provide personal services, e.g., dry cleaning, shoe repair; a supermarket is often the principal tenant.	30,000 to 100,000 sq. ft. of gross leasable area; 4 to 10 acres	Under 5 minutes driving time; 1- to 1½-mile range; 5,000 to 40,000 potential customers
Community shopping center	Stores that sell convenience goods, personal services, and shopper goods, i.e., goods that require comparison such as apparel and appliances; a junior department store or off-price/discount store is often the principal tenant; other tenants include variety or super drugstores and home improvement centers.	100,000 to 300,000 sq. ft. of gross leasable area; 10 to 30 acres (includes mini-malls)	5 to 20 minutes driving time; 3- to 5-mile range; 40,000 to 150,000 potential customers
Regional shopping center	Stores selling general merchandise, shopper goods, and convenience goods; one or more department stores are the principal tenants.	300,000 to 1,000,000 sq. ft. of gross leasable area; 30 acres; contains one or more department stores of at least 100,000 sq. ft.	20 to 40 minutes driving time; 10- to 15-mile range; 150,000 to 400,000 potential customers
Superregional shopping center	Stores selling general merchandise, apparel, furniture, home furnishings, and services as well as recreational facilities.	Over 750,000 sq. ft. of gross leasable area; contains at least three major department stores of at least 100,000 sq. ft. each	In excess of 30 minutes driving time; up to a 35-mile range; over 500,000 potential customers
Specialty or theme center	Boutiques and stores that sell design items, craft wares, and gourmet foods; a high-profile specialty shop is often the principal tenant; festival malls are a type of theme center.	Same range as a neighborhood or community shopping center	Similar to that of a regional shopping center
Power center	A minimum of three, but usually five or more, anchor tenants that are dominant in their categories.	Typically open-air centers of more than 250,000 square feet; almost all space designed for large tenants.	A minimum of 15 miles—typically a 20-minute range and a population of 400,000 to 500,000
Off-price outlet and discount center	Name brand outlet stores and/or wholesale grocery, hardware stores, etc.	60,000 to 400,000 sq.ft.	Similar to superregional center
Strip commercial* (a continuous row or strip along a main thoroughfare)	Convenience stores, fast-food restaurants, car dealerships, and service stations.	Varies according to trade area	Neighborhood or community
Highway commercial*	Motels, restaurants, truck stops, service stations; may stand as a single establishment within a cluster of other highway-related service facilities.	Varies	Passing motorists in need of highway-related services.

* Thoroughfare or highway-oriented retail developments are technically not shopping centers because they are not planned or managed in a coordinated manner. Furthermore, they do not generally benefit from the principle of cumulative attraction, which holds that a location in a retail cluster brings increased customer traffic.

Table 12.2

Trade Area Breakdown by Total Sales and Driving Time

	Primary	Secondary	Tertiary
	The geographic area immediately adjacent to the facility, from which approximately 60% to 80% of its sales/customers are derived.	The geographic area adjacent to the primary trade area, from which an additional 20% to 40% of its sales/customers are derived.	The farthest outlying segment of the trade area, from which the remaining percentage of the facility's sales/customers are derived.
Neighborhood shopping centers	Under 5 minutes	5 to 15 minutes	
Community shopping centers	5 to 20 minutes	20 to 35 minutes	
Regional shopping centers	20 to 40 minutes	40 to 60 minutes	
Superregional shopping centers	40 minutes plus		

THE MARKET ANALYSIS PROCESS FOR A SHOPPING CENTER

Table 12.3 presents an overview of a fundamental, Level C market analysis for a shopping center. The six-step process includes analysis of the subject property, analysis of the subject's trade area, an estimate of existing and potential demand, an inventory of competitive supply, analysis of market equilibrium, and the estimated of subject capture. The market analysis provides essential data used in the three approaches to value. Each of the six steps has been further divided in substeps. For example, the nine substeps of Step 3.2, identified as Steps 3.2(1) through 3.2(9), describe the segmentation process used to estimate demand in the retail center's primary and secondary trade areas. The case study application follows the sequence of steps shown in Table 12.3.

CASE STUDY DESCRIPTION

The following case study illustrates the application of the market analysis process. The purpose of the study is to lend support to the highest and best use conclusion and to furnish information for the valuation approaches applied to estimate mar-

Table 12.3
The Market Analysis Process for an Existing Shopping Center

Step 1: Analyze property productivity

  1.1 Analyze the site and building for competitive strengths and weaknesses.

  1.2 Analyze the location of the subject property.

  1.2(1) Investigate land use(s) and the linkages of the subject property.

  1.2(2) Determine the position of the subject property within the patterns of urban growth.

  1.2(3) Identify the location of the competitive supply.

  1.2(4) Rate the subject location in comparison with the location of the competition.

Step 2: Delineate the market of property users

  2.1 Define the trade area.

Step 3: Forecast demand

  3.1 Analyze trends (inferred analysis).

  3.2 Segment demand (fundamental analysis).

  3.2(1) Forecast number and size of households in the primary trade area.

  3.2(2) Estimate mean/median household income and total income for primary trade area.

  3.2(3) Estimate the percentage of household income that is spent on retail items.

  3.2(4) Estimate the percentage of retail purchases typically made at a shopping center of the subject's type.

  3.2(5) Estimate the percentage of sales retention in the primary trade area from the total potential sales for the primary trade area.

  3.2(6) Repeat Steps 3.2(1) through 3.2(5) for the secondary trade area.

  3.2(7) Determine total demand in the primary and secondary trade areas.

  3.2(8) Estimate the supportable square footage of retail space by dividing total demand by required sales volume per square foot.

  3.2(9) Adjust the estimate of supportable retail space to reflect the normal vacancy rate for the market.

  3.3 Analyze demand by the ratio method (fundamental analysis).

  3.4 Reconcile findings and forecast final demand.

Step 4: Measure competitive supply

  4.1 Inventory existing competition, competitive properties under construction, proposed competitive properties, and likely additional competitive space.

  4.2 Rate the supply of competitive properties according to the following criteria: size, access and location, quality of merchandise, reputation, rental rates, vacancy, and tenant mix.

Step 5: Analyze market equilibrium/disequilibrium

  5.1 Estimate residual or marginal demand.

Step 6: Forecast subject capture

  6.1 Analyze capture by inferred methods, including
  - Historical capture of subject
  - Capture of comparable properties
  - Secondary data surveys and forecasts
  - Impact of residual or marginal demand on subject
  - Local economic analysis

  6.2 Forecast capture by fundamental methods.

  6.3 Reconcile subject capture indications derived by inferred and fundamental analyses.

The forecast capture rate for the subject is then employed as a basis for the highest and best use conclusion. In particular, a forecast of timing is needed to test feasibility. Forecast capture is also essential data in the three valuation approaches.

Note the numbering system employed in this six-step process. Substeps are indicated with sequential numbers in parentheses. Thus, Step 1.2 is followed by Steps 1.2(1), 1.2(2), 1.2(3), etc.

ket value. The question of use is not a major element of this study because the subject retail center is relatively new and currently occupied. The value of the land as though vacant is far less than the value of the property as improved. Alternative uses that would require remodeling are not feasible.

Because the income approach depends on forecasting, the market analysis provides valuable support for this valuation approach. Questions of future rents and occupancy, which are critical to the income capitalization approach, form a principal part of the market study conclusions. The market study also provides support for the sales comparison approach by answering the following question: Are the comparables' prospects for future benefits similar to those of the subject? If not, the market study will indicate the need for an adjustment. Information from the market study can be used in the cost approach to help estimate external obsolescence.

Subject property

The subject of the case study is a shopping center located in a small town with a growing population. The property is six years old and has 55,000 square feet of gross leasable area. It is currently leased at 80% of total occupancy, has a typical design for this city, and is in good condition. The mix of tenants at the subject center includes a small anchor supermarket (which sells only food), a video cassette shop, a fast-food restaurant, an auto parts store, a dry cleaning establishment, a variety store, and a hobby shop.

The subject had a good leasing history during its first four years and occupancy reached 95%. Last year, however, two specialty stores (an electronics store and a shoe shop) moved out and the space has not been re-leased. Although the center's rental rates may be considered competitive, they are among the highest in town. The rents have not been lowered since the center opened and have generally increased with the rate of inflation.

A new mall has been announced recently and a new bypass is being built which will direct traffic away from the subject. These factors contribute to the uncertainty surrounding the subject's future.

Location

The subject shopping center is located in a community with a population of 45,000. Over the past decade the community has experienced steady growth averaging 5% per year. The economic base of the community includes a good mix of manufacturing industries (electronics, office equipment, appliances) and suppliers (food and paper). Given its solid economic base, the town is expected to continue to grow at a rate similar to that experienced over the past decade.

The subject is located on a major thoroughfare that feeds into the central business district, which is approximately four miles away. As mentioned previously, the city is planning to open a traffic loop around the town in three years.

Except for commercially zoned areas along the thoroughfares on which the shopping center stands, the surrounding area is zoned for residential use and improved primarily with single-family dwellings. The housing density is fairly uniform.

Immediately north of the subject is moderate- to low-income housing that is approximately 30 years old. South of the subject is a 20- to 30-year-old subdivision of moderate- to high-income housing. These residential subdivisions are in good condition due to a high level of maintenance and upkeep.

Competition

The subject is located in one of four major retail areas serving the community. Development of two additional centers is planned. A new mall four miles south of the subject and a 100,000-sq.-ft. shopping center one-half mile west of the subject are expected to open in five years, after the new bypass is completed. There are some scattered, stand-alone retail stores in the town, but very few.

STEP 1 ANALYZE PROPERTY PRODUCTIVITY

Step 1.1 Analyze the site and building for competitive strengths and weaknesses

The purpose of this step is twofold: to inventory the attributes of the subject and to make a preliminary assessment of the functional problems and competitive advantages or disadvantages of the subject property. The subject is assessed in light of current trends in retail shopping centers. The importance of current industry standards underscores the dynamic nature of retail real estate. Properties can quickly become outdated, which significantly impacts future demand and, in turn, value.

Current industry standards

The industry standards described here are not applicable to every retail use or even, perhaps, to the subject retail center. The items cited are typical concerns that might appear on an appraisal checklist. Such a list should be continually updated to reflect trends in the industry. Trade associations,[8] trade magazines, interviews with leasing agents, and study of newer retail centers might reveal further information on industry standards. If new center types cannot be found in the subject area, a national search for data may be needed. For example, in the 1970s appraisers were investigating what was being built in California since the rest of the country could be expected to follow its lead in five to 10 years. Retailing has changed since then, however; now different trendsetters have emerged

---

8. Trade associations are listed in the *Encyclopedia of Associations*, published by Gale Research, Inc., and in *U.S. Industrial Outlook*, published annually by the U.S. Department of Commerce.

in different parts of the country. A notable example is the retail trend Sam Walton started with his Walmart stores in Bentonville, Arkansas.

The following discussion covers the attributes to be considered in the first part of the productivity analysis, which focuses on the subject improvements. The analyst's objective is to determine to what extent the subject improvements meet current retailing needs.

Site characteristics

Ratio of Land to Building Area

Typical land-to-building ratios may be calculated by analyzing the four basic components of shopping center acreage: gross leasable area, landscaping and walkways, parking area, and buffers and setbacks.

The landscaped and walkway area is generally about 10% of the gross leasable area. Thus, a 200,000-sq.-ft., one-story center would have about 20,000 square feet of landscaping and walkways.

Approximately 6½ parking spaces per 1,000 square feet of gross leasable area is a good rule of thumb. This guideline assumes half of the cars parked are compact models. Thus, for a property with 200,000 square feet of gross leasable area, approximately 1,300 parking spaces would be needed (200,000 ÷ 1,000 x 6.5).

With efficient use of space, 325 square feet per car is needed for the parking and maneuvering of compact cars. For larger car models and less efficiently designed space, 400 square feet is required. Thus, the area needed for 1,300 parking spaces would range between 422,500 square feet (1,300 x 325) and 520,000 square feet (1,300 x 400).

A 15-ft. perimeter around a site is usually set aside for bufffers and setbacks.

Building Area

As an overall rule of thumb, the ratio of gross building area to land area should be about 10,000 to 15,000 square feet of *GBA* for each 43,560 square feet (one acre) of land.

Parking

The availability of parking space is critical. Parking area is related to the gross floor area or gross leasable area of the center and the tenantry. A neighborhood center with convenience stores has a high rate of turnover for each parking stall and thus may require less overall parking area than a larger center with specialty shops and stores selling shopper goods.[9]

---

9. Urban Land Institute, *Parking Requirements for Shopping Centers: Summary, Recommendations and Research Summary Report* (Washington, D.C.: ULI, 1982).

Parking areas should be conveniently located in relation to the shopping center's stores. The preferred distance between the parking area and stores falls between 300 and 350 feet, with 400 feet as the maximum distance.[10]

Frontage and Visibility

Shopping centers should have sufficient frontage to ensure ease of access. Visibility is more dependent on location. Both frontage and visibility can be critical to the success of a retail center. A center with poor visibility may never be able to compete regardless of the marketing strategies implemented.

Topography

The topography of the site should be level or slightly sloping. Steep grades are hard to maneuver and may create runoff problems. Difficult maneuvering can cause customers to go to competitive centers that are more accessible. Runoff problems increase maintenance costs and can create an unseemly appearance that discourages customers.

Utilities

Utilities should be adequate and convenient. The costs of linking up utilities may render a project infeasible. In some municipalities the requirements for utility service vary with the center's tenants; restaurants and appliance stores may require more utility service. The setup of utilities at the subject property could restrict future tenant flexibility.

Landscaping

The term *shopping center* often suggests a sea of asphalt. The use of landscaping to upgrade a center's exterior appearance and define traffic lanes, however, has recently begun to change the image of shopping centers, especially more expensive ones. Good landscaping can help draw customers, improve a center's image, generate higher rents, and improve traffic flow and parking access. Poorly planned landscaping, on the other hand, may obstruct the center's visibility, impede circulation, and result in higher maintenance costs. Zoning often regulates landscaping and should be considered in regard to proposed centers and the expansion of existing centers.

Design and Building Layout

The design and layout of the building or buildings in the shopping center must project a modern, functional appearance if the center is to compete effectively. A

---

10. The Urban Land Institute cites the following guidelines for base parking area: 4 spaces per 1,000 square feet of gross leasable area for centers with 25,000 to 400,000 square feet of gross leasable area; 4 to 5 spaces with an average of 4.5 spaces per 1,000 square feet of gross leasable area for centers with 400,000 to 600,000 square feet of gross leasable area; and 5 spaces per 1,000 square feet of gross leasable area for centers with more than 600,000 square feet of gross leasable area.

center's design and layout should reflect current marketing trends. A flexible layout is important because marketing concepts change continually.[11]

Amenity Features

Amenities are features that enhance a property's attractiveness or increase the satisfaction derived from its use. Although amenity features do not constitute an essential part of the property, they can give a shopping center a competitive advantage in drawing customers. Amenities range from the skating rinks found in regional centers to the small, attractively landscaped eating areas in community centers.

Store Size

The variety of the retail tenant mix is more important in drawing customers than the size of any particular store. Centers with a variety of tenants are generally more successful than those with only a few large stores.[12] Store size and design change over time. As retail marketing techniques evolve, the appraiser must assess an existing center's overall capability to compete with more modern facilities.

Store Width

There is no standard width for a particular store tenant.[13] Landlords often try to restrict the widths of mall stores to provide mall frontage to as many tenants as possible.

Store Depth

Store depth may range from 40 to 120 feet depending on building requirements and feasibility. The ability to provide stores of varying depths is an asset to any center. Small stores may be carved out of deeper space, leaving rear areas for larger neighboring stores. Greater store depth is needed if shopper traffic moves along two frontages, if deliveries are made at the back of the store, or if the center has no basements and ground-level storage facilities have to be provided. Less depth is required if storage and service facilities are in a basement area or if pedestrian traffic passes on only one side of the store. Regional centers with specifically planned uses such as large, high-quality stores or multi-screen theaters are generally designed with greater store depths.

Signage

Shops should be clearly identified by signage that conforms to the center's design and image. Poor sign control can be counterproductive; inappropriate sig-

---

11. Urban Land Institute, *Shopping Center Development Handbook*, 69.

12. Ibid., 80-88.

13. Data on median store sizes (in gross leasable area) by tenant classification are provided in *Dollars and Cents of Shopping Centers*, published triennially by the Urban Land Institute.

nage may block views, emphasize the wrong anchor, and give the center a cheap or second-rate appearance.

Truck Service Facilities

Delivery areas for the loading and unloading of trucks should be screened from the view of customers.

Tenant Mix and Marketing Attributes

A center's ability to attract customers is a function of the type, mix, location, and reputation of the tenants. Anchor tenants have long been the key tenants in a center, but this may be changing. Anchor tenants are the major stores within a shopping center that attract or generate the vast majority of customers for the facility.

The presence or absence of secondary stores is also important. There are two types of secondary stores. One type includes stores that complement and broaden the selection of the anchor store. The second type consists of convenience stores that serve the customers who come to shop at the anchor and complementary stores. These convenience stores may include fast-food restaurants, pharmacies, and card shops. Whether a secondary store is to be considered complementary or not depends on the mix of stores in the vicinity and the location of the store within the center.

The location of tenants should ensure the proximity of compatible stores and take advantage of access linkages. Richard Nelson refers to this design factor in the context of "pedestrian interruptions."[14] For example, it is desirable to have a women's apparel store adjacent to a men's apparel store; if the stores are separated by a driveway to the parking area, however, the benefit is canceled out.

The principle of compatibility is closely related to the principle of cumulative attraction. Both of these principles of retail association rest on the premise that the grouping of two or more compatible stores is beneficial when it creates more business for the retail facilities. The size of the stores, however, must also be addressed. While some degree of interchange usually occurs between two stores of a given size, this may not guarantee a market large enough to support both stores.

The image of a shopping center depends on consumer perceptions of its tenants. The factors influencing these perceptions include the age of the center, the price and quality level of the goods sold, the security provided, and the promotional activities of the retailers. A new center can generally expect to attract customers for a period just because it is new. A center in a high crime district cannot expect to compete with a store in a safer area. A center that is actively promoted by its developer may attract a larger share of the potential market than its size would warrant.

---

14. Nelson, 58-78.

Legal Constraints and Opportunities

Legal constraints and opportunities vary. Long-term leases may be detrimental. For example, a center may have tenants located in the wrong place but be unable to move them because of their leases. Zoning restrictions may also create leasing problems. For example, a center designed for small retail shops may be prevented from leasing to restaurants, for which there is market demand, because the parking was originally planned for retail shops. According to the municipal zoning regulations, there are not sufficient spaces for restaurant parking.

Subject property rating

The purpose of rating the subject property is to document, organize, and assess the subject's strong and weak points systematically. A rating is different from a description of the subject. This step is analytic, not descriptive. The attributes of the subject and the location are not easy to analyze quantitatively, so how does the appraiser proceed? The appraiser begins by recognizing how the data from this analysis, combined with data produced in subsequent analyses, will eventually be used.

This analysis provides input for identifying competitive centers because the subject's attributes (along with location) determine, in large part, which centers are considered competing centers. It also helps the appraiser determine the subject's specific advantages or disadvantages. With the information in this analysis, the appraiser can establish a relative scale for rating the subject. Used in combination with future analyses, this scale helps narrow the study and refine the data until it is possible to arrive at specific estimates of:

- Functional and economic obsolescence in the cost approach
- Adjustments in the sales comparison approach
- Rents and occupancy rates in the income capitalization approach.

To assess the subject's productive qualities, some comparative standard or scale must be used; otherwise the appraiser's task would be descriptive rather than analytical. In this example the subject is rated relative to current industry standards. Some appraisers choose to compare the subject property to the most dominant competition in the area. Either technique can be used, but the dynamic nature of retail shopping centers is one reason to base the comparison on current industry standards. In retailing, the primary competition can be expected to differ from future centers as much as other current centers. Fundamental market analysis techniques are future-oriented. For this reason, the case study property is rated relative to current standards, not in relation to the competition. The rating scale applied here is both narrative and quantitative. In practice, an appraiser might select either form or apply several other rating methods.

The rating process begun at this early stage in the market analysis is further refined in the subsequent steps of location analysis and competitive supply analysis. The successive ratings rank the subject vis-a-vis the competition and contribute data to support the share-of-the market forecast required in the appraisal. The rating grid in Table 12.4, like the others employed throughout the market analysis, represents a screening process in which the characteristics of the subject and the competition are successively analyzed and ranked until the appraiser is ready to formulate conclusions to be used in the three valuation approaches. This is the first step in a rating process in which data are scaled, refined, and evaluated. These successive ratings build upon one another and help form the final value opinion. As the late James Graaskamp wrote, "In fact, each step in the appraisal process is a screening and ranking of alternatives."[15]

Application of Step 1.1

Using a checklist like Table 12.4, the appraiser inventories the subject's attributes and rates the relative impact of each. Guidelines for completing this particular rating chart follow.

First, the analyst must determine which items to rate. The list will vary with the center type. The attributes listed in the table can serve as a starting point. The analyst must research detailed sources for current industry standards. These sources may include recent publications from the Appraisal Institute, the Urban Land Institute, and retailing trade groups that correspond to the subject's tenancy.

Second, an item-by-item comparison of the subject attributes to current industry standards is made. To help in this assessment, the analyst might develop a comparison grid for the subject and newer centers serving a similar market. These newer centers may be in the subject area or in other locations around the nation. Use of such a grid is recommended to help the analyst identify new trends that may not have reached the subject city. Data on newer centers can be obtained from the Urban Land Institute, trade publications, and discussions with other appraisers. A comparison grid listing the major attributes of the centers can be used to determine whether the subject is similar or dissimilar in each attribute. This comparison can suggest what attributes the subject center may be lacking and identify whether the subject is typical, inferior, or superior. If, for example, the new trend is toward bigger anchor stores and the subject's anchor is smaller, the subject would be rated inferior.

Third, the analyst must weight the factors. Factors are weighted in two ways. First, the number of factors to be rated in each category is itself a form of weighting. The more factors in a category, the greater the weight given to that category. In Table 12.4, for instance, the category titled "Tenant Mix and Marketing Features" contains five factors to rate. For the other categories, between two and four factors are listed. Thus more weight has been given to "Tenant Mix and Marketing Features."

---

15. *The Appraisal of 25 N. Pickney Street: A Demonstration Case for Contemporary Appraisal Methods,* (Madison, Wis.: Landmark Research, Inc., 1977), 3.

Factors are weighted in a second way by assigning a numerical score to attributes judged inferior or superior. This ranking technique measures the item's impact on the subject's productivity, i.e., retailing ability. After initial scores are assigned to all of the factors, these scores are further refined. In the initial comparison the analyst considers whether the subject is equal, inferior, or superior. The adverse or beneficial impact of inferior and superior characteristics is then judged to be slight, moderate, or high. All factors judged equal must have the same impact score. If a factor is superior to another factor, it must have a higher impact score; if inferior to another factor, it must have a lower score.

In this case, the subject's street visibility and anchor size were both judged inferior to current industry standards. However, the size of the anchor store could have a much more detrimental impact on the center's success than the lack of good street visibility. Thus, the size of the subject's anchor is given a highly detrimental rating (with a category score of 0 for that factor), but street visibility is given only a slightly detrimental rating (with a category score of 4).

The magnitude of the difference among the assigned scores should be noted. Many scoring systems can be used. In this system, a single point represents the difference between an average and an inferior or superior rating. A one-point differential allows for smoothing in situations where the distinctions among attributes are very fine. The ranking system described helps define these distinctions.

The scores assigned to the subject are compared to the score given the industry standard. Using the categories in Table 12.4, the industry standard score is 90, calculated by multiplying the 18 factors rated by an average score of 5 for each factor. The final step in the ranking is to calculate each item's score by multiplying the number of factors in each score category by the scoring number given that category.

Note the column on the left designated "Veto Factor." The purpose of this column is to highlight a feature or features that are so bad, and so important, that they put the subject at a distinct competitive disadvantage. In short this column specifically identifies an item that would necessitate an alternative use or a major corrective program.

The following discussion provides an interpretation of the rating analysis shown in Table 12.4.

Comments and Conclusions

The subject property, a six-year-old, 55,000-sq.-ft., community-type shopping center, was rated for all factors in Table 12.4. The center was considered average or standard in comparison to a modern retail center in all respects but the four characteristics described below:

1. Topography (grade). Traffic from the street must climb a steep grade, thus restricting ease of access.
2. Visibility. Due to the steep grade, subject visibility is poor.

Table 12.4
Subject Retail Building Rating

Comparison to Standard		Inferior			Typical	Superior		
Impact on Productivity	Veto Factor	High	Mod.	Slight	Average	Slight	Mod.	High
Site								
Grades (topography)				X				
Land-to-building ratio					X			
Exterior access (curb cut, etc.)					X			
Landscaping						X		
Parking								
Number of spaces					X			
Interior circulation					X			
Building Improvements								
Exterior appearance & quality					X			
Signage appearance					X			
Design flexibility					X			
Street visibility				X				
Tenant Mix & Marketing Features								
Size of anchors		X						
Drawing power of anchors		X						
Tenant compatibility mix					X			
Image of center					X			
Amenity features					X			
Shopper Access								
Shop to shop					X			
Cars to shops					X			
Other								
Legal constraints/opportunities					X			
Number of items		2	0	2	13	1	0	0
Times category score		0	2	4	5	6	8	10
Subtotal score		0	0	8	65	6	0	0
Total subject score								79

3. Anchor—The anchor is a grocery store, which is small in comparison to newer grocery store anchors. It does not provide the variety of goods found in anchor grocery stores built in the last two to three years in similar communities across the country. This rating reflects industry standards, not the current competition. In this case, the subject anchor is typical of area competition, so why should the analyst consider other parts of the country? The answer lies in the ever-changing nature of retailing. The analyst studies the retail business to predict possible changes in future competition. The supply analysis performed in Step 4 will consider existing and planned competition in greater detail. This initial rating is one of the analytical building blocks that the analyst will use to form a judgment about the planned competition in the supply analysis.

4. Landscaping. The subject site was carved out of a hill covered with many large trees. This is one of the most attractively landscaped sites in town.

These four factors are rated on a relative scale to assess the subject's advantage or disadvantage in the market. The factors considered standard each received an average score of 5. Of the four nonstandard factors, three are negative and one is positive. The ratings were weighted to reflect the relative importance of each factor to the future marketability of the subject.

The market trend toward bigger anchors with a broader product mix is by far the most important factor, but how do topography and visibility rate? Is topography (ease of access) more or less important than visibility? Comparison of rents, discussions with retailers, and similar research can sometimes provide a clue. In this case, topography and visibility received the same scoring weight of 4, compared to the inferior anchor size, which was weighted at 0.

A summary of the weighting factors is shown in Table 12.5.

Table 12.5
Summary of Property Ratings

Rated Item	Quantitative Score	Qualitative Score
Anchor	0	Highly inferior
Topography (ease of access)	4	Slightly inferior
Street visibility	4	Slightly inferior
Landscaping	6	Slightly superior
All other features	65	Average
Subject score	79	On balance, moderately inferior
Industry standard score	90	

Interpreting the Data

How does an appraiser interpret the results of this analysis? At this preliminary stage, no final judgments are made. This is just the first in a series of screenings that continue throughout the appraisal and help the appraiser arrive at a final value conclusion. The analysis does indicate that the subject center is inferior in comparison to the typical competition and current industry standards. (This fact may or may not account for its occupancy rate of only 80%.) The ratings also provide a relative scale for the subject's competitive position. The subject rating was 88% of the industry standard (79 ÷ 90).

In the next step, location analysis, the analyst examines the impact of location on the subject's current and future occupancy.

Step 1.2 Analyze the location of the subject property

Retail shopping centers need to attract customers to survive. The attributes of a shopping center account for its ability to draw customers. When more customers spend money at the stores in a facility, the value of the shopping center real estate tends to increase. A center's ability to attract customers also depends in part on how far the shopping center is from the customers. In retailing, this distance is measured in time. A final consideration is the proximity of any competing center that might interfere with the subject's draw. All these issues relate to location. For shopping centers, the urban setting is the economic terrain where the competition for customers takes place. Since value is the present worth of future benefits, the appraiser must understand the current and future urban setting. This section describes some ways to assess how location affects the subject's productivity.

Location analysis focuses on the following questions:

- Where does the subject fit in the overall growth pattern? To answer this question the analyst studies the current land use pattern, the future land use pattern, and the direction of growth.
- Where does the subject's market come from? The center's linkages to demand must be identified.
- Where is the subject's competition located? The analyst studies the market's linkages to supply.
- How does the subject's location vis-a-vis demand compare to the location of the competition now and in the next five to 10 years?

These questions can be addressed with graphic analysis, which includes several mapping techniques:

1. Maps of the current and forecast land use patterns are created. The analyst considers current land uses and transportation routes as the primary determinants of the land use pattern that will emerge over the next 10 years. For appraisals, the short-term future land use pattern is the most critical. Known changes in transportation, land use, and institutional ac-

tivity are the main factors that will affect the current land use pattern over the short term.

2. Growth areas are isolated by placing dots on a map to represent new developments within the past five to 10 years. These dots can identify new retail and/or residential areas. The clustering of the dots indicates the boundaries, direction, and intensity of growth.

3. A map is drawn to show where demand is located and the driving times from demand sources to area shopping centers.

4. A map is marked to identify the location of existing and potential competition.

The graphic analysis techniques applied will focus on existing and future linkages between the subject center and areas that generate demand, i.e., residential subdivisions, office clusters, centers of major economic activity, and other retail developments. The subject's current and future linkages are compared to those of the competition to determine the relative drawing power of each center. Traffic counts and the traffic volume passing a site are also important. The appraiser investigates current land use trends in the neighborhood, which may lead to changes in the customer base of retail centers. The age and condition of nearby buildings and the relative degree of conformity characterizing the neighborhood also indicate change.

The maps created in this step provide a base for further analysis of locational factors.

Step 1.2(1) Investigate land uses and the linkages of the subject property

Richard B. Andrews' theory of situs relationships[16] may be adapted and used to prepare a checklist for this investigation. (For a discussion of the concept of situs, see Chapter 4.) Among other things, Andrews' concept affirms that certain types of land uses require the support of complementary land uses nearby (i.e, within the neighborhood), while other land use associations can be more distant from one another.

The subject property has the same size and tenant mix as a neighborhood retail center except for the presence of the fast-food restaurant. Because of its location on a major east-west thoroughfare and its proximity to office buildings, however, the subject may have the drawing power of a community center. What key land use associations should be identified? How is the subject affected by these key associations? Do the essential linkages between the subject and complementary land uses exist? A list of requisite support facilities and demand generators based on situs relationships can be developed. A possible list for the subject center is shown in Table 12.6, where the linkages for the subject property are rated.

---

16. Richard B. Andrews, *Urban Land Economics and Public Policy* (New York: The Free Press, 1971), 33.

Table 12.6
Land Use Linkages Between a Community or
Neighborhood and a Retail Center

Rating of Current Land Use Linkages of the Subject

Desirable Nearby Land Uses	Poor	Fair	Average	Good	Excellent
Number of residential units to support a retail center (measured in travel time and travel distance)				X	
Traffic volume by the subject site				X	
Complementary retail uses in the immediate area				X	
Service support, i.e., post office, branch bank, transit stop				X	
Complementary neighborhood support, i.e., churches, schools, community recreation centers			X		
Quality of adjacent land uses			X		
Desirable Areawide Land Uses					
Proximity to traffic generators such as employment centers and major residential areas				X	

In conclusion, the subject is rated above the city average in most respects and therefore should be a highly competitive center.

Step 1.2(2) Determine position within urban growth patterns

Next the analyst examines the rate and direction of urban growth by identifying where retail clusters are forming, where new and existing centers of economic activity (i.e., peak value intersections, critical mass centers, and development nodes) are developing, and where housing is being built.

Urban growth is influenced by the natural and man-made features of an area, the economic base, and the local political situation. For example, a political entity can influence the direction of growth by approving a larger share of infrastructure development for certain areas of the city.

Anticipated development of residential subdivisions and business centers and projected linkages (e.g., new freeways and major thoroughfares) indicate changes in land use patterns. These changes will affect the market area and the linkages on which a retail center depends. For example, the current rent structure and occupancy level of a community retail center may be jeopardized if new roads will soon redirect traffic to another area. The direction of growth determines both future population patterns and the timetable for population increases in market areas. Growth also affects income potential. In growth areas, retail sales increase; when growth slows, retail sales generally level off. Thus locations closer to expanding centers or at peak value intersections experience higher rates of occupancy, and consequently higher land values, than locations in declining nodes or at less intensely developed intersections.

The study of growth patterns also helps the analyst assess the validity of the population projections used in the demand analysis in Step 3.

Location Analysis Techniques

The map shown in Figure 12. 1 is the result of one type of graphic analysis applied to the subject market area. Growth was plotted by mapping recent preliminary plats as well as actual development that has occurred in the last five years. The map also identifies the location of the competition. Together these data describe the general pattern of growth expected in the next five to 10 years.

A new source of real estate market data is the Geographical Information System (GIS), which spatially delineates legal, physical, and economic factors on a map base. The GIS system makes possible the depiction of productivity, location, and market factors in an appraisal report.

Rate of Growth Analysis Technique

The appraiser may compare aerial photographs of the area taken over a period of time to determine the amount of acreage that has been developed. Census tracts or other population data should be analyzed for long-term trends. Appraisers are cautioned to look beyond short-term cycles, which may not be typical. The appraiser may also consider using an analog to which the subject area can be compared. The analog may be an adjacent area or an area in a nearby city which has already reached the population anticipated for the subject's city in the next five to 10 years. If the location and economic base of the subject city are similar to the analog, a comparable rate of growth may be anticipated.

Step 1.2(3) Identify the location of the competitive supply

In this step of the market analysis, competitive supply may be approached either in a general or detailed manner. In our example, supply has been considered in a general way. This is a practical course of action since the subsequent demand analysis undertaken in Step 3 may show that some facilities which were initially considered primary competition are actually secondary competition. Accordingly, it may be impractical to spend a great deal of time compiling detailed survey data this early on. However, some practitioners might undertake a detailed survey at this point.

Figure 12.1
Map Showing Direction of Growth and Location of Competition

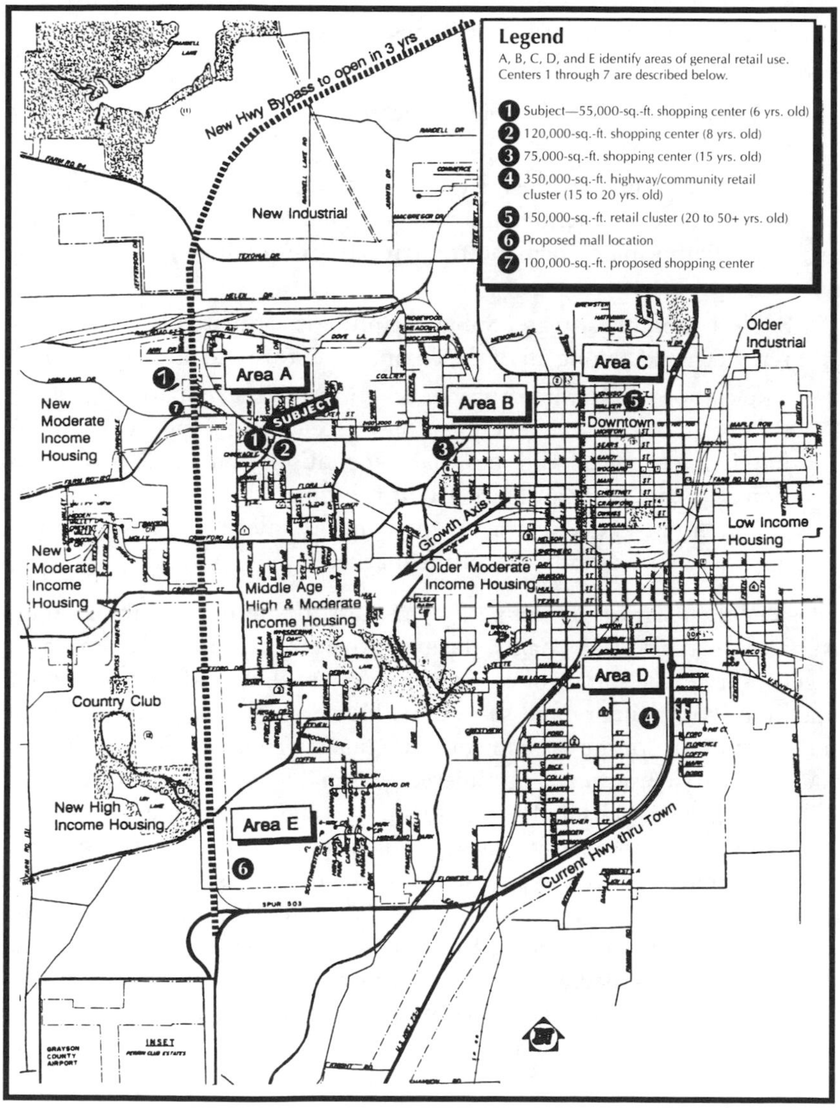

The choice of approach is a matter of judgment. The sequence of steps in the process is not at issue. The point to be emphasized is that analysis of the location of competitive supply is only the first component in a four-part supply analysis. As each component is added, the supply analysis becomes more refined. The competitive supply analysis contributes to four principal areas of the overall market analysis.

1. Location analysis. The subject's location is compared to the location of the competition.
2. Equilibrium analysis (the relationship between supply and demand). Current, under-construction, and planned competition is compared to existing and anticipated demand to arrive at a residual or marginal demand estimate.
3. Subject capture estimate. Subject capture is estimated by dividing total retail demand among all of the competitive stores (including the subject).
4. Application of the three approaches to value (the valuation models). In the cost approach, the functional obsolescence of the subject is estimated in relation to the condition of the competition. In the income capitalization approach, current market rent is estimated through analysis of the competition. The adjustments made in the sales comparison approach are based on the standards of the market.

Besides the location of competitive centers, the appraiser notes their approximate size, the typical tenants, the amenity features, and the major anchors. As a general rule, the survey of competitive centers should identify all potential competition, both primary and secondary. However, survey requirements vary with the complexity of the assignment. The subject property is located in a small town, so a citywide survey is considered reasonable. In a larger metropolitan area, however, the appraisal of a 55,000-sq.-ft. community center would probably not require a comprehensive survey, which could be rather time-consuming. Usually secondary data are available for areawide analyses and the survey focuses on the primary competition in the immediate market area. Even for an appraisal conducted in a small town, a precise survey of the secondary competition may not be as critical as the analysis of the primary competition. In many cases the only information required concerning the secondary competition are the property locations, approximate sizes, and typical tenants.

Application of Step 1.2(3)

The locations of all competitive centers are plotted on a map and survey sheets with basic data (i.e., size, tenants, amenities, and anchors) are attached. The locations of the subject's competition are indicated on the map in Figure 12.1.

Step 1.2(4) Rate the subject's location in comparison with the competition

In this example the location analysis concludes with a location rating. The success of a retail center depends on its location as well as individual property characteristics such as tenant mix and amenities. Changes in the location can rapidly lessen the appeal of a shopping center. A well-designed center that has very little competition in the immediate area may be harmed by changes in city growth patterns that drain clientele from the center's trade area.

In a fundamental market analysis, the analyst may need to rate quantitatively the locational attributes of the subject and competitive properties in the subject's primary and secondary trade areas. In a later stage in the market analysis, the competitive location rating is used to estimate the share of the market in the primary area that the subject is likely to retain.

The analysis in Step 1.2(4) provides input for Step 2, the definition of the subject's primary and secondary trade areas. The location rating also helps the analyst assess the likelihood that new competition will develop in other parts of the city. The prime retail areas of many American cities have relocated over time.

Use of a rating technique is one approach to location analysis. Ten factors that affect the subject and competitive facilities are considered in the location rating. (The factors described below are used in the sample rating chart shown in Table 12.7.)

1. The number of households in the trade area. The trade area of each competitive center is defined, the number of housing units in each trade area is estimated, and each center is rated according to whether the number of units in its trade area is approximately equal to, greater than, or less than the number of units in the trade area of other competitive centers.

2. Proximity to new retail development. The locations of all retail stores less than five years old are identified on a map. Areas with the greatest retail concentrations receive the highest ratings.

3. Location in the path of growth—i.e., new or projected residential development. The direction of urban growth is identified. (See the discussion of the four social ecology theories in Chapter 5.) Then finalized plats in the area are reviewed and preliminary plats are examined to project growth five to 10 years in the future. Each area is rated based on the relative amount of plat activity.

4. Proximity to major roads. Centers are rated for advantages such as a location on a major thoroughfare or intersection and disadvantages such as a location on a collector road or one-way street.

5. Traffic counts by each center. Sites with the heaviest traffic volume are rated the highest. Forecast traffic counts are used to derive a five- to 10-year rating.

6. Proximity to the market. People tend to travel along the same routes to existing shopping areas. All things being equal, the center along the route that is closest to the broadest customer base (the intercept location) tends to capture more of the market. The appraiser determines

where the greatest concentration of customers is located and identifies the traffic routes over which these customers travel. The primary axis for customer shopping trips is thus established. The subject location is compared with the locations of the competitive centers to determine which facilities should attract the greatest number of customers.

7. Size and drawing power of the anchors. Current trends show that location and anchor type are critical to a center's retailing ability. The number and mix of anchor stores may be as important as their size. In this case, the diversity of the merchandise available was considered a principal factor in rating a center's drawing power. The product mix may be provided by one anchor or by several stores at a particular location node.

8. Tenant mix and compatibility. The appraiser considers the tenant mix of nonanchor stores and the compatibility of all merchandising operations, including those of the anchor.

9. Effective age and reputation of the centers. Both the appearance (level of maintenance) and the image (prestige, safety) of the shopping area are considered.

10. Special amenity features. Amenity features may be associated with the center(s) or the trade area. A center may have a community attraction such as a performance area. A trade area may be located next to a scenic lake or near recreational activities that draw people.

Rating Procedure

The appraiser rates each area as equal, superior, or inferior to competing retailing areas. The procedure involves these six steps:

1. First, two clusters are rated, e.g., Area A is compared to Area B and judged equal to, better than, or worse than the other trade area. At this initial stage, the degree of difference between the two areas is not specified.

2. This procedure is repeated with another cluster—e.g., Area C is rated relative to Area A. Again, the degree of difference is not specified.

3. Next the ratings of the second and third clusters are reconsidered. For example, Area B and Area C both were compared to Area A, but not to each other. The degree of difference between the two centers, which may have received superior or inferior ratings compared to Area A, are now measured quantitatively—e.g., 3 indicates the area is better than 2, 2 is rated better than 1, and the same score goes to areas that are equal.

4. The ratings are completed by analyzing the specific relationships between all possible pairs of competitive areas. Five competitive areas are studied in the example (see Table 12.7) so 10 possible sets are compared.

5. The factors are weighted after all the combinations have been compared. The ranking number for each factor is then multiplied by the weight as-

Table 12.7

Competitive Location Analysis Chart

Rating Element	Factor Rated	Area A (Subject)	Area B	Area C (CBD)	Area D	Area E*	Rank by Importance	Importance Weight
1.	Households in trade area	1†	1	1	1	2	6	14%
2.	Proximity to new retail (existing or approved)	2	1	2	1	3	5	12%
3.	Location in path of growth (platting activity and sites under construction)	1	2	3	1	3	5	12%
4.	Proximity to major roads (existing or approved)	3	2	2	1	4	4	10%
5.	Traffic count by site	2	2	2	1	3	6	14%
6.	Proximity to market (interceptor sites)	2	1	1	1	3	3	7%
7.	Size and drawing power of anchors	2	3	2	1	3	7	17%
8.	Tenant mix and compatibility	3	2	1	1	2	3	7%
9.	Effective age and reputation of center	3	2	3	2	3	1	2%
10.	Special amenity features	1	1	1	1	1	2	5%
Total (individual score times weighting)		79	75	76	43	117	42	100%
Weighted average score (total/42)		1.88	1.79	1.81	1.02	2.79		
Percentage of total scores (total/390)		20%	19%	20%	11%	30%		

* Area E includes a proposed mall. Rating assumes the bypass is finished and the new mall has been completed in Area E.

† A rating of 3 is better than 2; 2 is better than 1. If two centers are similar with respect to a specific item, they may have the same rating.

signed to the factor. The weighted scores for each area are added up and converted into a percentage using the total of all weighted scores as a base. Each area score is divided by the base number to obtain a percentage.

6. The individual score for each area is calculated by multiplying each area score by its weight. The total score for each area is shown at the bottom of Table 12.7.

Rating Technique Suggestion

The amount of data and analysis required for each factor rated will vary with the complexity of the assignment and the importance of the factor. As a general rule, the ratings developed in a Level C analysis can be based on a moderate amount of data on the factors rated rather than an exhaustive analysis of each factor. For example, in rating the number of households, the analyst will usually need to know which trade area has the most households, not exactly how many each area has. Typically a minor difference in the number of households will not produce a major miscalculation in the trade areas' overall buying power. Usually the only data needed to analyze and rate this factor is an aerial photograph or a detailed street map of the area that shows the findings of a customer spotting survey. As a general guide, an appraiser refines the trade area circle by modifying its boundaries to take into account major streets and physical features. Trade areas are then compared visually. If the comparison is too close to call without counting each rooftop, the areas are rated similar.

The rating technique described here is intended to target major differences, not to gauge the differences with mathematical precision. A Level D analysis may require greater exactitude, but most Level C assignments do not. As with other sections of the appraisal, the extent of data collection and analysis required is determined by the client and the appraiser in light of the costs and benefits that greater precision will bring to the analysis.

Application of Step 1.2(4)

The subject area was rated against four competitive areas in Table 12.7. The ratings at the bottom of the table suggest that the subject's future share of citywide retailing will be approximately 20%, assuming that the new mall is built in the next five years. The subject's current share is approximately 29% because the new mall planned for Area E has not yet been built. Using the scores for the other four areas, the subject's current percentage is calculated in Table 12.8.

STEP 2 DELINEATE THE MARKET OF PROPERTY USERS

Step 2.1 Define the trade area

The purpose of trade area analysis is to determine where the people who are likely to patronize the subject center live. The area is indicated on a map to iden-

Table 12.8.

Calculation of Market Share

	Area	Wt. Avg. Score		Total of Wt. Avgs. (Areas A—D)	% of Total Scores
(Subject area)	A	1.88	÷	6.50	29%
	B	1.79	÷	6.50	27%
	C	1.81	÷	6.50	28%
	D	1.02	÷	6.50	16%
Total		6.50			100%

tify the districts for which forecast data will be generated. Three basic methods of analyzing the trade areas of retail centers are presented: trade area circles, gravitational models, and customer spotting. All three should be applied, if possible, so the results of the different methods can be reconciled.

Trade Area Circles

The delineation of trade area circles begins with preliminary zonal boundaries, which the analyst adjusts and refines. The method may be broken down into three steps:

1. Identify the subject center type.
2. Draw circles around the areas from which the subject may typically be expected to draw customers (primary, secondary, and perhaps tertiary).
3. Adjust the circles to reflect the data and the specific characteristics of the area as well as economic, demographic, and geographic factors.

Identification of the subject center type. Shopping centers may be differentiated by size and tenantry. (See Table 12.1.) Each type of center has a trade area of a typical size that can be depicted as a range or circle. A 55,000-sq.-ft. center with a supermarket as an anchor tenant would be classified as a neighborhood shopping center, which typically has a trade area of one to one and one-half miles. Although the subject has the size and tenant mix of a neighborhood shopping center, it functions as part of a retail cluster that attracts comparison shoppers. This feature increases its drawing power. Such a retail cluster may be classified as a community shopping center. The sizes of the primary trade areas for three types of centers are shown below:

Neighborhood shopping center	1- to 1.5-mile range
Community shopping center	3- to 5-mile range
Regional shopping center	10- to 15-mile range

The type of center should be identified in terms of the retail node or cluster of which it is a part. Retail establishments are often found in clusters within a small geographic area. Understanding the reasons for these clusters is important to sound retail market analysis. Clustering may result when stores selling similar goods (e.g., auto dealerships, furniture, and appliance stores along arterial streets) locate in proximity to one another to offer customers a wider selection. Although these establishments sell similar goods, consumers can differentiate among their products and the owners of the establishments feel that the benefits of increased consumer traffic outweigh the negative effects of proximity to competitors.

Shopping centers represent another type of retail cluster. A shopping center usually contains stores that are not directly competitive with one another, although some stores may sell products that are close substitutes. There are several dimensions to this relationship that merit closer examination.

Shopping centers are based on the principle of cumulative attraction.[17] They generate more consumer traffic for each individual retail establishment within the center than the establishment would generate if it were located by itself. The composition of a shopping center depends on its *size*. Smaller neighborhood centers contain retail establishments that stock convenience goods, while large regional and superregional malls have a greater proportion of retail establishments that sell shopper goods. Each store in a shopping center is affected by the presence or activity of other stores in the center. The tenant mix should ensure maximum compatibility.

A property's location is studied to determine whether it is part of a cluster. Once this is determined, as in the case of the subject, the analyst can proceed to the next step, the drawing of primary and secondary trade area circles.

Drawing preliminary trade area circles. Regular trade area circles drawn with the retail facility at the center are based on erroneous assumptions.[18] These assumptions include:

- Easy accessibility to the retail facility from all points on the plane
- A uniform distribution of consumers
- Consumers that share the same characteristics, e.g., income and preferences
- Transportation costs that are directly proportional to distance

Since none of these presuppositions reflect the real world, an ideal geometrical shape such as a circle cannot describe a trade area. Thus the shape and size of the trade area circle must be adjusted.

Adjusting trade area circles.[19] Trade area circles are refined to take into account

---

17. Nelson, 59.

18. Neil Carn, Joseph Rabianski, Ronald Racster, and Maury Seldin, *Real Estate Market Analysis: Techniques and Applications* (New York: Prentice-Hall, 1988), 184-185.

19. According to the theoretical work of Lösch, Berry, and Isard, a hexagon is the most efficient shape for a market area. See the discussion of urban structure in Chapter 5.

- The specific characteristics of the area in terms of land uses, terrain, and transport systems
- The distribution of population and purchasing power
- The fit of the available data (e.g., county, census tract, and block data)
- The interrelationships among the area's geography, demography, and economy (e.g., population density and its effect on purchasing power)

The specific characteristics of an area that the appraiser considers include the system of transportation (mode, capacity, accessibility, and quality); the transportation network (area served and current or committed development); any physical barriers to the flow of traffic (natural features and man-made barriers); and psychological barriers (undesirable land uses).

The next problem encountered in drawing the trade area boundary is that the initial line drawn is not likely to conform to the geographic areas for which data are available. Secondary data are generally obtainable for counties, census tracts or zip code areas, and blocks. County data may be used if the retail facility is a regional shopping mall that draws on a relatively large area or is part of a commercial cluster in a rural area. Census tract or zip code area data may be suitable if the facility is a community shopping center or a commercial district located along a main metropolitan arterial. Block data are used to demarcate the trade areas of neighborhood shopping centers. The primary and secondary trade areas of these centers may be enclosed within a single census tract or portions of the trade areas may spread across two or more census tracts.

Rarely do trade areas and census tracts coincide. The appraiser must understand the relationships affecting the subject property and make judgments concerning the use of aggregate census tract data.

Gravitational Models

Trade area circles do not consider the full effect of competition. Gravitational models attempt to address this weakness. The gravity model traditionally employed in market analysis is Reilly's law of retail gravitation.[20] To paraphrase Reilly's law, a center's ability to draw customers varies with both the size of the center and the distance of the center from its competitors. Distance, however, is of greater consequence than size. (An application of Reilly's law can be found in Chapter 7.)

By calculating the trade area boundary between all major competing retail stores or clusters, the appraiser can draw a gravitational boundary for the subject trade area. The application of Step 2.1 on the following page shows how the boundary is determined.

Customer Spotting

Customer spotting can also be used to define the trade area of the subject and

---

20. William Reilly, *Methods for the Study of Retail Relationships* (Austin: University of Texas, 1959), 16.

competitive retail centers. The customer spotting procedure can be broken down into five steps:

1. Obtain the home addresses of the customers of the retail facility using intercept interviews, sales receipts, mailing lists, charge account information, or license plates. Addresses may be difficult to locate in a large metropolitan area, so the customers may be asked to identify the major intersection nearest their address. (Note some of these techniques are more appropriate for advanced, Level D fundamental analyses. Like most appraisals, the case study application relies on a survey of license plates and general data obtained from the store manager.)

2. Spot (i.e., identify) the addresses on a map.

3. Calculate the primary and secondary (and tertiary, if applicable) trade areas based on the distances and travel times between the homes of the customers and the store.

4. Examine the distances and linkages in relation to the attributes of the facility's location.

5. Draw the boundary of the facility's trade area based on this analysis.[21]

Conclusion

An appraiser may use all three methods of delineating a trade area and check them against one another. Any divergence or inconsistency in the proposed trade area boundaries should be reconciled.

Application of Step 2.1

Trade area circles/customer spotting. The subject property has the size and tenant mix of a neighborhood shopping center, but the locational characteristics of a community shopping center. (It is located at the intersection of two major thoroughfares, functions as part of a retail cluster, and sells shopper goods.)

The first task of the appraiser is to forecast the typical tenants expected in the subject center over the next three to 10 years. The key word is *typical* tenants, not *specific* tenants. This is one of the subtle differences between a market study in appraisal and a study conducted in other fields. A market analysis for an appraisal is based on what is probable—i.e., average or typical retail management—whereas specialized market studies consider specific managers, individual retailing objectives, and specific retail types.

The type of tenants currently occupying the subject center will probably continue their leases because

• The subject has had a fairly successful track record with these tenants.

---

21. William Applebaum, "Methods for Determining Store Trade Areas, Market Penetration, and Potential Sales," in *Readings in Market Research for Real Estate* (Chicago: American Institute of Real Estate Appraisers, 1985).

- Customer spotting by means of a sample license plate survey indicates that 65% of the customers come from within two miles of the subject. This seems reasonable given that the subject's tenants stock convenience goods which are typically bought by customers from nearby.
- The location rating indicates that the new mall area will probably serve the future shopping needs of the community. It is unlikely that the subject or the adjacent center will attract more retail tenants oriented toward shopper goods.

Therefore, the primary trade area for the subject is preliminarily identified as the immediate residential area within a one- to two-mile radius. This approximation will be refined using a gravitational model and the conclusions will be adjusted to reflect the available data.

Adjustment for competition. The gravitational model is used to adjust the preliminary trade area boundary established by the trade area circle and customer spotting analyses. In the case of the subject property, distance and travel time were similar for all parts of the city. The gravitational model was used to compare the drawing power of the stores in four areas by size. Since the CBD has very little retail space, the CBD was not analyzed in detail.

The gravitational model is based on the following formula:

$$TAB = t/(1 + \sqrt{Sa/Sb})$$

where

TAB is the trade area boundary, measured as either the travel time or distance from Store A to Store B
t is the travel time (or total distance) between Store A and Store B
Sa is the size (area) of Store A
Sb is the size (area) of Store B

The subject property is located in Area A. The following specific data on distance and square footage were input into the formula.

Distance between Area A and Area B = 1.5 miles
Distance between Area A and Area D = 4 miles
Distance between Area A and Area E = 5 miles

Size of stores in Area A   = 175,000 sq. ft.
Size of stores in Area B   = 75,000 sq. ft.
Size of stores in Area D   = 350,000 sq. ft.
Size of stores (planned) in Area E = 400,000 sq. ft.

The formula indicates the distance of the trade area boundary between Area A and Areas B, D, and E as follows:

Area A and Area B = 0.90 mile from A
Area A and Area D = 1.66 miles from A
Area A and Area E = 2.0 miles from A

Conclusions

The results of the alternative analytical techniques are described below.

1. The radius of the trade area circle extends one to one and one-half miles.
2. Customer spotting indicates that 65% of the subject's customers come from within two miles.

   Note: This refers to the number of customers, not the dollars spent per customer. Level D survey techniques could reveal how total purchases break down by area. Customers outside the primary trade area may drive to the grocery store and make big dollar expenditures, while nearby customers may make frequent trips but spend fewer dollars per trip. Thus, customer spotting must be considered along with other factors.
3. The radii of the gravitational models extend approximately one to two miles.

None of the techniques identify a trade area that corresponds to specific census tract boundaries and the results are not definitive. After reconciling the findings, the preliminary boundary for the primary market area is adjusted in a number of ways.

1. The boundary has been adjusted to reflect major natural and man-made barriers including parks, lakes, and major thoroughfares.
2. The market area has been extended to the west to include the most urbanized area of existing housing. The subject has better linkages to these customers than the competition does.
3. The final primary market area has a conservatively drawn southern border because a planned mall, which will be identified as Center 6, will open in three years and Center 4 is now serving this area. It appears that Center 4 will feel the impact of competition from Center 6 to a far greater extent than will the subject.
4. If the proposed retail mall, Center 7, is developed, the western trade area boundary of the subject will remain the same, but the subject's capture will be reduced.

The final trade area boundary is indicated by the circle drawn on the map in Figure 12.2.

A final thought. Defining the trade area is important because this information is critical to the subsequent analysis. The appraiser collects and analyzes data from the defined trade area as the analysis proceeds. Appraisal is a screening process which focuses on the most important factors affecting value. In retail analysis, the greatest capture and greatest competition are usually found in the primary trade

Figure 12.2
TRADE AREA BOUNDARY

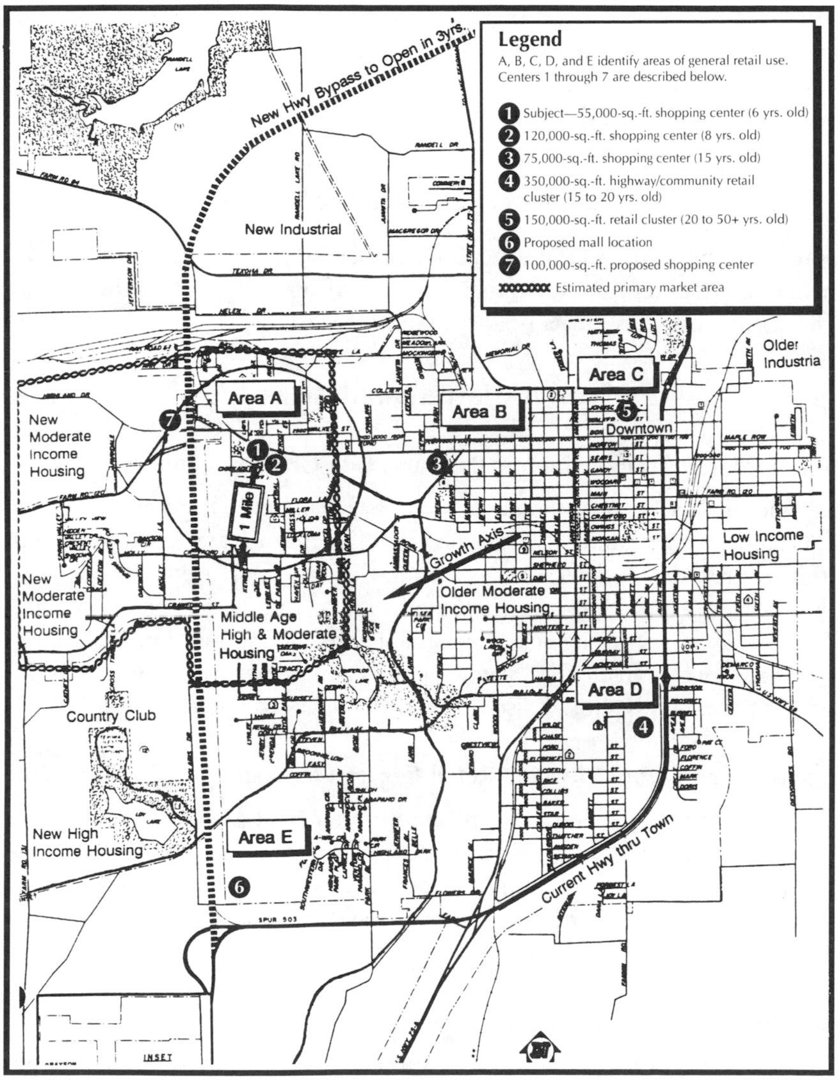

area. Thus the boundary of the primary trade area defines the area from which data are drawn to forecast buying power and other demographic characteristics. It also indicates where the appraiser must gather precise data on supply (competition). This is not to suggest that the appraiser can merely guess at the number of households and the extent of competition in the secondary area. However, less precision is needed in the secondary trade area because any error in the data will have less impact on the study.

STEP 3 FORECAST DEMAND

Demand will be analyzed with methods employed in inferred (trend) and fundamental analyses. Level C analysis makes use of both types of methods and reconciles the conclusions into a final demand forecast.

Step 3.1 Analyze trends (inferred analysis)

Demand Inferred from Economic Base and City Growth Trends

The economic base of the community was described at the beginning of the chapter. The subject community had a good employment mix and good prospects for continued growth. On average, the population has increased 5% per year for the last decade. Local industries continue to grow, and there is no indication that the trend will change in the next 10 years. Therefore, population growth of 5% per year is a reasonable expectation for the city; this growth indicates that demand for retail goods should also grow in the years to come.

Demand Inferred from Citywide Retail Center Occupancy

Retail occupancy citywide has been steadily increasing over the past 10 years, from approximately 80% in the early part of the decade to about 90% today. Since the city is expected to continue to grow, it can be surmised that citywide occupancy will continue to increase and that the subject will realize a share of this increase.

Demand Inferred from Competitive Centers Occupancy

The center across the street from the subject is operating at 95% occupancy. Similar centers around the city also have good occupancy rates, which suggests that demand for centers like the subject is strong in the city.

Step 3.2 Segment demand (fundamental analysis)

The fundamental demand for retail space is a function of the following factors:

- The overall population of the trade area
- The number of households

- The average household income
- The percentage of average household income spent on retail purchases
- The percentage of retail purchases typically made at a subject-type shopping center
- The percentage of purchases made at the shopping center allocated to the primary and secondary trade areas
- The volume of sales per square foot of retail area required for the facility to remain profitable or supportable
- The normal vacancy rate in the market

These variables are calculated in Steps 3.2(1) through 3.2(9)

Step 3.2(1) Forecast number and size of households in primary trade area

The appraiser starts by compiling various population forecasts for the market area. Typical data sources include government agencies, public utility companies, and commercial data vendors. Projections vary widely, so the appraiser should not simply accept the first one found. Multiple projections should be analyzed to judge which forecast is the most reliable. This judgment is critical because the population forecast is one of the most sensitive variables in an appraisal. One procedure for analyzing forecasts is described below.

1. Compare forecasts with local area trends to determine how reasonable the forecasts are. To evaluate forecasts in terms of economic base factors, the appraiser asks: How does the change in employment break down by sectors? Are trends in household growth and buying power consistent with employment trends and trends in the regional economy?

   In evaluating forecasts in terms of location factors, the questions are: Is the development of the city infrastructure consistent with the forecast? Is the land use pattern consistent with the area demographics? For example, a forecast indicating a large percentage increase in high-income population cannot be applied to an area of the city dominated by moderate-income housing.

2. Talk to the forecaster to identify the data sources employed and determine if they are reliable and appropriate. The methodology used to develop the forecast should be scrutinized. Is the technique state-of-the-art? Are the assumptions reasonable? Is the method appropriate? For example, the use of linear regression to analyze rapid growth or decline may overstate the rate of change. It may not be reasonable to apply a previously compounded rate to estimate future change because the base has changed. The appraiser should ascertain that the population figures forecast for subareas add up to the population forecast for the overall area.

3. Analyze the motivation of the forecaster. Most water districts make high forecasts to ensure that the community will never go without water. A

health department may make low forecasts to curtail the costs of public hospital services and efficiently ration health care to the indigent. Chambers of commerce sometimes make high forecasts to promote their cities.

4. Make a simple, original forecast to get a feel for the numbers. This can help the appraiser to judge the sensitivity of the variables.

5. Compare the absolute growth of an analog city with the absolute growth forecast for the subject city. Ideally, the analog should be a nearby city with a similar economic base that has reached the population that is forecast for the subject city. The time frame of the forecast can then be compared to the actual growth of the analog city over a similar time span. This analytical method can be used as a test of reasonableness for the absolute growth forecast.

6. Reconcile the data, considering their reliability and applicability, and choose a final forecast range for the market study. (This step is similar to the reconciliation procedure in the sales comparison approach.) It should be noted that forecasts in appraisals typically cover a longer time frame than forecasts in specialized market studies. A specialized study usually has a short-term focus. For example, the analyst may ask: Can the retail center lease up within the next three years? Is there current demand for a clothing store? The questions an appraiser asks relate to a longer term and are more concerned with probability: What is the present value of future benefits given the most probable tenants, the most probable competition, and the most probable customer base over the economic life of the project? The emphasis is different because a typical appraisal is performed for lending purposes and lenders make a long-term commitment. For this reason most lenders now require a 10-year discounted cash flow (DCF) analysis for appraisals. A specialized market study, on the other hand, may be undertaken to assess the prospects of selling men's clothing at a particular location for the next five years. More advanced, Level D analysis is more specific and usually requires a shorter time frame.

Application of Step 3.2(1)

From census data the appraiser estimates the number of households in the subject's primary trade area to be 2,560 (i.e., total primary trade area population of 6,144 divided by 2.4, the average household size). Data from a commercial source were compared with both local forecasts and the appraiser's own simple forecast, in this case based on trend analysis and comparison with an analog city. The appraiser concluded that the subject city should continue to grow 4% to 6% in the next decade. Thus, in five years the number of households is projected to be between 3,100 and 3,400 and a point estimate of 3,267 is chosen—i.e., total primary trade area population of 7,841 divided by 2.4, the average household size. (This figure is shown under Step 3.2(1) in the summary of demand analysis in Table 12.14. Only one forecast is shown in this table to simplify the presentation. In practice, the development of high-, low-, and mid-range forecasts is recommended.)

Step 3.2(2) Estimate mean/median household income and total income for primary trade area

Total potential retail sales volume is a function of population, income level, and the propensity to spend income which, in turn, depends on the level of income and the characteristics of the population (age, family size, tastes, and preferences).

Sources

Data on mean or median household income may be obtained from the following sources:

- The U.S. Census of Population provides data on the mean or median income per capita and per family gathered in each decennial census.
- *Current Population Reports* publishes data on per capita income every two years.
- The U.S. Commerce Department's *Survey of Current Business* provides data on per capita income for counties and metropolitan areas.
- The "Annual Survey of Consumer Buying Power" in *Sales and Marketing Management* magazine presents data on household income for counties, metropolitan areas, and major cities.
- Commercial data vendors can also supply income data.

Procedure

If current income figures for the subject trade area are not available, they can be estimated in several ways.

First, the per capita, household, or family income for the subject can be calculated by adjusting available estimates for a larger metropolitan area such as the city or county. In the example presented in Table 12.9, the appraiser estimates the current median income in the census tract by extrapolating the rate of increase (146%) from the percentage change in the ratio between the census tract and metropolitan statistical area ($3,942/$2,700).

Second, current income may be inferred from house prices in the trade area. If the average house price is $100,000 and we assume that 26% of income is spent on housing, the typical area household income can be estimated with the following calculations:

$100,000 house, minus 10% down payment = $90,000 mortgage
@ 10% for 30 years requires $789.81 monthly payment

Table 12.9
Per Capita Median Income

	Previous Census	Most Recent Census	Current	Forecast
Trade area (Tract 101)	$2,500	$3,000	Unknown	$3,942
MSA	$2,000	$2,200	$2,700 (known)	Not available
Census tract as % of MSA	125%	136%	Unknown	est. 146%

Plus 20% for ad valorem taxes and insurance
Indicates a total yearly expenditure on housing of
approximately $11,500.

$11,500 \div 0.26 = $44,230

Equals the approximate total annual household income required
to support housing in the $100,000 price range.

Third, if the trade area comprises a number of census tracts, the most accurate procedure is to calculate the income for specific subsections using block data. This is particularly important for convenience-type centers because the majority of their customers will come from the immediately adjacent area. For a Level C analysis, however, aggregate income data can be compiled by weighting the representative mean or median income of each census tract in the trade area by the percentage of the population to be captured in that tract. This procedure is illustrated in Table 12.10.

Table 12.10
Median Income Weighted for Capture

Primary Trade Area	Current Population	Current Median Income	Estimated Percentage of Capture		Weighted Average
Census Tract 101	10,000	$3,942	x	0.30	$1,183
Census Tract 102	8,000	3,000	x	0.24	720
Census Tract 103	9,000	3,300	x	0.27	891
Census Tract 104	4,000	3,500	x	0.12	420
Census Tract 105	2,000	2,700	x	0.07	189
	33,000			100%	$3,403

Mean Versus Median Income

Both the mean and the median are measures of central tendency. In most communities, the mean income will be greater than the median income. This is true because most communities have a few people with large incomes and a great number of people with low and moderate incomes. In other words, the distribution of incomes is skewed toward the few higher incomes. If income were distributed evenly, then the average income (mean) and midpoint income (median) would be the same. This is rarely the case. Thus, some analysis of the difference between the mean and median income is advisable to determine which measure of central tendency gives the more reliable picture of purchasing power in the subject center. The extent of skewness can be calculated by subtracting the median from the mean. If the result is a negative amount, the data are skewed to lower incomes; if the result is positive, to higher incomes. If the difference is relatively large, then the data are significantly skewed; if the difference is relatively small, then the data are more evenly distributed.

The compilation of census data generally shows that family income is higher than household income. A household may comprise only one individual, but a family must have two or more members.

Inflated Dollars Versus Constant Dollars

Forecasts of income are generally based on rates extrapolated from data for larger areas and adapted to reflect the profile of households in the trade area. In an inflationary environment, real income does not necessarily increase. Real median income in the United States did not grow between 1973 and 1994. If the appraiser uses income projections based on inflationary dollars, then he or she should also employ data on the required volume of sales per square foot that reflect inflationary expectations. Alternatively, an appraiser may use a constant dollar approach, which considers real growth only, not inflation.

Application of Step 3.2(2)

The appraiser estimates local median household income to be $37,500. (See Step 3.2(2) in Table 12.14.) The subject trade area is split between two census tracts. The census tract north of the subject has fewer households and is populated by residents at the lower end of the moderate-income range. The census tract south of the subject consists of moderate-income households immediately adjacent to the subject and higher-income households some distance away. Median household income was estimated using three different methods and the results were reconciled.

First, the median incomes of the two census tracts were weighted by the estimated number of houses in each census tract within the subject's primary trade area. The number of houses in the census tracts was estimated by means of aerial photographs.

To apply the second method the analyst estimated the number of houses and the house values at three different price levels (low, medium, and high) in the primary trade area. The incomes required to own the houses at each level were then calculated and weighted according to the number of houses at that level.

The third method for estimating median income relied on data purchased from a commercial source. These data pertained to households in the two-mile ring around the subject property.

The results derived from the three methods were reconciled into a point estimate of the most probable median income. The forecast median income shown in Step 3.2(2) in Table 12.14 is expressed in constant dollars.

Step 3.2(3) Estimate the percentage of household income spent on retail items

Procedure

To estimate the percentage of average household income spent on retail purchases, the analyst first deducts taxes from gross household income to determine net disposable income, or effective buying income. Nonretail expenditures are then deducted from this figure to arrive at retail buying power. A representative breakdown of gross household income indicates the following percentages.

For households in the subject's primary trade area, taxes average 22% of gross household income. Nonretail expenditures account for 36.3% of gross household income and 46.6% of effective buying income. The remaining 41.7% of gross household income, and 53.4% of effective buying income, is spent on retail purchases.

Using these percentages, gross household income for the primary trade area is disaggregated in Table 12.11. Income is based on citywide data, while the percentages are based on general data for the region.

Application of Step 3.2(3)

The appraiser estimates that approximately 45% of household income in the subject trade area is spent on retail purchases. This estimate is based on the analysis of primary market area incomes in the previous step, which suggested that more lower-income households than higher-income households are located in the subject primary trade area. Lower-income households typically spend a greater percentage of their income on basic retail goods. In the subject center, there are more stores selling necessary retail goods than stores selling luxury items. The breakdown of retail expenditures in Table 12.11 was based on metropolitan data and, in some cases, national survey data. Such data can be used only as guidelines for the subject trade area. As a further check, the appraiser studied information from a commercial data source which estimated a similar mean income and retail buying power for the subject's primary trade area. (See Step 3.2(3) in Table 12.14.)

Table 12.11

Household Income and Buying Power (in Current Dollars)

			Percentage of Gross Income
Gross household income		$31,615	
Less taxes on gross income		6,955	22.0%
Net disposable income or effective buying income (*EBI*)		$24,660	78.0%
Less nonretail expenditures:			
Housing	26.0% of *EBI*	$6,412	
Medical	9.1%	2,244	
Personal insurance and professional services	3.5%	863	
Personal services	3.0%	740	
Recreation	2.0%	493	
Savings	3.0%	740	
Total nonretail	46.6%	$11,492	36.3%
Retail buying power	53.4% of *EBI*	$13,168	41.7%
Totals	100% of *EBI*		100% of gross income

Note: This breakdown varies over time and for different areas of the country. One good source for current data is the *Quarterly Consumer Expenditure Survey,* published by the U.S. Department of Labor, Bureau of Labor Statistics.

Step 3.2(4) Estimate the percentage of retail purchases typically made at a shopping center of the subject's type

The percentage of retail purchases typically made at a certain type of shopping center varies with the tenants in the shopping center. A fundamental demand study can segment the demand on a tenant-by-tenant basis according to the specific type of retail item(s) sold by each tenant. Then the demand for each retail category (identified by SIC code) can be studied and compared to the competition posed by corresponding retailers to assess current residual or marginal demand on a category-specific basis.

This type of study is conducted in a more detailed, Level D analysis. It is not described in this book because a Level D study is used principally by retailers making management decisions to introduce new products to the market or expand current capture by stepping up marketing efforts.

Appraisers may sometimes utilize this information. Indeed, in certain assignments it may be required. For example, if a major tenant is essential to the valuation of a shopping center, a forecast of that tenant's particular market segment may be needed. However, in most assignments the appraiser is primarily interested in a mid-range (10-year) economic forecast for the center as a whole. This range is compatible with the economic modeling typically used in the income approach. Given the 10-year time frame of the forecast, a center's value will be most influenced by the general tenant types in the center; it is unlikely to be affected to a large degree by any one tenant.

In a Level C analysis conducted for an appraisal, the segmentation of purchases usually begins with the major tenant types most likely to occupy the subject over the next 10 years. The analyst examines the subject to identify major tenant types that sell convenience goods and shopper goods. If the facility principally sells convenience goods such as groceries and pharmaceuticals and personal services such as dry cleaning and shoe repair, the percentage of retail purchases captured will differ from that of a facility that sells shopper goods or comparison items like appliances and apparel.

The appraiser next identifies unique tenant types (current and prospective over the next 10 years) on a category-by-category basis. After each category is noted, the anticipated percentages of expenditures spent at these shops are totaled. These data are input in calculating demand. Using this technique the analyst develops information about what percentage of expenditures from general tenant types is anticipated at the subject over the next few years (usually a 10-year DCF period). The analyst does not forecast specific tenants or specific tenant-by-tenant space demand, as might be done in a more detailed, Level D study.

There are many variations of the procedure described here. For example, one refinement uses general segmentation as a base, but takes the analysis a step further and segments demand between large space tenants and small space tenants.

Expenditure data on convenience and shopper goods are needed to complete this step in the analysis. Sources of this type of data include:

- U.S. Census of Business, *Retail Trade*, published every five years; contains a breakdown of sales for cities and counties by major retail categories
- U.S. Bureau of the Census, *Monthly Retail Trade Report*, reports monthly and annual department store sales for most metropolitan areas; also publishes sales tax data for states on a city or county basis
- U.S. Department of Labor, Bureau of Labor Statistics, *Consumer Expenditure Survey*
- Local sales tax data
- Commercial data vendors

The percentage of income spent on convenience goods and shopper goods depends on local income levels and general economic conditions and can change over time. Percentages that characterize consumer expenditures at a national or regional level may have to be adjusted to reflect local patterns.

A typical expenditure pattern is illustrated Table 12.12.

Table 12.12
Percentage of Retail Buying Power: Consumption per Household

Retail Commodity/ Establishment	SIC Code*	% of Retail Buying Power	% by Subsection	% Applicable to Subject
% Building Materials	52	5		
Hardware store	525		1	1
Other	521,523		4	
General Merchandise	53	10		
Department store	531		5	
Junior department store	531		3	3
Variety store	533		1	1
Misc. general merchandise	539		1	1
Food	54	25		
Supermarket	541		19	19
Other	542-549		6	6
Automotive	551-559	16		
Service Stations		7		
Apparel	56	4		4
Men's & boy's	561		1	
Women's	562,563,568		1.5	
Family-general	564,565,569		1	
Shoes	566		0.5	
Furniture & Appliances	57	4		
Furnishings	571		2.5	
Appliances	572		1.5	
Eating & Drinking	58	9		
Restaurant	581		3	3
Cafeteria	581		2	2
Fast food	581		4	4
Miscellaneous Retail	59	20		
Drugs	591		2	2
Liquor store	592		1	
Used merchandise	593		1	
Misc. shopping goods	594			
Jewelry			2	
Florist			1	1
Hobby & sporting			2	2
Radio, TV & music	595		2	2
Nonstore retailers	596		1	1
Office computer equipment	597		2	2
Other retail	599		6	6
Total		100.0%		60%

* Standard Industrial Classification Code

Explanation of Table 12.12

The percentages shown may vary over time because the spending habits of the population change. For example, more is now being spent on home computers than was spent in previous years. Percentages may also vary from area to area. Lower-income populations tend to spend a greater percentage of their income on basic living goods and food items.

The categories shown in the table are those identified in the Standard Industrial Classification (SIC) Code. Changes or supplementary categories are introduced from time to time. The material presented is provided as an example only. A detailed explanation of each SIC category is provided in the *Standard Industrial Classification Manual*, published by the U.S. Office of Management and Budget. Before applying these data, the appraiser should study the SIC definitions and the local percentage breakdown of buying power under each category. Expenditure patterns in local areas can be updated using sales tax data, which are available in most states by four-digit SIC code and for geographic areas by zip code. The other Department of Commerce sources previously mentioned are usually limited to counties or MSA areas.

For most Level C market analyses, use of the three-digit SIC code data shown in Table 12.12 is sufficient. Sometimes analysts refer to the two-digit entries that specify each general category. Retail commodities are classified under group numbers 52 through 59. The SIC number for hardware stores is 525, but sometimes reference is made to the two-digit SIC number, 25, under the 5 series. Similarly, the four-digit 5231 which details out paint, glass, and wallpaper stores is sometimes referenced as the three-digit entry, 231, under the 5 series. In this book the SIC numbers referred to are four-digit entries.

Application of Step 3.2(4)

The appraiser estimates that 60% of household retail purchases are made at shopping centers with a tenant mix like that of the subject. The appraiser must study the tenant mix of the subject and nearby centers, the subject's trade area, and trends in the area to determine who the subject's most probable future tenants are and estimate the percentage of retail expenditures typically made at this type of center. The total percentage is estimated by adding up the respective percentages of select items listed in Table 12.12. An estimate obtained in this manner cannot be considered conclusive since it cannot be corroborated without additional information about the composition of each category of goods. Moreover, there is no standard shopping center. Based on the general categories provided in the table, however, one possible solution is offered below.

The following categories from Table 12.12 were excluded from the analysis: other building materials, department stores, automotive/service stations, furniture and appliances, and some miscellaneous retail. The remaining categories indicate approximately 60% capture.

If the assignment warranted a Level D study, the appraiser would investigate all retail categories, estimate the demand for each, and compare each category with its respective competition. This level of study would help identify retail gaps (undersupplied retail areas), which could be used to target the most probable future tenants for the subject.

Step 3.2(5) Estimate percentage of sales retention in primary trade area from total potential sales for primary trade area

Industry sources[22] indicate that a shopping center will capture 70% to 80% of sales from its primary trade area and 20% to 30% of sales from its secondary and tertiary trade areas. The percentage of retail leakage outside the primary trade area includes purchases made on trips, purchases of specific items or alternative brands not available in the primary trade area, purchases made close to workplaces, and purchases made at competing centers that provide special amenities or offer a variety not found in the primary trade area.

The estimated retention of potential retail sales in the primary trade area is a difficult number to support in any study. At best, only a range can be estimated. Nevertheless, the techniques described below may be considered.

In Step 3.2(4) the appraiser estimates the potential retail purchases most probable at the subject community center by category. Many state and local governments compile sales tax data using similar categories and, in many cases, break down this information for small geographic areas by zip code. The tax data provide an indication of actual dollars spent, which can be compared to the estimate of potential retail purchases. The difference is one measure of the leakage out of the trade area.

Another method for estimating the retention of sales is to compare the trade area circles and the customer spotting analysis. Do the trade area circles of nearby competitors overlap the final boundaries chosen for the subject? If so, what percentage of households is involved? This number might be used to check retail sales retention.

A third technique makes use of the location rating of citywide retail areas developed in Step 1.2(4). The subject did not rate as the best retail location in town, but it came in a close second. The industry standard that holds that typical stores get 70% to 80% of their business from the primary trade area might be a good estimate. On the other hand, if the subject had rated considerably lower than nearby competitors, the retail sales retention could be lower than the 75% rule of thumb.

The final retention estimate represents a probable range. As in many other steps of the market analysis, estimates derived from alternative techniques should be compared and the final capture forecast should be based on the reliability and comparability of the data analyzed.

---

22. See text on pages 196-198 and footnotes 7 and 8 for sources such as the Urban Land Institute and Gale Research, Inc.

The techniques described can be applied in the analysis of an existing retail center or a specific proposed retail development. In an assignment that is not value-specific such as a feasibility analysis, the leakage might be attributed to poor design, insufficient marketing, or the tenant mix of the center. When such deficiencies are corrected, the center's retention might increase. This type of problem usually requires Level D-type analysis. The effect of marketing usually is not considered within the scope of a typical valuation appraisal.

In general, if the subject and competitive facilities are modern, convenience-good stores, they can be expected to retain a large percentage of the potential convenience-good purchases in the trade area. Retention of convenience-good purchases is common, even at levels above 80%. If the subject and competitive centers are oriented toward comparison shoppers, however, retention will probably be lower and depend on the competitive ranking of the shopping centers in adjacent trade areas.

There are other ways to consider the rate of retention for neighborhood and community centers. If the buying power and competition in the primary and secondary areas are similar, then the leakage out of the trade area might approximate the leakage into the trade area. In the case study example, a more detailed approach was applied.

Application of Step 3.2(5)

The appraiser estimates that the subject center will retain 75% of the total potential sales in its primary trade area, but this rate is forecast to decline once the new mall opens. The location rating in Step 1.2(4) assigned the subject a 29% rating today compared to a 20% rating five years out. Thus, after the new mall opens in five years, the subject's retention rate in the primary trade area may be expected to fall by about the same percentage (10%) to 65%. (See Step 3.2(5) in Table 12.14.)

Step 3.2(6) Repeat steps 3.2(1) through 3.2(5) for the secondary trade area

This step is shown in Table 12.14.

Step 3.2(7) Determine total demand in the primary and secondary trade areas

In this step, the appraiser adds the retail sales potential of the primary and secondary trade areas. (See Table 12.14.)

Step 3.2(8) Estimate the supportable square footage of retail space by dividing total demand by required sales volume per square foot

The subject's prospects for earning income (rent) are directly dependent on occupancy. Rents and occupancy are typically reported on a square-foot basis. To understand how total effective retail buying power relates to future rent and occupancy, the appraiser examines retail buying power in terms of how many sales are required per square foot of space at a specific rent for a store to turn a profit.

An estimate of the volume of sales required per square foot of retail area for a facility to remain profitable or supportable is used to translate dollar demand into estimated retail space. This estimate can be obtained from industry data on median sales per square foot of gross leasable area. Such data are often quoted along with data on the median rent per square foot of gross leasable area. Required sales volume per square foot of retail space is closely related to rent per square foot of retail space. If rents increase, greater sales volume is required to support the store. If rents decline, less sales volume is necessary for the store to remain in business.

Sources

Publications such as *Dollars and Cents of Shopping Centers*, put out by the Urban Land Institute, provide data for different tenant classifications. Table 12.13 shows typical store sales per square foot and store rents for the 20 types of tenants most frequently found in community shopping centers.

Forecasts of the sales required per square foot of retail space can be made in current (inflated) or constant (real) dollars. If the appraiser uses inflated dollars, the estimates of income and expenses must also be expressed in inflated dollars. The need for more *GLA* comes from a forecast of real growth in sales, not from inflation.

Application of Step 3.2(8)

The required sales volume per square foot of tenant space for the subject center can be estimated by weighting the anticipated rent from each of the tenants by the respective size of the tenant space. The weighted average estimate of the sales volume required came to approximately $200 per square foot of *GLA*. The sales volume data used can be taken directly from Table 12.13 and adjusted for inflation to the current date and for the subject rent range, if it is dissimilar. The appraiser then divides the total retail sales potential by the dollar sales required to support one square foot of retail space to derive the supportable square footage of retail space. (See Step 3.2(8) in Table 12.14.)

Step 3.2(9) Adjust the estimate of supportable retail space to reflect a normal vacancy rate for the market

This step recognizes that in a balanced market some vacant space for move-ins, move-outs, and short-term growth is necessary to maintain rents at competitive levels. Economists sometimes refer to normal vacancy as *frictional vacancy.*

The vacancy rate applied to the subject shopping center is 5%, the industry rule-of-thumb. This 5% figure is employed in estimating proposed construction (i.e., justifiable building space) and in analyzing market equilibrium.

Table 12.13
Sales and Rents for Typical Tenants

Tenant Classification	Rank	Average Number of Stores	Median GLA*	Median Sales Volume per Square Foot of GLA* (in Dollars)	Median Total Rent per Square Foot of GLA (in Dollars)
General Merchandise					
Junior dept. store	12	0.4	35,390	$110.29	$3.55
Discount dept. store	15	0.4	59,537	133.24	3.38
Food					
Superstore	13	0.4	37,430	346.95	4.48
Food Service					
Restaurant (w/out liquor)	8	0.6	2,807	135.12	10.00
Restaurant (with liquor)	2	0.8	3,537	138.28	10.57
Fast food/carryout	3	0.7	1,500	200.00	12.73
Clothing and Accessories					
Ladies' specialty	9	0.5	1,600	153.91	12.00
Ladies' ready-to-wear	1	1.2	3,000	124.87	8.75
Shoes					
Family shoes	5	0.6	3,000	118.88	9.00
Home Appliances/Music					
Radio, video, stereo (< 10,000 sq. ft.)	14	0.4	2,222	191.86	9.00
Gifts/Specialty					
Cards and gifts	7	0.6	2,600	101.30	10.00
Books	17	0.3	2,400	144.74	9.70
Jewelry					
Jewelry	6	0.6	1,260	265.25	14.20
Drugs					
Super drugstore	19	0.3	14,600	172.46	4.88
Drugs	20	0.3	7,532	182.48	6.18
Personal Services					
Beauty	4	0.6	1,300	96.94	10.59
Cleaners and dryers	11	0.4	1,600	86.42	11.34
Unisex hair	18	0.3	1,217	125.49	12.00
Videotape rentals	15	0.3	2,000	83.51	9.73
Financial					
Bank	10	0.5	2,955	3,356.22	11.80

* Supportable sales volume per square foot is related to the rents for retail space. If rents go down, *less* sales volume would be required to support the store and vice versa.

Source: Urban Land Institute, *Dollars and Cents of Shopping Centers,* 1990. (Appraisers should refer to the most recent version of this publication, which is published approximately every three years.)

Note that the appraisal question is primarily focused on the forecast of *actual* occupied square footage. The subject capture forecast uses the actual occupancy forecast (Step 3.2(8) in Table 12.14), while residual or marginal demand studies typically utilize data based on a balanced market assumption, i.e., that some vacant space is normal (See Step 3.2(9) in Table 12.14.)

Step 3.3 Analyze demand by ratio method or fundamental analysis

In the ratio method the appraiser applies the current amount of occupied retail square footage per capita to the future population forecast. This simple method is applicable when the amount of currently occupied space is known. When currently occupied space is not known, a time-consuming supply survey is required. In such a case, preparing a fundamental demand forecast would probably be more expedient.

The following ratio analysis makes use of the supply (competition) survey developed in Step 4 (see Table 12.16). The survey shows that currently occupied space totals 679,250 square feet (competitive space plus space in the subject). Since the town has a population of 45,000, there are approximately 15 square feet of retail space per person (679,250 ÷ 45,000). In the subject's primary market area (Area A), there are currently 6,144 people and 158,000 square feet of occupied retail space. This indicates a ratio of approximately 25 square feet of retail space per person. It appears that the subject area has strong capture from outside the primary trade area. (Only 13.65% of the town's population is found in the subject's area.) The subject area's capture rate is 23% (i.e., current actual occupancy of 158,000 square feet in Area A divided by citywide current occupancy of 679,250).

The subject area's capture seems consistent with the location rating derived in Step 1.2(4), which suggested that the subject area is currently the best commercial area in town. According to that rating method, however, it should be capturing 29% of all citywide demand. When that ratio is applied to the current actual occupied space, the current demand indicated for the subject area is 196,983 square feet (29% location rating x 679,250 square feet of current citywide occupancy). This suggests that either the subject should be capturing more or other factors may be eroding the subject's capture potential. Lower rents or better management of centers in other parts of town could be lessening the subject's capture. It is also possible that the rating analysis was a bit overly optimistic for the subject market (Area A). Given the expected margin of error in the data, the results of both methods may be considered to fall within a reasonable range.

The forecast data must now be examined. Over the next five years, the subject area is forecast to grow to 7,840 people. Based on the current 25:1 ratio, demand in Area A five years in the future should be 196,000 (7,840 x 25).

The end of the decade must also be considered. This may be accomplished by applying the ratio to the tenth-year population forecast. Before this is done, however, the ratio needs further analysis. Somewhere around the fifth year, two events

Table 12.14

Summary Chart of Demand Analysis (Mid-Range Estimate)

	Description	Current	In 5 Yrs.	In 10 Yrs.
Step 3.2(1)	Total number of households in primary trade area	2,560	3,267	4,100
Step 3.2(2)	Median household income	$37,500	$37,500	$37,500
Step 3.2(3)	Percentage of income spent on retail purchases	45%	45%	45%
Step 3.2(4)	Percentage of retail purchases made at a shopping center of the subject's type	60%	60%	60%
Step 3.2(5)	Percentage of sales retention in the primary trade area	75%	75%	65%
Retail sales potential in primary trade area		**$19,440,000**	**$24,808,781**	**$26,983,125**
Step 3.2(6)	Total number of households in secondary trade area	4,038	5,154	6,462
	Median household income	$32,500	$32,500	$32,500
	Percentage of income spent on retail purchases	45%	45%	45%
	Percentage of retail purchases made at a neighborhood shopping center	60%	60%	60%
	Percentage of sales captured in the secondary trade area	35%	35%	25%
Retail sales potential in secondary trade area		**$12,403,125**	**$15,829,931**	**$14,175,000**
Step 3.2(7)	Total retail sales potential in primary and secondary trade areas	$31,843,125	$40,638,712	$41,158,125
Step 3.2(8)	Sales required per square foot	$200	$200	$200
Supportable square footage of retail space		**159,216**	**203,194**	**205,790**
Step 3.2(9)	Estimate of the supportable retail space in primary and secondary trade areas adjusted for normal vacancy rate for the market (5%)	167,595 sq. ft.	213,888 sq. ft.	216,621 sq. ft.
	(Divide supportable retail space by 0.95.)			

are anticipated: the opening of a new mall in Area E and the addition of 75,000 square feet of space in the subject Area A. These developments will probably affect demand in the subject area. The location rating forecast indicated that the subject would become the second best area, falling from a 29% location capture rating to a 20% location capture rating. This is an approximately 30% drop in the location rating. Thus, instead of a 25:1 ratio, a 30% smaller ratio is probable for the fifth year through the tenth year. This changes the ratio to approximately 18:1. Multiplying the tenth year population forecast of 9,840 for Area A by 18 gives a fifth-year estimate of approximately 177,000 square feet of retail space for Area A.

The data imply that demand in the subject area will be leveling off in five years because of the new mall and the anticipated loss in current market share.

Step 3.4 Reconcile findings and forecast final demand

Each appraisal method has its strengths and weaknesses, so it is recommended that the appraiser use the suggested alternative methods and reconcile the results into a final conclusion. In the market analysis component of an appraisal, inferred (trend) analysis, fundamental analysis, and ratio analysis are the alternative methods to be applied and reconciled.

In the reconciliation of data into a final demand forecast, the appraiser should consider the strengths and weaknesses of each method. The strength of trend analysis is that the data are verifiable. The appraiser knows the previous occupancy rate of the subject, the previous occupancy rate of the competition, and any specific increases that have been realized. The method's weakness is that the data are historical and supply-oriented. This is a serious shortcoming because the appraisal concept of value derives from "future benefits." Another weakness of trend analysis is that the data are typically macro data and generally not specific to the subject's submarket.

The strengths of a fundamental analysis are twofold. The analysis is future-oriented and it is possible to segment forecast demand to reflect the specific submarket of the subject. The weakness of fundamental analysis stems from the need to make judgments at each substep in the data analysis process regarding the future demographics of the subject submarket. Thus, there is potential for error at several points. An analogy can be drawn to sales comparison analysis, in which the best value indicator is usually the sale requiring the smallest gross adjustment (unless an especially high level of confidence can be placed in the adjustments applied to other sales). Similarly, in data analysis fewer judgments may reduce the margin of error. Fundamental analysis focuses on segmenting data. Thus, it is critical that the analyst have confidence in the judgments made at each point in the development of the demand estimate.

The ratio method combines certain advantages of both fundamental analysis and trend analysis. In the ratio method current occupied space, a known fact, is compared with a future-oriented population forecast. It is a simple method and requires few adjustments. The first weakness of the ratio method is that it does not segment, in detail, all of the factors that make up retail demand. The dynamics of today's market may change tomorrow. Fundamental analysis, which segments demand data, provides a means to forecast change. By contrast, the ratio method is static, basically assuming that future ratios will follow current ratios.

The second weakness of the ratio method lies in the selection of a "proxy" ratio, the ratio for the comparable market to be used in the forecast. The choice of the proxy ratio depends on the quality of the appraiser's analysis. It is up to the appraiser to assess whether the proxy ratio is the best indicator of future relationships in the subject's submarket.

Having summarized the strengths and weaknesses of the methods applied, we can now consider the demand indicated by each (see Table 12.15).

Table 12.15
Recap of Demand Forecast

Method	Conclusion	
Trend method	Increased demand	
	Supportable occupied space:	
Fundamental method	In 5 yrs.	In 10 yrs.
(market segmentation)	203,194 sq. ft.	205,790 sq. ft.
Ratio method	196,000 sq. ft.	177,000 sq. ft.

The trend method does not provide a specific number, but from the data we can infer that demand for the subject will increase.

The reliability of the fundamental analysis can be checked by comparing the calculated current demand of 159,216 square feet, shown in Table 12.14, to the current actual occupancy of 158,000 square feet. The close correlation of these figures lends credence to the multiple estimates required by the fundamental demand model. The five-year forecasts of the segmentation and ratio methods are very close, differing by only about 7,000 square feet. This further supports the segmentation method.

For the five- to 10-year period, however, the conclusions of the segmentation and ratio methods vary by about 26,000 square feet. Both methods recognize the reduced market share anticipated by lowering the capture rate for Area A in Years 5 through 10, but two different methods were used to estimate the change in area capture. In the segmentation method, the estimate was based on interviews with the store managers who were asked what part of their customer base they felt could be maintained after the new mall is put into operation. The estimated area capture based on their average response is shown in Steps 3.2(5) and 3.2(6) in Table 12.14, which record sales retention and capture in the primary and secondary trade areas. In the ratio method the location rating was used to quantify the reduction in market share. Given the uncertainty of both methods and the level of detail in the case study, the analyst could choose a point estimate in the middle of the range. In this example, however, the appraiser will assign more weight to the fundamental analysis because the information obtained from the store managers is considered very reliable.

STEP 4 MEASURE COMPETITIVE SUPPLY

Supply data

A preliminary investigation of the competition was made for the location analysis and trade area definition in the first and second steps of the market analysis. In Step 4 competitive supply is analyzed in greater detail. There are three reasons for undertaking an in-depth supply study.

First, the analysis of competitive supply more precisely rates the competition in comparison with the subject. This rating generates more detailed information, which enables the appraiser to forecast the subject's prospects for earning income (rent) and capturing a specific share of the market.

Second, the inventory and forecast of competitive supply is used in the equilibrium analysis to determine marginal demand. Marginal demand represents the "window of opportunity" for new development, i.e., the point in time when all available and projected retail space has been absorbed and new net demand becomes apparent. Identifying this point in time is very useful; the information is employed in many parts of the appraisal. It may signal when rent increases and/or new competition can be anticipated. In the sales comparison approach, it supports the adjustment for a change in market conditions (time adjustment). In the cost approach, it provides a means of identifying and measuring external obsolescence.

Third, supply data on the overall retail activity in the city can be used in inferred demand analysis. For example, if retail centers have an overall occupancy of 90% and no new centers are planned, it might be inferred that the subject will increase its current occupancy. On the other hand, if a major center is planned (like the new mall in the case study), the appraiser might infer that occupancy at the subject will decrease in the near future.

Step 4.1 Inventory existing, under-construction, and proposed competitive space

Procedure

As part of the analysis of location, land use, and linkages in the first step of the market analysis, the appraiser identified the location of competitive shopping centers in the primary and secondary trade areas of the subject. By this stage, the appraiser is ready to examine the attributes of the specific competition in greater detail.

The survey at hand is limited to the competition, i.e., competitive facilities selling similar items that are readily substitutable for those sold at the subject center. For example, the stores in a multitenanted shopping center directly compete with stores in other multitenanted centers and with large, freestanding discount outlets in the area. Caution should be exercised in making judgments about competitive space in large stores such as super discount stores. The primary trade area for a discount store could be as large as that of a regional shopping center. Therefore, in the appraisal of a neighborhood or community shopping center, only a portion of the space in a large regional discount store should be counted as competitive space.

The geographic area in which the competitive facilities are located must correspond to the area used in the demand forecast. Otherwise, the estimate of marginal demand will be distorted. Nevertheless, data from outside the primary trade area may be useful for market share analysis and analysis of the secondary competition. In metropolitan areas, such data are usually available from secondary sources. The data survey conducted by the appraiser is usually concerned only with the primary trade area of the subject. A citywide survey of a small town such as the one in which the subject property is located can be accomplished within a reasonable amount of time. However, because competition in the primary trade area will affect the subject the most, the survey usually concentrates on the competition in the immediate area, even in a small town.

At this point the appraiser may select the competing centers to be used in the detailed market rent analysis developed in the income approach.

Planned and potential competition that may enter the market over the next five to 10 years must also be considered. This competition may be extremely difficult to identify. The appraiser might begin by investigating vacant competitive sites in the area. Who are the owners? Are these owners developers? Not all potential sites can be developed. For example, a parcel of land may be tied up in an estate. The appraiser should also look into possible zoning problems. What is the likelihood of a competitive site being rezoned if current zoning does not allow for retail development?

The appraiser should consult the personnel at municipal departments that issue building permits and those involved in city planning. These individuals can sometimes provide information on who may be considering development in the area.

A survey of preliminary plats may reveal long-term development patterns. Preliminary plats are more reliable than zoning because platting usually indicates a nonspeculative venture with money paid up front. Not all preliminary plats will be developed, but final plats often show a strong correlation with preliminary plats. Historical data may also indicate how many preliminary plats become final plats and how many are actually developed.

An appraiser can clip announcements of building starts and proposed developments from local newspapers and keep them on file to furnish data for subsequent assignments.

Small, stand-alone retail stores that are not adjacent to a shopping center are considered satellite stores. If the retail space in these stores has not been included in the demand calculations, it is not necessary to include this space in the supply survey. For example, the ratio method segments out such space because the ratio is based on a comparison of the space included in the survey and the current population. Since we are considering the demand for shopping centers, outlying stand-alone space need not be included in the ratio comparison. On the other hand, any cluster of small stores that functions as a shopping center should be included in the survey. In this case study application, the CBD (Area C) and the highway strip commercial (Area D), which are groups of stand-alone stores, have been included in the survey because they function as shopping center nodes.

Application of Step 4.1

The inventory of existing, competitive retail space in the city serving the target market totals 750,000 square feet. This total includes the four existing community shopping areas plus the 55,000 square feet in the subject property. Only 175,000 square feet of the total are in the subject's primary market area. A survey of citywide competitive retail space revealed a 90% occupancy rate.

An investor has just concluded a land purchase and has announced plans to construct in five years a 100,000-sq.-ft. center one-half mile west of the subject on the new proposed highway bypass. (This property was identified as Center 7 in Figures 12.1 and 12.2.) The developer has not yet secured financing or preleased any space. The owner of an existing shopping center on the current traffic route through town (Area D) indicates that 25% to 50% of his business comes from highway customers. Thus, if the proposed center is built, probably only one-half of the space will be competitive.

Table 12.16 summarizes the results of the citywide survey of retail activity. Detailed survey sheets are not shown here as this material is typically presented in the income approach section of the appraisal report, where actual rents and expenses are analyzed for the discounted cash flow forecast.

Step 4.2 Rate supply of competitive space

The in-depth competitive supply analysis in Step 4.1 provides information that complements the competitive rating developed in the location analysis in Step 1.2(4). Information derived from these analyses is used to estimate the current market rent for the subject property and to provide additional data for the share-of-the-market analysis to be performed in Step 6 of the market analysis.

Procedure

In competitive supply analysis the appraiser investigates property characteristics other than access, location, and design attributes, which have already been rated in the subject and location analyses. The subject's competitors in the primary

Table 12.16
Summary of Survey of Competitive Retail Space

Existing	Size (in Sq. Ft.)	Occupied Sq. Ft.	Vacancy Rate	Quoted Rental Rate	Typical Tenants
Area A Center 2	120,000	114,000	5%	$10 to $12	•Grocery anchor •Convenience
Center 1 (Subject)	55,000	44,000	20%	$10 to $12	•Grocery •Restaurants •Variety/junior department
Area B Center 3	75,000	71,250	5%	$10 to $12	•Hardware •Variety/junior department •Grocery
Area C CBD	150,000	120,000	20%	$ 8 to $10	•Department store (shopper goods) •Specialty
Area D Highway strip	350,000	330,000	5%	$ 9 to $11	•Grocery •Discount store •Restaurants •Specialty •Convenience
Total	750,000	679,250	10%		
Proposed					
Area A Estimated competitive space	75,000				•Restaurants •Shopping •Automotive •Convenience
Area E Estimated competitive space in proposed mall and anticipated satellite, first five years	300,000				•Department store (shopper goods) •Discount store •Specialty store
Total	375,000				

Note: The survey includes only major retail centers or clusters and the neighborhood centers cited above. Small convenience centers, small stand-alone retail space, and noncompetitive specialty retail space such as auto dealers are not included.

trade area are inventoried and rated against the subject using the following criteria: 1) size, 2) quality of merchandise sold, 3) image, 4) current vacant space, 5) rental rates, 6) tenant mix, and 7) reputation and merchandising characteristics of anchor. For share-of-the-market analysis, a rating is assigned to each center in the geographic area where demand data are forecast. For rent and expense analysis in the income approach, citywide competition is considered.

Application of Step 4.2

A detailed rating of the subject's primary competition, Center 2, is presented in Table 12.17. The rating is based on both qualitative and quantitative analyses. The quantitative technique applied employs a scoring system like the system previously used to rate the property against current industry standards. In this analysis, however, the subject becomes the focus of comparison and is assigned a base score of 5. The scoring is done on a seven-point scale, rating each characteristic of the competition as highly inferior (0), moderately inferior (2), slightly inferior (4), same as subject (5), slightly superior (6), moderately superior (8), or highly superior (10). The weighting procedure described previously is again applied with the largest scores assigned to items judged to have the most impact.

Center 2, which is across the street from the subject, is the only competitive center in the subject's primary trade area. This center scored 128 in the quantitative ratings. Qualitatively, Center 2 rates as moderately superior to the subject because in five characteristics it was judged superior and in only one characteristic, inferior. The drawing power of its anchor was judged to be a most significant factor, and thus a highly superior rating was assigned. The 115 score of the subject (23 factors x 5) compared to the competitor's score of 128 suggests that the competitor is approximately 10% superior (11.3% to be exact).

The superior rating and the financial incentive provided by the slightly lower rents of the competitor appear to explain the competitor's higher occupancy. The subject may need to lower its rents to stay competitive. A final opinion on this matter is left for the appraiser's reconciliation.

Final Thoughts on Analysis of the Competition

Rating the subject in comparison to the competition may be accomplished in several ways. Level C and D analyses usually call for quantification and documentation. The end results of competitive analysis include:

1. An estimate of the square footage of specific competition (This estimate is needed to calculate marginal demand.)
2. An estimate of the market rent the subject can expect to generate in the current market
3. A comparative ranking of the subject

Table 12.17

Rating of Primary Competition Compared to Subject

	Subject	Comparable 2
Gross leasable area *(GLA)*	55,000 sq. ft.	120,000 sq. ft.
Occupancy	80%	95%
Financial data comparison—rental rate and terms		
Actual	$8 to $11/sq. ft.	$6 to $10/sq. ft.
Reported	$10 to $12/sq. ft.	$10 to $12/sq. ft.
CAM rate	$1.50/sq. ft.	$1.50/sq. ft.
Rent concessions	none	1 month free
Tenant finish allowance	$9/sq. ft.	$7 to $10/sq. ft.

Comparison Rating	Comparable 2 Qualitative Rating	Comparable 2 Quantitative Rating
Location		
Proximity to major highway	similar	5
Proximity to residential housing	similar	5
Proximity to other sources of customers	similar	5
Traffic volume by site	similar	5
Parking		
Number of spaces	similar	5
Adequacy	similar	5
Exterior access	slightly superior	6
Curb cuts	similar	5
Landscaping	inferior	4
Visibility	slightly superior	6
Building improvements		
Exterior appearance	similar	5
Signage	similar	5
Design flexibility	superior	6
Tenant mix and marketing features		
Anchor size	superior	8
Anchor drawing power	highly superior	10
Tenant compatibility mix	similar	5
Image of center	moderately superior	8
Shopper shop-to-shop access	similar	5
Shopper car-to-shop access	similar	5
Amenity features	similar	5
Quality of merchandise	similar	5
Marketing programs	similar	5
Legal constraints and opportunities	similar	5
Total		128

Note: Subject base score is 23 items x 5 = 115

STEP 5 ANALYZE MARKET EQUILIBRIUM
OR DISEQUILIBRIUM

The purpose of the market analysis section of an appraisal is to identify the subject market and the subject's ability to capture a share of that market. The various steps in the analysis contribute information that will be used to answer these questions. One additional analysis is required—the residual demand analysis or marginal demand analysis,[23] which identifies the phase of the supply and demand cycle that the overall market is currently experiencing. This determination is useful to the final step, in which the analyst assembles various blocks of market data and forms a judgment concerning the subject's market share.

Step 5.1 Estimate residual or marginal demand

Residual or marginal demand is estimated by comparing the inventory of existing and anticipated competitive supply against the estimate of current and potential demand. The prospective date when marginal demand will register in the market corresponds to the point when all available and projected retail space will have been absorbed, thus opening a window of opportunity for new development as well as rent and occupancy increases.

Application of Step 5.1

The appraiser compares the estimate of supportable retail space with the existing and projected supply to gauge marginal demand. Table 12.18 describes the demand-supply situation.

These calculations of marginal demand suggest that the market will have an oversupply during the next one to two years, but should then register positive marginal demand for the next three to seven years. The table also indicates the possibility of another oversupply situation in five to 10 years. This marginal demand forecast will be used in the subject capture (share-of-the-market) analysis and in the valuation models—e.g., as support for the market conditions adjustment, the projected rent increase in the DCF analysis, and the estimate of economic obsolescence.

STEP 6 FORECAST SUBJECT CAPTURE

Retail capture is extremely difficult to forecast due to the dynamic nature of retailing. Consumer tastes and preferences can change rapidly and the effect on retail property is immediate. Change in office and housing markets tends to be felt more gradually. The capture rate is not only difficult to estimate, but it is one of the three most sensitive variables in the analysis. (The other two highly sensitive variables are the population forecast and the estimate of sales retention

---

23. This type of analysis may be called *residual analysis, gap analysis,* or *net demand analysis.*

Table 12.18
Marginal Demand Analysis

	Current	In 5 Yrs.	In 10 Yrs.
Estimate of supportable retail space in primary and secondary trade areas adjusted according to the vacancy rate for the market (5%)	167,595 sq. ft.	213,888 sq. ft.	216,079 sq. ft.
Deduct existing competitive retail space in Area A	175,000 sq. ft.	175,000 sq. ft.	175,000 sq. ft.
Deduct projected retail space in Area A		0	75,000 sq. ft.*
Marginal demand point estimate (supply excess) or supply shortfall in square feet	(7,405)	38,888	(33,921)
Probable range in square feet		35,000 to 43,000	(30,500) to (37,000)

* Center 7: 100,000 sq. ft. with an estimated 25% oriented to highway commercial

in the trade area.) As with other sensitive variables, use of a variety of techniques is recommended. The final capture rate estimate is derived by reconciling the results of alternative techniques into a probable range.

Level A and B analyses rely on an estimate of inferred demand. In Level C and D capture analyses, inferred methods are augmented with fundamental forecast data and specific quantifiable rating data.

Step 6.1 Analyze capture by inferred methods

The inferred demand data presented here include the following facts:

- In its first three years of operation, the subject achieved 95% occupancy, but in the last year occupancy has fallen to 80%.
- Comparable properties show occupancy rates of 90% to 95%, with the most competitive center across the street operating at 95% occupancy.
- Secondary data indicate that citywide occupancies have been 80% for all retail space and 90% for retail space of the subject type.
- Economic base and general growth trends suggest that the general economic outlook for the city is good. Population is forecast to increase at a healthy rate of 4% to 6%. The subject is located in the general direction of growth, although slightly on the fringe.

Step 6.2 Forecast capture by fundamental methods

The Market Outlook (Residual or Marginal Demand Study)

In Step 5 the analyst forecast an oversupply of competitive retail space for the next two years. The five-year forecast indicated strong marginal demand. This suggests the next phase of the market cycle in which the subject will be competing. The following analysis of the subject's specific capture or market share incorporates this market outlook.

Quantitative Ratings

Three quantitative ratings have been derived up to this point in the market analysis. First, in terms of current industry standards, the subject was rated slightly inferior. Second, when the subject and its locational attributes were rated against the citywide competition, the subject's location was rated the best currently, but only second best in five years. Finally, when the subject was compared to its main competition in the primary trade area, it was rated 10% inferior.

Each analytic technique produced its own conclusions. In each, the subject was ranked using different comparative data and varying levels of detail. The initial analysis identified attributes of the subject that were above or below average. The second analysis examined the relative strength of the subject's location. This test is important because real estate is extremely location-sensitive. If the subject's location is poor, leakage can be expected to increase and the subject's future capture may be weak. The third analysis assessed the relative strength of the subject compared to its primary competition. Each quantitative analysis conducted builds on the previous analysis. These consecutive ratings form a foundation for the final capture analysis.

Capture Estimate by the Size-of-the-Center Technique

The next step in the capture analysis is called the *share-of-the-market* or *size-of-the-center technique*. This method is based, in part, on Reilly's law, which states that the drawing power of a center is directly proportional to its size. According to this theory, if a center has 100,000 square feet and its existing competition has 500,000 square feet, the first center should draw a 17% share of the market (100,000 ÷ 600,000).

Of course, the base estimate of subject capture must be adjusted for several factors.[24] For example, if the subject property were a proposed project or a new center with low occupancy, its estimated share of the market would have to be adjusted for the time it would need to become established in the market. It might achieve a 25% share in the first year, a 28% share in the second, and a 31% share in the third. The relationship between the primary and secondary trade

---

24. Rocca, 25-30.

areas would also be considered. For a center to achieve an overall market share of 25% in the first year, it might have to capture 50% of all purchases in its primary trade area and 25% of purchases in its secondary trade area.

Two other possible factors to adjust for are the correspondence between the market areas of the subject and its competitors and any unique features that diminish the comparability of the subject and its competitors. If a competitor serves an area larger than the subject's market area, the estimate of the competitor's capture must be adjusted to be consistent. Moreover, the base for the data employed in the demand calculations must match the base for the data on the competition. This pertains to both the geographic area and the character of the retail product.

Matching the data on which the percentage spent at the subject center is based with the square footage of space inventoried for the competition provides a specific example. Assume that the subject is a community-type center that competes with a large discount store. Not all of the space in the discount store is competitive with the subject space. The discount store probably provides auto services and stocks appliances as well as many other shopping goods. These categories were excluded from the calculations used to identify the subject trade area. Thus it is reasonable to exclude the square footage in these centers devoted to noncompetitive retail sales from the inventory of the competition. Unique center characteristics such as design and amenities may also necessitate adjustments.

Application of the Size-of-the-Center Technique

The subject center contains 55,000 square feet of space and the existing competitors contain 120,000 square feet. Therefore, the subject represents 31% (55,000 ÷ 175,000) of the effective retail space in the primary trade area.

In the subject case, the need for some adjustment is apparent. Based on its size, the subject should be capturing 31% of the market. Previously the subject's actual capture was a fair (proportional) share of the market, but its current capture is slightly less than a fair share. Consider the following calculations:

Currently occupied space in Area A	= 158,000 sq.ft.
Occupied space in subject (at 80% occupancy)	= 44,000 sq. ft.
Subject capture	= 27.8% capture

The fair share method indicates that the subject should currently capture 31% of the actual, occupied, supportable retail space demanded in the subject's primary and secondary markets. However, in the analysis of competitive supply the subject was rated 10% inferior. Thus, the 27% capture range indicated by the adjusted fair share method may be the best estimate obtainable.

Now the analyst must consider the future, when the proposed center is scheduled to be built. If we assume that 50,000 to 75,000 square feet of retail space in the new center will be competitive with the subject, then the subject's fair share drops to between 22% and 24%. If we incorporate the findings of the competitive analysis that rated the subject to be 10% inferior to the competition, the fair share capture rate for the subject drops to between 20% and 22%.

Capture Analysis by the Ratio Method

The demand analysis revealed that the current ratio of occupied retail space per capita was 15 square feet per person citywide. The ratio method may be used to check the results of the size-of-the-center method since the ratio method segments demand to the subject center only. Demand that is being met by small, stand-alone satellite stores is not a part of the demand ratio and, therefore, an examination of this ratio reduces the potential for error in the subject capture forecast.

This method begins with the citywide population which is forecast to be 57,000 in five years. Utilizing the 15:1 ratio, citywide demand in five years should increase to about 855,000 square feet of major retail center space. The current supply citywide is only 750,000 square feet and no new space is planned in the next five years. The subject area is currently rated as the best in town. Therefore the city in general, and the subject in particular, should experience very good occupancy rates and rising rents.

The good market conditions of the next five years are forecast to change in the later part of the decade with the opening of the new mall south of the subject and the new center close to the subject. Both centers are scheduled to come on line in about five years. The population in 10 years is forecast at about 73,000. At 15 square feet of retail space per capita, demand for competitive retail space 10 years out is approximately 1,095,000 square feet. By this time, competitive space citywide is expected be about 1,150,000 square feet, so the market in general should still be good.

This may not be the picture for the subject, however. The subject area will be the second best in town after the opening of the new mall. In the quantitative location rating, the subject area, Area A, received a 20% capture rate. This would suggest that, in 10 years, there would be demand in the subject area for 219,000 square feet (1,095,000 x 20%) of space. By this time, Area A is expected to have 250,000 square feet of competitive space (see Table 12.18). This would give Area A an occupancy rate of about 88%. Because the subject was rated 10% inferior to the competition in Area A, its occupancy would likely be less than 88%, perhaps approximately 80%.

Step 6.3 Reconcile subject capture indications

Now the ratings and other results of the analyses must be reconciled. This process is similar to the appraiser's reconciliation of the value indications derived from the three approaches to value or the adjustment of comparable sale prices in the sales comparison approach. The appraiser forms a judgment based on the most reliable data. In a Level C or D fundamental analysis, additional techniques are employed beyond the general inferred methods used in Level A and B analyses. These fundamental methods provide the best means of arriving at a final judgment for reconciliation.

Residual analysis can be used to check the results of inferred methods as well as fundamental methods. Residual analysis provides an estimate of the sales remaining after all sales allocated to competitive facilities have been deducted. In an oversupplied or undersupplied market, more weight may be given to fundamental methods; in a relatively stable market, more consideration may be given to inferred methods.

Application of Step 6.3

This chapter has presented several techniques which, taken together, constitute an incremental approach to capture analysis. Table 12.19 summarizes the techniques applied and the conclusions reached.

Table 12.19
Summary of Capture Analyses

Analytical Technique	Conclusion
1. Property rating	Subject is slightly inferior to industry standard. The quantitative estimate is 12% inferior.
2. Location and competition rating	Subject is currently considered the best location in the city. In five years it should rate as the second best retail area citywide.
3. Primary competition rating	As one of two centers at this location, the subject is rated 10% inferior.
4. Supply survey analysis	
Citywide	90% occupancy
Primary competition	95% occupancy
5. Residual analysis	The market is characterized as moderately competitive for the next five years and highly competitive once the new mall adjacent to the center is completed.
6. Size-of-the-center analysis	31% capture of Area A demand
7. Current capture rate of subject	27% capture of Area A demand
8. Estimated future capture rate of subject	20% to 22% capture of Area A demand when new competition comes on line.

Conclusion of Capture Forecast

The subject does not appear to be capturing its fair share of the market. There are several possible reasons for this situation. The subject may have management problems, which would account for its poor merchandising record, inefficient service personnel, and costly merchandise. Alternatively, the competition may have very superior features which were not properly weighted in the rating analysis. For example, the competitive center across the street or a center in another part of town may have an especially dominant anchor store.

The appraiser cannot assume highly superior or inferior management; rather, the appraisal report should accurately reflect current conditions. One possible forecast is that if the current management is poor, it will improve in the future. This assumption might logically coincide with the more favorable market conditions two years out, which were forecast in the marginal demand analysis. Thus the income capitalization approach might logically project a capture rate of approximately 30% in two years. This higher capture rate might be further supported by the good, short-term location rating if the appraiser feels the data are reliable. The long-term capture rate will probably be lower, however, because competition will most likely increase significantly.

Also contributing to the subject's low capture rate are the rents for the subject, which are above market levels. So far rent levels have not been considered in detail. The income capitalization section of an appraisal report will usually include a detailed rent and expense analysis, which should support the appraiser's final judgment as to the subject's rents and, in turn, capture. The above conclusions may, therefore, be considered only tentative, pending the completion of additional steps in the appraisal. When the three approaches to value are applied later in the appraisal, the appraiser may refine these early conclusions before estimating a final capture rate for the subject.

Table 12.20 summarizes and concludes the capture estimate.

In this example, more weight was given to the fundamental analysis because it best accounts for new competition and the limited nature of total market demand.

Use of Conclusions

These conclusions are pivotal to the appraisal. They can be used to test alternative highest and best uses and provide forecasts required for the valuation models. In this case, alternative uses were unlikely, given the high occupancy of the subject and the absence of any indicated demand for an alternative use.

This market study will furnish the forecast needed to perform DCF analysis in the income approach. The conclusions of the residual or marginal demand study will be used in the sales comparison approach to adjust sales for market conditions as of the date of the appraisal. The quantitative ratings of the subject property's attributes are also useful in sales comparison. In the cost approach the analyst makes use of data from the residual or marginal demand study to estimate economic obsolescence. Lastly and most important, market analysis pro-

Table 12.20
Capture Estimate Conclusion

| Conclusions of Study Parts | Most Probable Subject Occupancy Conclusion | | | |
| | 0 - 5 Years | | 6 to 10 Years | |
	Occupancy	Rents	Occupancy	Rents
Trend (Inferred) Methods				
•Subject history: 80% to 95%	87%	Rising	90%	Rising
•Comparable across street: 95%	95%	Rising	95%	Rising
•Citywide occupancy: 90%	90%	Stable to rising	90%	Stable to rising
•Economic base good: 4% to 6% population growth	Rising	Rising	Rising	Rising
Fundamental Methods				
•Market conditions indicated by residual or marginal demand	Rising	Rising	Falling	Falling
•Quantifiable capture: 27% to 30% In 5 yrs., total occupied demand from trade area: 183,000 to 223,500 sq. ft.*	Occupancy rising to between 49,000 sq. ft. (90%) and 55,000 sq. ft. (100%)	Rising from market rate		
In +10 yrs., total occupied demand from trade area at 20% to 22% capture: 185,000 to 226,000 sq. ft.			Falling to between 37,000 sq. ft. (67%) and 49,720 sq. ft. (90%)	Falling
Final reconciled point estimate conclusion	87% average	Stable	80%	Falling

* The demand figures shown in Table 12.14 were 203,194 sq. ft. in Year 5 and 205,790 sq. ft. in Year 10. Table 12.14 was a mid-range forecast. This table includes the high and low ends of the range.

vides a basis for reconciliation, helping the appraiser judge the applicability and reliability of each valuation approach in light of the appraisal problem and the market conditions prevailing on the date of the appraisal.

THE MARKET ANALYSIS PROCESS
FOR AN EXISTING OFFICE BUILDING

—>•0•<—

- Analyze property productivity.

- Delineate the market of property users.

- Forecast demand.

- Measure competitive supply.

- Analyze market equilibrium/disequilibrium.

- Forecast subject capture.

CHAPTER THIRTEEN

⬦

Existing Office Building

This chapter presents a step-by-step procedure for analyzing the market for an office building as part of a valuation assignment. Recent developments in the office building market, basic concepts and terminology, and the analytical process are described. Then a case study application of the market analysis of an office building is presented as it might appear in an appraisal.

THE OFFICE BUILDING MARKET

In the past two decades, extensive office building development has occurred throughout the United States. The demand for new office space has been fueled by the expansion of the white-collar workforce, especially service sector jobs associated with business, finance, and the professions, and by the creation of employment opportunities in high-tech industries. This demand led to rapid office construction in the early 1980s and a surplus of office space in many American cities by the late 1980s.

Much of this new development has occurred in the suburbs. As recently as 10 years ago, development of office space in the suburbs was outpacing development in central business districts. In many areas office space was divided almost evenly, with about 45% of office space in the suburbs and 55% in the CBD. During the 1980s, however, this outward trend slowed in many cities because the rising cost of doing business in the suburbs had substantially reduced the savings achieved by moving out of the CBD. Suburban office space has become costlier over the past decade for several reasons: dramatic increases in rents relative to the rents charged for office space in CBDs, higher suburban real estate taxes to pay for infrastructure development, and higher wages to attract workers with the requisite skills. Suburban traffic congestion has become an irritant for commuters. Moreover, cities have started to offer corporations incentives to remain in the CBD.[1]

The distinctions between urban and suburban markets, which were once considered separate and competitive, seem to be fading. A three-tiered office market has emerged.[2] The first tier consists of companies that wish to maintain high visibility and seek the convenience of a central business location. Financial institutions; investment brokerages; and advertising, public relations, legal, and accounting firms are often willing to pay high rents for prime office space.

The second tier of the market includes cost-conscious tenants who do not require high visibility and firms that decide to separate their operations, locating certain office functions in the suburbs while keeping management downtown. Electronic linkages make such a separation possible. Satellite offices also allow these firms to recruit from the suburban workforce.

The third tier is composed of companies seeking a hedge against inflationary increases in operating costs. These firms often hold full or partial equity in their office space. Small firms may have condominium ownership of the office space they occupy, while larger firms often share the equity position with a developer.

A forecast of the market for office space made by the Urban Land Institute[3] in 1982 seems equally valid today. Location, access, and the availability of support facilities were identified as key elements in channeling market demand.

> The office space market will continue to be strongest in larger central business districts with effective mass transportation and in established suburban nodes where infrastructure and amenities are already in place. There will be fewer remote suburban office parks due in part to three major reasons: energy availability, transportation costs, and the lack of sewer and water capacity.

The prognosis developed by the Urban Land Institute also included extensive redevelopment of existing office space.

> Older office buildings in good locations will be rehabilitated... since these buildings were created with less costly capital, modernized space in them can often be marketed at much lower rents than new space. Many such structures can be refurbished with efficient and attractive space truly competitive with new buildings.

---

1. Ian Alexander, *Office Location and Public Policy* (New York: The Chancer Press, 1979) and *Chicago Tribune*, September 13, 1989.
2. Urban Land Institute, *Office Development Handbook* (Washington, D.C.: ULI, 1982), 213-214.
3. Ibid, 214-216.

Due to overbuilding and the changing lending criteria of the 1990s, these forecast trends are becoming apparent in many markets.[4]

CONCEPTS AND TERMINOLOGY

Market analysis for an office building requires the segmentation of demand and supply. The terms and concepts used in this segmentation are described below.

User or tenant categories

The market for office space may be subdivided according to the users, or tenants, who occupy office buildings. The institutional/professional category includes banks, insurance companies, and investment firms which generally occupy prime downtown office space. Accounting and law firms may also require offices in the highly visible buildings of a CBD. Central business districts may be the traditional downtown areas of older cities. In many metro areas, however, suburban nodes have developed to such a degree that they are functioning as CBDs. The general commercial category of office space comprises smaller buildings occupied by firms that have a strong sales orientation and require convenient automobile access and adequate parking facilities for both workers and clientele. Medical and dental offices are usually located in professional buildings, often near hospitals or residential areas that account for their patient base. Government offices are centrally located in or near city halls, civic centers, courthouses, and county seats. They may be owned or leased by the municipality or the county. Industrial space includes pure industrial office space, which is actually part of a manufacturing plant; quasi-industrial office buildings that are located in industrial parks, but house high-tech firms; and research and development space for industries unrelated to manufacturing.

Multitenant versus Owner-Occupant

Office buildings are also segmented into multitenant and owner-occupant offices. Owner-occupant space is usually associated with another use such as an office in a manufacturing plant.

---

4. From a more recent perspective, Anthony Downs writes "because the general economic expansion of the 1980s had an unprecedented length, so did the boom phase of the office space development cycle. Unfortunately, that length contributed to the creation of a massive supply of office space and other commercial real estate space that will overshadow activity levels in most U.S. markets for at least the first half of the 1990s. Even so, by closely observing the many factors influencing office space activity levels, participants in those markets will be able to anticipate when an overbuilt phase will end, to be inevitably replaced by a gradual absorption phase, and ultimately by another boom phase." "Cycles in Office Space Markets," *The Office Building: From Concept to Investment Reality*, John Robert White, ed., a joint publication of the Counselors of Real Estate, the Appraisal Institute, and the Society of Industrial and Office Realtors® Educational Fund, Chicago, 1993.

Classes of office buildings

Office buildings can be differentiated qualitatively by their location, construction, condition, management, tenants, and amenities.[5] Class A space is characterized by excellent location and access. It attracts high-quality tenants and is professionally managed. Class A space offers numerous amenities and support facilities such as restaurants, hotels, and retail stores. The construction materials and design of Class A buildings are also of good quality, and the condition of the building is good to excellent. Rent for Class A space is competitive with the rents for space in new buildings.

Class B buildings have good location, management, and construction. Tenant standards are high, but rents are lower than rents for space in newly constructed buildings. Class B buildings may suffer some physical deterioration or functional obsolescence. Class C buildings are generally older (15 to 25 years). With reasonably high occupancy levels, Class C buildings are still part of the active supply of office space. Older buildings may have to be brought into compliance with current building codes, but they often suffer considerable physical deterioration and functional obsolescence. In addition to these three classes of office buildings, rehabilitated buildings constitute a separate category. Restoration can return a building to a satisfactory condition without changing the floor plan, form, or style of the structure.

The actual segmentation of Class A, B, and C space is market-specific. For example, the Class A buildings in Dallas, Texas, may exceed Class A standards in Austin. It is imperative that the appraiser classify demand and supply in the subject market consistently.

Segmenting the office study

The classification of office space provides a framework for analyzing the supply of competitive office buildings within the overall metropolitan area as well as the specific district or node in which the subject property is located. An appraiser should identify the percentage of office space of each class within both the metropolitan area and the subject node. Generally buildings compete with other buildings in the same class. Thus an oversupply of Class A space will have a far greater effect on new office construction than excess space in Class B or C buildings.

The configuration of the overall office market must also be considered. In prosperous times some tenants may move up from Class B to Class A space or from Class C to Class B space. (When a firm moves, it will generally rent or buy 10% to 20% more space than it currently occupies.) This phenomenon is known as *move-up demand*. In some overbuilt markets, excess Class A space may impact Class B space—i.e., the surplus of Class A space may reduce the income prospects for Class B buildings. Rents in Class B buildings will have to be lowered in re-

---

5. Urban Land Institute, 18-19.

sponse to the surplus of Class A space, or additional costs will have to be incurred to ensure that Class B buildings remain competitive.

A 1:2 ratio seems reasonable in many cities: one Class A building for every two Class B or C buildings. If the ratio of Class A space to other space is 1:4 or greater, the market may soon be able to absorb twice the current amount of Class A space and achieve a more typical ratio.[6]

Office space per employee

Another consideration in office building analysis is the amount of space required per office worker. The amount of office space per worker varies with the industry, the rank of the employee, the state of the economy, and current rental rates. Typical standards for office space are: 220 square feet per worker in high-tech industries; 200 square feet per employee in offices associated with manufacturing and distribution; and 136 square feet per employee in financial and governmental offices.[7]

Broken down by employee rank, the average space allotment per general office worker is 65 to 80 square feet; per supervisor, 100 to 120 square feet; per administrative assistant, 150 square feet; per executive assistant, 300 square feet; and per executive, 400 to 500 square feet. The Building Owners and Managers Association (BOMA) considers 175 to 200 square feet per office worker an average area requirement. Until recently, the amount of office space per worker was increasing. Current ratios are expected to remain relatively stable or to decline in response to rising building costs and rents. According to some corporate executives, the cost of office space must get back to what it was in the 1960s and 1970s, when the space allotment was 150 square feet per employee.[8]

The ratio of office space per worker must be estimated separately for each specific market since supply and demand, economic conditions, and industry needs vary in different market areas and are continually changing. The problem is compounded for appraisers who must use the ratio in the forecast of office space demand, which usually covers a 10-year period. This extended period means that the forecast must reflect successive office market cycles. During periods of overbuilding, space per employee usually goes up; when space is scarce, the amount allotted per employee usually declines.

Office building terms

Key office building terms are defined below.

Gross building area. The total floor area of a building measured from the exterior of the walls, including below-grade space but excluding unenclosed areas.

---

6. Ibid., 18.
7. Ibid., 69, and *Office Space Supply Study*, Technical Report 978, Texas A&M Real Estate Center, February 1993.
8. "Office Tenants Face Squeeze Play," *Dallas Morning News*, December 6, 1991.

Rentable area. The tenant's pro rata share of the entire office, excluding elements of the building that penetrate through the floor to areas below such as stairs and elevators. Measurement of the rentable area varies with the locality. In tight markets, more area is included as rentable.

Rented area. The amount of space under lease(s) in a building.

Usable area/space. The amount of area or space that can be occupied by tenants. Usable space can vary over the life of the building.

Efficiency ratio. The rentable area (the space used and occupied by tenants) divided by the gross building area (total building area measured from the exterior of the walls, including below-grade space but excluding unenclosed areas).

THE MARKET ANALYSIS PROCESS FOR AN OFFICE BUILDING

An overview of the market analysis process applied in this office building application is presented in Table 13.1. The basic six-step process includes: 1) an analysis of the productivity of the subject property, 2) a delineation of the market of property users, 3) an estimate of existing and anticipated demand, 4) an inventory of competitive supply, 5) an analysis of market equilibrium, and 6) the capture estimate for the subject. Each of the six steps is further divided into substeps. The results of the six-step process are applied in the appraisal, in testing highest and best use alternatives, and in the three approaches to value. The case study example follows the sequence described.

The market analysis process is not static. It varies with the availability of data, the techniques chosen by the appraiser, and the changing conditions of the market. For example, different techniques might be used to analyze markets of differing size. Demand is typically estimated on a citywide basis, but capture estimates will vary with city size and the growth pattern for office complexes. In large metropolitan areas, demand is usually segmented to reflect the specific node and building class. For a smaller city, the appraiser may forecast demand and analyze competitive buildings citywide. In this case, demand is not segmented to a specific node, but only to the class of competitive buildings.

The case study property is located in a larger metropolitan area with an established CBD and two suburban office building nodes. To obtain an estimate of subject capture, aggregate demand is segmented by means of three different ratings: a preliminary rating of the site and building relative to the typical competition and/or industry standards (Step 1.2), a rating of the office building nodes in the metropolitan area (Step 1.3(1)), and a rating of the subject compared to competitive buildings in the same node (Step 4.2).

CASE STUDY DESCRIPTION

The following application is a Level C market analysis for the appraisal of an existing office building. An alternative use for the subject is not being considered. The purpose of the study is to support 1) the future rent and occupancy

Table 13.1
Market Analysis Process for an Existing Office Building

Step 1   Analyze property productivity

1.1   Identify the type of office building by tenancy and class.

1.2   Analyze the site and building. Rate the subject in relation to the typical competition and/or the industry standard.

1.3   Analyze the location.

    1.3(1)   Analyze the macro location. Identify the clusters or nodes of office buildings within the metropolitan matrix and the pattern of urban growth. Rate the cluster or node in which the subject is located relative to other competitive clusters or nodes within the metropolitan area in terms of land use linkages and the direction and rate of urban growth.

    1.3(2)   Analyze the micro location of the subject, i.e., the characteristics of the subject's location within its node.

Step 2   Delineate the market of property users

2.1   Identify the market of property users by studying the tenants in the building and the clientele they draw. Most office markets do not have a contiguous market area; the market area is generally diffused over a broad metropolitan area. The tenancy and clientele will vary with the character of the cluster or node.

Step 3   Forecast demand

3.1   Conduct trend analysis using inferred methods.

3.2   Conduct fundamental analysis using segmentation method.

    3.2(1)   Forecast the workforce occupying office space. Forecast employment by occupational category and multiply this figure by the percentage of employees in each category occupying office space.

    3.2(2)   Estimate the size of the workforce occupying space in the subject's class of office building. Multiply the figure derived in Step 3.2(1) by the specific percentage for that class of building.

    3.2(3)   Estimate the requisite space per office worker.

    3.2(4)   Calculate the demand for the specific class of office space by multiplying the number derived in Step 3.2(2) by the figure derived in Step 3.2(3).

    3.2(5)   Adjust demand for the "normal" vacancy rate.

3.3   Conduct fundamental analysis by the ratio method.

3.4   Reconcile the results of the various methods applied and forecast demand.

Step 4   Measure competitive supply

4.1   Inventory current competitive supply. This will include office building space within the subject's building class as well as competitive buildings that are under construction and proposed. The competitive supply inventory may also be affected by demolitions, renovations, and the adaptation of space under other uses to office use.

4.2   Analyze competitive supply. Rate the subject against competitive properties within the same cluster or node.

Step 5   Analyze market equilibrium/disequilibrium

5.1   Compare supply and demand to determine marginal demand.

Step 6   Forecast subject capture

6.1   Derive a preliminary (inferred) estimate of subject capture. Analyze the competitiveness of the subject vis-a-vis the competition in view of the marginal demand forecast. Examine historical occupancy rates for the subject and competition against historical marginal demand.

6.2   Derive a capture rate for the subject by fundamental analysis. Reconcile the competitive rating in Step 4.2 with the inferred capture rate of the subject derived in Step 6.1.

6.3   Reconcile subject capture indications.

Note the numbering system employed in the six-step process. Substeps are indicated with sequential numbers in parentheses. Thus, Step 3.2 is followed by Steps 3.2(1), 3.2(2), 3.2(3), etc.

forecast needed in the income approach, 2) the adjustments made to comparable sale properties from different markets in the sales comparison approach, and 3) the estimate of economic obsolescence (if relevant) in the cost approach. Thus the appraiser must forecast the demand for Class A space and estimate the share of this demand that the subject will likely capture over the next 10 years.

The subject is a five-year-old, 100,000-sq.-ft., multitenanted, Class A office building in the CBD of a town of 180,000. The town has experienced steady growth over the past decade and this growth is expected to continue. The building houses institutional/professional, general commercial, and quasi-industrial tenants.

The stable central business district where the subject is located is one of three office nodes in the city. The central business district contains banking institutions, investment and accounting firms, law offices, advertising and public relations agencies, and municipal offices leased by the city. Class A office buildings account for 15% of the buildings in the CBD; Class B space makes up 40%; and the remaining 45% is Class C space. A combination of retail buildings, a courthouse, two hospitals, a sports complex, a public library, and a newspaper office give the CBD its diversity. Although it is not characterized by dynamic growth, the CBD may be considered a stable area with good potential for long-term redevelopment.

A node of office buildings associated with a regional shopping center is located southwest of the CBD. The office buildings contain professional offices with typical tenants that include physicians, dentists, financial planners, and real estate agents. Half of these are Class A office buildings while the other half is Class B space. A node to the northeast contains offices that house computer operations for companies that have management headquarters in the central business district. High-tech and research and development firms are located here. Most of the buildings are single-tenanted office buildings; a few are multitenant buildings. About half are Class A and the other half are Class B buildings.

STEP 1 ANALYZE PROPERTY PRODUCTIVITY

Step 1.1 Identify the type of office building by tenancy and class

As stated in the case study description, the subject is a Class A office building with institutional/professional, general commercial, and quasi-industrial tenants.

Step 1.2 Analyze the site and building

A preliminary rating is developed by comparing the subject office building to the typical competition and/or the industry standard. The purpose of this rating is to assess the subject building's major strengths and weaknesses. In this step of the analysis the appraiser focuses on the subject building; ratings are also derived in location analysis and supply analysis. Besides providing a general understanding of the subject property, the preliminary rating helps identify the characteristics to look for in determining which properties constitute the competitive supply. Subsequent ratings will enable the appraiser to estimate subject capture and to segment demand by location and building class.

The subject should be analyzed to assess how it compares to the competition today and in the near future. The overall productivity of an office building depends on the successful integration of diverse components into an efficient product. These components include physical items such as building design and construction materials as well as nonphysical items such as management and the reputation of building tenants. The following discussion highlights the factors to be considered in a typical office building analysis.[9]

Physical Items

Building design and construction materials. The structural and design features of office buildings are constantly changing in response to new technology and human preferences. In building design, flexibility and efficiency are critical. Flexibility refers to the adaptability of the space to changing tenant requirements. The efficiency of a building's layout is measured by the ratio of rentable area to gross building area. The higher the ratio, the greater the efficiency.

Signage. Signs are an integral part of the design of an office project. Poor signage reflects on the quality of the buildings. Functional exterior and interior signage is essential to direct pedestrian and vehicular traffic to and within the office complex.

Exterior lighting. Exterior lighting of the building(s), pedestrian walkways, and parking areas promotes public safety and enhances the image of the office complex.

Street layout. Access to the office building or office park is important and helps a building maintain a competitive advantage. The layout of the adjacent streets should readily accommodate vehicular traffic at peak hours.

Utilities. The availability and capacity of the utility lines providing service to a project are important factors in the property analysis. Fire codes often determine the size of the pipes that constitute the water system. The sprinkler system and adequacy of standpipes (for the attachment of long hoses) should also conform to building standards.

Sewage systems comprise sanitary and storm sewers. The capacity of the system and any user fees for sewer maintenance or disposal service should be considered.

The capacity of existing utilities to provide adequate electricity, gas, and telephone service should be investigated. Utility lines installed underground are gen-

---

9. The discussion of site and building attributes is based on material in the Urban Land Institute's *Office Building Handbook*, 45-85.

erally preferable to poles running along easements or within street rights-of-way. The maintenance and repair of underground lines will require excavation, so landscaping should be placed accordingly.

Parking. In urban areas the need for parking is tempered by the availability of mass transportation and the limited area of urban sites. In suburban areas on-site, surface parking is essential to the success of an office park. There is no standard indicator of the number of parking spaces required, but a general rule of thumb would allow four spaces for each 1,000 square feet of rentable area or approximately one space for every two employees. A ratio of 3.5 spaces per 1,000 square feet would be the absolute minimum unless public transportation is available to the site.

Lotting and building lines. In urban areas an office building typically covers 100% of the site at grade, although prestige buildings usually have some of the ground plane devoted to plazas, landscaping elements, or arcades. In suburban projects approximately 25% to 30% of the site is generally covered by the building. A typical, two-story garden office will have about 17,000 to 20,000 square feet of building area on one acre of land.

Landscaping and grading. Landscaping gives identity to a project and can impart a sense of unity to a complex that comprises uncoordinated buildings. Office developments are usually landscaped with plants that stabilize the soil and define the space around the buildings. Trees and shrubbery can be added to upgrade the image of a complex and enhances its value.

Grading is necessary to promote drainage, create a proper site for buildings, and enhance the aesthetic qualities of the land. Poorly graded surfaces are subject to erosion and the sedimentation produced by the effects of wind and water.

Office space layout. To be effective, the interior layout of the building must address five factors: the availability and placement of space, the users for whom the space is designed, the activity taking place in the space, the need to accommodate future change, and energy efficiency.

The availability of space is determined by fixed building elements—i.e., floor areas, ceiling heights, and the location of the building core and supporting columns. There are closed-office, open-office, and combination open- and closed-office layouts. The closed-office layout is the traditional office building design, characterized by closed offices located around a central building core. The open-office layout, in which partitions are used to create modular units, originated as a means to facilitate office design changes.

The subject building should be analyzed to determine if it addresses the specific needs of the tenants and the work flow patterns within and among the office departments. To accommodate a diversity of activities, offices must include conference rooms as well as private space. One contemporary example of a new activity necessitating design change is the use of computer terminals and electronic equipment, which increased tremendously during the 1980s.

Tenant finish. Tenant finish refers to the modifications or remodeling that a tenant requires before occupying leased space. Normally the cost of some changes is covered by the developer or landlord. When an office complex is under construction or space is re-leased, the developer usually makes some modifications free of charge. These changes, known as *building standard installation*, may include partitioning, painting, augmentation of the electrical capacity, and installation of various appointments (e.g., doors, hardware, acoustical ceilings, floor covering, lighting, electrical and telephone outlets, plumbing connections, closets, blinds, ducts for the HVAC system). The design of a building should be analyzed in terms of its ability to accommodate alteration. A building that is easily adapted to changing tenant needs has a competitive advantage over a building that is less adaptable.

Floor sizes. Optimum floor sizes in mid- and high-rise speculative office buildings can range from 16,000 to 30,000 square feet per floor. Since such buildings may be occupied by a single anchor tenant or multiple tenants, a floor area design that is flexible enough to accommodate both full-floor users and small-space users has a competitive advantage.

Stairways, corridors, and elevators. In a low-rise, garden office building, the stairway or escalator often creates a visitor's first impression of the building. Stairways should be well lighted and clean. Each floor should be marked on stairwell doors and a floor directory should be provided. Corridors must be maintained. The elevator service in mid- and high-rise buildings must meet the needs of the users. The elevators should be dependable and waiting time should not be excessive.

Electrical system. Electrical components need sufficient capacity to support the ever-increasing advances in technology being incorporated into office buildings.

Heating, ventilation, and air conditioning (HVAC). Generally HVAC equipment is accommodated in the space between the ceiling of one floor and the floor of the next. HVAC systems control the level of heat and cooling in the building's interior and perimeter space. Most systems divide a building into zones. The recommended standard is one thermostat zone for each 1,200 square feet of area. The criteria for replenishing office space with fresh air have been reduced in recent years to conserve energy. The recommended flow of outside air into general office space is approximately 0.15 cubic feet per minute per square foot.

Amenities. The support facilities provided in an office building or within walking distance give the building a competitive advantage. These facilities may include convenience retail stores, professional and business services, cafeterias and restaurants, transient lodging, conference halls, and physical fitness centers. Providing support facilities within a project contributes to tenant satisfaction. Other types of special amenities include cultural or aesthetic attractions such as prominently displayed art, special exhibits, and garden atriums.

Security. Tenant security may be considered a special amenity feature. Security includes both low-profile measures such as entry card systems and high-profile measures such as closed- circuit television and alarm systems. Security concerns are governed by the number of entrances and exits in the building, the absence or presence of fencing, the accessibility of the parking area, and the presence or absence of security personnel.

Nonphysical Items

Although the layout and physical condition of an office building are important considerations, nonphysical items such as building management and the quality and mix of tenants are equally significant.

Building management. Professional on-site management is generally preferable to off-site management. Most Class A buildings are managed onsite and, thus, have a competitive advantage over buildings with off-site management.

Tenant quality. A location near a building occupied by a major tenant such as a Fortune 500 company is a competitive advantage. This is attributable to the sense of prestige and stability that the market associates with long-term, major tenants and to the economic advantage of being able to serve such companies. Class A buildings are characterized by their long-term tenants.

Application of Step 1.2

The subject property contains 100,000 square feet of rentable area, has a high efficiency ratio, and is in excellent condition. Based on information gathered from a preliminary analysis of office buildings in the subject's class, the appraiser was able to rate the subject according to the property characteristics described above. Table 13.2 lists the factors used to rate the subject. In a Level C study, a quantitative method is generally applied to structure the analysis and help the reader follow the reasoning. In this case the subject was considered average in all categories and a rating of 5 was assigned for each factor. (For a more complete discussion of this rating method, refer to the shopping center application in Chapter 12.)

Step 1.3 Analyze the location

Because the demand for office space is diffused over a broad metropolitan area, the analysis must first consider the subject's macro location.

Step 1.3(1) Analyze the macro location

Macro location analysis encompasses the overall metropolitan matrix, reflecting urban growth patterns, the clusters or nodes of office buildings, and the quality of the vital linkages that connect these buildings to the community and support facilities. The analyst's objective is to identify the subject node and to determine how it compares to competitive office nodes now and in the future.

Table 13.2

Subject Office Building Rating

Comparison to Standard:		Inferior			Typical	Superior		
Rating Factors	Veto Factor	High	Mod.	Slight	Average	Slight	Mod.	High
Site								
Parking					X			
Access					X			
Visibility					X			
Proximity to support facilities					X			
Building								
Construction quality					X			
Design and exterior appearance					X			
Size (leasable area)					X			
Efficiency ratio					X			
Condition and effective age					X			
Obsolescence					X			
Quality of tenant finish					X			
Property Management and Tenancy								
Management					X			
Quality of tenants					X			
Number of items	0	0	0	0	13	0	0	0
Times category score (weighting)		0	2	4	5	6	8	10
Subtotal score					65			
Total subject score								65

Urban growth patterns are examined to discern the direction and rate of development. The appraiser investigates where office, retail, and residential growth has occurred in the last five to 10 years; where large public expenditures on infrastructure development have been made; and where future growth is most likely to occur.

In location analysis for office buildings, the metropolitan market is divided into clusters or nodes of office buildings. In most metropolitan areas, office buildings tend to cluster around established centers of economic activity or principal transportation arteries.[10] Office space is the primary property use in downtown business districts. Financial institutions, corporation headquarters, and government offices remain the anchors in most CBDs and ensure the CBD's viability. If these institutional, corporate, and municipal offices stay downtown, other tenants are likely to follow suit and the stability or growth of the CBD will continue.

Within a metropolitan area, additional nodes may form and relieve congestion in the CBD. An uptown node is such an area. Uptowns result from an intra-urban shift. Often this type of node is located along an arterial that provides access to the suburbs. Its shape is likely to be linear, reflecting the importance of the artery along which it has developed.

Another type of node accommodates a specialized activity. Offices serving attorneys and title companies often cluster around major government buildings such as courts and public record repositories. Medical offices tend to be found near hospital complexes, assuring doctors easy access to patients. University areas attract research and development firms that seek proximity to technical expertise and laboratory facilities. Companies that depend on air service may rent space in office buildings near airports.

Office parks house tenants oriented toward research and development activity or local manufacturing. Major corporations without local connections may choose to locate in office parks to take advantage of their attractive park-like surroundings or an especially enticing rental offer negotiated with the developer.

Shopping centers are nodes of activity that support office building development. They may be especially attractive to tenants with modest space requirements. Generally the users of such offices serve the needs of the residential households within the trade area of the shopping center.

Application of Step 1.3(1)

The three office nodes in the city are rated in terms of their competitiveness. The node in which the subject property is located may be ranked against competitive nodes for its quality of linkages, ease of access, reputation, and visibility and for the availability of support facilities. The appraiser focuses on the time workers and management must spend commuting to the buildings in the node, traffic conditions, proximity to mass transit systems and airports, proximity to clients or

---

10. This discussion has been adapted from John McMahan's *Property Development: Effective Decision Making in Uncertain Times* (New York: McGraw-Hill, 1976), 182-183.

associated facilities such as courthouses and hospitals, nuisances in the area, any scenic or natural advantages that the node may possess, and the size of the node, which strongly affects its drawing power.

Based on information about the three competitive office building nodes, the appraiser was able to assign the macro-locational ratings shown in Table 13.3. These ratings will provide support for the allocation of citywide demand among the CBD and the competitive office nodes.

Table 13.3
Macro-Locational Rating by Node

	Central Business District (Subject Node)	Southwest Node	Northeast Node
Current travel time to executive housing	1	2	3
Expected travel time to executive housing in next 10 years	2	3	2
Current travel time to airport	2	2	3
Expected travel time to airport in next 10 years	same	same	same
Support facilities (stores, hotels)	3	2	1
Visibility/prestige (e.g., proximity to branch offices of Fortune 500 companies)	3	1	2
Recent office building construction	1	2	3
Public expenditures on infrastructure in last 5 years	3	1	2
Amount of Class A office space	1	2	2
Total	16 (33%)	15 (31%)	18 (37%)

Note: In this table, 3 is the highest (best) rating; 1 is the lowest rating.

The comparative ratings suggest that the CBD remains a highly attractive area for tenants. Note the high rating for public expenditures. The city is spending considerable funds on CBD infrastructure which, among other advantages, will improve access to the CBD. Thus high ratings are recorded in the future access categories. The location rating is future-oriented because value is the present worth of future benefits.

After completing the macro-locational analysis of the node in which the subject property is located, the appraiser investigates the micro location of the subject building.

Step 1.3(2) Analyze the micro location

Micro location refers to the following attributes: the subject's relative location within the node, traffic conditions around the subject site (e.g., one-way streets, curb cuts, median cuts), pedestrian access to and from the support facilities for the subject building, adjacent land uses, the availability and convenience of parking, nuisances, natural amenities (e.g., an especially scenic view from the subject), the subject's future location within the projected pattern of growth for the node, and any special building amenities the subject may possess. This information will be employed to rate the subject relative to the competitive supply in Step 4.2.

Application of Step 1.3(2)

The subject is easily accessible within the CBD. Unlike many older office buildings, it has adequate parking facilities. The other Class A office buildings in the CBD have comparable access and parking facilities.

STEP 2 DELINEATE THE MARKET OF PROPERTY USERS

Step 2.1 Identify the market of property users

Most office buildings do not have the contiguous market or trade areas that characterize retail facilities (i.e., concentric trade circles defined by time-distance relationships and sales volume percentages) and residential subdivisions (i.e., commuting time to employment centers). The clients of financial institutions, investment firms, and professional offices are attracted more by the reputation of the firm or the practitioner than by the convenience of the firm's location. The users of office space tend to be diffused over a broad metropolitan area.

Application of Step 2.1

The subject is a multitenanted, Class A office building suitable for institutional/professional, general commercial, and quasi-industrial tenants and the clientele and employees such tenants will draw. In view of this fact, the appraiser will consider office-based employment for the entire metropolitan area in the demand forecast.

STEP 3 FORECAST DEMAND

Step 3.1 Conduct trend analysis using inferred methods

The analyst studies trends in both city growth and office space occupancy. The city has seen a steady increase in population and employment over the past 10 years. All signs point to continued growth, so it can be inferred that demand for Class A office space will continue to increase.

Current citywide occupancy for all types of office space is approximately 80%; Class A space is doing better at 84% occupancy. During the past five years, Class A occupancy went up to 95%, but due to some moderate overbuilding three years ago, the market experienced a downturn resulting in the current 84% occupancy. Nevertheless, during this time positive net absorption has been reported. (Net absorption is calculated as move-ins minus move-outs.) Therefore it can be inferred from these data that demand for Class A office space has been increasing; if the current trend continues, demand will continue to increase.

Step 3.2 Conduct fundamental analysis using segmentation method

Step 3.2 has five substeps in which the future workforce is identified and quantified, the office space demand is estimated and segmented by class, and the final demand figure is adjusted for vacancy.

Step 3.2(1) Forecast the workforce occupying office space

Composite or aggregate data on monthly employment for selected metropolitan areas are published by the U.S. Department of Labor, Bureau of Labor Statistics.[11] Employment projections are also provided by the Bureau of Labor Statistics and by local government agencies and commercial vendors. Such aggregate data must be analyzed, adjusted, and refined to forecast employment in the future.[12] The employment forecast must then be adjusted by the appraiser to reflect the workforce occupying office space of the subject type.[13]

In analyzing employment data, the appraiser should carefully review the parameters of the data, particularly to determine whether the data refer to individuals who are locally employed or to employed individuals who are local residents. For example, census data provide information on the employment of local residents, but these data do not necessarily indicate that these residents work locally. The demand forecast for an appraisal focuses on local employment; it is not as concerned with where the employees live.

The Bureau of Labor Statistics uses the Standard Industrial Classification (SIC) codes for its occupational breakdown. The SIC system identifies nine employment sectors: agriculture; mining; construction; manufacturing; transportation and public utilities; wholesale and retail trade; finance, insurance, and real estate; services; and public administration. The sample data in Table 13.4 relate to the case study application.

---

11. *Employment and Earnings*, published monthly by the U.S. Department of Labor, Bureau of Labor Statistics (Washington, D.C.: U.S. Government Printing Office) and *Handbook of Labor Statistics*, Bulletin No. 2217, published by the U.S. Department of Labor, Bureau of Labor Statistics (Washington, D.C.: U.S. Government Printing Office).

12. Employment forecasts are developed using procedures similar to those outlined for the population forecast in Chapter 12.

13. The following discussion has been adapted from the article, "Office Space Demand Analysis," by J.R. Kimball and Barbara S. Bloomberg in *The Appraisal Journal* (October 1987), 567-577.

Table 13.4

Locally Employed Individuals

SIC Classification	Current Estimate	Five-Year Projection	Growth in Five Years
Agriculture	1,980	2,295	315
Mining	990	1,148	158
Construction	7,920	9,182	1,262
Manufacturing	38,610	44,760	6,150
Transportation and public utilities	19,800	22,954	3,154
Wholesale and retail trade	4,950	5,738	788
Finance, insurance, and real estate	11,880	13,772	1,892
Services	7,920	9,182	1,262
Public administration	4,950	5,738	788
Totals	99,000	114,769	15,769

In each of these nine broad employment categories, a specific percentage of workers will be employed in freestanding office buildings. Not all office employees work in freestanding office buildings. Some office workers occupy space in facilities such as manufacturing plants and agricultural warehouses.

Estimating Procedure

An estimate of the number of employees in each category who will work in freestanding office buildings can be derived with two calculations. The annual figures provided by the Bureau of Labor Statistics break down the workers in each category by type of job—i.e., executive, administrative and managerial, sales, administrative support (including clerical), machine operators, assemblers, inspectors, and so forth. The number of worker types most often found in offices may be divided by the total number of employed workers to derive a ratio.

For example, of the 2,295 agricultural workers counted in 1984, 88 were expected to work in offices:

Total employed in agriculture	2,295
Office employees	
Executive, administrative, and managerial	12
Sales	15
Administrative support (including clerical)	61
Agricultural office employees	88

Thus the ratio of agricultural workers employed in offices is:

$$\frac{\text{Office employees}}{\text{Total employees}} \quad \frac{88}{2,295} = 3.834\%$$

This ratio must be adjusted to indicate the number of agricultural employees who will work in freestanding office buildings since the preliminary figure includes all types of office space. Research indicates that about two-thirds of all office employees work in freestanding office space.[14] A second calculation refines the ratio.

$$0.67 \times 3.834\% = 2.568\% \text{ or } 2.6\% \text{ (rounded)}$$

So 2.6% of agricultural employees work in freestanding office space.

Using this procedure the typical percentages of office workers in freestanding office buildings can be estimated for each of the nine employment sectors. Table 13.5 provides these percentages. This breakdown of the employment data is based on statistics that were published by the Bureau of Labor in 1983. These percentages are provided only as examples. Such data change over time and from one market to another.

Table 13.5
Workers in Freestanding Office Space by Category

SIC Classification	Percentage in Office Buildings
Agriculture	2.6%
Mining	18.8%
Construction	14.6%
Manufacturing	17.0%
Transportation and public utilities	30.2%
Wholesale and retail trade	16.8%
Finance, insurance, and real estate	59.0%
Services	19.0%
Public administration	28.3%

Percentages such as these can be applied to five-year growth estimates to determine how much additional demand for office space will exist. Applying the percentages to the employment forecast yields a forecast of the number of employees who will occupy multitenant office space. (Note, in this example only

---

14. Ian Alexander, *Office Location and Public Policy* (New York: The Chancer Press, 1979). Research on this subject is limited so in most cases the appraiser will have to rely on local studies.

the mid-range forecast is shown. In practice, it is recommended that high- and low-range forecasts also be prepared.) The results of the calculations are shown in Table 13.6.

Table 13.6
Estimate of Additional Office Space Demand

SIC Classification	Five-Year Growth Estimate	Percentage in Offices	Number in Offices
Agriculture	315	2.6%	8
Mining	158	18.8%	30
Construction	1,262	14.6%	184
Manufacturing	6,150	17.0%	1,046
Transportation and public utilities	3,154	30.2%	953
Wholesale and retail trade	788	16.8%	132
Finance, insurance, and real estate	1,892	59.0%	1,116
Services	1,262	19.0%	240
Public administration	788	28.3%	223
Projected number of new workers in office buildings			3,932

Alternative Procedure

If local data on occupied multitenanted office space are available and the future employment mix in the area is expected to remain stable, the appraiser may estimate the percentage of the total workforce occupying multitenanted office space in three steps:

1. Divide the total amount of occupied multitenanted space by the average square footage of space per worker to find the overall local office employment.
2. Divide the overall local office employment by the total local employment to obtain the percentage of the total workforce occupying multitenanted space.
3. Apply this percentage to the employment forecast.

Note, this procedure is similar to the ratio method presented in Step 3.3.

Application of Step 3.2(1)

The metropolitan area has a population of 180,000. Population and employment are projected to increase by 3% per year. Current data indicate that 99,000 workers (55% of the population) are employed locally and that 24,750 workers

(25% of those locally employed) have jobs requiring office space. It is anticipated that high-tech industry in particular will experience growth, ensuring a new source of employment for the community.

The five-year growth in demand for office space is calculated at 3,932. Thus total demand in five years may be forecast at 28,682 (current demand of 24,750 plus growth of 3,932). Area forecasts by the local council of governments and a commercial data vender both indicate that the size of the citywide workforce occupying office space will increase over the next 10 years by approximately 3% per year. Thus demand for the next 10 years may be projected based on an expected growth rate of 3% per year (see Table 13.7).

Step 3.2(2) Estimate the size of the workforce occupying space in the subject's class of office building

This step is accomplished by multiplying the figure derived in Step 3.2(1) by the specific percentage for that class of building.

Application of Step 3.2(2)

In this metropolitan area, Class A office buildings have a higher-than-average occupancy level and make up 32.5% of the existing inventory of office space. This figure reflects the percentage of office workers using Class A space and may be used to determine the number of citywide workers in Class A space: 32.5% x 28,682, or 9,322 (see Table 13.7).

Step 3.2(3) Estimate the requisite space per office worker

After the number of office workers occupying space in a specific class of office building has been estimated, this figure is multiplied by the standard area required per office worker, which was estimated at 180 square feet based on a recent BOMA survey. If local historical data on the amount of office space and number of office workers are available, a more representative figure may be obtained by dividing occupied space by the current number of employees. Since this figure will vary at different points in the market cycle, an average allotment over the forecast period should be considered.

Application of Step 3.2(3)

The average area per office worker is estimated at 180 square feet (see Table 13.7).

Step 3.2(4) Calculate demand for the specific class of office space

The number of Class A workers estimated in Step 3.2(2) is multiplied by the average area per office worker derived in Step 3.2(3) to determine the Class A space presently in demand.

Application of Step 3.2(4)

Multiplying the 9,322 Class A workers by the average area of 180 square feet per office worker indicates that 1,677,960 square feet of Class A space will be in demand in five years (see Table 13.7).

Step 3.2(5) Adjust demand for "normal" vacancy rate

The demand figure is adjusted to reflect the typical vacancy rate for the specific class of buildings. The result is a gross estimate of supportable Class A office space. This figure is used in marginal demand studies and proposed construction feasibility analyses. In many appraisal applications, however, the subject capture forecast figure derived in Step 3.2(4) is not adjusted for normal vacancy.

Application of Step 3.2(5)

The forecast demand figure of 1,677,960 square feet is adjusted upward by the normal vacancy rate of 5% (see Table 13.7).

The calculations in Table 13.7 illustrate the procedure for estimating existing and anticipated demand.

Table 13.7
Estimate of Existing and Potential Demand

Step	Current	Forecast in 5 Years	Forecast in 10 Years
3.2(1) Forecast citywide workforce occupying office space	24,750	28,682	33,250
3.2(2) Percentage of above total in Class A office buildings	32.5%	32.5%	32.5%
Citywide Class A office workforce	8,044	9,322	10,806
3.2(3) Average square footage per office worker	180	180	180
3.2(4) Actual demand for Class A office space (occupied space)	1,447,920	1,677,960	1,945,080
3.2(5) Plus normal vacancy for Class A buildings *	76,206	88,314	102,373
Gross estimate of total supportable Class A office building space	1,524,126	1,766,274	2,047,453

* For proposed construction, an adjustment for building efficiency should also be considered.

Checking Reasonableness of Demand Forecast Model

The reasonableness of forecast demand calculations can be checked using known data, which is sometimes called *model calibration*. Inferred methods based on a general comparison of forecast data to historical data can also be used.

The calibration method utilizes the demand forecast for known data. In this case the supply survey indicates a current estimate of 1,430,040 square feet of occupied Class A space (see Table 13.9). The current demand (occupied space) indicated in Table 13.7 is 1,447,920 square feet. These two figures are very close and, thus, the demand model is considered reliable. (A more extensive calibration analysis could be made by comparing data over the past 10 years.)

The accuracy of the demand model can also be checked with inferred analysis. Projected demand is compared with historical net absorption. If there is little difference between the two and the forecast employment is similar to past employment, the model would appear reasonable. Considerable variation in the figures may indicate that the market has recently undergone a significant upturn or downturn, that additional growth is expected, or that the projections in the model are not well founded.

Step 3.3 Conduct fundamental analysis by the ratio method

All appraisal methods have technical weaknesses. Thus alternative approaches applied throughout an appraisal can serve as checks on one another. The alternative method applied here is based on a ratio of total employment to total occupied space. This method cannot be considered a true fundamental method because the analyst neither segments future employment according to mix nor assesses the space needs of workers. These weaknesses must be recognized. Nevertheless, the ratio method does serve as a check on the segmentation method.

Total employment in the subject city is currently 99,000 workers. The supply survey that follows (Step 4.1) indicates that the city has 1,430,040 square feet of occupied freestanding Class A office building space. Thus current demand in the city is approximately 14.5 square feet of office building space per employee (1,430,040/99,000). The city's forecast indicates a total of 115,000 jobs in five years (Step 3.2(1)). Thus, using the ratio method, total demand in five years should be 1,667,500 square feet of Class A office space. Assuming that employment continues to grow at an annual rate of 3%, total employment in 10 years may be forecast at 133,000 workers. Using the same ratio (14.5 square feet per worker), total demand for Class A office space in 10 years is calculated at 1,928,500 square feet (133,000 x 14.5). Comparing these results to those of the segmentation method (Table 13.7), the analyst finds that the methods produce almost identical forecasts. The procedure may be further refined by comparing the 14.5 ratio with the average ratio over the past five years.

The underlying assumptions of this method, i.e., that the future mix of employment and the current ratio of office space per employee will remain the same, are possible weaknesses.

Step 3.4 Reconcile the results of the various methods and forecast demand

Table 13.8 summarizes the demand conclusions developed.

Table 13.8
Demand Forecast Summary

Method	Conclusions
Trend (Inferred) Methods	
• Growth trends	Positive
• Historical occupancy	Moderately positive citywide
Fundamental Methods	
• Segmentation method	1,677,960 occupied sq. ft. in 5 years and 1,945,080 sq. ft. in 10 years
• Ratio method	1,677,500 sq. ft. in 5 years and 1,928,500 in 10 years.

In this example, historical demand and forecast demand are very similar. The appraiser should compare the rate of growth in employment during this period to the rate indicated in the forecast. It is reasonable for the forecast rate to approximate the historical rate.

The segmentation method and the ratio method produced very similar results. In theory, the segmentation method is more reliable because it accounts for more of the variables. In practice, however, the reliability of the segmentation method depends on an accurate estimation and forecast of all the variables. Since the methods applied in the case study application yielded similar results, further refinement of the forecast is not necessary.

STEP 4 MEASURE COMPETITIVE SUPPLY

Step 4.1 Inventory competitive supply

The appraiser must obtain local data on existing office space, current occupancy and vacancy levels, office buildings under construction, and proposed or likely office buildings. Although data on existing buildings and office space under construction are generally readily available, data on proposed office buildings may be difficult to gather. Collecting the data is only part of the problem. The timing of possible building starts must be forecast as well as the amount of new space expected. The following list describes a possible procedure for this analysis.

1. Research planned projects.

   - Interview building officials and planning department staff in the local jurisdiction regarding recent inquiries concerning planned projects.
   - Review preliminary and final plats submitted for office use and determine their status.
   - Review announcements of proposed buildings in local newspaper(s) and information from the Chamber of Commerce to determine current status of projects.
   - Survey brokers, lenders, and developers active in the area.

2. Compile a list of possible projects and assess the probability that they will be developed. For each project, consider

   - Who is the developer and what is his or her track record?
   - How close is the developer to obtaining permission?
   - How much space has been pre-leased?
   - Does the developer have multiple projects?
   - How attractive is the location?

3. Analyze the probability of other projects being developed.

   Compare marginal/residual demand against existing buildings and projects under construction only. This helps the analyst discern what market participants are thinking about windows of opportunity in the future. If it appears that the market sees the potential for high marginal/residual demand, it is probable that some new competition can be expected during this period.

4. Complete a probability forecast of new space.

Other factors that may change the supply situation should also be considered. The demolition of office buildings, the rehabilitation and upgrading of office buildings, and the adaptation of older buildings to office use all affect the potential supply of office space.

Application of Step 4.1

There are currently 5,435,000 square feet of office space citywide and the overall occupancy rate is 80%. The average area currently allotted to an office employee is about 180 square feet. Class A office space in multitenanted buildings accounts for 32.5% of total office space; Class B and owner-occupied buildings account for the remainder of the citywide total.

Approximately 2,720,000 square feet of the citywide total are in the central business district. Multitenanted Class A buildings account for approximately 15% of the CBD space. The CBD has an overall occupancy rate of 79%.

The southwest node has about 1,357,500 square feet of space with an 85% occupancy rate. The northeast node also contains approximately 1,357,500 square feet and has an 85% occupancy level. Approximately 48% of the office buildings in both suburban nodes is Class A space. An additional 125,000 square feet of office space is under construction in the northeast node and will begin to lease up in a year. Because of low occupancy citywide and the current restrictive lending policy, no additional competitive space is anticipated.

Current competitive supply is measured by adding up the Class A space in the CBD and the two suburban nodes (see Table 13.9). The additional 125,000 square feet of Class A office space currently under construction should be included in the supply projections.

Table 13.9
Current Occupancy Survey of Class A Multitenant Space

	Net Rentable Sq. Ft.	% of Total Sq. Ft.	Occupied Sq. Ft.	% of Total	% Occupied
CBD	408,000	24%	322,320	22%	79%
Southwest node	651,600	38%	553,860	39%	85%
Northeast node	651,600	38%	553,860	39%	85%
Total	1,711,200	100%	1,430,040	100%	81% (avg.)

Step 4.2. Analyze competitive supply

In addition to the inventory of existing and future competitive supply, supply analysis provides information that may be used with the findings of the location analysis in inferred demand analysis.

Location and Supply Analysis

The information in Table 13.9 can be compared to the location rating derived in Step 1.3(1) and shown in Table 13.3. The location rating indicated that the CBD should be capturing 33% of citywide demand, but the survey of actual capture shows the CBD is capturing only 22%. Is the rating wrong? Perhaps it is, but it has served one purpose—to make the analyst investigate further. A wider range of office products are typically built in suburban nodes than are available in the CBD. In the subject case, the CBD is dominated by four large multitenanted office buildings with large floor plans, whereas the suburban nodes offer large and small spaces with a mix of amenities. Thus location alone may not indicate potential capture. In the location rating, two factors concerning future conditions were rated. The supply analysis, on the other hand, is historical. The two perspectives must be reconciled. In the final analysis, however, the appraiser is more interested in future benefits than historical experience.

Analyzing the Competition

Analysis of the competition can indicate a range for the subject's expected rent and occupancy (inferred demand). Thus the supply analysis supports the more involved lease analysis and rent forecast required to perform discounted cash flow analysis in the income approach. (In DCF analysis scheduled rent is investigated in light of lease terms, the tenant finish allowance, and the building services included in the base rent.)

In supply analysis the subject and competitive buildings are compared with regard to the following characteristics: size (gross building area or rentable area), age, vacancy level, access, parking, tenant quality, management, building quality and condition, amenities, and support facilities.

Application of Step 4.2

The subject property rents for $14 per square foot, which is competitive with the rent charged for similar buildings. The subject has an 80% occupancy rate, average for Class A buildings, and is easily accessible within the CBD. Unlike many older office buildings, it has adequate parking facilities. The other Class A office buildings in the CBD have comparable access and parking facilities. In Table 13.10 the subject is rated with respect to the other major Class A buildings in the CBD.

In the comparative rating of major Class A professional office buildings in the CBD, the subject received an intermediate score. In the next step of the market analysis, the subject's future capture will be estimated based on the reconciled results of this rating and the other data considered.

STEP 5 ANALYZE MARKET EQUILIBRIUM/DISEQUILIBRIUM

Step 5.1 Compare supply and demand to determine marginal demand

In many parts of the appraisal, the appraiser considers the point in the real estate cycle the market is experiencing. Marginal demand analysis helps the analyst make this judgment.[15]

To determine marginal demand the appraiser begins by comparing data on existing and future competitive supply with the estimates of current and anticipated demand. This is done with two objectives in mind. First, the appraiser must identify whether there is unsatisfied, or marginal, demand. Marginal demand is the demand that remains after all available space is subtracted from the

---

15. Information on the market cycle is used in the income capitalization approach to project increases or decreases in the subject's rent and occupancy and to assess what portion of the discount rate represents risk. It is also used to support the market conditions adjustment in the sales comparison approach.

Table 13.10

Rating of Competitive Class A Office Buildings in the CBD

	Subject	Score	Competitor 1	Score	Competitor 2	Score	Competitor 3	Score
Rentable area	100,000 sq. ft.	2	125,000 sq. ft.	3	100,000 sq. ft.	2	83,000 sq. ft.	1
Average rent	$14 per sq. ft.		$14 per sq. ft.		$14 per sq. ft.		$14 per sq. ft.	
Vacancy	20%		14%		25%		28%	
Access	good		similar		similar		similar	
Parking	adequate		similar		similar		similar	
Tenant quality	AAA		similar		similar		similar	
Management	on-site	3	off-site	2	off-site	2	off-site	2
Construction	good	2	excellent	3	good	2	good	2
Design	conventional	2	high-profile	3	conventional	2	conventional	2
Condition	well-maintained		similar		similar		similar	
Support facilities	convenient		similar		similar		similar	
Total		9 (26%)		11 (31%)		8 (23%)		7 (20%)

A rating of 3 is better than 2 and 2 is better than 1; if two factors are similar, they are rated the same.

projected demand for space. Marginal demand cannot be satisfied unless additional space, over and above proposed and newly constructed space, is added to the inventory.

Second, the appraiser seeks to determine how long the absorption of existing vacant office space and space under construction will take. This determination depends on the growth of demand. The point in time when existing vacant space, space under construction, and proposed office space will be absorbed represents a window of opportunity when new development might be expected.

Application of Step 5

Marginal demand is estimated by subtracting the competitive existing and projected supply citywide from supportable current and projected Class A office space.

Table 13.11
Citywide Marginal Demand Over the Next 10 Years

	Current	Forecast in 5 Years	Forecast in 10 Years
Estimate of total supportable Class A office building space in sq. ft. (from Table 13.7)	1,524,126	1,766,274	2,047,453
Less total competitive supply citywide (from Table 13.9)	1,711,200	1,836,200	1,836,200
Marginal demand estimate (excess) or shortage	(187,074)	(69,926)	211,253

The time needed to absorb the existing vacant space and space under construction may be calculated by dividing the total excess space by the square foot demand per year.

Total excess space
187,074 (available vacant space)
+ 125,000 (space under construction)   312,074 sq. ft.

Square foot demand per year
$$\frac{242,148 \text{ sq. ft.* (the anticipated growth in demand)}}{5 \text{ years}}$$ 48,430 sq. ft.

312,074/48,430 = 6.44 years

* Five-year forecast of supportable demand minus total current supportable demand (see Table 13.7).

Thus the current office space surplus of 187,074 square feet and the 125,000 square feet under construction should be absorbed over the next six to seven years. Note that market occupancy during this period is forecast to average 95%. The forecast also suggests that the next six years will be highly competitive and rents will stay relatively stable. Occupancy at the subject property will be slow to rise. This information is used in the next step, the subject capture estimate, to provide a context for the capture forecast. Expectations for the next six years will necessarily be on the conservative side, while the projection for the following years might be more optimistic.

STEP 6 FORECAST SUBJECT CAPTURE

This step can be considered a reconciliation of the market analysis section of the appraisal. It could also be seen as a marketability analysis for the subject property. At this point, all the pieces of the market study are refocused on the competitive outlook for the subject property. The capture estimate becomes the launch pad for the last part of the appraisal, application of the three approaches, in which the appraiser determines how the subject's capture affects property value.

A forecast of the subject's capture is made after examining all the data, including the historical capture rate of the subject, the marginal demand forecast for the total market, and the ratings assigned in the first and fourth steps of the market analysis process.

Step 6.1 Derive a preliminary (inferred) estimate of subject capture

Growth trends for the subject city appear to be positive. City employment and population are forecast to grow at a rate of 3% per year. It can be inferred that subject occupancy will continue to increase at a similar rate. If this is so, the subject should attain a 90% occupancy level in four years.

Current market occupancy is 81%, similar to the subject's occupancy. Thus the subject may be considered typical of the Class A market and the analyst may infer that subject occupancy will increase at a rate similar to the market rate.

Step 6.2 Derive a capture rate by fundamental analysis

The marginal demand estimate suggests that the subject should expect little or no increase in occupancy or rent levels for the next six to seven years. This outlook is at odds with the inferred analysis. Consequently, a more detailed fundamental forecast and capture analysis will be required to reconcile and support the specific income forecast in the income capitalization approach section of the appraisal.

A good starting point for a fundamental capture analysis is the current capture rate of the subject. The subject has a current occupancy level of 80%, and there is total citywide demand for 1,447,920 square feet of space (see Table 13.7), so the subject capture rate is 5.5% (80,000/1,447,920). This capture estimate can be applied to forecast Class A space (see Table 13.12).

Table 13.12
Citywide Capture Analysis:
Mid-Range Forecast

	Current	In 5 Years	In 10 Years
Actual demand for			
Class A space	1,447,920 sq. ft.	1,677,960 sq. ft.	1,945,080 sq. ft.
Current subject capture rate	5.5%	5.5%	5.1% (reduced since the subject is full)
Indicated subject occupancy	79,636 sq. ft.	92,288 sq. ft.	99,200 sq. ft.

Only the mid-range forecast is presented here. High- and low-range estimates are omitted for the sake of brevity. Nevertheless, it is recommended that the appraiser present a complete analysis, including the range of the estimates, to improve the reliability of the forecast and to reflect the probability of each outcome.

This analysis suggests that it will take the subject five to 10 years to achieve full occupancy. This information can be used to reinforce or modify the general conclusions of the inferred analysis. It can also be used to form more specific judgments about the likely timing of lease-up.

If the appraiser felt the subject would compete equally with all the buildings in all the areas of town, the analysis might stop here. However, there is a question concerning whether or not the CBD will capture citywide Class A office space in the future at the same rate it has in the past. It does not appear that the CBD is maintaining its fair share (see Table 13.9). The CBD represents 24% of the current Class A space, but only 22% of the capture. That is close to a fair share, but there may be a problem since growth is occurring in the suburban nodes and not in the CBD. An additional 125,000 square feet of space is to be built in the northeast suburban node within the next few years. Table 13.13 suggests that the CBD's pro rata share of the market will be shrinking.

Step 6.3 Reconcile subject capture indications

CBD Capture Conclusions

The implication of the fundamental analysis is that, on a pro rata basis, the CBD will be losing 10% of its historical share (from 24% to 22%) when the new Class A space is built. The location rating in Table 13.3 suggested a 33% capture for the CBD, but that conclusion was predicated on the improved access into the CBD that was assumed to result from increased municipal expenditures. Thus, the appraiser might conclude that the current capture of 24% is the low-

Table 13.13
Inventory of Existing Competitive Class A Office Buildings and Forecast of Potential Supply

	Current	% of Total	Forecast in 5 Years	% of Total Space	Forecast in 10 Years	% Total Space
Square feet in CBD	408,000	24%	408,000	22%	408,000	22%
Square feet in SW node	651,600	38%	651,600	36%	651,600	36%
Square feet in NE node	651,600	38%	776,600	42%	776,600	42%
Citywide total	1,711,200		1,836,200		1,836,200	

range estimate and the 33% capture based on improved access is the high-range estimate. Nevertheless, the appraiser may still consider adjusting the capture estimate 10% downward to account for the new construction in the northeast node. Based on this reasoning, a CBD forecast capture range of 20% to 30% seems reasonable.

Subject Capture Within the CBD

Based on actual occupancy in the CBD (see Table 13.9), the subject is capturing 24.8% of the CBD market (80,000/322,320). The appraiser must determine if the subject's capture will continue at this rate. The comparison rating of competitive CBD buildings shown in Table 13.10 indicated a subject capture rate at 26%, which is within a reasonable range of the current actual capture of 24%. No additional space was planned in the CBD, so future competitive space was not considered.

Calculating Capture by Segmenting Demand in CBD

One way to consider future capture is to allocate demand to the CBD and then estimate the subject capture rate from the current competition. The conclusions derived from applying this method are shown in Table 13.14.

Conclusions

The citywide capture analysis in Table 13.12 and the subject capture derived from segmenting CBD demand in Table 13.14 yield similar results. The inferred methods suggest a slightly more optimistic scenario. The results of the future-oriented fundamental analysis are typically given more weight. In fundamental analysis, the more sensitive variables are considered. These include questions such as:

Table 13.14

Subject Capture Estimate: Mid-Range Forecast

	Current	In 5 Years	In 10 Years
Citywide demand for Class A space	1,447,920 sq. ft.	1,677,960 sq. ft.	1,945,080 sq. ft.
Times % captured by CBD	22.3%	20% to 30%	20% to 30%
Actual occupancy*	322,900 sq. ft.	335,600 to 503,400 sq. ft.	389,000 to 583,500 sq. ft.
Times % subject capture	24.8%	26%	26%
Subject estimated occupancy*	80,000 sq. ft.	87,250 to 100,000 sq. ft.	Fully occupied

* Rounded

- Is the employment forecast consistent with current market expectations?
- Are adequate data available to segment out demand for office space of the subject type—i.e., Class A space?
- Is the method used to estimate the capture rate based on sound assumptions and data? In the case study application, the ability of the CBD to capture its share of future demand is critical to the subject's leasing prospects. Based on its historical capture of 20%, the subject would only maintain its current occupancy rate of approximately 80%. However, the CBD's capture rate could increase if improved access helps the CBD as much as the appraiser indicated it would in the location rating. Thus the final capture estimate is largely dependent on the weight given the location rating.

The final conclusions of this case study application are set forth below.

Low-range forecast *Occupancy*: Level to slightly increasing Years 1 through 5, then slowly increasing Years 5 through 10 to 85% occupancy. *Rents*: Declining at real rate of 0.5% per year to maintain a slight increase in occupancy.

Mid-range forecast *Occupancy*: Improving to 90% occupancy between Years 5 and 7 and then leveling off and dropping slightly in Years 7 to 10. *Rents*: Must remain level or decline slightly over the next five years if a slow increase in occupancy can be reasonably expected. After Year 7, a slight real rate of increase can be expected once citywide marginal demand appears positive.

High-range forecast *Occupancy*: Increasing to 95% in five years and maintaining this rate through Year 10. *Rents*: Real rate of increase to remain level over the next five years, then increase 2% per year for Years 5 through 10.

Note. The high- and low-range forecasts are presented for illustration. The calculations are not shown. The estimating procedure is the same, but low and high employment projections are used.

The mid-range forecast is compared to the subject's current capture ratios in Table 13.15 as a final check on reasonableness.

Table 13.15
Estimates of Subject Capture

	Current	Forecast In 5 Years	Forecast In 10 Years
Subject capture as percentage of supportable Class A space at current and projected occupancy levels	80,000 sq. ft. of 1,447,920 sq. ft. of supportable Class A space	90,000 sq. ft. of 1,677,960 sq. ft. of supportable Class A space	90,000 sq. ft. of 1,945,080 sq. ft. of supportable Class A space
	5.5%	5.4%	4.6%
Subject capture as percentage of total available Class A space in CBD	80,000 sq. ft. of 408,000 sq. ft.	90,000 sq. ft. of 408,000 sq. ft.	90,000 sq. ft. of 408,000 sq. ft.
	19.6%	22.1%	22.1%
Subject space as percentage of total available Class A space in metropolitan area	80,000 sq. ft. of 1,711,200 sq. ft. of total Class A space	90,000 sq. ft. of 1,836,200 sq. ft. of total Class A space	90,000 sq. ft. of 1,836,200 sq. ft. of total Class A space
	4.7%	4.9%	4.9%

THE MARKET ANALYSIS PROCESS FOR AN EXISTING APARTMENT COMPLEX

—⇒•⇐—

- Analyze property productivity.

- Delineate the market of property users.

- Forecast demand.

- Measure competitive supply.

- Analyze market equilibrium/disequilibrium.

- Forecast subject capture.

CHAPTER FOURTEEN

—————⟶◦⟵—————

Existing Apartment Complex

This chapter demonstrates the step-by-step procedures applied in a market analysis for a residential property. Concepts and terminology unique to the residential property market are reviewed and the analytical process is presented. Each step of the process is then applied to demonstrate the market analysis of a residential apartment complex.

Apartment buildings and subdivisions are residential properties that fall into the categories of income-producing and speculative real estate. A subdivision appraisal is not presented here, but it would include most of the same procedural steps. A market analysis for a subdivision differs from a market analysis for an apartment building in only two ways: data are segmented for owner-occupied housing rather than rental housing and several of the rating attributes used to estimate subject capture are different.

THE RESIDENTIAL MARKET

Residential properties constitute the building blocks of communities. Because of the far-reaching social benefits that accrue from stable communities, the government has traditionally promoted home ownership, most notably by allowing income tax write-offs for personal home mortgage interest. Residential real estate development is a mainspring of the economy, so government organizations have long worked to improve conditions in the housing market as a means of stimulating general economic growth. As an economic commodity, residential property has a dual character, being both a usable good and a material asset. Traditionally residential property has been considered a consumer good, a means of satisfying basic needs for shelter and comfort. In the inflationary environment of the past two decades, however, residential property was increasingly perceived as an investment instrument. More recently, many home owners have discovered that the residential market has a cycle like any other market. The current downward phase of the cycle has cancelled out many of the investment benefits of home ownership.

To understand the cycles of the residential real estate market, a historical perspective is needed. In the mid-twentieth century the character of residential development underwent a profound transformation. An economic depression, which nearly brought construction to a standstill in the 1930s, and the diversion of national resources to the war effort during the early 1940s created a severe housing shortage after the war. Pent-up demand and the rapid rate of household formation after World War II triggered an unprecedented building boom. Despite short-lived cyclical contractions in housing starts, postwar levels of building activity have been maintained to the present day. Sixty-five million units of privately owned housing were built between 1946 and 1988.[1]

Postwar development centered on suburban areas. The typical pattern of residential development[2] combined the creation of lots with the building of houses to produce complete unit packages, each consisting of a finished single-family house on an improved lot. During the 1950s and 1960s, subdivisions typically contained uniformly spaced, detached single-family houses. In the 1970s, several factors brought about changes in development patterns. Concern for the environmental impact of development and energy conservation as well as escalating costs led to more intensive residential development, reflected in smaller houses, more attached units, and cluster plans. Sophisticated design techniques were used to maintain the privacy and individuality of units and preserve other amenities associated with low-density housing. During the 1980s, however, the size of new detached houses began to increase again.

Factors influencing demand

Changes in demographics, lifestyles, consumer preferences, and economic circumstances continue to affect the demand for residential development. Over the past 25 years, the median age of the U.S. population has been increasing, while average household size has decreased. Consequently, the need for larger single-family houses may decline over the long term. Considerable demand for residential property has been generated by the baby boom generation, those people born between 1946 and 1966 who account for one-third of the population of the United States. Demand for housing is expected to slacken somewhat over the next decade as fewer new householders succeed the baby boomers. Older

---

1. The most recent economic recession bottomed out in 1991. Between 1988 and 1994, there were approximately 4.8 million housing starts (single-family units). *Source:* U.S. Department of Commerce, Bureau of the Census, *Construction Reports* (January 1980 and February 1989) and First Union Group, *The Real Estate Analyst* (January 1974), 71-72.

2. Urban Land Institute, *Residential Development Handbook* (Washington, D.C.: ULI, 1978), 1-4.

suburbs built in the postwar years have taken on the character of empty-nester communities. In the 1980s the real price of houses (in constant dollars) actually declined. Lower interest rates between 1989 and 1994 also contributed to making homes more affordable.

Gentrification, the renovation of older homes, and the conversion of multiunit rental properties into condominiums and cooperatives have helped stabilize many metropolitan neighborhoods. The proportion of single Americans in the population, including people who are divorced, widowed, or never married, has increased. Their preference for smaller residential units has been felt in both suburban and urban markets. The influx of women into the workforce has also significantly influenced housing development. Working couples want housing that requires minimal maintenance and often consider smaller units to be more efficient and practical. Affluent, double-income households with the disposable income to satisfy their demands may also require more residential amenities.

The employment and income levels of the population affect the affordability of residential property. In the inflationary environment in the United States after 1973, real median income actually stopped growing. Certain segments of the residential market, often younger households, did not have the requisite income to purchase new homes. Consequently, an affordability crisis was created. The decline in interest rates during the early 1990s helped reverse this situation.

Factors influencing supply

Supply-side factors such as the amount of available housing stock and the costs of new development and construction also affect residential housing. Housing market inventories keep track of vacancy and absorption rates for properties on the market as well as losses in existing stock and conversions of properties from nonresidential uses. Such data are especially important in estimating supply in older Rust Belt cities. Several northern cities with high replacement needs and low vacancy rates have been able to support considerable housing construction.[3]

The cost of vacant land and the expenses associated with financing have increased over the past two decades. Twenty-five years ago the cost of raw land represented approximately 18% of the price of an overall property; between the late 1970s and the late 1980s, however, the building site accounted for an average of 26% of the total sale price.[4] During the real estate market decline of the 1990s, this trend reversed itself and land value as a percentage of overall property price fell. The cost of underwriting construction loans and homebuyer mortgages today represents a larger percentage of the sale price than it once did. Typically, 5% to 10% of the sale price is now required to fund the financial costs of producing a new home.

---

3. Dowell Myers, "Housing Market Research: A Time for Change," *Urban Land* (October 1988), 19.
4. Kiplinger Washington Editors, Inc., "Your Home," *Changing Times* (December 1988), 22 and Urban Land Institute, *Residential Development Handbook* (Washington, D.C.: ULI, 1978), 307-309.

CONCEPTS AND TERMINOLOGY

Compared to markets for other types of property, the residential real estate market has an especially strong consumer orientation. To be successful, developers, investors, and underwriters must stay attuned to shifts in consumer tastes and preferences and to changes in household formation patterns and lifestyles. The marketability of housing depends heavily on accessibility and the availability of public utilities and support facilities (e.g., schools, shopping centers, recreational areas). The residential market can be broken down into the following types of properties: single-family residential, rental apartments (two- to four-unit buildings and multitenanted projects), retirement housing, and cooperatives and condominiums.

Single-family residential properties

Detached single-family housing is still the preference of the typical residential consumer. Residential demand may be segmented according to the size, age, and income of the household. For example, there are starter households with or without small children that generally have limited means, move-up households whose growing size requires more space, established households with older children that are affluent enough to afford a variety of amenities, and empty-nester or move-down households that seek smaller accommodations. Over the next decade, ownership rates for single-family homes are expected to decline modestly because of the higher costs of home ownership, the affordability gap, and the declining number of households due to demographics.

A single-family residence is a consumption good with an economic life that generally extends over many decades. As an investment instrument, single-family residential properties fared better in the 1970s. While the median price of residential property continued to rise in the 1980s, inflation rather than appreciation accounted for the price increase. In 1988, the median price of a new, detached single-family house was $112,500; the median price of an existing house was $87,000. The price of housing between 1980 and 1988 rose 75%, outpacing inflation. Since that time, many markets have seen significant drops in the average price of housing. For example, the average house price in the Dallas/Fort Worth area in 1987 was $95,746; by 1990 it had dropped to $69,602, but then started to rebound in 1991 to an average price of $77,933.[5] The market for housing, and all other categories of real estate, is cyclical over time.

Detached single-family residential houses encompass a wide array of sizes, types, and styles. Common designs include one-story (ranch, rambler, and bungalow), one and one-half story (Cape Cod), two-story, bi-level (raised ranch), and split-level houses.

---

5. The Burton Center for Development Studies, University of Texas at Dallas, 1991.

Rental apartments

Rental apartments range from small, two- to four-unit properties to multitenanted developments. Like office buildings, apartment complexes may also be divided into building classes based on their location, construction, condition, management, tenancy, and amenities. These qualities determine the level of rent an apartment building is capable of generating.

Three principal demographic groups create demand for apartments: the young and upwardly mobile; a growing class of moderate-income, permanent renters; and empty-nesters, who require less space and want to keep maintenance to a minimum. The demand for rental apartments is expected to decline in the 1990s. In fact, the vacancy rate for multitenanted apartments has generally been rising since 1981. The vacancy rate for the nation peaked at 11.4% in 1988, fell to 9.6% in 1990, and rose again to 10.3% in 1991. Overbuilding has prevented many Class A apartments from achieving commensurate rents and has necessitated many rent concessions.

Retirement housing

Retirement housing options include scaled-down townhouses, senior apartments, and congregate living facilities. This last category may be further divided into adult congregate living facilities (ACLF), for those who are able to maintain a semi-independent lifestyle, and continuing-care retirement centers (CCRC), for those who require care. Although the performance of retirement housing in the 1980s did not come up to industry expectations, demand for rental retirement housing is expected to grow as the baby boom generation ages.

Cooperatives and condominiums

Empty-nesters and affluent singles are the two main groups that constitute the demand for cooperatives and condominiums. Many amenity-laden condominiums are well beyond the means of starter households. Since the mid-1980s, sales of existing condos have shown strength, but many markets are overbuilt and the median price of condominiums has not increased as much as that of single-family residential properties.

Residential measurements

Four terms are used in describing the area of residential properties: gross living area, gross building area, gross leasable area, and net leasable area. These terms are defined below.

Gross living area (*GLA*), which is sometimes referred to as *above-grade living area* (*AGLA*), is the total area of finished, above-grade residential space. Unfinished areas and attics are not included. Gross living area is the most common measurement applied to houses.

Gross building area (*GBA*) is the total area of all floor levels, measured from the exterior of the walls. The floor area of the superstructure and the substructure basement are included in gross building area.

Gross leasable area (*GLA*), also referred to as *gross rentable area* (*GRA*), is the total floor area designed for the occupancy and use of tenants, including basements, corridors, and stairways.

Net leasable area (*NLA*), which is sometimes referred to as *net rentable area* (*NRA*), is the amount of space rented to the individual tenants, excluding common areas such as basements, corridors, and stairways.

TRENDS IN MARKET ANALYSIS FOR RESIDENTIAL PROPERTY

Appraisers should be advised that several parts of a residential market analysis call for special care in the application of procedure and judgment. These areas include the demand estimate, the supply inventory, and the market forecast.[6]

In estimating demand, the analyst must consider the demographic characteristics of household formation. Various age groups within a population form households at different rates. The traditional method of dividing total population by average household size produces a general estimate which ignores different rates of household formation among cohort groups. The rate of household formation also varies with income. For example, high rents may discourage household formation among young, unmarried adults.

The use of small-area population projections, which are usually made without consideration of basic development conditions (e.g., utilities, infrastructure, land prices, or available acreage), can also be misleading. The analyst should study projections for the overall metropolitan area and the development potential these projections support. Small-area demand should then be forecast based on how supportable development will likely be allocated among the various communities in the metropolitan area. Local capture rates and the availability of vacant land and infrastructure will determine the allocation formula. Because small-area demand is important, the case study application stresses detailed location analysis.

In calculating changes in the competitive supply inventory, the analyst must adjust for vacancy, lost units, and units added through conversions. Data on loss of units and conversions are especially difficult to obtain. Losses and conversions are generally higher in older Rust Belt cities than in Sun Belt cities.

The appraiser's market forecast should identify long-term trends rather than short-term indicators, which may be poor predictors. Short-term factors include current mortgage interest rates, vacancy or absorption rates, and the inventory of available competitive supply and space under construction. Mortgage rates are extremely volatile and vacancy rates cannot be forecast with any accuracy be-

---

6. Dowell Myers, "Housing Market Research: A Time for Change," *Urban Land* (October 1988), 16-18.

yond two to five years. The appraiser should instead consider factors that are bellwethers of long-term trends: the economic base, which indicates the future growth potential of the community and the likely progression of economic cycles; planned infrastructure improvements; and demographics. Reasoned judgment should be applied to the data available, even if these data are fragmented.

The forecasting process must be tempered by the realization that the future may be a significant departure from the past. For example, the demand for multifamily apartments in recent years was driven by the baby boom generation, but this demand has now shifted to single-family houses. Any forecast based on the continuation of recent occupancy rates in multifamily apartments could overstate the strength of that demand. Moreover, such a forecast would seriously underestimate the demand for single-family houses.

MARKET ANALYSIS FOR A RESIDENTIAL PROPERTY

Table 14.1 outlines the process to be applied in the case study application. Only the market analysis portion of the appraisal is presented.

CASE STUDY DESCRIPTION

The following application describes a Level C market analysis prepared as part of an appraisal assignment. The subject property is an existing, 312-unit apartment complex located in Leadville, a major metropolitan area. The complex consists of 18 detached, two-story buildings and is called the Pine Grove Apartments. The apartment project is 80% occupied. The appraiser will need to examine the current and anticipated demand/supply situation to determine whether the property will maintain, lose, or increase its present occupancy and income levels. The purpose of the market analysis is to provide information to be used in the three approaches to value.

STEP 1 ANALYZE PROPERTY PRODUCTIVITY

The appraiser begins the market analysis by investigating the legal, physical, and locational attributes of the subject apartment complex.

Step 1.1 Analyze the legal attributes of the property

The subject site is zoned for multifamily residential use, and the existing buildings meet the density requirements set forth in the zoning ordinance. The leases on the apartment units are of one-year duration, so they do not have any significant impact on the property's marketability.

Conversion of the complex to condominium units is a possibility, but this would require a zoning change. The city has had one condominium project which was not successful; thus proposals for conversion to condominiums have been received negatively by city planners.

Table 14.1
The Market Analysis Process for an Existing Apartment Complex

Step 1   **Analyze property productivity**
     1.1   Analyze the legal attributes of the property.
     1.2   Analyze the physical attributes of the property.
     1.3   Analyze the locational attributes of the property.

Step 2   **Delineate the market of property users** Identify the characteristics of likely residents by studying the consumer profile of occupations, income levels, and the ability to afford housing.
     2.1   Determine the boundaries of the market area based on time-distance relationships. Distances to employment and support facilities (e.g., shopping centers, schools) are important as are the locations of competitive housing that appeals to the same consumers as the subject.
     2.2   Analyze the tenant profile of the subject property and neighborhood.

Step 3   **Forecast demand**
     3.1   Conduct inferred (trend) analysis. Compile data on general growth, market occupancy and rent trends, and the subject history to infer future demand.
     3.2   Conduct fundamental analysis.
          3.2(1)   Estimate the current and projected population within the defined market area.
          3.2(2)   Establish the current and projected average household size and divide the population estimates by the household size averages.
          3.2(3)   Segment the number of current and projected households to identify those headed by owners and those headed by renters.
          3.2(4)   Segment the number of households by income levels to determine the percentage of households that are or will be able to meet the monthly rent on the rental unit.
          3.2(5)   Adjust the demand forecast for a normal vacancy rate. (This step is optional.)

Step 4   **Measure competitive supply**
     4.1   Inventory existing competitive properties, properties under construction, planned properties for which building permits have been obtained, and proposed properties. Tally the inventory of existing and anticipated competitive supply for the projection period.
     4.2   Analyze the competitive supply. Rate the subject against competitive subdivisions, districts, or apartment buildings according to criteria such as location, age, and amenities.

Step 5   **Analyze market equilibrium/disequilibrium** Compare existing and potential demand with current and anticipated competitive supply to determine marginal demand.
     5.1   Input data on existing and anticipated demand for the subject property (Step 3).
     5.2   Input data on existing competitive properties and properties under construction, planned properties for which building permits have been obtained, and proposed properties (Step 4.1).
     5.3   Subtract the total inventory of existing and anticipated competitive supply for the projection period (Step 5.2) from the estimate of existing and anticipated demand for the subject property (Step 5.1) to determine the net excess or shortage in the market.

Step 6   **Forecast subject capture**
     6.1   From inferred demand and the fundamental demand market forecast, estimate the subject capture in terms of future occupancy expectations and the corresponding rent required to realize that capture.

Note the numbering system employed in this six-step process. Substeps are indicated with sequential numbers in parenthesis. Thus, Step 3.2 is followed by Steps 3.2(1), 3.2(2), 3.2(3), etc.

Step 1.2 Analyze the physical attributes of the property

Site and Improvement Description

The apartment buildings stand on a rectangular site of 14.5 acres (631,620 square feet). Site drainage and utilities meet the standards of the municipal code. The apartments are set back from the intersection of two public roads (i.e., a primary, six-lane thoroughfare and a secondary, four-lane street) and are accessible by means of two private roadways. The subject complex is clearly visible from the primary road and a billboard on the secondary road helps drivers locate the complex from that direction.

Each of the 18 buildings in the 312-unit apartment complex has an exterior entry. In addition to the buildings housing apartment units, there are two other buildings, one of which contains an office and recreation room and the other, a laundry. Total gross building area is 235,582 square feet; total net rentable area is 234,208 square feet. The average unit size is about 751 square feet. Each building has siding of brick and wood and a composition roof. The style is best described as modern vernacular. The project was built in 1988, and the overall condition and quality of the units are average. The effective age is the same as the physical age—six years. Project amenities include a tennis court, a swimming pool, and one covered parking place per unit. Each unit has a porch or patio. The 312 apartment units in the complex are of three types:

- 152 units with one bedroom and one bathroom (678 square feet of net rentable area)
- 80 units with two bedrooms, one bathroom, and one lavatory (800 square feet of net rentable area)
- 80 units with two bedrooms and two bathrooms (907 square feet of net rentable area)

Subject Improvement Analysis

The purpose of the productivity analysis is to identify the submarket the real estate product serves and its competitiveness within this market. The improvement analysis is the first step in this determination and is accomplished by rating the subject against current industry standards. The rating chart in Table 14.2 provides both a checklist of items to be studied and a starting point for the analysis of the subject's productivity attributes.

Conclusion of the Improvement Analysis

The subject improvements are generally in good condition and may be considered competitive with modern projects. However, the subject swimming pool and recreation building are moderately inferior to most newer apartment complexes in the metropolitan area.

Table 14.2
Subject Apartment Building Rating

Comparison to Standard:		Inferior			Typical	Superior		
Impact on Productivity	Veto Factor	High	Mod.	Slight	Average	Slight	Mod.	High
Design and appearance of property					X			
Quality of construction (materials and finish)					X			
Condition of improvements					X			
Room sizes and layout					X			
Closets and storage					X			
Plumbing (adequacy and condition)					X			
Electrical and appliances					X			
Unit amenities					X			
Recreation amenities			X					
Parking					X			
Number of items	0	1	0		9	0	0	0
Times category score (weighting)	0	2	4		5	6	8	10
Subtotal score	0	2	0		45	0	0	0
Total subject score								47

Note: A more complete description of the rating technique applied is presented in Chapter 12.

Step 1.3 Analyze the locational attributes of the property

The subject's location is considered in terms of natural features, land use trends, linkages, local support services, and proximity to major cities in the region. No natural features distinguish the northwest sector, where the subject is located, from other areas of the city where competitive apartment projects are found.

The zoning patterns in the subject area are consistent with city planning policies. The abutting land uses are complementary and nearby retail centers, schools, recreational facilities, and professional offices adequately serve the residents of the subject apartments.

A breakdown of the developed acreage in the community indicates a land use mix that supports housing. Approximately 35% of the developed acres in the community are residential and there has been a 30% increase in residential development since 1980. In analyzing land use, the appraiser has also investigated growth trends in specific sectors of the community.

Identification of Submarkets

The competitive submarkets were identified in analyzing the direction of overall growth. Leadville, the subject city, is divided into four submarkets: northeast, northwest, southwest, and southeast. (The subject is in the northwest submarket.)

The northwest (subject) sector is expected to remain a stable, moderate-income residential area with some additional development of single-family housing. By contrast, the northeast sector has minimal support facilities and is largely underdeveloped, so existing multifamily complexes in that area do not represent serious competition for the subject. Moreover, because there is little likelihood of further development in the northeast sector, it is not likely to compete with the subject area in the future. The southwest sector, like the subject area, is rated a good growth area, but it is primarily single-family and the city has discouraged further apartment development in the area.

The southeast sector has the largest concentration of apartment projects in the community. This sector constitutes the corridor of growth for the area. A regional mall, a mixed-use development, and two office buildings have all either been recently completed or are under construction. The southeast sector, therefore, represents the main competition for the subject area.

The northwest (subject) sector has good access linkages. Traffic counts indicate that the subject is located just south of one of the most heavily traveled thoroughfares in the community. Congestion may become a problem for the apartment complex, but it seems that this will have no effect in the short term. Plans to develop employment centers in the southeast sector of the city are likely to put the subject at a competitive disadvantage.

Location Rating

As part of the location analysis, a competitive location rating of the city is prepared (see Table 14.3). This rating procedure has two steps. First, each area of the city is compared with another area with regard to various factors. For example, Area A and Area B are compared to determine whether Area A is better than, equal to, or worse than Area B with regard to each specific factor. The higher the rating assigned to an area, the higher its score. This process is then repeated for other paired areas. Second, the four districts are ranked relative to one another using a calibrating process. The resulting scores are then totaled. (The capture percentage used in Step 6 of the analysis is supported, in part, by this ranking.) A higher score identifies an area considered superior. The rating procedure focuses on general urban growth characteristics, not a specific land use. Nevertheless, urban growth is extremely relevant to residential uses.

Table 14.3
Location Rating Analysis (by Submarket)

Rating Factor	NW	NE	SW	SE
Proximity to existing development	2	1	2	3
Public planning/ development support	2	1	2	3
Path of growth	2	1	3	4
Reputation/prestige	2	1	2	3
Access/linkages (now and in 10 years)				
Schools	3	1	3	1
Restaurants/shopping	2	1	2	3
Employment centers	1	1	1	2
Higher-income housing	2	1	2	2
Recreational facilities	2	1	2	2
Aesthetics—natural features	3	1	2	2
Infrastructure—existing and committed	2	1	2	3
Score	23	11	23	28
% of total scores	27%	13%	27%	33%

STEP 2 DELINEATE THE MARKET OF PROPERTY USERS

The market of property users must be delineated before demand and competitive supply are analyzed. The purpose of market delineation is to focus the demand forecast and competition rating on the specific users, or submarket, of the subject property. In this step the appraiser identifies the characteristics of the likely users—i.e., status (owner or renter), occupational profile, and income level, which indicates their ability to afford the housing. A more in-depth analysis of demand is carried out in Step 3. In this analysis the appraiser disaggregates data on existing and projected demand for the market area to establish what percentage of owners/renters have income levels sufficient to meet the monthly mortgage or rent payments on the subject units. Competitive supply is also considered in Step 2, as an indicator of the boundaries of the market area.

Step 2.1 Determine the boundaries of the market area

After analyzing the time-distance between the subject and employment and support facilities as well as the market area for competitive housing, the appraiser concludes that the market area for the subject apartment project coincides with the boundaries of the city in which the project is located. The citywide market area corresponds to the area where competitive projects are found and constitutes the area from which data will be gathered to forecast population in the demand analysis.

The community of Leadville covers a fairly compact area of approximately 20 square miles. Of the local population, 70% commute to work in three nearby cities. The length of the commute from the subject to these major employment centers is about the same as the commute from any of the major clusters of multifamily housing in the community. In fact, the time-distance relationships to employment centers are similar for all of the residential areas.

Step 2.2 Analyze the tenant profile of the subject property and neighborhood

By conducting a random survey and analyzing management records, the appraiser develops the following percentage breakdown of the current tenants of the subject property.

> 40% - Single professionals under 30
> 30% - Married couples under 30 without children
> 20% - Married couples under 35 with children
> 10% - Retired couples

Tenant Income

Tenant income is estimated based on current rents. The subject units rent for $350 to $475. It is generally estimated that the average household in this market spends about 26% of their income on housing. Thus, the subject tenants' income range is estimated at $16,000 ($350 x 12 mos./0.26) to $22,000 ($475 x 12 mos./0.26).

Citywide Income

The income pattern for the city is studied since the competitive market area is assumed to be citywide. The current income pattern for the city is shown in Table 14.4. A review of these data indicates that about 21% of the population cannot afford the subject rents (5.1% + 13.9% + 20% of 10.4%). Because it takes a minimum income of $16,000 to afford an apartment in the subject, it is estimated that 20% of households with incomes of $15,000 to $24,999 cannot afford the subject rents.

Table 14.4

Percentage Distribution of Household Income

Less than $10,000	5.1%
$10,000 to $14,999	13.9%
$15,000 to $24,999	10.4%
$25,000 to $34,999	12.4%
$35,000 to $49,999	27.0%
$50,000 to $74,999	21.1%
More than $75,000	10.1%

Source: XYZ Data Co. and U.S. Census *Buying Power Index.*

Consumer Spending Patterns

To prepare the table, the appraiser compared data on spending patterns within local zip code areas obtained from XYZ data service with the purchasing patterns indicated in a national survey. The XYZ data showed that the subject area surpassed national averages in nearly all categories. In comparion with apartment dwellers across the nation, residents of the subject were above-average consumers in the following areas: sporting goods (28.9%), dining out (17.8%), auto and accessories (19.2%), and apparel (21.2%). These spending patterns suggest a lifestyle on par with or superior to the typical apartment dweller's lifestyle.

Age Distribution and Household Size

Table 14.5 provides an age breakdown of the population of the subject city.

Table 14.5

Age Distribution (%)

0-4 yrs.	7.8%
5-14 yrs.	17.0%
15-24 yrs.	17.6%
25-34 yrs.	17.1%
35-44 yrs.	17.6%
45-54 yrs.	11.6%
54-64 yrs.	6.4%
65-74 yrs.	3.2%
75+ yrs.	1.7%

Source: XYZ Data Co. and U.S. census data

About 60% of the residents are below the age of 35. A young population is beneficial to the subject apartment project because this group constitutes the likely occupants of apartments. The age distribution suggests a large market base for the subject and further confirms the occupant profile. However, nearly 25% of the city's population is under the age of 14, which suggests a large number of families, who typically seek single-family units rather than apartments.

STEP 3 FORECAST DEMAND

The appraiser studies the existing and anticipated relationships between the demand for and competitive supply of apartment units within the community. Future demand will be forecast using the inferred and fundamental methods listed below.

Inferred Methods

- General area growth trends
- Residential construction trends
- Historical absorption
- Real rental rates

Fundamental Methods

- Forecast studies of multifamily residential demand based on the segmentation of population growth between single-family and multifamily households and the ability to afford the subject units

Step 3.1 Conduct inferred (trend) analysis

Demand Based on General Area Growth Trends

Table 14.6 shows the historical growth pattern of the city of Leadville, where the subject is located.

Table 14.6

Population Growth of Leadville

1984 population	24,273
Est. 1994 population	46,500
Annual growth rate	6.7%

Source: Council of Governments

Historical growth data from 1984 to the present show that Leadville has grown at a compound annual rate of 6.7% percent. The projected population growth for the city is also positive.

Conclusions based on growth trends The population growth for the market area is quite high relative to other, comparable-sized cities. Based on the historical pattern of population growth and the expectation that this rate will continue, demand for future multifamily uses is considered very positive. Next year the subject should be leasing at a rate above 95%.

Demand Based on Residential Construction Trends

Figure 14.1 illustrates multifamily residential building activity from 1985 to the present. Construction activity was highest in 1988 and 1989, dropping slightly in 1990 and 1991. Activity dropped again in 1992 and came to a standstill in 1993 and 1994. As of the date of valuation, no construction permits had been issued for three years. (The Leadville Planning Department provided this information.) The average number of units constructed in the 10-year period studied was 650 units per year.

Figure 14.1
Multifamily Units Added in Leadville

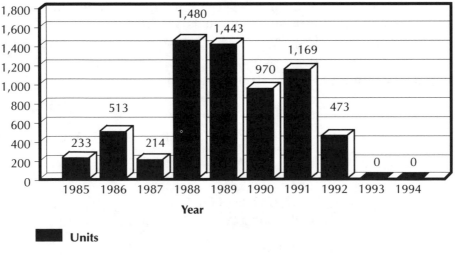

Source: City Planning Department.

314

Conclusions based on new construction It can be inferred from the building permit data that demand for new multifamily units is weak. No permits have been issued for the past three years, and no plats or building permits have been released this year. Overbuilding in the late 1980s has caused construction to fall off in the past several years. This overbuilding is obviously the reason for the high vacancy rates citywide. Given the lack of recent construction activity and the continued growth in population, however, the subject should lease up in the next year or two.

Demand Based on Historical Absorption

Another indicator of demand is the current trend in occupancy levels. XYZ data service conducts annual apartment surveys, which can be used to discern historical occupancy levels. Table 14.7 indicates the occupancy trend in the Leadville market since 1991.

Table 14.7
Occupancy Levels in Leadville

1991	75%
1992	78%
1993	80%
1994	85%

Occupancy levels in Leadville for multifamily units have increased from the 1991 level, when the full impact of the overbuilding in 1988 and 1989 was felt. During the past year, occupancy has increased significantly.

Conclusions based on absorption trends Compared to the past several years, the demand for multifamily units appears to be increasing. An XYZ company survey reported that approximately 5,800 of the 6,900 units available were occupied in the fourth quarter of 1994. This 85% occupancy rate is consistent with the appraiser's survey in Step 4.2, which reveals an 83% occupancy rate. According to the XYZ survey, only 5,300 units were occupied in the fourth quarter of 1992. This indicates that approximately 500 units were absorbed over the previous two years, an average of 250 units per year. In 1994 there was a 5% increase in occupancy. Based on increasing occupancy rates and subsequent absorption, the demand for multifamily units in Leadville appears to be very positive. A 5% annual increase in occupancy for the subject may be inferred based on these data. Thus in two years the subject should achieve 95% occupancy.

Demand Based on Real Rental Rates

Actual rental rates can also be used to infer demand for multifamily units. Rents are typically related to occupancy levels—i.e., as occupancy levels increase, rents are also expected to increase. Data on historical and current rent levels are presented here to check if occupancy levels are an appropriate indicator of demand. Rent levels are used later in the equilibrium analysis (Step 5) to indicate when new construction is expected to occur. Table 14.8 summarizes the rental rates in the city of Leadville from 1991 to 1994. The rates are adjusted for inflation using the metro area CPI; thus the figures reflect real rates, exclusive of inflation.

Table 14.8
Rental Rates in Leadville

Year	Real Rate per Sq. Ft.	% Increase
1991	$0.55	
1992	$0.49	–11%
1993	$0.50	2%
1994	$0.55	10%

Source: XYZ Data Co. Figures represent fourth quarter survey results.

Conclusions based on real rental rates The recent increase in rent levels may be considered a consequence of the rapid increase in occupancy levels in the Leadville apartment market. These occupancy level increases are believed to reflect an increase in real demand, not an increase in occupancy resulting from special marketing or rent inducements. For the subject property, the trends in occupancy and rents are very positive.

Step 3.2 Conduct fundamental analysis

A fundamental forecast is based on the premise that an area's ability to support multifamily units is a direct function of the number of people and composition of households in the area, both current and anticipated over the next few years. To conduct this type of study, data on existing and projected demand in the market area must be disaggregated to establish the percentage of renters with income levels sufficient to meet the monthly rent for units in the subject property. The appraiser estimates demand by paring down aggregate demographic and income data to isolate the population segment that matches the profile of a typical consumer who may be expected to rent an apartment and can afford the subject rents. Table 14.9 illustrates the application of Steps 3.2(1) through 3.2(5) in developing a demand estimate.

Step 3.2(1) Estimate the current and projected population

Measuring the current and forecast population within the market area is the appraiser's first step. In this case, the local council of governments was the main source of data on area population. Population forecasts from the City of Leadville, the State Highway Planning Department, and XYZ Data Co. were also studied.

In the past 10 years, the population has grown at an average rate of 6.7% per year, resulting in an increase of 22,227 people. Population is expected to continue to grow even though the economy appears to be slowing down slightly. The most reliable forecasts of growth in Leadville in the next 10 years indicate increases of 14,000 to 30,000 people, with a mid-range forecast of approximately 22,000 people, a repetition of the growth experienced in the last decade.

Step 3.2(2) Establish the current and projected average household size

Household size declined from 2.8 members 10 years ago to 2.7 currently and is expected to continue to decline by .011% annually (0.10/9). (The average household size figures shown in Table 14.9 have been rounded to two decimal places.)

Step 3.2(3) Segment current and projected households to identify owners and renters

The percentage of renters in the community over the past decade has averaged 39% of the population and this percentage is forecast to remain constant. The subject area, the northwest part of town, has about the same percentage of renters as the rest of the city. Thus, the citywide average will be used. If the subject area had a significantly different percentage of renters, then a population forecast for the subject area would be developed and the percentage of renters in the submarket would be utilized.

Alternatively, the ratio of apartment units to other types of housing (e.g., condominiums, single-family detached, single-family duplexes) can be used to segment demand. In this study, the ratio between renter and owner households corresponds to the ratio between apartment units and other housing.

Step 3.2(4) Segment households by income levels to determine percentage that can meet monthly rent

For a household to pay $350 in monthly rent, the lowest rent for a subject unit, its income must exceed $16,000. Approximately 80% of the households in the community have incomes above $16,000. (See the tenant profile discussion in Step 2.2.) In addition to disqualifying the 20% of households with incomes below $16,000, some analysts would also segment out the households with incomes above $22,000, the high end of the income range for the subject property. In this analysis, however, the appraiser has chosen not to segment out the

Table 14.9

Demand Calculations Summary: Mid-Range Forecast

Line	Year 0	Year 1	Year 2	Year 3	Year 4	Year 5	Year 6	Year 7	Year 8	Year 9	Year 10
1. Population (Step 3.2(1))	46,800	49,048	51,295	53,543	55,790	58,038	60,285	62,533	64,780	67,028	69,275
2. Population increase		2,248	2,248	2,248	2,248	2,248	2,248	2,248	2,248	2,248	2,248
3. Persons per household (Step 3.2(2))	2.70	2.69	2.68	2.67	2.66	2.65	2.64	2.63	2.62	2.61	2.60
4. Total number of households (Line 1 / 3)		18,233	19,140	20,053	20,973	21,901	22,835	23,776	24,724	25,680	26,643
5. Percentage of renter households (Step 3.2(3))		39%	39%	39%	39%	39%	39%	39%	39%	39%	39%
6. Demand for subject unit type (Line 4 x 5)		7,111	7,465	7,821	8,180	8,541	8,906	9,273	9,643	10,015	10,391
7. Plus normal vacancy (Step 3.2(5))		0	0	0	0	0	0	0	0	0	0
8. Total demand for subject housing (Lines 6 + 7)		7,111	7,465	7,821	8,180	8,541	8,906	9,273	9,643	10,015	10,391
9. Affordability percentage (Step 3.2(4))		80%	80%	80%	80%	80%	80%	80%	80%	80%	80%
10. Total demand for occupied units (Line 8 x 9)		5,689	5,972	6,257	6,544	6,833	7,124	7,418	7,714	8,012	8,313

higher income range for two reasons. First, Step 3.2(3) segmented out the apartment dwellers from the single-family households so the top income households, which are likely to occupy single-family housing, have already been segmented out for the subject market. Second, the apartment market in the case study is fairly homogenous—there are no more expensive apartments for higher-income households. However, in more stratified markets, segmentation of the top end of the market should be considered.[7]

Step 3.2(5) Adjust for normal vacancy

At any given time, some units will be vacant because of seasonal occupancy or the need to refurbish units. A vacancy rate of about 5% is often applied to the demand forecast to reflect a market in equilibrium. In nonvaluation studies such as feasibility analyses for proposed construction, this adjustment is used to estimate the supportable project size. In this case study application, however, the appraiser is mainly interested in the subject's capture of the actual occupancy. Therefore this adjustment is not made in Table 14.9.

Other Potential Adjustments

Two other types of demand—move-up demand and latent demand—should also be considered.

Move-up demand is demand generated by the upward mobility of lower-income households. The subject apartment complex is an average multifamily residential project and is unlikely to attract much "move-up" demand. Furthermore, the apartments are not located in the southeast growth corridor and may lose some of their tenants to complexes in that sector of the city. Move-up gains and lateral losses may be expected to cancel each other out.

Latent demand, which is also called *pent up demand*, typically results from underbuilding in an area. If, over the last few years, apartment building had not kept pace with the population increase and, more importantly, the 39% of the population desiring (or needing) rental units had been forecast to increase, latent demand might be present. This is not so in the case study application.

Table 14.9 presents the demand calculations described in Steps 3.2(1) through 3.2(5).

STEP 4 MEASURE COMPETITIVE SUPPLY

The first part of the analysis calls for an inventory of available and anticipated competitive supply. Quantitative supply data may be obtained from many sources. Apartment associations, private market research companies, and some

---

7. Segmentation of low-end and high-end households is typical in most single-family markets. These households show more extremes in the income levels of both home owners and renters. Also note that it may be more reliable to segment households by income before segmenting by household type (owner/renter). The inavailability or costliness of data often makes this impractical. In this case study, the nature of the market allowed us to apply the more traditional sequence, segmenting by type of household first.

municipal governments maintain lists of existing apartments and unit totals. City planning commissions may be able to provide information on anticipated supply. The appraiser can also conduct a survey to obtain data not available from secondary sources.

In the second part of the supply analysis, a qualitative ranking of competitive apartments is developed. The appraiser relies on judgment to complete the qualitative survey and rate the subject against the competition.

Step 4.1 Inventory existing competitive properties, properties under construction, planned properties, and proposed properties

Existing Properties

Using quantitative data obtained from municipal lists of existing apartments and unit totals, the appraiser estimates citywide supply at 8,000 multifamily units. Not all of these units are competitive with the subject. Some units are occupied by tenants with household incomes below the range specified for the subject. To obtain more data, the appraiser conducts a survey of 30 large apartment complexes of more than 25 units. (The 8,000 total cited above includes smaller complexes such as four-plex units.) The appraiser's survey compiled data on 6,969 units, about 87% of the total multifamily units in the city. The appraiser's survey indicates that the occupancy rate for apartment projects in the community averages approximately 83%, while the occupancy rate for the subject is 80%. This suggests the subject capture is slightly below the market average.

Planned Projects

The appraiser has learned from the city planner that no new plats or building permits for apartments have been filed in the past year. Because the lending market has recently become more restrictive, few development loans are being made in the metropolitan area. Thus, new competition in the next couple of years is unlikely. However, there are signs that the lending climate is easing up and occupancy and rents are increasing. The possibility of new construction in two to four years must be considered. This prospect will be further examined in the equilibrium analysis in Step 5.

Step 4.2 Analyze competitive supply and rate the subject against the competition

To obtain an inventory of apartment buildings that are competitive with the subject, the noncompetitive supply must be deducted from the total inventory of available and anticipated supply. In this step, noncompetitive supply is identified in the rating process.

The appraiser has rated the 30 apartment complexes surveyed in the city in terms of three major criteria: location, age, and amenities.

Location

Each of the areas where apartment buildings are clustered was assigned a rating on a scale of 1 to 4. The better the location within the community, the higher the rating. The areas were scored based on the results of the location rating in Step 1.3 (see Table 14.3). The southeast sector received the highest rating of 4, while the northwest and southwest were both rated 3. Because the northeast sector had a significantly inferior location rating, it was rated 1.

Age

The ages of the apartment complexes were rated 1 to 5. Complexes constructed in the last three years received a rating of 5. Those constructed four to six years ago were rated 4. A rating of 3 was assigned to complexes built seven to nine years ago. Those constructed 10 to 15 years ago received a rating of 2, and older projects were assigned a rating of 1.

Amenities

For rating purposes, amenities were divided into three groups. First the appraiser considered the amenities within the apartment units. When a greater variety of amenities (e.g., appliances, fireplaces, patios) was provided, a higher rating was assigned to the unit. The second category covered the amenities found on the site (e.g., swimming pool, tennis court, sauna/hot tub, clubhouse). The third category included the amenities within walking distance of the apartment complex (e.g., shopping areas, restaurants, recreation facilities, employment areas). Each of the three amenity categories was rated on a scale of 1 to 5. Scores were assigned based on the number of amenities in each category and then the totals were divided into five groups with ratings from one to five. In Table 14.10, the 30 properties included in the appraiser's competitive supply survey are rated.

Table 14.10
Competitive Supply Survey and Rating

Name and Location	Year of Construction	Number of Units	Average Rent per Sq. Ft.	Occupancy Rate	Amenities	Rating	Class
1. Arbor Apts., SE	1988	300	$0.53	85%	P, LR, S, CL, O,DD WD, CF, F, C, SC, PB	19.0	B
2. Atrium Apts., NW	1984	244	$0.45	83%	P, LR, T, S, CL, DD WD, CF, F, C, SC, PB	19.0	B
3. Berkshire, SW	1976	232	$0.43*	90%	P, LR, S DD, C	11.0	D
4. Beacon Hill, NW	1989	180	$0.55	86%	P, LR, S, CH, DD, WD CF, F, C, O, SC, PB	20.0	B
5. Bryn Mawr, NW	1989	356	$0.47	84%	P, LR, S, CL, HT DD, F, C, PA	18.0	C
6. Chestnut Hill, SE	1987	212	$0.54	90%	P, LR, S, CL DD, WD, CF, F, C	18.5	B
7. Devonshire, SE	1987	126	$0.46	85%	P, LR, S, CL, O DD, WD, F, CF	18.0	C
8. Dorchester, SW	1988	70	$0.47	83%	P, LR, CL DD, WD, F, CDD, WD, F, C	15.0	C

Note. Amenities *in the apartment units* include: dishwasher/disposal system (DD), washer/dryer connections (WD), ceiling fan (CF), fireplace (F), cable TV—landlord pays (CL), tenant pays (CT)—burglar alarm (B), microwave oven (M), patio (PA), and other (O).

Amenities *on the site* include: pool (P), laundry room (LR), covered parking (CP), tennis court (T), security (S), clubhouse (CH), hot tub/sauna (HT), racquetball court (RB), and other recreational facility (O).

Amenities *within walking distance* include: shopping center (SC), park (PK), and professional office building (PB).

* HUD-subsidized

Table 14.10

Competitive Supply Survey and Rating (continued)

Name and Location	Year of Construction	Number of Units	Average Rent per Sq. Ft.	Occupancy Rate	Amenities	Rating	Class
9. Fairfax, NW	1984	160	$0.48	80%	P, LR, CL DD, WD, F, CF	16.0	C
10. Hillcrest, NE	1975	152	$0.37*	100%	P, LR, O D, CT	10.5	D
11. Kensington, SW	1977	48	$0.40	74%	CT	2.5	D
12. Lake Forest, NE	1992	282	$0.45	70%	P, LR, S, CL, HT, DD, WD CF, F, B, C, PA, SC, PB	20.0	B
13. Maplewood, SE	1986	176	$0.52	80%	P, LR, T, CL, DD WD, CF, F, B, C	17.5	C
14. Oak Park, SE	1990	300	$0.57	85%	P, LR, S, T, CL, HT, DD WD, CF, F, B, C, SC, PK, PB	22.0	A
15. Old Orchard, NW	1986	248	$0.59	83%	P, LR, T, O, CL, DD WD, CF, F, CT, B, SC, PB	19.0	B
16. Pine Grove, NW (subject)	1988	312	$0.51	80%	P, LR, T, CP, S, CL DD, WD, F, C, SC, PB	20.0	B
17. Plaza, NW	1988	250	$0.51	80%	P, LR, T, CP, S, CL DD, WD, CF, F, C, SC	20.5	B
18. Rainbow, NW	1991	180	$0.56	83%	P, LR, TC, S, CL, HT, DD, WD CF, F, C, M, O, SC, PK, PB	23.5	A

* HUD-subsidized

323

Table 14.10

Competitive Supply Survey and Rating (continued)

Name and Location	Year of Construction	Number of Units	Average Rent per Sq. Ft.	Occupancy Rate	Amenities	Rating	Class
19. Savoy, SE	1988	485	$0.49	80%	P, LR, S, CL, HT, O DD, WD, CF, F, C, SC	20.0	B
20. Seton Hall, NW	1991-92	372	$0.59	90%	P, L, S, CL, O, HT, CW, DD WD, F, CT, SC, PK, PB	21.0	A
21. Sleepy Hollow, NW	1989	230	$0.58	70%	P, LR, S, CL, HT, DD WD, CF, F, B, C, SC	20.0	B
22. Somerset, SE	1990	256	$0.54	90%	P, LR, T, S, CL, HT, DD WD, CF, F, B, C, SC, PK	23.0	A
23. Turtle Creek, SE	1986	240	$0.50	80%	P, LR, T, CL, DD WD, CF, F, C, M, O	17.0	C
24. Village Green, SW	1977	136	$0.42	80%	LR, D, CT	8.0	D
25. Wellington, NE	1975	50	$0.51	75%	LR, D, CT	8.0	D
26. Westend, NE	1977	240	$0.44	85%	LR, S, D	12.5	D
27. Willow Grove, NW	1990	270	$0.57	79%	P, LR, CL, O, HT, DD WD, CF, F, B, C, SC, PK	21.0	A
28. Winchester, SE	1990	300	$0.59	80%	P, LR, CL, RB, HT, DD WD, CF, F, C, SC, PK, PB	21.0	A
29. Woodale, NW	1990	334	$0.56	90%	P, LR, T, S, CL, HT, O, DD WD, CF, F, C, SC, PK	26.0	A
30. Yorkshire, SE	1989	228	$0.52	80%	P, LR, T, S, CL, HT, DD WD, CF, F, C, SC	19.0	B
Total		6,969		Avg. 83%			

The location ratings, the age ratings, and the three amenities ratings were added to produce the ratings shown in Table 14.10. Using their competitive supply ratings, the 30 apartment complexes were grouped into four classes: A, B, C, and D. Table 14.11 shows the breakdown of the apartment complexes by class and the characteristics, or property profile, or each class. Table 14.12 shows where the various classes of apartment units are located within the city of Leadville.

Table 14.11
Breakdown of Apartment Complexes into Four Classes

Rating Class	No. of Units	% of Total Units	No. of Complexes per Class	% of Total Complexes	Rent Range ($/SF/Mo.)	Avg. Rent	Avg. Occu-pancy	Rating Scores
A	2,012	29%	7	23%	$0.54-$0.59	$0.57	85%	21-26
B	2,971	43%	11	37%	$0.45-$0.59	$0.52	81%	19-20
C	1,128	16%	6	20%	$0.46-$0.52	$0.48	82%	15-18
D	858	12%	6	20%	$0.37-$0.51	$0.42	84%	2-13
Totals	6,969	100%	30	100%				

Table 14.12
Location of Units

City Sector	Class A	Class B	Class C	Class D	Totals
Northwest	12%	21%	7%	0	40%
Northeast	0	4%	0	6%	10%
Southwest	0	0	0	6%	6%
Southeast	17%	18%	9%	0	44%

Conclusions of Competitive Analysis

Pine Grove, the subject, is a Class B apartment complex with a rating of 20 and an average monthly rent of $0.52 per square foot. The 10 other Class B complexes are most competitive with the subject. Nevertheless, the ratings for Class A, Class B, and Class C properties were fairly close and all of the projects are of recent construction. Therefore, the appraiser included Class A and Class C apartments in the competitive supply inventory. Only Class D apartment complexes, with ratings 7 to 18 points below the subject, were not part of the competitive supply.

Class D units represent 12% of the total units surveyed. Since the citywide demand forecast includes all likely occupants of rental units with sufficient income to afford the subject units (80% of all renters), the appraiser must consider the total citywide competition.[8] The subject city is relatively young, as cities go, and the population is fairly uniform in its characteristics. Therefore, the 12% of Class D space found in the survey was judged to represent the percentage of Class D units citywide. The competitive inventory was tallied at approximately 7,000 units (8,000 total multifamily units minus 960 noncompetitive Class D units).

STEP 5 ANALYZE MARKET EQUILIBRIUM/DISEQUILIBRIUM

Steps 5.1, 5.2, and 5.3 Compare demand and competitive supply

Table 14.13 shows a projection of demand and competitive supply over the next four years. In Steps 5.1 and 5.2, the findings of the demand analysis (Step 3) and competitive supply analysis (Step 4.1) are entered into the equilibrium analysis grid. The difference between supply and demand is calculated in Step 5.3, where either a net excess or shortage is identified. The four years shown in the projection represent the time over which demand and supply are in balance, assuming a mid-range forecast. Although the calculations indicate excess demand, the market may be considered in balance since the demand calculation was not adjusted for normal vacancy in Step 3.2(5). The excess demand in Year 4 represents a vacancy rate of 6.5% which is approximating a balanced market.

Observations on Equilibrium Analysis

The calculations in Table 14.13 suggest that in four years the market will reach equilibrium.[9] The way an equilibrium analysis is used in a valuation appraisal differs from the way such an analysis is used in a feasibility study for proposed construction. With regard to proposed construction, the equilibrium point is the point in time when construction is most likely feasible. In this housing application, lease-up is estimated based on the anticipated capture of excess demand.

In appraisals of existing properties, equilibrium analysis is used to forecast rent cycles and new competition. In the case study application, new construction can be expected when the market shows a positive net demand. Rents may also peak at this time. The relationship between rent increases and new construction should be considered in greater detail.

8. In performing market analysis it is important to ensure that all segmented demand-side data are consistent with segmented supply-side data.

9. Only the mid-range population forecast is presented here. High- and low-range forecasts are omitted because the analysis is presented simply to demonstrate the analytical technique. Calculations for high- and low-range forecasts can be developed using the same steps. The high and low ranges are significant to the analysis because the actual equilibrium will vary around the forecast midpoint.

Table 14.13
Marginal Demand Projection: Mid-Range Forecast

Line	Year 0	Year 1	Year 2	Year 3	Year 4
1. Population (Step 3.2(1))	46,800	49,048	51,295	53,543	55,790
2. Population increase		2,248	2,248	2,248	2,248
3. Persons per household (Step 3.2(2))	2.70	2.69	2.68	2.67	2.66
4. Total number of households (Line 1 / 3)		18,233	19,140	20,053	20,973
5. Percentage of renter households (Step 3.2(3))		39%	39%	39%	39%
6. Demand for subject unit type (Line 4 x 5)		7,111	7,465	7,821	8,180
7. Plus normal vacancy (Step 3.2(5))		0	0	0	0
8. Total demand for subject housing (Lines 6 + 7)		7,111	7,465	7,821	8,180
9. Affordability % (Step 3.2(4))		80%	80%	80%	80%
10. Total demand for occupied units (Line 8 x 9)		5,689	5,972	6,257	6,544
11. Current & estimated competitive supply (Step 4.1)		7,000	7,000	7,000	7,000
12. Estimated new competitive supply		0	0	0	0
13. Total competitive supply (Lines 11 + 12)		7,000	7,000	7,000	7,000
14. Net (excess) shortage (Line 10 - 13) (Step 5.3)		(1,311)	(1,028)	(743)	(456)

New Construction and Required Rent Analysis

Based on the relationship between projected demand and the current supply of units, the demand for multifamily units justifies the construction of new units in approximately four years. However, rents must be high enough to support the project and to obtain financing. Table 14.14 shows the calculation of the rent level required to make construction of a new, multifamily, Class A development feasible. The analysis assumes a new apartment building of typical size with a typical number of units and on-site amenities.

The calculations indicate that rent levels of $0.65 to $0.75 per square foot per month are needed to support construction of a new multifamily develop-ment. The appraiser should recognize that the level of required rent may change depending on the construction cost, design, density, land cost, and expenses as-

MARKET ANALYSIS FOR VALUATION APPRAISALS

Table 14.14
Rent Level Required for New Multifamily Construction

Assumptions

Average unit size	600 sq. ft.
Number of units	175
Total net leasable area (*NLA*)	105,000 sq. ft.
Construction cost	$28,000 per unit; $46.67 per sq. ft. of *NLA*
Land size	7 acres
Land and site cost	$850,000; $2.79 per sq. ft.
Overall cap rate	9%
Operating expenses	40% of gross income
Construction cost 175 × $28,000	$4,900,000
Land and site cost	$850,000
Total cost	$5,750,000
Required *NOI* $5,750,000 @ 0.09	$517,500
Required effective gross income $517,500 ÷ 0.60	$ 862,500, say $ 860,000 @ 95% occupancy
Required rent per square foot $860,000 ÷ 105,000 sq. ft. of *NLA*	$8.19 per square foot per year, or $0.68 per square foot per month

sociated with the project as well as the investors' perceptions. Nevertheless, the figure derived is considered a good gauge of the rent required to justify new construction.

Current rent levels in the Leadville market, which were established in the survey of Class A, B, and C apartment units (Step 4.2), averaged $0.52 per square foot per month. According to XYZ Data Co., current monthly rents average $0.55 per square foot. The appraiser's survey is considered more reliable. Rent levels will need to increase approximately 30% in real terms before new construction is anticipated. Assuming rents will be able to increase at the 8% to 10% rate experienced in this market in the past year, it will be approximately three years before construction is feasible. Should rents increase at a faster rate or developers find a way to reduce costs, new construction might be feasible earlier, say in one to two years.

Forecasting the future date when new construction will commence requires consideration of other supply-side factors in addition to rent. These factors include the availability of land and financing, proper zoning, and a market that is attractive to developers. By way of example, consider two comparable metro areas. One area attracts development, while the other area does not despite high rents, good zoning, and generally favorable circumstances. In such a case developers may continue to build in the proven market because a perception of risk associated with the latter.

Final Conclusion on New Construction

Based on the marginal demand and rent analysis, significant new construction is anticipated to occur in two to five years, say four years.

The quantity of new construction is another question. Over the past 10 years, an average of 650 units per year have been built in this market (Step 3.1). This overbuilding is not expected to continue in the future because of new, more stringent lending rules. Thus, construction of 300 to 450 units per year, on average, is probable over the four- to 10-year forecast period.

STEP 6 FORECAST SUBJECT CAPTURE

The subject market was analyzed with both inferred and fundamental methods. The appraiser's conclusions are summarized below

Inferred Methods

- General growth trends. Strong lease-up potential was indicated for the subject property.
- New construction. The lack of recent construction suggests less competition for the subject and is therefore another positive indicator of the subject's potential for quick lease-up, given the strong growth trends cited above.
- Historical absorption. Over the previous two years, absorption averaged 250 units per year. If last year's trend continues and the subject's capture increases by 5% annually, the subject will achieve 95% occupancy in two to three years.
- Rent increase. Last year real rents increased 10%, thus it can be inferred that the subject's rents will increase accordingly.

Fundamental Methods

Fundamental methods were used to estimate the subject capture rate, which was then applied to the forecast of the real demand for space in the market.

The subject's capture rate can be analyzed in number of ways. Three methods are presented here and the results are reconciled:

- The subject's current capture rate. Current capture is calculated as follows. Of the approximately 7,000 competitive units citywide, about

83% to 85% are occupied, indicating 5,810 to 5,950 occupied units, say 5,880. The subject currently has 250 occupied units. Thus the subject's capture rate is 250 / 5,880, or 4.2%.

- The pro rata share method. This method employs the ratio of subject units to competitive units. There are 7,000 competitive units, including the 312 subject units. Thus the subject's pro rata share is 4.5% (312 / 7,000). Comparing the current capture rate of the subject with its pro rata share suggests that the subject's performance is slightly below average.

- Competitive rating method. The scores shown in the supply survey and rating chart (Table 14.10) are examined. The subject had a rating, or score, of 20, and the scores of all Class A, B, and C projects surveyed totaled 474. Based on these figures, the subject's indicated percentage of capture is 4.2% (20 / 474).

Given the indications described above, it is reasonable to conclude that the subject's current actual capture rate will continue until new competition materializes. The prospect of new construction may necessitate an adjustment of the capture rate. The previous equilibrium analysis forecast probable construction of approximately 350 units annually beginning in two to five years. The pro rata share method may be used to gauge how the new units will impact the subject capture rate. The subject's current pro rata share is 4.5% (312 / 7,000), but with 350 units added, the pro rata share will be reduced to approximately 4.3% (312 / 7,350). If construction continues to add an average of 350 units annually, as expected, a similar reduction in the subject's pro rata share can be expected each year.

Step 6.1 Estimate subject capture

In Table 14.15 the subject's possible capture is calculated based on the mid-range population forecast presented earlier in the case study.

Final Conclusions on Subject Marketability

The preceding analysis was based on a mid-range population forecast and employed both inferred and fundamental methods. The inferred methods suggested strong lease-up potential for the subject. The fundamental methods generally supported this conclusion, but with two significant exceptions. First, these techniques indicated that lease-up would not be as strong as indicated by the inferred methods. Second, the fundamental methods revealed a cyclical trend that is expected to peak in five years, with the subject at 94% occupancy (i.e., 294 units occupied in Year 5 divided by 312 total units). The subject's occupancy rate will then begin to decline, assuming new construction comes on line as forecast.

The major purpose of this analysis is to forecast future income for a valuation appraisal. The conclusions drawn from the inferred methods are based on

Table 14.15
Marginal Demand Projections: Mid-Range Forecast

	Year 0	Year 1	Year 2	Year 3	Year 4	Year 5	Year 6	Year 7	Year 8	Year 9	Year 10
1. Population	46,800	49,048	51,295	53,543	55,790	58,038	60,285	62,533	64,780	67,028	69,275
2. Population increase		2,248	2,248	2,248	2,248	2,248	2,248	2,248	2,248	2,248	2,248
3. Persons per household	2.70	2.69	2.68	2.67	2.66	2.65	2.64	2.63	2.62	2.61	2.60
4. Total number of households (Line 1 / 3)		18,233	19,140	20,053	20,973	21,901	22,835	23,776	24,724	25,680	26,643
5. Percentage of renter households		39%	39%	39%	39%	39%	39%	39%	39%	39%	39%
6. Demand for subject unit type (Line 4 x 5)		7,111	7,465	7,821	8,180	8,541	8,906	9,273	9,643	10,015	10,391
7. Plus normal vacancy		0	0	0	0	0	0	0	0	0	0
8. Total demand for subject housing (Lines 6 + 7)		7,111	7,465	7,821	8,180	8,541	8,906	9,273	9,643	10,015	10,391
9. Affordability %		80%	80%	80%	80%	80%	80%	80%	80%	80%	80%
10. Total demand for occupied units (Line 8 x 9)		5,689	5,972	6,257	6,544	6,833	7,124	7,418	7,714	8,012	8,313
11. Current & estimated competitive supply		7,000	7,000	7,000	7,000	7,000	7,350	7,700	8,050	8,400	8,750

Table 14.15

Marginal Demand Projections: Mid-Range Forecast (continued)

	Year 0	Year 1	Year 2	Year 3	Year 4	Year 5	Year 6	Year 7	Year 8	Year 9	Year 10
12. Estimated new competitive supply		0	0	0	0	350	350	350	350	350	350
13. Total competitive supply (Lines 11 + 12)		7,000	7,000	7,000	7,000	7,350	7,700	8,050	8,400	8,750	9,100
14. Net (excess) shortage (Line 10 - 13)		(1,311)	(1,028)	(743)	(456)	(517)	(576)	(632)	(686)	(738)	(787)
Capture Estimates for Pine Grove Apartments (Subject Property)											
15. Estimated % of total demand captured by subject	0.0%	4.4%	4.4%	4.4%	4.4%	4.3%	4.1%	3.9%	3.7%	3.6%	3.4%
16. Estimated total subject capture in units (Line 10 x 15)	0.0	250.3	262.8	275.3	287.9	293.8	292.1	289.3	285.4	288.4	282.6

historical data which described a period of unprecedented building activity. Since the forecast data are considered reliable, the conclusions based on the fundamental methods have been given more weight in estimating future occupancy and rent levels.[10]

Low-end estimates *Occupancy:* Level to slightly rising Year 1 through Year 5, then slowly increasing to 85% occupancy Year 5 through Year 10. *Rent:* Declining at real rate of 0.5% per year to maintain the slight gain in occupancy.

Mid-range estimates *Occupancy*: Increasing to 94% in Year 5. New construction occurs, and from Year 6 to Year 10, occupancy declines. By Year 10, occupancy reaches 90%. *Rent***:** Increasing at a real rate of 4% per year for three years. From Year 4 to Year 10, rents decline at a rate of 0.5% per year to maintain occupancy.

High-end estimates *Occupancy:* Increasing to 95% in five years, and maintaining this level through Year 10. *Rent:* Remaining level at the same real rate over the next five years; increasing at 2% per year for Years 5 through 10.

Note that the high- and low-end estimates are included for illustration purposes. The calculations are not shown. The calculation procedure is the same as the procedure demonstrated, but low- and high-end population projections are used.

---

10. Some appraisals and many Level D analyses require further segmentation of supply and demand by tenant types and unit mixes. The Level C analysis seemed adequate to the needs of the case study for several reasons. The city had a fairly uniform population and the competition was also uniform. Further segmentation of demand usually requires the use of small area data based on secondary sources, which are typically less reliable.

PART III

*Highest and Best Use
Applications*

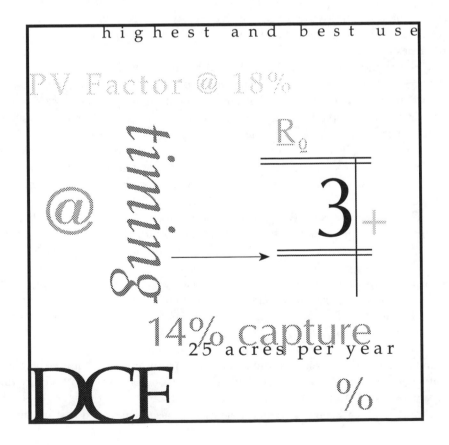

INTRODUCTION

———⇒•⇐———

The three case studies presented in Chapters 15, 16, and 17 provide a link between the mathematical models employed to test financial feasibility and the data inputs required in these models, specifically the forecast of occupancy and rent for the subject property. Part III underscores the leitmotiv of the book, that market analysis is a process, not a mechanical procedure. The process provides the estimates of effective demand, subject capture, and timing, which are critical to the conclusion of highest and best use and the application of the three approaches to value.

The applications in Part III show that the traditional four criteria used to determine highest and best use and the six-step market analysis process presented in this book are interrelated. The conclusion of highest and best use requires an additional step, the financial analysis of alternative probable uses to determine which use results in the highest value. Thus, the six-step market analysis process plus the financial analysis of alternative probable uses (Step 7) make up the comprehensive study process applied to determine highest and best use. The highest and best use conclusion is completed by the specification of the use, timing, and market participants.

This book focuses on the twofold purpose of market analysis in valuation appraisals. First, market analysis serves as support for the capture forecast required for each alternative probable use in highest and best use analysis. Second, market analysis provides the economic information needed to apply the three approaches to value, i.e., the economic forecast used in the income approach, the analysis of property productivity considered in the sales comparison approach, and the estimate of functional and economic obsolescence incorporated into the cost approach.

The level of market analysis required to support the three approaches to value differs with market conditions and the type of appraisal. Similarly, alternative probable uses considered in highest and best use analysis may require different levels of study. Thus, the appraiser also considers the level of study appropriate for each alternative probable use. Because highest and best use analysis is a decision-making process, each alternative probable use should be studied in sufficient detail to allow the analyst to make a logical, supportable decision on that use in terms of specification, timing, and identification of market participants. Five of the six case studies in the book represent Level C analyses. (The final case study, in Chapter 17, is a Level B analysis.)

Those who criticize appraisals of improved properties do not usually argue that the conclusion among alternative probable uses is wrong, but that the forecast developed in the income approach is not adequately supported. On the other hand, the most frequent criticism of appraisals of vacant land is that the alternative probable uses have not been adequately analyzed and, in particular, the timing for each use has not been given sufficient attention. This criticism suggests that the factors with the greatest impact on value require the most detailed market analysis.

For properties that have improvements that are relatively new and are operating at, or have a reasonable potential for, a positive net operating income (*NOI*), alternative uses are not a critical concern. Of course, alternative uses must still be considered, but the extent of market analysis undertaken to assess these alternative uses may, in many cases, be less detailed. The highest and best use of the land as though vacant has to be considered. However, since demolition of the improvements is unlikely and the land value is usually a relatively small portion of overall property value, it is reasonable that the analysis of the land as though vacant be less extensive. On the other hand, future capture rates and rent levels are critical to the determination of the value of improved properties, both prospective properties and currently leased properties. Therefore, in the valuation of improved properties, the focus of market analysis is on the property as improved, rather than the land as though vacant.

The appraisal of vacant land is different. The specific use among alternative probable uses that is selected as the highest and best use is identified as the use that results in the greatest value. When valuing vacant land, each alternative probable use must be considered for its impact on the value of the land. A highest and best use is chosen from among alternative probable uses, under which land value may vary widely. The market analysis for each highly competitive alternative use requires an equally detailed level of study.

Below are guidelines on the level of market analysis and degree of documentation required in a given assignment.

- For improved properties that are relatively new and are operating with a positive *NOI* (or for which a positive *NOI* is highly probable in the near future), an in-depth, typically Level C study of current use is almost always necessary. The purpose of market analysis for these properties is to support the three approaches to value.

- For appraisals of vacant land, an equally detailed level of market analysis is required for each highly competitive alternative use. Several alternative uses may be eliminated from consideration during productivity analysis. Thus, only one or two market segments may need to be considered in the analysis of demand, competitive supply, and capture.

337

- For appraisals of both vacant land and improved property, moderately competitive alternative uses are typically analyzed in less detail; usually a Level A or B analysis is adequate.
- For appraisals of vacant land and improved property, alternative uses that are only slightly competitive require even less extensive study. Usually Level A analyses of property productivity, demand and competitive supply, and capture are appropriate. These Level A analyses in combination with threshold testing (as described in Chapters 16 and 17) are considered sufficient.
- For appraisals of vacant land and improved property, remotely competitive alternative uses require only cursory study of property productivity, demand and competitive supply, and capture. Limited documentation is usually adequate.

The case studies presented in Part III include two applications involving vacant land and one application of an improved property that has not leased up. The first application, in Chapter 15, illustrates how the timing of a mix of uses impacts the highest and best use decision. Chapter 16 presents a situation in which the highest and best use of a vacant tract must be decided from two alternative probable uses. The case study in Chapter 17 demonstrates that the use of an unleasable improved property may not be the same as the use envisioned for the property when it was built.

THE MARKET ANALYSIS PROCESS FOR VACANT LAND (OPTIMAL USE MIX)

———◆———

- Property productivity analysis

- Market area definition

- Analysis of demand for each prospective use

- Analysis of supply under each prospective use

- Marginal demand/equilibrium analysis

- Subject capture estimate

- Financial analysis and optimal land use plan

CHAPTER FIFTEEN

Vacant Land

In valuing vacant land, appraisers often face the following problems:

- The most probable use of a property may not be the same as the use currently zoned. If nearby properties developed under the same permissible use are experiencing high vacancy rates, a different use may be indicated.
- The only comparable sales available to the appraiser involve buyers who had a specific use or uses in mind for the properties they purchased. If the subject's highest and best use, however, is as a long-term holding, a significant time adjustment will be required. How does the appraiser support a time adjustment without recent sales of very similar properties?
- Properties that represent truly comparable sales may be hard to identify since the use or timing of the use for the subject has not been established.
- Appraisers are required by clients, and sometimes by professional standards, to support the economic feasibility and probable timing of the land use. How can this be accomplished without recent comparable sales to users?

These are only a few of the problems confronting appraisers of vacant land. Highest and best use determination is a special challenge in the appraisal of vacant urban land. Sometimes the highest and best use is apparent, but the timing for that use is difficult to establish. Unfortunately for the appraiser, timing has a great effect on value. Because vacant land does not have an income stream, its current value must be derived from its future use.[1]

To reflect value accurately, comparable sales must have a similar use potential and similar timing for that use. *Timing* refers to the absorption of the completed property. Timing is a critical element of the development approach to value, which is a variant of the income capitalization approach. It is used as an alternative to the sales comparison approach when sales data are unavailable. The development approach requires detailed support for the anticipated timing of development.

The complexity of an appraisal increases when the subject has mixed-use potential. As mentioned earlier, the current zoning for a property may not reflect the highest and best use of that property. Excess vacancies in nearby properties under the use or uses allowed by the current zoning may indicate that another use, or combination of uses, should be considered for the property.

The dynamics of a market in which land parcels are sold to user-investors in anticipation of development may be very different from those of a market in which tracts of vacant land are held by speculator-investors. The nature of demand for raw land varies with the motives of its most probable buyers. A user-investor will either purchase and develop the property immediately or buy the land to develop it within the next few years. Such an investor regards the land as a component of a property that will yield an anticipated return after it is developed. A speculator-investor considers an undeveloped parcel differently. Some such investors will purchase land only to resell it for short-term gain. Short-term speculators are at the mercy of real estate cycles; they will reap big profits if the speculative land market goes up and incur big losses if the speculative land market goes down. Other speculator-investors use vacant land to warehouse capital assets over a long term.

The forces constituting the demand for vacant land generally interact with one another because they have a common interest. The ultimate success of the user-investor and the long-term investor depends on the demand for land by ultimate users. The success of a short-term speculator-investor is dependent on his or her ability to predict short-term market cycles, which may or may not be driven by user economics. Although economic theory suggests that short-term land markets are driven by the real demand of users, in reality other market forces are at work. Short-term market fluctuations reflect real estate's response to zoning and lending regulations and the tendency of participants in real estate markets to make decisions based on imperfect information.

In the 1980s, abundant investment capital increased the demand for land. In the 1990s, however, user-investors have generated very little demand. The decline in the value of short-term speculative land experienced in the 1990s may be attributed to both an increase in supply resulting from government liquidations

---

1. John S. Mitchell, "What Is Land Worth?" *Urban Land* (June 1988).

and a decrease in investment capital. In the late 1980s, the government became the controlling landowner in many markets, with a mandate to dispose of the REO holdings of insolvent institutions as quickly as possible. Thus, supply increased significantly. At the same time, financing for land purchases almost disappeared, significantly reducing the price of speculative land.

The activity of speculator-investors in short-term, boom markets often drives the prices of raw land up so high that they exceed what may be considered a reasonable economic cost to current user-investors. The resulting constriction of supply, however, acts to sustain high price levels. Eventually user-investors may find the high land prices justified—once the increasing pressure of user demand makes development economically feasible. On the other hand, if the pressure of demand is insufficient to support the high price level, speculator-investors will likely lower their asking prices to bring them in line with user-investor economics. The appraiser must understand not only the character of the short-term market for a vacant parcel, but also the long-term user demand for the tract of land. Is the market driven by user-investors or by speculator-investors? How do these two types of demand forces interact?

The case study presented in this chapter shows how market analysis can address these questions in an appraisal. The methodology employed to determine the highest and best use of the parcel has been adapted from the technique described in an article by Richard Peisner.[2] To apply this technique the appraiser obtains market data on the annual absorption rates for the specific uses and calculates the present value of the land under each use over the projection period. The appraiser examines the discounted land values from the various uses in conjunction with estimates of the acreage absorbable under each use to determine which mix of land uses will bring the greatest return. The case study that follows also illustrates the linkage between market analysis, highest and best use analysis, and the three approaches to value.

CASE STUDY DESCRIPTION

An appraiser has been retained to estimate the market value of a 66-acre tract of vacant land with a potential for mixed use. The subject is located along two major thoroughfares in a rapidly growing metropolitan area. It is three-quarters of a mile west of a major north-south freeway that is lined with new, multistory office and retail buildings. It is approximately one-quarter of a mile south of a proposed north loop interchange, which will be completed in the next three to five years. The current zoning specifies office and retail use, but the highest and best use of the property may not correspond to the zoning. The vacancy rate for office and retail buildings in the overall metropolitan area is high.

---

2. Richard B. Peisner, "Optimizing Profits from Land Use Planning," *Urban Land* (September 1982), 6-10.

The only comparables available are older sales of land bought by speculator-investors who anticipated a short-term gain from its resale. Unfortunately for the investors, this gain was not realized.

Over the past few years, development in the area approaching the subject tract has ceased. Until about three or four years ago, development had been booming, particularly just east of the subject on the north-south freeway. Even before the boom years, there was steady development in the general direction of the subject area. Recently, however, speculative activity has declined dramatically, while past speculative investment has restricted the available supply, driving up land prices. The pressure of demand would have to increase substantially to justify the high land prices of the recent past in terms of user-investor economics.

HIGHEST AND BEST USE ANALYSIS

The analysis of highest and best use is a screening process for examining alternatives uses. The use considered most probable is selected for further analysis.

The study begins with an economic overview and scoping analysis. In this step the appraiser focuses the study and quickly eliminates the alternatives that are obviously not feasible.

The detailed part of the study begins with productivity analysis of the subject tract. In this step the appraiser investigates how the attributes of the tract define the range of possible uses and identify which use(s) may be especially suitable. The subject's attributes include physical attributes (shape, size, contour, and drainage); legal and regulatory attributes (zoning and easements); and locational attributes (accessibility, linkages, adjacent land uses, relation to urban growth patterns, and locational ranking according to use-specific criteria). The productivity analysis eliminates uses deemed inappropriate from consideration. Those uses that are not eliminated are examined in subsequent steps — market delineation, supply and demand analysis, equilibrium analysis, and subject capture analysis. The appraiser considers the specific market for each probable use.

If it is clear that the subject site has mixed-use potential, the appraiser must specify the optimal land use plan, i.e., the mix of uses that will result in the highest return on the land given the acceptable level of risk. Future area demand and the subject's probable capture rate are the major parts of this study. In the final step of the analysis, the appraiser estimates the value per acre of land under each type of land use (user value less development costs), the amount of acreage to be developed under each specific land use, and the timing for each use. The timing estimate is based on the marginal demand outlook for each land use, or how much acreage is likely to be absorbed in the coming years. The appraiser uses projected absorption rates in conjunction with financial analysis to determine the land use mix that indicates the highest present value.

The study process described here parallels the four tests of highest and best use. In the productivity analysis, the appraiser establishes that the use mix is physically possible and legally permissible. Location analysis rounds out the study of productivity, which establishes a foundation for testing financial feasibility in the supply and demand analysis. The last step, in which the appraiser considers the mix of uses resulting in the highest present value, is a test of maximum profitability, the fourth and final test of highest and best use.

The process applied in the case study is illustrated in Figure 15.1. The highest and best use analysis process includes the six steps in market analysis plus a seventh step, financial analysis to detemine maximum profitability.

1. Property productivity analysis
2. Definition of the market for each use
3. Analysis of the demand for each prospective use (For the subject tract, these uses are multifamily apartment use, moderate-intensity retail use, garden office use, and light industrial use.)
4. Analysis of the supply of properties under each prospective use
5. Equilibrium analysis/marginal demand for each use
6. Estimate of subject capture for each market
7. Financial analysis and optimal land use plan

STEP 1 PROPERTY PRODUCTIVITY ANALYSIS

Step 1.1. Site analysis

In site analysis the appraiser identifies specific restrictions on the use of the site as well as potential opportunities to develop the site under alternative land uses. The four factors to be considered in site analysis are:

1. Immediate access to the site
2. Physical restraints and/or advantages
3. Immediately adjacent land uses
4. Legal restraints and/or advantages

Description of Site

Among the physical characteristics of the subject tract are its shape, size, contour, and drainage. The subject is a 66-acre rectangular site aligned with the surrounding grid of land parcels. Its dimensions are approximately one-half mile (2,640 feet) by one-fifth of a mile (1,090 feet). The slope of the site is moderate and would not present any impediment to development. Two existing ponds on the site are fed by a creek that flows across a narrow floodplain. The ponds could be used as a retention facility to capture additional runoff after the site is developed. However, constructing such a facility would reduce the developable area of the tract by at least two and one-half acres. An alternative solution would be to fill in the ponds and channelize the creek with culverts. Current electricity, water, and sewer service is adequate.

Several regulatory constraints and legal entitlements are associated with the subject tract. The site is subject to two different zoning ordinances. The frontage

Figure 15.1
Highest and Best Use Analysis Process

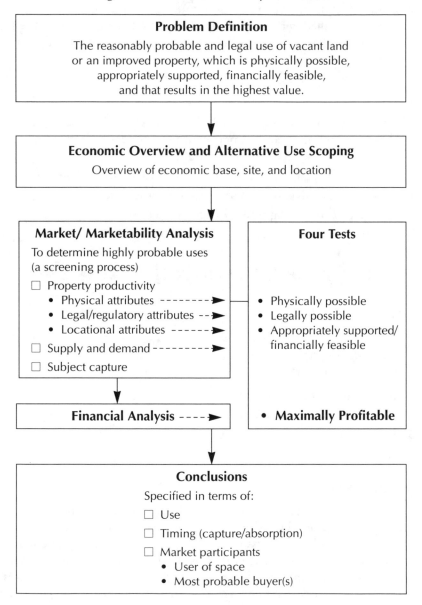

Problem Definition
The reasonably probable and legal use of vacant land
or an improved property, which is physically possible,
appropriately supported, financially feasible,
and that results in the highest value.

Economic Overview and Alternative Use Scoping
Overview of economic base, site, and location

Market/ Marketability Analysis
To determine highly probable uses
(a screening process)
☐ Property productivity
  • Physical attributes -------▶
  • Legal/regulatory attributes --▶
  • Locational attributes ------▶
☐ Supply and demand --------▶
☐ Subject capture

Four Tests

  • Physically possible
  • Legally possible
  • Appropriately supported/
    financially feasible

Financial Analysis ----▶

  • **Maximally Profitable**

Conclusions
Specified in terms of:
☐ Use
☐ Timing (capture/absorption)
☐ Market participants
  • User of space
  • Most probable buyer(s)

along the two thoroughfares is zoned for general retail use, while the remainder
is zoned for garden office use. The city planning department is not adverse to
changing the zoning, either by reducing the allowable density to accommodate
multifamily apartments or by increasing the density to allow for light industry
(i.e., office showrooms and industrial flex space). Thus, there are no serious legal

constraints on the potential development of the tract. Local floodplain regulations require that runoff be contained. A right-of-way will run with the access road that connects with St. James Place, the tract's western border. It is up to the developer, however, to decide whether to install such an access road.

Analytic Process

One way to begin site analysis is with a map. The analyst prepares a topographic map of the subject, outlining features that represent restraints upon its use as well as features that present opportunities for its development. Site features can be mapped individually on transparencies which are then overlaid to produce a graphic analysis of site areas where opportunities or problems may arise. This procedure is similar to the McHarg overlay technique.[3] The checklist shown in Table 15.1 indicates the site characteristics studied in site analysis. A map depicting the characteristics of the subject site is presented as Figure 15.2.

Conclusions derived from the graphic analysis of the site characteristics (Figure 15.2) are cited below:

- Views and slopes. The northern half of the tract is suitable for residential development.
- Access points. Curb cuts are required 250 feet from major corners, but this requirement should not limit land use. If an interior east-west street is desired, it will have to connect to Virginia Avenue on the west side of the subject. This street cannot be extended to an eastward connecting street, however, because there are existing apartments to the east of the subject. The interior street cannot exit to the south since the connection with New York Avenue, a major thoroughfare, would be too close to another major north-south street, St. James Place. Therefore, the only possible exit would be at Virginia Avenue. To avoid the cost of bridging the creek, the interior street should be located to the west of the creek area.
- Floodplain. The amount of area in the floodplain raises questions about the development costs. To justify the costs of floodplain modification, the land use selected must be fairly intensive and well supported. The situation is further complicated because the city requires retention features for floodplain modification, i.e., the runoff flow must meet the specific parameters set for residential use. The creek and existing ponds could be worked into the design of the tract and provide scenic amenities for residential and possibly office use. However, these features divide the tract into a two halves: one to the north of the creek and another to the south.
- Abutting land uses. To the west of the subject is single-family residen-

---

3. I. McHarg, *Design with Nature* (New York: Natural History Press, 1969).

Table 15.1

Site Analysis Checklist

Characteristic	Comment
☐ Slopes	The slopes of different areas of the site are shown on the map. Analyzing the slope of the site provides a basis for identifying probable uses. For example, slopes of less than 2% are best suited for retail and industrial uses. Slopes of more than 15% are not recommended for road grades. Steep slopes may be preferred for residential development.
☐ View	View is a function of both the site characteristics and the off-site perspective. The subject is at the top of a ridge. The primary concern is whether the off-site view puts the site at a disadvantage. A good view is considered positive for residential, office, and restaurant uses.
☐ Access points	Access to a vacant tract is controlled by curb cut regulations and the parcel's alignment with existing or platted streets. These features should be marked on the map of the site. A connection with the road may be required at a specific point, but in most cases, the alignment with interior roads is flexible.
☐ Floodplain	Usually a 100-year flood line is drawn on the site map. Existing or planned ponds and other drainage features should be indicated as well.
☐ Abutting land uses	Adjacent land uses go a long way in determining the ultimate use of the land. In the site analysis, these uses are usually labeled and their borders with the subject are measured. The exact land use should be cited. In the subject case, apartment buildings are a nearby land use. The land immediately adjacent to the subject is an open, landscaped area, which could be used by occupants of the subject for recreation. This abutting area helps shape the land use possibilities for the subject.
☐ Legal/ regulatory	Zoning does not represent a constraint on development. Floodplain regulations specify containment of runoff. A right-of-way will run with the road that connects with St. James Place, the tract's western border. (Construction of this road is the developer's option.)
☐ Noise contours	Sites near major generators of noise may have a noise contour above 65 decibels. A 65-decibel contour is the recognized limit for residential uses. Higher levels indicate that noise abatement measures will be required to accommodate other uses.
☐ Utilities	The capacity of, distance to, and access points for utilities should be marked on the site map. For large tracts under less costly uses such as residential, the access point is usually in the area developed during the first phase of the project. High-intensity land uses such as office and retail use can sometimes support the higher costs of an off-site extension. The interior area of the subject tract has substantial residential potential, but the most probable use of the front of the tract is for retail development. The absence of any current demand for a retail use could change the prospects for residential land use. If the demand for residential use is immediate but the cost of an off-site utility extension makes it unfeasible to develop the back part of the tract at this time, then the retail use at the front of the site may have to be reconsidered. If the tract has an alternative use as a long-term holding, future demand will have to be high enough to justify the holding costs.
☐ Tree cover	The portion of a site covered by trees should be marked on the site map. The cost of clearing is included among construction costs. Tree-covered areas are a positive amenity feature for uses such as residential subdivisions and office parks.
☐ Soil/rock patterns	Underlying soils and rock strata that differ significantly from those of competitive tracts can impact land use. Extensive rock deposits can make construction of sewer lines very expensive and discourage residential use. High shrink-swell type soils can present an obstacle to industrial land use. This feature is considered in relation to the competition and the engineering costs to correct deficiencies.

Figure 15.2
Site Analysis Map

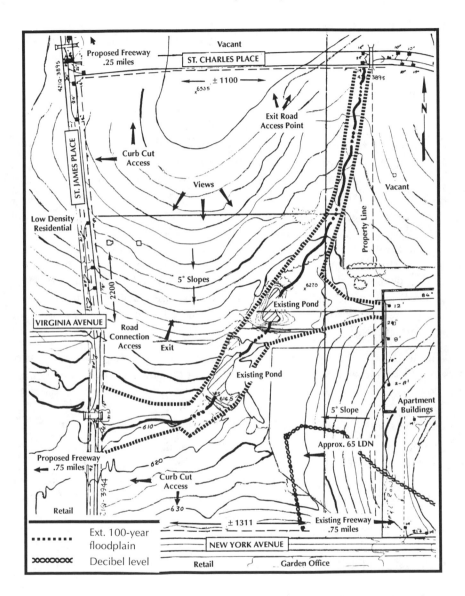

tial use, to the east are apartments, and to the south are retail/office units, which are 50% occupied. The land to the north is vacant but zoned for office use. For the subject, the land use question is whether the higher-density uses will connect from south to north, or the less-intense residential uses will connect from east to west. This question cannot be resolved in the site analysis, in which the appraiser only identifies the site and abutting land uses and indicates that either alternative or some combination of uses is possible.

- Noise contours. The commuter airport near the subject creates decibel readings of more than 65 in the southeast corner of the site. This suggests that a residential use for this area is doubtful.

- Utilities. The access point for utilities can be a major factor in phasing the development of large tracts. In this case, utility connections have already been installed at the site, so utility access is not a determinant of use.

- Natural features (e.g., trees, soils). The presence or absence of certain natural features can significantly influence land use decisions. Trees are not found on the subject site, which is typical of the area. The subject soils have high shrink-swell properties, but so do the soils of all the competitive tracts in this area. The shrink-swell problem can be corrected with proper engineering. Thus, these features have no impact on alternative land uses.

Table 15.2 summarizes the site analysis. So far, the appraiser's analysis has focused only on the specific site. Further analysis of the subject's location may alter the conclusions presented in this table.

Conclusions

The table reveals that many site features are conducive to residential development of the northern half of the subject. The southern half of the tract appears to have greater potential for retail and office use, primarily because it fronts on one of the most heavily traveled east-west thoroughfares in the city and properties across the street have been developed under similar uses. Nevertheless, the site analysis has not eliminated any uses. Therefore, the appraiser must continue to consider the full range of use possibilities for the subject. The next step, location analysis, will help focus the study on the most probable uses.

Step 1.2 Location analysis

The locational attributes of real estate tell us where growth is most likely to occur. The demand and supply analysis performed in Steps 3, 4, and 5 will help the appraiser estimate how much growth might be expected. The areas with locational features most favorable to growth will tend to capture growth at a faster rate than other areas.

Table 15.2
Summary of Site Analysis Conclusions

Northern half of tract   **Impact on:**

	Single-Family Use	Apartment Use	Retail Use	Office Use	Industrial Use
Slopes	positive	positive	neutral	neutral	negative
View	positive	positive	neutral	positive	neutral
Access	positive	positive	negative	negative	positive
Floodplain	positive	positive	negative	negative	negative
Abutting land uses	positive	positive	negative	negative	negative
Noise	positive	positive	positive	positive	positive
Utilities	positive	positive	positive	positive	positive
Tree\soils	neutral	neutral	neutral	neutral	neutral
Legal	positive	positive	positive	positive	positive

Southern half of tract   **Impact on:**

	Single-Family Use	Apartment Use	Retail Use	Office Use	Industrial Use
Slopes	positive	positive	neutral	neutral	negative
View	positive	positive	neutral	positive	neutral
Access	slightly negative	positive	highly positive	positive	positive
Floodplain	positive	positive	negative	negative	negative
Abutting land uses	negative	positive	highly positive	positive	slightly positive
Noise	highly negative	negative	neutral	neutral	neutral
Utilities	positive	positive	positive	positive	positive
Tree/soils	neutral	neutral	neutral	neutral	neutral
Legal	positive	positive	positive	positive	positive

Location comprises both static and dynamic features. Static features include linkages and land use associations. *Linkages* refer to the movement of people, goods, services, and information to and from the subject site. They are measured in terms of time and cost. Land use associations may be complementary or incompatible. In terms of growth, complementary uses have a positive impact, while incompatible uses have a negative effect. Because locational relationships change over time, the dynamic aspects of location also need to be addressed. Dynamic features include the character of urban growth as well as its direction and rate.

Step 1.2(1) Description of the subject's location

Major thoroughfares provide access to the 66-acre site along its southern and western borders. A secondary street provides access along the northern side of the tract. Commuters traveling from suburban communities in the north to the office park districts further south account for much of the traffic on the thoroughfares. To provide direct access to the site, curb cuts will have to be made along the two thoroughfares, and an east-west access road to the interior of the tract will have to be built to line up with an adjacent east-west secondary street.

Linkages with other sectors in the metropolitan area are readily available. A major north-south freeway lies three-quarters of a mile to the east, and the site of a proposed north loop freeway is approximately one-fourth of a mile to the north. The freeway should be completed in three to five years. The subject does not have direct access to these freeways, but linkages to the subject will be improved with the completion of the freeway. The traffic count in the immediate vicinity of the subject is now approximately 20,000 vehicle trips per day and is expected to double in the next 10 to 15 years. Traffic congestion in the area could, therefore, become a problem and might negatively impact the tract's potential for residential use.

The subject is located along the northern periphery of a major metropolitan area. Land uses in the immediate area include residential and strip commercial development. To the north and the northeast, there are moderate-income, family-type apartment complexes. Middle-income residential communities extend five miles to the northwest of the tract. Beyond these communities lie higher-income neighborhoods. A middle-income, single-family, patio home development is located to the southwest of the subject. If residential development is considered for the tract, it would likely appeal to middle-income, rather than upper-income, residents.

Retail facilities to the south of the subject include a local shopping center, several strip developments, and convenience stores. These represent support facilities for the residents in the area. Light industrial flex space has been planned for an area one-half mile to the southeast of the subject. This area was platted with streets a year ago, but no lots have been sold nor has any construction started.

With respect to metropolitan growth patterns, the tract lies three-quarters of a mile west of the north-south freeway, a major corridor lined with multistory office buildings. This office corridor has an excellent reputation both locally and nationally. The completion of the proposed north loop freeway northwest of the subject tract will likely stimulate further office development in the vicinity.

An understanding of the metropolitan matrix and major regional employment centers also helps the appraiser assess the probable character of development for the tract. The central business district, which is approximately 20 miles south of the site, contains 30 million square feet of office space. A second concentration of office buildings three to four miles southeast of the subject is centered around an interchange on the north-south freeway. The office corridor that lines the freeway is an extension of this node. The second office district contains 10 million square feet of office space as well as retail and light industrial space. A third office node is located eight miles west of the subject tract. It has 10 million square feet of office space plus retail, hotel, and light industrial space.

Step 1.2(2) Application of the location analysis

The location analysis focuses on probable future land use(s) for the subject given the broad trends in area growth. Growth trends are analyzed in a number of ways. In one analytic approach, locational factors are examined under four major categories:

- Existing land uses and linkages
- Direction of growth and land use intensity
- Growth rate (dynamic attributes)
- Zoning and planning

The examination of these four factors, together with the location rating developed in Step 1.2(3), form the basis for the neighborhood use forecast.

Different analytical techniques may be applied. The example shown here is based on a graphic analysis in which the appraiser maps the specific elements being considered, e.g., land use linkages, land use patterns, historical growth rates. As a final step, a narrative summary and future land use map are compiled.

Land Uses and Linkages—Projected Roads and Thoroughfares

Figure 15.3 is a map of existing roads in the area of the subject and roads that will be completed within the next five years. A five-year time frame was selected because the subject is located in an area where substantial development has occurred within the last five years. If the land use of a tract located some distance from current development were being considered, then roads projected for completion in five to 10 years might be mapped. For still more distant tracts, roads planned 20 years into the future could be mapped, using the city's long-range thoroughfare plan as a guide. Most roads indicated on the long-range thoroughfare plan will not be in place until after the subject property is developed so this plan is given little weight in the location analysis. Land use is influenced more by immediate linkages than by linkages that may exist in 20 years. (The 20-year plans of some cities represent long-range wish lists rather than expectations of thoroughfares that will be actually completed 20 years in the future.)

A land use map is important for identifying potential critical mass locations (corners or strips), which are sometimes called *major intensity nodes*. Urban growth models suggest that growth occurs along transportation linkages and that concentrations of different socioeconomic groups also influence growth

Figure 15.3
Land Use Linkages

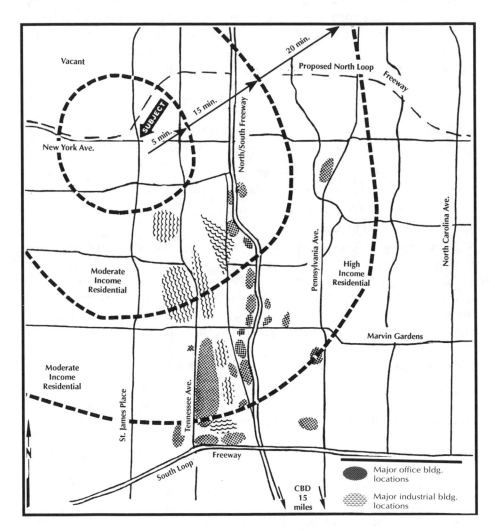

Note. Not to scale. Driving times are indicated by concentric circles.

patterns. Figure 15.3 shows land use linkages and the moderate- and high-income residential developments located in the subject area. The only new road of significance is the proposed north loop freeway to be completed just north and west of the subject in the next few years. This new freeway will help link the subject to other complementary land uses and open up new markets for the subject. On the downside, more intense land uses may develop at the major intersections of the new freeway and draw clientele away from the currently developing retail node on the southwest corner across from the subject. Such development would also tend to relegate the retail uses around the subject to small-scale, drive-by retail establishments rather than larger destination retail centers.

Direction of Growth and Intensity of Land Use

The analyst identifies current growth trends, focusing on patterns in the intensity of use to determine if the subject will be located in a high-, medium-, or low-intensity area. Will the subject be located in an area where intense land uses such as multistory office or retail use dominate? Again, the analytical technique demonstrated is graphic, mapping land uses by intensity. The following categories are identified on the existing land use map (Figure 15.4):

- High-intensity commercial—multistory office buildings and regional retail centers.
- Moderate-intensity commercial—concentrations of garden office (e.g., doctors' offices, insurance offices), community retail, and restaurant facilities. Small, scattered, neighborhood retail uses are not usually included in this category because they do not typically set the growth pattern of an area. Of course, there may be exceptions. If neighborhood retail use is able to expand in one location, it may evolve into a community retail node. When such situations are found, they are identified on the map as moderate-intensity commercial.
- Moderate-intensity industrial—industrial park and flex space buildings. All industrial land uses in the subject area are considered to be in this category. The graphic analysis technique identifies concentrations rather than isolated industrial land uses.
- Moderate-intensity apartment—20 to 35 apartment units per acre. All the apartments in the subject area are considered moderate intensity.
- Low-intensity residential—one- to four-family units.

Based on these classification criteria, the pattern for development in the subject area is plotted in Figure 15.4. The contour lines on the map set the boundaries of the high-intensity growth area. In the case study application, high-intensity land use is of major concern. The subject is zoned for moderate-intensity land use (general retail and garden office), and the analysis of growth patterns confirms that a high-intensity use is not probable. High-intensity land uses have been developed on a north-south axis along the freeway, in keeping

Figure 15.4
Existing General Land Uses

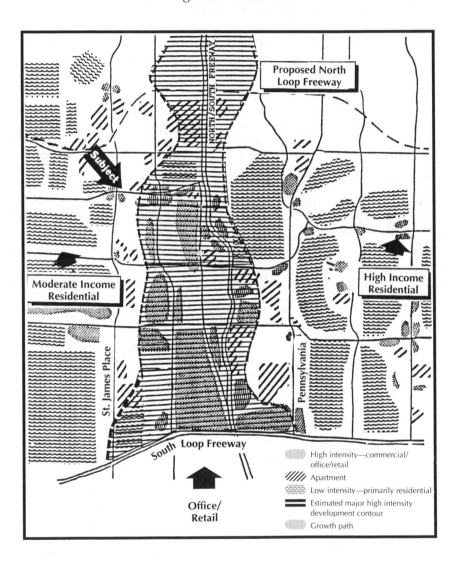

with the radial corridor growth model. Land uses in the immediate area of the subject, however, are likely to be moderate- to low-intensity.

From this analysis of land use patterns, the following conclusions can be drawn. High-intensity land use can be seen on both sides of the north-south freeway corridor between St. James Place to the west and Pennsylvania Avenue to the east. The greater the distance from the north-south freeway, the lower the land use intensity, as evidenced by the presence of apartment and residential uses.

The development pattern in the areas to the east and west of the north-south freeway resembles a funnel. The highly intense development at the intersection of the south loop freeway and north-south freeway tends to constrict north of the intersection. Based on proposed developments, the high-intensity corridor is likely to expand in the vicinity of the proposed new freeway intersection.

Based on this analysis, it appears that the subject lies in a transitional area between the more intense uses to the east near the north-south freeway and the area of less intense land use to the west. The contour line shown in Figure 15.4 indicates the probable area to be developed under high-intensity land use.

Growth Rate Analysis

Rate of growth is another significant factor. The rate of growth is a function of infrastructure, regulatory trends, demographics, and demand. At this stage in the process, the analyst takes a preliminary look at the rate of growth from a locational perspective. The technique presented here maps the areas of urban growth over time. The historic boundaries shown in Figure 15.5 indicate when most of the land came under development — e.g., by 1970, 1980, or 1990. This information was compiled by studying aerial photographs taken over a period of time. An urban area was defined as an area in which at least 60% of the land was developed. The periphery of urban growth at the beginning of each decade is shown on the map. The growth rate for the area within the contour lines of the growth corridor is then estimated from the timing and direction of previous development.

The subject area is not located within the path of the growth corridor, but at its edge. Assuming demand continues, the subject will become part of a growing urban area within two to five years.

Zoning and Public Planning

The zoning of the subject and adjacent areas and the probability of a change in zoning are analyzed next. The portion of the subject tract along the two thoroughfares is currently zoned for general retail use; the remainder is zoned for garden office use. The adjacent areas to the east and northeast of the subject are zoned for multifamily, neighborhood retail, and office uses. The area to the west of the subject has a more residential character, with retail uses limited primarily to major intersections of the proposed north loop freeway.

The area just southeast of the subject is zoned for light industrial/office park use. This area has been platted and streets were finished within the last year and

Figure 15.5
Historical Rate of Growth

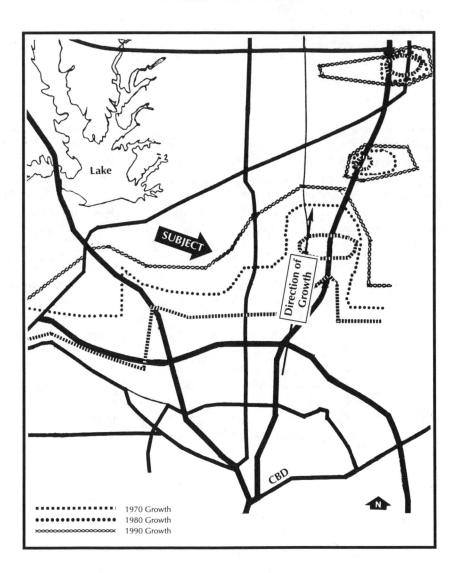

1970 Growth
1980 Growth
1990 Growth

a half, but no lots have yet been sold. South of the subject is a development of single-family and patio homes with some garden office facilities. Northeast of the subject, at the intersection of the north-south freeway and the proposed new north loop freeway, a tract has been zoned for a shopping mall. Zoning to the northeast, northwest, and west of the subject is predominantly residential mixed with some commercial uses to support residential development.

The analyst must consider the likelihood of a change in the current zoning of the subject and adjacent sites. The first step in this analysis is to eliminate uses that are clearly not compatible with existing uses in the area as well as uses that have been previously denied in the subject area or comparable areas of the city. In the second step the analyst draws on the productivity analysis of the subject to prepare a preliminary land development forecast for the subject area. If the subject site is not zoned for the probable alternative uses indicated by this forecast, these uses must be considered in conjunction with the likelihood of the required zoning change. In rating probable alternative uses for the subject tract, the analyst considers the following conditions:

1. The subject site may not be suitable for the use under the current zoning, but it is physically suitable for the forecast use.
2. The forecast use is compatible with adjacent land uses.
3. The forecast use conforms to the city's comprehensive land use plan.
4. Conditions in the subject area have changed since the current zoning became effective.
5. The forecast use of the subject contributes to the public good (e.g., a police station, firehouse, playground, school) and is supported by civic or public interests.
6. Zoning changes for comparable properties in similar locations in other parts of the city have been approved.
7. No nearby neighborhood association opposes the zoning change required to accommodate the forecast use.

If the forecast alternative use or uses satisfy all these conditions, the probability of a change in the zoning may be considered very high. If some of these conditions are met, the probability is moderate. The analyst should note, however, that the probability of a zoning change is almost never 100% certain. The typical approval time should also be considered. If it is extremely long, the estimated timing for the use should account for the time required for rezoning.

In conclusion the zoning and public plans for the subject area are conducive to mixed-use development of the tract. Given the requisite demand, all potential uses seem to fit the current development pattern with the exception of high-intensity uses. Analysis of the contour lines in Figure 15.4 indicates the need to eliminate high-intensity land uses from consideration. The zoning of nearby sites also suggests that rezoning for any of the proposed uses would not be a problem, with the exception of regional retail and light industrial uses.

Step 1.2(3) Subject use potential by location rating

The purpose of the location rating is to relate the subject's locational features to the most probable use. At this point in the analysis, demand has not been considered. In the next section the analyst will screen probable uses on the basis of demand.

In the rating procedure, specific criteria are applied to evaluate various potential uses of the subject site. According to the analysis, the subject location is most suitable for multifamily, garden office, and community retail uses; moderately suitable for an industrial park; and least suitable for regional retail, single-family, and multistory office uses. The rating procedure is shown in Table 15.3.

Table 15.3
Summary of Subject Location Analysis

	Ratings				Relative
	1 Poor	2 Average	3 Good	4 Excellent	Relative Score
Multistory Office					
Proximity to major activity nodes (Linkages to other offices & support facilities)	X				
Proximity to major transportation linkages (freeway)		X			
Proximity to executive housing	X				
Proximity to Fortune 500 firms	X				
Direction of multistory office growth	X				
Public planning and zoning	X				
Total score					7
Garden Office (Doctors, Insurance, etc.)					
Proximity to housing market				X	
Proximity to major thoroughfares				X	
Proximity to complementary retail uses				X	
Proximity to office occupants' housing		X			
Direction of garden office growth			X		
Public planning and zoning			X		
Total score					20
Regional Retail					
Proximity to regional housing market		X			
Traffic volume by site		X			
Proximity to major activity center (office, etc.)	X				
Proximity for direct access to freeways	X				
Direction of regional retail growth	X				
Public planning and zoning	X				
Total score					8

Table 15.3
Summary of Subject Location Analysis (continued)

	Ratings				Relative Score
	1 Poor	2 Average	3 Good	4 Excellent	
Community Retail					
Proximity to housing				X	
Traffic volume by site			X		
Proximity to other community shopping facilities			X		
Density of area housing			X		
Direction of community retail growth			X		
Public planning and zoning			X		
Total score					19
Multifamily					
Proximity to employment		X			
Proximity to cultural activities (restaurants, entertainment, etc.)				X	
Proximity to views/amenities			X		
Proximity to other apartment communities				X	
Direction of multifamily growth				X	
Public planning and zoning				X	
Total score					21
Single-Family					
Proximity to employment		X			
Proximity to schools/ community facilities	X				
Proximity to neighborhood shopping		X			
Proximity to quiet streets/privacy	X				
Direction of single-family growth	X				
Public planning and zoning	X				
Total score					8
Industrial Park					
Proximity to major transportation (particularly freeways, truck routes)		X			
Proximity to labor force			X		
Neighborhood acceptance of industrial park		X			
Proximity to service and material suppliers			X		
Direction of industrial park growth		X			
Public planning and zoning	X				
Total score					13

The site and location analyses indicate that all uses are probable alternatives for the subject site, with the exception of multistory office, regional retail, and single-family residential. The top-rated uses are:

1. Multifamily residential
2. Garden office
3. Community retail

An industrial use is also possible. Given the lack of public support for industrial zoning and the typically low prices of land under industrial use, this use is not highly probable, but it should not be eliminated from consideration.

Figure 15.6 shows the most probable development of the subject, under a mix of apartment, garden office, and community retail uses.

Conclusions of Site and Location Analyses

The subject appears to be in a transitional area with lower land use intensity than the high-intensity development along the north-south freeway corridor. The east side of the freeway is more developed than the west side. Studying current land use on the east side can provide a good indication of what can be expected in the subject area in the future, with one difference. The purchasing power (income level) of residents on the west side of the freeway is lower than the purchasing power of residents on the east side. This suggests lower rents and less retail development. With this in mind, some conclusions can be reached.

The predominant land use west of the subject will probably be residential since the east side of the freeway has been developed residentially. Nine planned developments of more than 50 acres were approved by the city in the last three years, and six were predominantly residential in nature.

The subject's corner location strongly suggests that its frontage should have a retail orientation. The existing retail/garden office development across the street from the subject provides the best example of what might be expected for the subject's frontage.

The back, or northern, portion of the subject has potential for a great variety of uses. From a locational perspective, this area could accommodate multifamily, patio home, moderate-intensity commercial/garden office, and light industrial uses. The key determinant of use, therefore, appears to be marginal or residual demand, which is examined in a subsequent section.

Conclusions Tested

The last step in the location analysis is to test the conclusions and ratings by developing an area land use plan. The subject's land uses must be compatible with the neighborhood's development potential, so the future land use of the neighborhood must be investigated. The same locational determinants of use applied to the subject tract are now applied to the immediate area of the subject.

The analyst first identifies where the network of thoroughfares and critical mass locations (corners and strips) will be. In this case the logical place would be

Figure 15.6
Projected General Land Uses Given Locational Characteristics

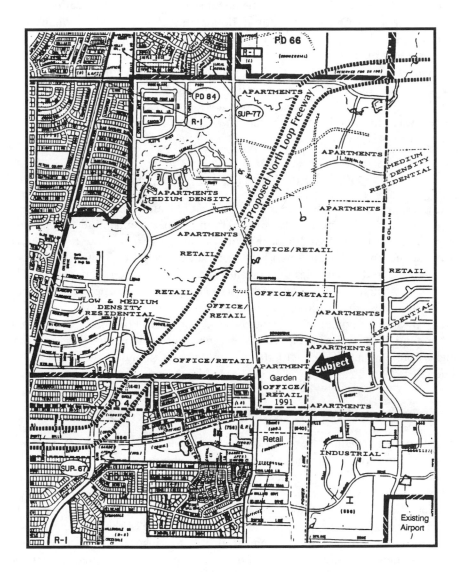

adjacent to the new proposed north loop freeway. Next, land uses adjacent to the critical mass locations must be studied to determine whether a major activity node could be developed. If so, the possible zoning for these locations is explored. Physical features, both natural (floodplains, topography) and man-made (utilities), are also examined in determining the likely use of the critical mass locations. Once the nodes of major activity have been identified, the fill-in areas are considered. The same locational determinants are considered in this analysis. Finally, a long-range development plan for the subject area can be drawn up. Figure 15.6 illustrates the conclusions of such a land use analysis applied to the subject tract. In the subsequent supply and demand analyses, the timing of these probable uses is investigated.

OVERVIEW OF STEPS 2, 3, 4, AND 5

The appraiser's analysis has identified four possible land uses based on the characteristics of the site and its location: multifamily apartments, moderate-intensity retail use, office use, and light industrial use (flex space). Now the potential demand and timing for these uses is studied. The appraiser estimates the demand for each use and inventories the current supply and planned competition. The timing is calculated by considering the relationship between supply and demand, which indicates when residual or marginal demand will exist. In the last step in the analysis, the optimal mix of land uses is determined. For a tract with mixed-use potential, the most probable combination of uses is the mix that yields the highest present value. Therefore, the timing of the residual demand must be considered.

STEP 2 MARKET AREA DEFINITION

A market area is defined by the specific use or uses of the property and the users it is likely to attract. The tenants and clientele who constitute the demand for the mix of uses in the subject tract will not all be drawn from areas with identical boundaries. Available data often have to be adjusted to correspond to the market areas defined by the location of property users. In this application, the overall city may be considered the market area for three of the prospective uses: the multifamily residential development, the light industrial use, and the office. Citywide demographics are used to measure the potential demand for these uses—i.e., the potential tenants of multifamily housing and the work force for a light industrial plant or office. The demand for retail space, the fourth potential use, is largely a function of the effective purchasing power of the population in the area of the retail facility. Thus the boundaries of the market area for a moderate-intensity, commercial use are defined based on the demographics of adjacent neighborhoods and local traffic counts, which will describe the likely clientele of prospective retail stores.

STEPS 3, 4, AND 5 DEMAND AND SUPPLY UNDER EACH PROSPECTIVE USE AND EQUILIBRIUM ANALYSIS

The appraiser gathers data on the demand for and supply of properties under the four uses deemed most suitable, i.e., multifamily apartment, moderate-intensity retail, office, and light industrial.

Multifamily apartment

Demand Analysis

The entire city constitutes the market area for multifamily apartment units. Based on a study of various demographic forecasts, the current citywide population of 67,500 may be expected to increase to 85,200 in four years and 107,585 in eight years. Household size now averages 2.58 persons, but is expected to decline at a rate of 1% annually. Thus, in four years, there should be 33,543 demand units (85,200/2.54) and in eight years, 43,034 demand units (107,585/2.50). Multifamily tenants account for 35% of the residents in the community, while single-family home owners account for 65%. Thus, total potential demand for multifamily units in four years will approximate 11,740 tenant households (0.35 x 33,543) and in eight years, 15,062 tenant households (0.35 x 43,034).

If the multifamily units considered for the tract are to appeal to middle-income tenants, approximately 25% of the potential demand should be disaggregated from the total projection to represent high-income tenants who seek more expensive apartments and low-income tenants who cannot afford the rents. The actual potential demand for middle-income apartment units would amount to approximately 8,805 tenant households (0.75 x 11,740) in four years and 11,296 tenant households (0.75 x 15,062) in eight years.

Table 15.4 shows how the projections of actual unit demand were derived.

Table 15.4
Projected Demand for Multifamily Residential Use

	Current	In 4 years	In 8 years
Citywide population	67,500	85,200	107,585
Divided by household size (declining at 1%/yr.)	2.58	2.54	2.50
Total unit demand	26,162	33,543	43,034
Times percentage of renters	x 0.35	x 0.35	x 0.35
Total tenant households	9,157	11,740	15,062
Less 25% high- or low- income households	2,289	2,935	3,766
Actual tenant households in middle-income range	6,868	8,805	11,296

Supply Analysis

There are currently 10,750 existing multifamily units. Of these, approximately three-quarters fall within a rental range affordable to middle-income tenants. Thus, the available competitive supply of 8,062 units (0.75 x 10,750) exceeds existing demand (6,868) by 1,194 units. The vacancy rate in the market area is at 15% and no new units are under construction or planned.

Marginal Demand Analysis

In four years there should be marginal demand of approximately 743 tenant households (8,805 – 8,062) and in eight years it should approximate 3,234 tenant households (11,296 – 8,062). (It is highly unlikely, however, that supply will remain static.) Thus, in approximately one to three years there should be positive marginal demand for apartments in the subject market area. An estimate of 2.5 years is reasonable (demand for 1,194 units divided by average annual demand of 484 units, as indicated in the next section). Some level of vacancy characterizes even balanced markets. Assuming a frictional vacancy rate of 5%, 361 units would be vacant in the current year. Residual demand for the multifamily residential use is calculated below:

	Current	In 4 years	In 8 years
Demand for multifamily units	6,868	8,805	11,296
Supply of multifamily units	8,062	8,062	8,062
(Excess)/shortage	(1,194)	743	3,234

Forecast Demand Compared with Historical Absorption

The average annual demand equals 484 units per year (8,805 – 6,870 = 1,935 which, divided by 4 years, equals 484). At 20 units per acre, the average annual demand for land would be 24.2 acres. The current number of excess units (1,194) divided by the 484 average annual demand for new units indicates a two and one-half year supply of units. In the last 10 years, approximately 250 acres have been developed for apartment units in the city.

Forecast Growth Conclusion

The development of 25 acres per year into apartment units seems reasonable, given the rapid population growth and liberal lending practices of the past 10 years. This pace of development did not result in overbuilding because population growth continued. The growth forecast is considered reasonable and is supported by the historical absorption rates. Thus, citywide growth in apartment unit development can be forecast as follows:

Conservative	—	an average of 15 acres annually
Most probable	—	an average of 25 acres annually
Optimistic	—	an average of 35 acres annually

There will be sufficient marginal demand to begin new apartment unit development in one to three years. It should be noted that any forecast of the timing of new construction typically includes feasibility analysis to determine whether future rents justify the construction. These analyses are presented for the highest and best use applications, but are not shown here. The above forecast is consistent with the feasibility analysis of future rents.

Moderate-intensity retail

Demand and Supply Analyses

A community retail facility on the subject site would probably have a market area with a three-mile radius. The number of supportable square feet of retail space is primarily a function of the purchasing power of the households within this three-mile area. Approximately one quarter of the city's residential population lives within this defined area. Thus, the current population of the market area is 16,875 (0.25 x 67,500), or approximately 6,540 households (16,875/2.58). Another 125 units were added to the total to represent commuters who may patronize the retail facility.[4]

Average area household income is $43,600 and has increased at an annual rate of 3% over the past decade. Approximately 57% of this income is spent on taxes and nonretail items, so the effective purchasing power per household is 43% of $43,600, or $18,748. About 50% of this effective purchasing power will go toward expenditures at a local retail complex. Demand projections for moderate-intensity retail use are shown in Table 15.5.

---

4. A percentage of the commuters who pass the site on a daily basis may be considered part of the potential demand supporting the retail use. The traffic count past the site is 20,000 vehicle trips per day, and this figure is expected to double in the next 10 to 15 years. Half of this total reflects local traffic (from the households within the three-mile radius), and the other half represents commuter traffic. The 10,000 commuter vehicles that pass the site each day include trips both to and from work, so 5,000 commuters pass the site daily. If 2.5% of the commuters who pass through the trade area stop to make purchases, 125 demand units may be added to the potential demand forecast.

Table 15.5
Projected Demand for Retail Use

	Current	In 4 years	In 8 years
Average area household income (increasing 3%/yr.)	$43,600	$49,000	$55,230
Times effective purchasing power per household	x 0.43	x 0.43	x 0.43
	$18,748	$21,070	$23,750
Times percentage of purchases at a local retail complex	x 0.50	x 0.50	x 0.50
	$ 9,374	$10,535	$11,875
Times number of households plus 2.5% of commuters	x 6,665	x 8,511	x 11,075
Total effective purchasing power	$62,477,710	$89,663,385	$131,515,625
Divided by sales/sq. ft. required to support retail (increasing at 3%/yr.)	$200	$225	$253
Total supportable sq. ft. of retail space	312,389	398,504	519,825

Marginal Demand Estimate

The appraiser estimates the total available retail space within a three-mile radius of the subject to be 350,000 square feet. An additional 30,000 square feet of retail space are expected in the future, indicating a future supply of 380,000 square feet.

Demand will exceed supply as the following calculations demonstrate:

	Current	In 4 Years	In 8 Years
Supportable retail space (in sq. ft.)	312,389	398,504	519,825
Supply of retail space (in sq. ft.)	350,000	380,000	380,000
(Excess)/shortage	(37,611)*	18,504	139,825

*16,441 sq. ft. of which is frictional vacancy, leaving 21,170 sq. ft. of oversupply.

Forecast Demand Compared with Historical Absorption

The forecast for four to eight years in the future indicates that approximately three acres of new retail space will be needed within the market area each year.

519,825 sq. ft. – 398,504 sq. ft.	=	121,321 sq. ft.
121,321 sq. ft./10,000 sq. ft. per retail acre	=	12.13 acres
12.13 acres/4 years	=	3 acres per year

According to the city planning department, 250 acres of retail space has been developed citywide in the past 10 years. This indicates an average of more than 25 acres per year, about eight times the retail acreage forecast for the subject area.

Forecast Growth Conclusion

In reconciling historical absorption with forecast demand, the appraiser gave far greater weight to the forecast, which is based on fundamental analysis. The appraiser reasoned that because the last decade was characterized by liberal lending practices, construction was not driven by fundamental demand. These conditions are not expected to be repeated in the next eight years. Moreover, the citywide data may be less indicative because they include all types of retail development (e.g., a major new mall) and are not segmented to reflect the center type or market area of the subject. The citywide data also described a larger area than the subject's market area.

Thus, the average annual growth in retail demand for the subject market area indicates that development should occur in about four years under one of the following scenarios:

Conservative	—	an average of one acre annually
Most probable	—	an average of three acres annually
Optimistic	—	an average of five acres annually

Feasibility analysis of future rents supported this timing.

Office market

Demand Analysis

The city boundaries encompass most of the market area identified for the subject. Thus, current and future employment citywide is studied to establish the demand for office space. Table 15.6 shows a projection of employment prospects for the city. The demand for office space is projected in Table 15.7, based on the employment projection and the office space needs of typical users.

Table 15.6

Trends in and Projections of Local Employment
by Standard Industrial Code

| Classification | Actual | Forecast | |
		In 4 years	In 8 years
Manufacturing	8,469	9,801	13,240
Mining	868	1,005	1,358
Construction	3,094	3,581	4,837
Transportation, communications, and public utilities	3,025	3,500	4,729
Wholesale trade	4,324	5,005	6,761
Retail trade	4,024	5,917	8,455
Finance, insurance, and real estate	1,575	2,170	4,105
Services and miscellaneous	3,463	4,770	9,024
Government	1,685	2,321	4,392
Total	30,527	38,070	56,901

Sources: Council of governments, employment commission, and the appraiser's analysis of city economic development data.

Supply Analysis

The local planning department estimates that there are currently 4,100,000 square feet of existing multitenanted office space in the subject city. This figure does not include office space in owner-occupied buildings and industrial buildings (flex space) or office space in retail shopping centers. According to a *Real Estate Data Company Report*, Northwest County Area #10 has about 4,039,300 square feet of multitenanted office space. Area #10 does not include all areas within the city, which accounts for the difference between the report's figure and the estimate provided by the city planning department. Neither study included the north-south freeway area in the adjacent suburban township, which has more than 9,797,000 square feet of office space, of which only about 62% is currently occupied.

A share of the citywide employment projection must be segmented to the subject market area. Because of the amount of vacant space nearby, reliable market segmentation is critical or a significant margin of error could result. The city planning department has processed final plats for an additional 712,000 square feet of office space in the subject market area, but there is no information on when development will begin. Given the current oversupply, construction is not anticipated in the near future.

Table 15.7
Office Space Demand Projection

Classification	Current	In 4 Years	In 8 Years	% in Offices*	Current Number of Office Workers*	In 4 Yrs. Number of Office Workers*	In 8 Yrs. Number of Office Workers*
Manufacturing	8,469	9,801	13,240	20%	1,694	1,960	2,648
Mining	868	1,005	1,358	20%	174	201	271
Construction	3,094	3,581	4,837	25%	773	895	1,209
Transportation, communications, and public utilities	3,025	3,500	4,729	39%	1,179	1,365	1,844
Wholesale trade	4,324	5,005	6,761	40%	1,730	2,002	2,704
Retail trade	4,024	5,917	8,455	40%	1,610	2,366	3,382
Finance, insurance, and real estate	1,575	2,170	4,105	70%	1,102	1,519	2,873
Services and miscellaneous	3,463	4,770	9,024	60%	2,078	2,862	5,414
Government	1,685	2,321	4,392	60%	1,011	1,392	2,635
Projected number of office workers					11,351	14,562	22,980
Average sq. ft. per office worker					x 200	x 200	x 200
Estimated total demand (in sq. ft.)					2,270,200	2,912,400	4,596,000

*In detached, multitenanted office space

Equilibrium Analysis

A comparison of supply and demand suggests that it will take more than eight years before supply and demand might achieve a reasonable balance. The calculations are shown in Table 15.8.

Table 15.8
Comparison of Demand and Supply

	Current	In 4 years	In 8 years
Demand in square feet	2,270,200	2,912,400	4,596,000
Supply in square feet	4,100,000	4,100,000	4,100,000
Residual demand in square feet	(1,829,800)	(1,187,600)	496,000

Yearly Average Demand		
Demand in 8 years	4,596,000	
Current demand	2,270,200	
New demand in 8 years	2,325,800	
Divided by	8 years	
Annual average demand	290,725	

Typically, 12,000 to 20,000 square feet per acre are developed under garden office use, so the annual office demand averages 14.5 acres (290,725 ÷ 20,000).

Forecast Demand Compared with Historical Absorption

Over the last 10 years, the city has seen an average of 10 acres platted for multitenanted office use each year. This shows that citywide office space has doubled over the last decade (10 acres x 20,000 sq. ft. per acre = 2,000,000 sq. ft.). However, a closer look at the data shows that 80% of this office space (1,600,000 sq. ft.) was created in the last five years, indicating an average of 16 acres per year (1,600,000 sq. ft. / 5 years = 320,000 sq. ft.; 320,000 sq. ft. / 20,000 sq. ft. = 16 acres).

Forecast Growth Conclusion

Based on fundamental analysis, a high-range forecast of the annual demand for new office space indicates 290,725 square feet over the next eight years. At this rate, new demand will fill up the current 1,829,800 square feet of vacant space in six years. Nevertheless, a closer look at the forecast shows that the major surge in employment will not occur until the latter part of the eight-year forecast period. Thus, new demand will not be realized for close to eight years. As Table 15.8 indicates, the annual average of 290,725 square feet of new demand over the next eight years comes to 14.5 acres per year. This figure is very close to the actual growth experienced over the last decade. Unfortunately, office building construction outpaced actual growth in employment, creating an overbuilt market.

It now appears that it will take up to eight years to absorb the current supply of vacant space. After this time, building can be expected to resume as the city has excellent long-term growth potential.

Due to a continuing strong outlook for the city, the appraiser forecasts demand at more than the historical average of 10 acres, but not more than the fundamental forecast of 14.5, say 15, acres per year. Fifteen acres per year is chosen as the top end of the range because the forecast is a little on the optimistic side, compared to actual historical occupancy levels. Thus, the final conclusion for citywide growth in demand starting eight years out is

Conservative	—	10 acres per year
Most probable	—	12 acres per year
Optimistic	—	15 acres per year

Light industrial

Supply and Demand Analysis

The demand for light industrial units is estimated based on citywide employment projections. The Bureau of Labor Statistics compiles statistical projections for production categories that correspond to light industry. While the projection years for which data are provided are not identical to those considered in the market analysis, interpolation may be used to obtain data for these years.

This case study application employs another method. The appraiser estimates the ratio of light industrial employment to employment in broader occupational categories, based on current occupied space. The first problem in forecasting the demand for industrial space is to define what is being forecast. *Industrial* is a broad term encompassing everything from factories to so-called flex space.[5]

Most of the industrial space in the subject city is used for specialized distribution, research and development (R&D), and light manufacturing, or as flex space. There is no heavy industrial manufacturing or warehouse space. The city has more than 4,500,000 square feet of industrial space, of which about 4,000,000 square feet are occupied. Dividing 4,000,000 square feet by 410 square feet, the average area per employee,[6] yields an employment estimate of approximately 9,750 employees. Most of these employees are classified under manufacturing; transportation, communication, and public utilities (TCU); or wholesale trade. Referring back to the employment data presented in the office analysis, we find 15,818 people employed in these three categories. Thus the 9,750 employees represent 61.6% of the total employment in these three cate-

---

5. *Flex space* refers to the conversion of flexible industrial space to nonindustrial uses, typically office use.

6. The average square footage per employee varies significantly for industrial uses, particularly if factory and bulk storage areas are included. The amount of space per employee can vary from 100 to 3,000 square feet. In this case, metro area data from local studies were used.

gories. Using this ratio and the employment forecast from the office analysis (Table 15.6), we can estimate probable future demand for light industrial space.

Table 15.9
Employment Projections for Subject-Type Industrial Uses

	Current	In 4 years	In 8 years
Number of employees			
(Manufacturing, TCU, wholesale trade)	15,818	18,306	24,730
Times % in light industrial use	x 0.61	x 0.61	x 0.61
Times sq. ft. per employee	x 410	x 410	x 410
Demand for light industrial space (in sq. ft.)	3,956,081	4,578,330	6,184,973
Supply of light industrial space (in sq. ft.)	4,500,000	4,500,000	4,500,000
(Excess)/shortage	(543,919)	78,330	1,684,973

Demand Forecast

The above forecast indicates an average annual demand of approximately 99 acres for industrial development in the next four through eight years. Demand is calculated as follows:

Demand in 8 years in sq. ft.	6,184,973
Minus demand in 4 years in sq. ft.	4,578,330
Plus excess demand in 4 years	78,330
Equals estimated new demand	1,684,973
Divided by average sq. ft. per acre of light industrial use	17,000
Equals total new demand for acreage under light industrial use over eight years	99 acres

The four-year demand forecast is 4,578,330 square feet and current and future supply is 4,500,000 square feet. Thus, marginal demand will begin to materialize in about four years. New construction is likely to occur within this period. Demand for the 99 acres will be felt four to eight years out, indicating demand of 25 acres per year for this later period.

Forecast Demand Compared with Historial Absorption

The forecast demand estimate is compared to the industrial development in the city in the past 10 years. During this time, more than 150 acres were developed under light industrial uses, most in the last five years. The analyst must ask: Will history repeat itself or is the downward trend indicated by the employment out-look for the next eight years more plausible? After analyzing the assumptions of the forecast and taking note of current conditions, the analyst chooses to give greater weight to the forecast. Thus, the final forecast calls for new construction starting in four years and three possible estimates of demand for industrial acreage:

Conservative	—	10 acres per year
Most probable	—	15 acres per year
Optimistic	—	25 acres per year

For a longer-term forecast, say 10 to 12 years, the lower range would be used. For a shorter-term forecast, say four to eight years out, the middle or higher range would be used.

Recap of citywide demand conclusions

Use	Most Probable New Development Start	Average Yearly Demand
Apartment	2.5 years	25.0 acres/year, say 15 to 35 acres/year
Retail	4.0 years	3.0 acres/year, say 1 to 5 acres/year
Office	8.0 years	12.0 acres/year, say 10 to 15 acres/year
Industrial	4.0 years	15.0 acres/year, say 10 to 25 acres/year

Apartment and retail uses have the most predictable short-term use potential. Demand for office use is eight years out and an industrial use is more problem-atic. An industrial use for the subject tract is eliminated from further considera-tion because of the following factors:

- Demand for an industrial use is questionable.
- Land values under retail and office uses are six times higher than the value of land under an industrial use.
- In locational analysis the tract was assigned a marginal rating for an industrial use.
- Zoning the tract for an industrial use is questionable.
- An industrial park was developed just southeast of the subject last year, but no lots have yet been sold.

In the subsequent capture estimate and financial analysis of the land use mix, retail/office and multifamily apartment uses are the only uses selected for fur-ther consideration.

STEP 6 SUBJECT CAPTURE ESTIMATE

Competitive tracts rating method

In addition to investigating the specific markets for the three remaining prospective land uses, the appraiser identifies competitive tracts of vacant land with a potential use mix similar to that of the subject. The number of competitive tracts that could be developed with a use mix similar to that contemplated for the subject is a principal factor in determining the demand/supply equation. The availability of many competitive tracts with a similar use mix potential will diminish the likelihood of the subject capturing a significant share of the market. If few competitive tracts have a use mix potential similar to that of the subject, it is more likely that the subject will capture a significant share of the market.

The appraiser first identifies all competitive tracts in the citywide area. The size and use potential of these tracts should be comparable to the subject's, and the tracts should be marketable and competitively priced. The tracts should also have accessibility comparable to the subject's and be located on thoroughfares equivalent to those that border the subject. Once identified, the competitive tracts are rated according to different use-specific criteria. A sample survey sheet for the competitive tract inventory follows:

Identification no.:	_____
Location:	Corner location, ½ mile west of subject on New York Avenue.
Owner:	ABC Development Company Comment/analysis: Company has good track record of developing land as retail centers.
Status:	Owner plans to develop as mixed-use development when market improves.
Land area:	55 acres
Zoning:	All commercial; zoning allows for multifamily and garden office uses.
Utilities:	All at site
Land condition:	Level; no floodplains

Based on the data gathered, seven tracts are identified as competitive with the subject. The capture potential of these tracts is analyzed using two methods: the rating matrix method and the pro rata share method.

Rating Matrix Method

Rating competitive tracts in relation to the subject provides a method of gauging the share of the market that the subject will likely capture. The compatibility matrix shown in Table 15.10 ranks six competitive tracts and the subject on a scale of 1 to 4, with 1 being the worst rating and 4 being the best.

Table 15.10
Competitive Tract Ranking

Criteria	Competitive Tracts						Subject
	1	2	3	4	5	6	
Proximity to other apartment complex or planned apartment development	2	4	4	4	2	2	4
Proximity to retail facility or planned retail development	3	4	4	2	3	3	3
Proximity to office development or planned office development	2	3	3	2	2	2	2
Volume of traffic by tract (current and in five years)	2	4	3	2	2	2	3
Driving time to major employment centers	3	3	3	3	3	3	3
Owner's ability to market the tract	3	3	3	2	3	3	4
Current public support for growth in the area	3	4	3	3	3	3	3
Existing or planned (funded) infrastructure/road network in immediate area	2	4	4	3	2	2	3
Quantity of available land in tract (tract size)	2	3	3	2	3	3	3
Reputation/prestige of area	2	4	4	3	2	2	3
Totals	24	36	34	26	25	25	31

Of the six competitive tracts, two were rated to be superior to the subject, and the remaining four were rated inferior. Thus, the subject is considered above average in comparison to competitive tracts suitable for mixed use development.

Pro Rata Share Capture Method

To apply this method the appraiser identifies the major competitive tracts and miscellaneous smaller tracts, estimates their acreage, and then assumes the subject will capture its proportionate share by size.

Acreage of major competitive corners	225
Acreage of miscellaneous smaller tracts	50
Plus acreage of subject	66
Total acreage	341

$$\text{Subject's share = acreage of subject / total acreage}$$
$$= 66 / 341$$
$$= 19.4\%$$

Capture Rate Conclusions

According to the pro rata share estimate, the subject's share is 19.4%. The ranking analysis indicates that the subject is significantly superior to most competition, so the pro rata share is adjusted upward to approximately 23%.

Now the subject's capture for the highest and best use mix indicated by the appraiser's marginal demand analysis can be estimated.

Use	Total Market Demand/Year	Subject Capture at Midpoint	Subject Yearly Avg. Capture (Rounded)	Start Date
Apartment	15 to 35 acres	23%	6 acres	+2 years
Retail	1 to 5 acres	23%	1 acre	+4 years
Office	10 to 15 acres	23%	3 acres	+8 years

Additional note about forecasting capture

The approach presented here is based on economic modeling rather than a forecast of the actual sequence of development, which is the procedure applied in feasibility studies. Economic modeling is used because the long-term predictions made in forecasting the actual phasing of development are often unrealistic.

The appraisal is of a vacant tract with an optimal land use mix based on a probability model. In the case study application, office use is included in the mix of potential uses, but office space is seldom developed on a per-acre basis. In the subject market, development in six-acre phases is most typical. However, marginal demand for office use is forecast to be eight years out. Market-wide demand averages 10 to 15 acres per year, with a mid-range point estimate of 13 acres; subject capture at 23% suggests approximately three acres per year. Thus, if demand is forecast eight years out, it will be 10 years before a six-acre phase of garden office development can begin on the subject tract, allowing time for demand to increase to sufficient levels. Of course, the exact date for the subject could be earlier or later than forecast.

The economic modeling technique demonstrated here does not attempt to forecast a specific date for the absorption of six acres. Instead, it establishes the average annual demand for each specific use. In other words, the subject might be the first tract to be developed or the last tract. This tends to smooth out forecast cash flows and their probable timing. In a market value appraisal, highest and best use is essentially a probability study, not a feasibility study for actual development. This is the rationale for using an economic modeling approach. An alternative would be to forecast the exact timing of development, which many appraisers do. Other appraisers undertake even more detailed analyses, estimating cash flows and actual construction and lease-up costs.

STEP 7 FINANCIAL ANALYSIS AND OPTIMAL LAND USE PLAN

Financial analysis of land use mix

To perform financial analysis the appraiser assigns user values (i.e., the value of the developed land under a specific use, sometimes called *retail value*) and absorption estimates to each possible land use. The mix of uses that yields the highest present value is the highest and best use. Site analysis has revealed seven possible use mixes, or models, all of which require approximately the same development cost (see Table 15.11). Development costs, holding costs, and sales expenses are ignored in the analysis, which assumes that the dollar figures under each use would be approximately the same. The analysis does not result in a value per se. The dollar amounts are only a means for comparing the use mixes and determining the most probable land use mix for the subject property.

In each of the seven models, nine of the 66 acres (14%) are allocated to interior roads and the floodplain identified in the site analysis. To determine the optimal land use mix on the remaining 57 acres, the following procedure is performed.

Input assumptions

First, the appraiser selects a discount rate and estimates typical user values.

> Discount rate: 12%
> User values:
> Multifamily use   @ $ 4/sq. ft. per acre
> Retail use   @ $10/sq. ft. per acre
> Office use   @ $15/sq. ft. per acre

Next development costs are considered and adjusted if significant. (In this application, the development costs for all seven uses were assumed to be the same.) Then the appraiser forecasts the average absorption of alternative uses over time. Absorption is assumed to begin when demand exceeds supply. The results of the financial analysis are shown in Table 15.11.

Table 15.11
Financial Analysis of Alternative Land Use Mixes

Use Mix	$/Sq. Ft.	Avg. Acres per Year	Start Date	Present Value of Land* @ 12% (Rounded)
Model 1				
42 acres multifamily	@ $ 4/sq. ft.	6 acres/year	+2 years	$ 4,260,000
15 acres retail	@ $10/sq. ft.	1 acre/year	+4 years	$ 2,112,000
57 acres			Total	$ 6,372,000
Model 2				
36 acres multifamily	@ $ 4/sq. ft.	6 acres/year	+2 years	$ 3,838,000
12 acres retail	@ $10/sq. ft.	1 acre/year	+4 years	$ 1,920,000
9 acres office	@ $15/sq. ft.	3 acre/year	+8 years	$ 2,130,000
57 acres			Total	$ 7,888,000
Model 3				
24 acres multifamily	@ $ 4/sq. ft.	6 acres/year	+2 years	$ 2,835,000
12 acres retail	@ $10/sq. ft.	1 acre/year	+4 years	$ 1,920,000
21 acres office	@ $15/sq. ft.	3 acres/year	+8 years	$ 4,047,000
57 acres			Total	$ 8,802,000
Model 4				
36 acres apartment	@ $ 4/sq. ft.	6 acres/year	+2 years	$ 3,838,000
21 acres office	@ $15/sq. ft.	3 acres/year	+8 years	$ 4,047,000
57 acres			Total	$ 7,885,000
Model 5				
57 acres apartment	@ $ 4/sq. ft.	6 acres/year	+2 years	$ 5,128,000
Model 6				
57 acres office	@ $15/sq. ft.	3 acres/year	+8 years	$ 6,531,000
Model 7 (as currently zoned)				
27 acres retail	@ $10/sq. ft.	1 acre/year	+4 years	$ 2,463,000
30 acres office	@ $15/sq. ft.	3 acres/year	+8 years	$ 5,010,000
57 acres			Total	$ 7,473,000

* Discounted with reversion factor (present value of $1)

Note: The land values estimated are not as critical as the ratio between land values.

Conclusion of financial analysis

The mix of multifamily, retail, and office uses proposed as Model 3 results in the highest present value. Model 3 would be the "best economic fit" to develop the highest and best use concept plan if all the forecasts had equal probability. However, highest and best use is not arrived at by a mechanical process. The financial analysis will provide input data to be further scrutinized. The risk associated with each value in the financial analysis must be assessed. For example, the land use mix specified in Model 2 is similar to that of Model 3. Model 2, which is 10% less valuable than Model 3, has a greater amount of acreage allocated to multifamily use and is less risky than Model 3 because there is some current demand for multifamily space. Whereas office space represents 46% of the value of Model 3, it is only 27% of the value of Model 2. Office use is the most uncertain because of its long projection period.

The element of uncertainty or risk can be addressed in three ways: the discount rate can be adjusted, the forecast for the more uncertain land uses can be revised along more conservative lines, or the different risks and values can be reconciled. Each method has its advantages and disadvantages. Adjustment of the discount rate for different land use mixes is the approach most often used, but it is sometimes difficult to support the rate adustment. Appraisers, like investors in the market, do not always agree on the trade-off between risk and the expected returns.[7] The use of a common discount rate to evaluate alternatives perceived to be within the same risk category does allow for a more consistent comparison of the data input and the assumptions underlying the decision-making process.[8] This application utilizes such a method and makes the final adjustment for risk in reconciliation.

Reconciliation of the financial analysis

The value of Model 3 is about 12% greater than that of Model 2, but 46% of the value of Model 3 depends on office space. If Model 1 and Model 2 are compared, the value of Model 2 is found to be 24% greater than that of Model 1. The relative percentage change in the potential present values of Model 1, Model 2, and Model 3 is decreasing while the risk is increasing. The higher allocation of multifamily use in Model 2 is less risky since there is current demand for multifamily space. Increased residential use in the area will also generate greater demand for retail space. Accordingly, the risk for the retail projection is reduced and its probability is increased. Therefore, the land use allocation in Model 2

---

7. Gaylon E. Greer and Michael D. Farrell, *Investment Analysis for Real Estate Decisions*, 2d ed. (Chicago: Dearborn Financial Publishers, 1988), 114.

8. This technique "controls risk rather than adjusts for risk." See Wayne E. Etter, "Putting a Leash on Risk: Towards Evaluating Commercial Properties," *Tierra Grande: Journal of the Real Estate Center at Texas A&M University* (Spring 1994), 12. See also the discussion of the incorporation of risk analysis into policy guidelines in the Greer and Farrell text, page 294.

seems more reasonable in terms of probability as well as from an economic stand-point. It should also be noted that the land use allocation in Model 7, which cor-responds to the current zoning of the tract, is only 5.5% less valuable than Model 2. However, there is greater risk associated with Model 7 since 67% of its value depends on office use, which is the land use with the longest forecast period.

Thus, the land use allocation of Model 2 or some combination of Model 2 and Model 3 may be considered the best financial alternative for the subject tract.

To conclude the analysis, the appraiser returns to the tract and fits the cho-sen mix to the physical constraints of the site. While the financial analysis of land use mixes provides guidance on the allocation of acreage among specific land uses, the land use model must be adapted to the physical features of the site. The map presented in the next section (Figure 15.7) represents the concept plan for the highest and best use of the tract.

HIGHEST AND BEST USE RECONCILIATION

This section brings together the site, location, supply and demand, capture, and financial analyses to identify the most probable use for the subject property. The land use conclusion forecast for the subject is based on its site characteristics and locational attributes and on the supply and demand relationships in its mar-ket. The land use conclusion is *not* an engineering study or a specific development plan. The *land use concept plan is for valuation analysis purposes only*; it must not be construed as the proposed development plan. The actual developer may have special financing advantages or anticipate revenues from an anchor tenant with drawing power that is not typical of the market. The developer could utilize this study as a starting point, but would need to commission a detailed engi-neering plan and feasibility analysis before development could proceed. Lengthy discussion with the city would also be required before the land use plan of the tract could be finalized. This highest and best use study does, however, indicate the long-term development potential of the site, given the market conditions at the time of the appraisal. The supply and demand study indicated that any non-residential use for this site will not be realized for at least four to six years.

Land use conclusions and major considerations

The land use conclusion recognizes five major specifications for the design of the tract that were considered earlier in the site analysis.

1. Access to the interior from St. James Place, which runs along the western boundary of the tract, should be at the Virginia Avenue intersection.
2. The frontage and adjacent land use along New York Avenue suggest a higher-intensity use. The logical dividing line between less intensive resi-dential land use to the north and more intensive retail/office land use to the south would be the access road connecting St. James Place to the

interior. Physical constraints can often necessitate modification of the allocation of acreage in the financial analysis. This means less multifamily acreage than the financial model suggested. The 36-acre allocation in the model is reduced to a 28-acre allocation in the concept plan. The reduction in multifamily acreage results in an increase in the acreage to be developed under retail and garden office use. The 21-acre allocation in the model is increased to an allocation of 29 acres in the concept plan.

3. An outlet is needed to St. Charles Place, which runs along the northern boundary of the tract.

4. In all probability, the city will discourage an outlet road from the interior directly onto New York Avenue, which runs along the southern boundary of the tract.

5. The topography and drainage of the tract will likely necessitate that some type of retention facility be constructed in the general location of one of the existing ponds, preferably the upper pond.

6. A lake park of 5.6 acres is recommended both as drainage for the residential development in the northeast quadrant and as an amenity feature aesthetically designed to give the project a competitive advantage and increase its absorption in this highly competitive market. The box culvert in the southwest quadrant allows for drainage of the acreage under proposed garden office and retail use.

Location

Location analysis showed the subject is located in a transition area between more intensive land uses along the north-south freeway to the east and less intensive residential use to the west. More intensive uses such as multitenant office use were not probable for the site.

Market Demand

Market analysis indicated long-term demand for all the land uses, but short-term demand only for apartment units.

Marketability

The subject site is one of the more competitive sites in the market area and can be expected to have an above-average capture rate.

Financial Analysis

Financial analysis suggests an optimal land use mix of apartment, retail, and office space, with apartment units the dominant use. The mix is similar to Model 2. The highest and best use concept plan shown in Figure 15.7 represents the appraiser's conclusion of the subject's highest and best use.

Figure 15.7
Concept Plan for Highest and Best Use of Subject Tract

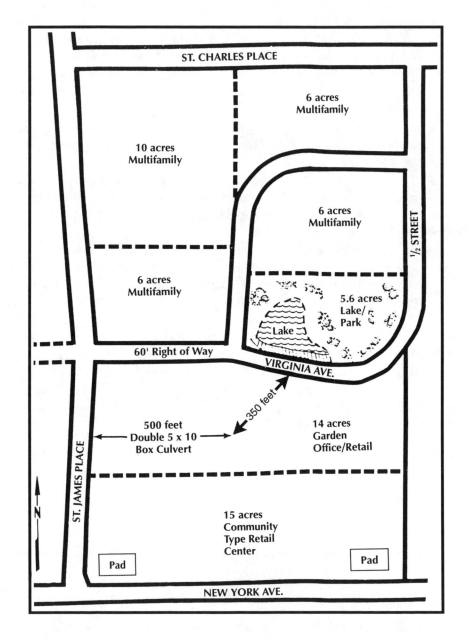

Land Concept Plan

The current zoning of the frontage along New York Avenue and the results of the location analysis both suggest a community retail center should be built on this part of the tract. From a location standpoint, the back portion of the tract shows potential for residential or office use. The financial analysis indicates that a multifamily residential use would yield the highest present value because residual demand for that use will be realized much sooner than demand for the other potential uses.

Highest and Best Use Specification

Based on the results of the site, location, and market analyses, a forecast of the most probable land use for the subject is made. This forecast is illustrated in Figure 15.7. Note that the subject has two especially competitive corners (pads) which would most probably accommodate land uses complementary to community retail—i.e., a fast-food restaurant, bank, or gasoline station.

Timing for Use

The market analysis projected the following schedule of residual demand for various uses of the subject tract:

Apartment	—	1 to 3 years
Retail	—	3 to 5 years
Office	—	6 to 15 years

The subject location was rated superior for all uses, so the subject should have a capture rate superior to most of its competitors.

Market Participants

The users of the property will reflect the categories of market demand for each of the proposed uses, i.e., moderate-income apartment residents, the local clientele of a community retail center, and community residents who use the services provided by occupants of a garden (neighborhood) office development. In view of the development potential for the land, the most probable buyer for the subject would be a speculative investor who plans to hold it and resell it.

THE MARKET ANALYSIS PROCESS FOR A PROPOSED RETAIL CENTER

———⟫•⟪———

- Property productivity analysis and alternative use scoping

- Market area definition

- Demand forecast

- Competitive supply inventory

- Marginal demand estimate

- Subject capture estimate

- Financial feasibility analysis/threshold testing

CHAPTER SIXTEEN

———◆◆◆———

Proposed Retail Center

This highest and best use study is based on a Level C market analysis of a vacant land tract that has potential for a neighborhood shopping center/supermarket. The study process includes these seven steps:

1. Property productivity analysis and alternative use scoping. The physical, design/amenity (shape of the tract), legal/regulatory, and locational attributes of the vacant land are examined to establish the potential use(s) of the parcel. The most likely use of the subject parcel was determined to be retail, specifically a neighborhood shopping center/supermarket; multifamily housing represented a less probable, alternative use.

2. Market area definition. The primary and secondary trade areas of the retail facility are identified.

3. Demand forecast. An estimate and a forecast are made of the population for the market area, probable per capita food expenditure, and net leakage out of the market area. The demand for the goods sold at a neighborhood shopping center is also estimated with an alternative ratio technique.

4. Competitive supply inventory. The square footage of current and anticipated competitive space in the subject's market area is inventoried.

5. Marginal demand estimate. Existing and forecast demand is compared to current and anticipated supply to determine the net market support for the supermarket.

6. Subject capture estimate. The likely share of the market that the subject retail center will capture is estimated.

7. Financial feasibility analysis/threshold testing. After property productivity and supply and demand analyses have been completed, a financial feasibility test is conducted by means of threshold testing. The potential values of the land resulting from development under retail use and multifamily housing use are identified. The retail use was found financially feasible, but the multifamily residential use was not. The retail use was substantially more profitable.

STEP 1 PROPERTY PRODUCTIVITY ANALYSIS

To conduct property productivity analysis, the appraiser examines the physical, design/amenity (shape of the tract), legal/regulatory, and locational attributes of the site. After a thorough examination, a preliminary highest and best use conclusion can be developed.

Step 1.1 Analysis of physical attributes

The subject tract is a 10-acre site with physical attributes that are well suited to a variety of different land uses, including multifamily housing, an office building, a warehouse, and a neighborhood shopping center/supermarket.

Step 1.2 Analysis of design/amenity attributes

The property is relatively level with a slightly irregular shape. It was purchased as a portion of a larger tract and its irregular shape was part of the purchase agreement submitted by the buyer, who bought the tract for use as a neighborhood shopping center. The tract's boundaries were designed with the contours of a neighborhood shopping center in mind. This shape ensures that excess land will be kept at a minimum when the land is developed as a shopping center.

The tract offers no special features for alternative land uses, but it could also accommodate an apartment complex, an office building, or a warehouse.

Step 1.3 Analysis of legal/regulatory attributes

A special benefit comes with the tract that most of the competitive properties do not have. The local zoning ordinance permits the sale of beer and wine on the tract. When the city voted on the zoning, the tract was already located within the city limits. Competing tracts had not yet been incorporated into the city at the time of the vote, and therefore did not receive this legal benefit. Such an important legal attribute will have a significant effect on any supermarket that anchors the neighborhood shopping center. For alternative land uses, the legal/regulatory attributes of the tract offer no special advantages.

Under the cumulative zoning ordinances in the city, both office and multifamily residential uses would be acceptable. Warehouse development is not allowed under the existing zoning, and a change would have to be requested. Members of the city planning staff have indicated that they would oppose such a change.

Step 1.4 Analysis of locational attributes

The attributes of both the micro location and the macro location appear favorable for the development of either a multifamily apartment complex or a neighborhood shopping center. Micro-locational features include ease of ingress to and egress from the tract and its location on the beltway around the city. Complementary land uses for both multifamily housing and a shopping center are relatively close by.

Office and warehousing uses require different micro-locational attributes. Although access to the tract is excellent for both uses, complementary land uses are seriously deficient. Most office and industrial space is found in other areas of the city, and it appears that the tract's location would not be favorable for either of these uses.

The tract's macro location is in the city's northeast quadrant, within the secondary growth path of development. Although growth has been in abeyance for the past several years, this particular growth axis is well established, and as soon as the current economic slump ends, new development in the northeast quadrant of the city is very likely to resume.

The prospect of economic recovery bodes well for both multifamily housing and retail uses. For warehouse and office uses, the tract's macro-locational attributes are less than desirable. Most warehouse, distribution, and manufacturing uses are found to the south and west of the site, while new office space has tended to cluster around the new mall to the southeast.

Step 1.5 Preliminary highest and best use

While the physical attributes of the tract support a number of land uses, other attributes indicate that a multifamily apartment project or a neighborhood shopping center is the most likely use. Furthermore, it appears that the shopping center has the advantage. Three features are favorable to development of the tract as a shopping center:

1. The boundaries of the tract were designed to accommodate a neighborhood shopping center.
2. The zoning advantage permits beer and wine to be sold on the tract, giving it a monopolistic edge over other competitive sites.
3. The micro and macro locations are well-suited to a neighborhood shopping center.

In Table 16.1 the attributes of the subject tract are rated on their suitability for multifamily housing and a neighborhood shopping center. The grid suggests that the retail use would be more likely although a multifamily apartment project remains a potential alternative use. The rating of the attributes does not completely eliminate the multifamily residential use from consideration. Use of the tract as a multifamily housing project will be reexamined in the financial feasibility analysis (Step 7) by means of threshold testing.

Table 16.1

Property Productivity Analysis Rating Grid
Alternative Land Use Ratings

Attributes	Subject's Features	Effect on Multifamily Housing	Rating	Effect on Neighborhood Shopping Center	Rating
Physical:					
Size	10 acres	Positive	+3	Positive	+3
Topography	Level	Positive	+3	Positive	+3
Design:					
Shape	Designed for neighborhood center	Negative	-1	Positive	+3
Legal/Political:					
Beer/wine sales	Permitted	Neutral	0	Positive	+3
Zoning	Retail	Negative	-1	Positive	+3
Location:					
Access/ visibility	Excellent	Positive	+2	Positive	+3
Linkages	Excellent	Positive	+2	Positive	+2
Neighborhood	Good	Positive	+1	Positive	+1
Direction of growth	Good	Positive	+1	Positive	+1
Ratings totaled			+10		+22

Threshold testing is an analytical procedure employed in highest and best use studies in which an alternative use is tested using especially optimistic forecast data (i.e., marginal demand projection and capture rate) to give the use every possible chance to succeed. If threshold testing reveals that the alternative use does not compare favorably with the other financially feasible uses, the alternative use can be eliminated from further consideration.

In Table 16.1 numbers from +3 to -3 are used to rate the suitability of the subject tract for the two uses. A rating of +3 indicates that the attribute has a strong positive rating whereas a -3 suggests the tract is undesirable in this regard. A zero indicates the effect is neutral. The land use with the highest total rating is the one best suited to that tract of land. The numerical ratings do not indicate that the retail use is 2.2 times better than the multifamily residential use. The ratings only suggest that the shopping center use is likely to be the more profitable use of the land at the time of the appraisal.

DEMAND AND SUPPLY ANALYSIS

Based on the property productivity analysis, the appraiser decides to test the market for the retail use. If the market did not indicate support for a retail use, the market for multifamily residential use would be tested. In the financial feasibility analysis (Step 7), threshold testing of both uses is undertaken to determine whether the multifamily housing project is indeed a viable alternative use.

In Step 2, the primary and secondary market areas for the subject are defined. The market areas of major competitors are also identified. The supply and demand analysis performed in Steps 3 through 5 investigates whether market support exists for a neighborhood shopping center. In these steps, two market areas are defined (Market Area 1 and Market Area 2) based on population data from several different sources. Then independent demand and supply estimates are developed to establish the extent of demand for a retail center in the designated market area and the competitive supply (Steps 3 and 4). Finally, an estimate of the marginal demand for retail space in the market area is made in Step 5 and the supportable retail space is allocated among a supermarket, general retail stores, and pad site(s).

STEP 2 MARKET AREA DEFINITION

The primary and secondary market areas for the subject are identified. The primary market area is defined as the area within a three-mile radius of the subject. The primary market area is identified with Census Tracts 1 and 2. The secondary market area covers the northeast quadrant of the city, extending from the center of the downtown area to the suburban periphery about 25 miles out. Census Tracts 1, 2, 3, and 4 define the primary and secondary market areas.

Figure 16.1 shows the subject's retail market area and the retail market areas for the major competing supermarkets. The breakpoints between the market areas for the various stores have been estimated using a retail gravitation model. The identification of these breakpoints allows the analyst to plot the individual market areas.

STEP 3 DEMAND FORECAST

Macro demand

Population growth in the city has been variable, but continuous, for the past 30 years. Figure 16.2 shows historical and forecast population growth for the overall city.

Figure 16.1

The Subject and Competing Market Areas

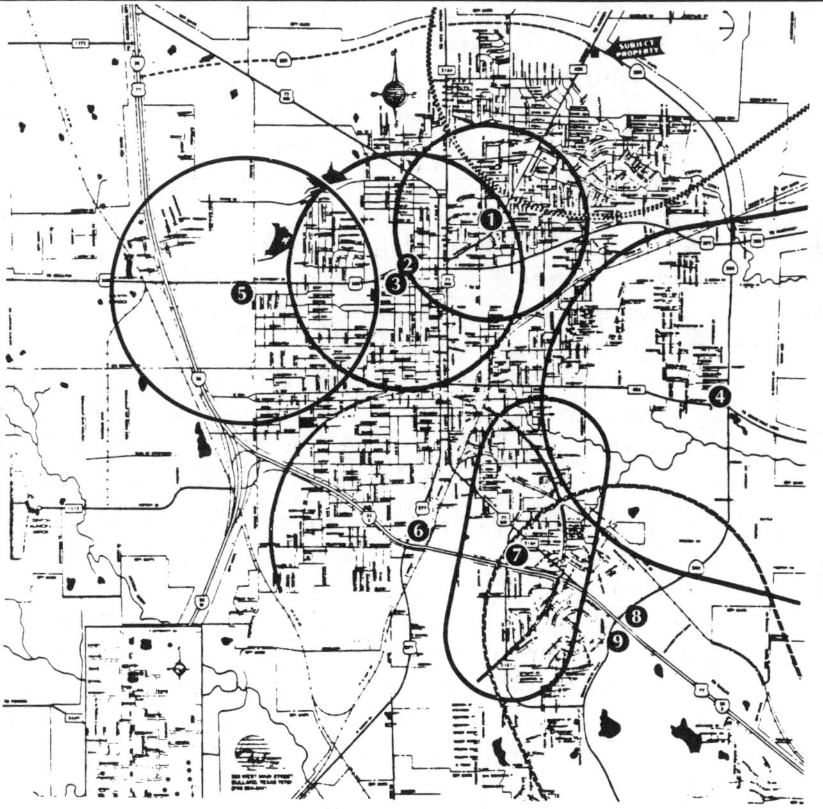

Competing Supermarkets

Super-Market	Name	Location	Distance/Time from Subject	Size in Sq. Ft.
1	Piggly Wiggly	Sherman Drive	1.8 mi./4 min.	30,750
2	Kroger	University Dr. @ Carroll Blvd.	2.8 mi./7 min.	45,750
3	Winn Dixie	Sunset Blvd. @ University Dr.	3.0 mi./8 min.	26,280
4	Piggly Wiggly	McKinney St. @ Loop 288	3.7 mi./5 min.	20,740
5	Skaggs	University Dr. @ Bonnie Brae	4.3 mi./10 min.	45,000
6	(Proposed) Albertsons	Ft. Worth Dr. @ IH-35	4.5 mi./10 min.	N/A
7	Winn Dixie	Teasley Ln. @ IH-35	4.7 mi./15 min.	45,100
8	Kroger	Loop 288 @ IH-35	6 mi./11 min.	44,400
9	Skaggs	Loop 288 @ IH-35	6.8 mi./12 min.	66,400

Figure 16.2
Citywide Population Trends

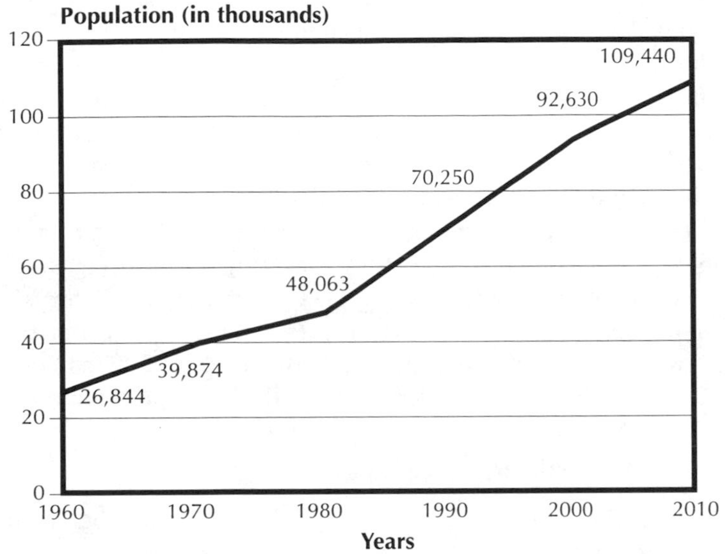

Population (in thousands)
120
100
80
60
40
20
0
109,440
92,630
70,250
48,063
39,874
26,844
1960
1970
1980
1990
2000
2010
Years

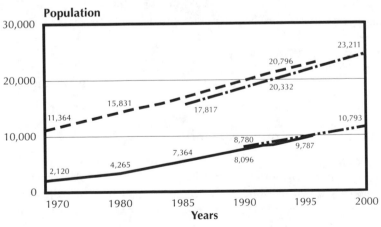

Market area demand

Historical population trends for Market Areas 1 and 2 are graphed in Figure 16.3.

Figure 16.3
Market Area Population Trends

Population
30,000
20,000
10,000
0
23,211
20,796
20,332
15,831
17,817
11,364
10,793
8,780
9,787
7,364
8,096
4,265
2,120
1970
1980
1985
1990
1995
2000
Years
1. National Planning Data Services data—Market Area 1
2. National Planning Data Services data, Denton-Tioga Polygon—Market Areas 1 and 2
3. North Central Texas Council of Governments data—Census Tracts 1 and 2
4. North Central Texas Council of Governments data—Census Tracts 1, 2, 3, and 4

Seven data sets were employed to estimate demand for the proposed super-market. Only two are analyzed here. Steps 3.1 through 3.4 explain the methods the analyst applied to estimate supportable supermarket space in the market area. An estimate is made for the food expenditures of the area population. Continuing with the demand estimate derived, the analyst inventories competitive supply in Step 4 and estimates marginal demand in Step 5. Table 16.2 (p. 397) shows the process employed to refine the demand data and arrive at the marginal demand estimate. Estimates of supportable supermarket space derived from the seven different data sets are shown in Table 16.3 (p. 398)

To estimate demand for retail goods (excluding food) sold at a neighborhood shopping center, an alternative method employing a ratio technique is applied. This method is demonstrated in Steps 3.01, 3.02, and 3.03. Steps 4.01 and 5.01 show how this alternative demand estimate is adjusted for competitive space and a marginal demand estimate is derived. Table 16.4 (p. 399) shows the steps in the process of refining the data derived from this alternative ratio technique.

Demand analysis (supermarket space)

To estimate market demand for a supermarket, the appraiser spoke with the real estate specialists for several supermarket chains. Most of the supermarket personnel offered little help, preferring not to divulge information about their company's location strategy. Only two supermarket chains were willing to talk about their customer bases. From these discussions, the appraiser concluded that the chains would be willing to develop a store in an area with 5,000 customers as the minimum level of support. One chain targeted weekly sales at $6.00 per square foot, or $312.00 per square foot annually, as sufficient demand.This information and other figures derived in developing the demand estimate (Steps 3.1 through 3.4) are applied in the calculations in Table 16.2.

Step 3.1 Population in trade area

Population in the primary and secondary trade areas is estimated for 1994 and 1999.

Step 3.2 Per capita food expenditures

Annual per capita expenditures on food are estimated using data from the Bureau of Labor Statistics' *Consumer Expenditure Survey Results*. Although the economy had taken a downturn since the data were published, no adjustment of the data appears to be warranted. The neighborhood is an upper-income area of the city so an average of the two highest deciles for the data are used.

Multiplying the annual per capita expenditure for food by the estimated population in the market area indicates that the total expenditures on food in the market area will be $14,817,384 in 1994 and $16,390,992 in 1999.

Step 3.3 Net leakage

In the preceding step, the total potential expenditure on food in the market area was estimated. However, some of these expenditures will not be made at supermarkets in the defined market area. Expenditures will leak out to other market areas and stores. In Step 3.3 the appraiser estimates this loss of sales to stores outside the market area to be 25%. The 25% figure is high relative to rule-of-thumb estimates, which range between 10% and 25%, depending on the structure of the market area and the design of the store. A 25% leakage estimate was used because there is vacant land surrounding the site.

Step 3.4 Estimated demand

Leakage is subtracted from the per capita expenditures to arrive at an estimate of supermarket expenditures for the market area. The calculations are

$$\$14,817,384 - (\$14,817,384 \times 0.25) = \$11,113,038$$

STEP 4 COMPETITIVE SUPPLY INVENTORY

Step 4.1 Total competitive supply

Figure 16.1 indicated the sizes and estimated market areas of the competitive supermarkets. Each competitor has its own market area. That figure showed no competitive supermarkets in the subject's market area and only one planned supermarket (Albertson's). The map in Figure 16.4 shows competitive vacant sites in the subject's market area.

STEP 5 MARGINAL DEMAND ESTIMATE

To arrive at an estimate of marginal demand for supermarket space, the competitive supply is subtracted from the supportable supermarket space. Since the defined market area has no competing supermarkets, zero appears on the line for competitive space in Table 16.2.

If there had been competitive space, the estimated demand would have had to be adjusted to obtain the estimate of marginal demand (i.e., net demand required to support new supermarket space). For example, if there had been an existing 30,000-sq.-ft. supermarket in the defined market area, its annual sales could be estimated at $9,360,000 ($312 in sales per square foot per year x 30,000 square feet).

Demand was estimated in Step 3.4 at $11,113,038, of which the 30,000-sq.-ft. supermarket would be absorbing $9,360,000. The $1,753,038 difference, representing marginal demand, would not be enough net consumer expenditure to warrant a new supermarket. Marginal demand, which is the focus of Step 5, is the measure of excess demand in the market area, calculated as supportable demand minus competitive supply.

Figure 16.4
Competitive Vacant Sites

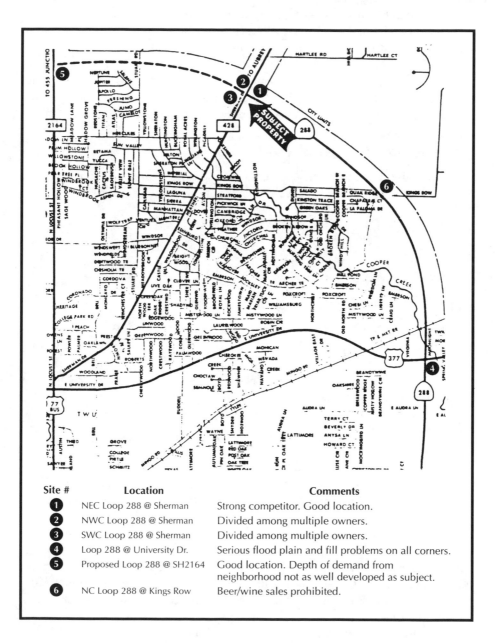

Site #	Location	Comments
1	NEC Loop 288 @ Sherman	Strong competitor. Good location.
2	NWC Loop 288 @ Sherman	Divided among multiple owners.
3	SWC Loop 288 @ Sherman	Divided among multiple owners.
4	Loop 288 @ University Dr.	Serious flood plain and fill problems on all corners.
5	Proposed Loop 288 @ SH2164	Good location. Depth of demand from neighborhood not as well developed as subject.
6	NC Loop 288 @ Kings Row	Beer/wine sales prohibited.

Step 5.1 Net market support

Using the average estimated supermarket sales required per square foot, the appraiser can calculate the amount of new supermarket space that market area demand can support. In Table 16.2, supportable supermarket space is calculated at 35,619 square feet for 1994 and 39,401 square feet for 1999. Thus, between 35,000 and 40,000 square feet of supermarket space can be supported in the market area.

Table 16.2
Demand for Supermarket Space in the Market Area—Data Set 1

	1994	1999
Demand Estimate		
Step 3.1 Primary trade area population*	9,774	10,812
Step 3.2 Annual per capita food expenditure[†]	$1,516	$1,516
	$14,817,384	$16,390,992
Step 3.3 Net leakage estimated @ 25%[‡]	−$3,704,346	−$4,097,748
Step 3.4 Estimated demand	$11,113,038	$12,293,244
Supply Inventory		
Step 4.1 Total competitive supermarket space in trade area	00	00
Step 5.1 Net market support—excess demand (demand minus supply)	$11,113,038	$12,293,244
Average sales/sq. ft.[§]	$312	$312
Supportable supermarket space in trade area	35,619 sq. ft.	39,401 sq. ft.

* Primary trade area consists of Census Tracts 1 and 2. Data are taken from the North Central Texas Council of Governments (NCTCOG) *Dallas-Fort Worth Economic Outlook: Recent Trends and Long-Range Forecasts to the Year 2010. Traffic Survey Zone Level Forecasts* (Arlington, TX: March 1989). The data for the primary trade area were adjusted to reflect only the portions of the traffic survey zones that are in the trade area.

[†] Annual per capita expenditures are based on Bureau of Labor Statistics, Department of Labor, *Consumer Expenditure Survey Results* (Washington, D.C.: U.S. Government Printing Office). Because the market area has a high median income level, the fourth and fifth decile food expenditures were averaged.

[‡] Net leakage is the estimated amount of food expenditures that will be lost to stores outside the trade area. Although 25% is a high leakage factor, it is considered reasonable because of the nature, extent, and size of the trade area.

[§] A rough guide employed by supermarket site location specialists is $6/sq. ft. per week, or $312/year. This will vary depending on a variety of factors.

In an attempt to double-check the estimates derived, the appraiser used several different population data sets and generated various ranges for the forecast. The results of this sensitivity analysis are shown in Table 16.3.

Table 16.3
Seven Forecasts of Supportable Supermarket Space (in Sq. Ft.)

Data Set No.	1994	1999
1	35,619	39,401
2	37,593	36,453
3	28,507	34,469
4	48,331	76,929
5	42,949	62,895
6	33,412	36,953
7	44,862	49,181
Average size	37,735	49,469
Standard deviation	+7,040	+15,419
Range	28,507 to 48,331	34,469 to 76,929
Mean plus 1 standard deviation	30,695 to 44,775	34,050 to 64,888
Recommended supermarket size:	35,000 to 45,000 sq. ft.	

ALTERNATIVE TECHNIQUE FOR ESTIMATING DEMAND

The appraiser applies an alternative technique to population data for Market Areas 1 and 2 to estimate the demand for the neighborhood shopping center. The steps followed in applying the technique are outlined below. Table 16.4 illustrates how the market demand data derived from the alternative ratio technique are refined into an estimate of marginal demand for the neighborhood shopping center.

Step 3.01 Per capita expenditure on retail goods

The per capita expenditure on retail goods at a neighborhood shopping center, excluding supermarket sales, is estimated based on sales tax data and population estimates. (Sales tax data for counties are available from the state.) Selected categories of retail sales considered pertinent to the subject were identified in the tax data. From the selected categories on the tax receipts, the appraiser estimates the total per capita sales for the county to be $435.22 ($122,340,419 in sales divided by the county population of 281,100).

Step 3.02 Retail sales per square foot

From data in *Dollars and Cents of Shopping Centers*, the appraiser obtained an estimate of $142.33 in retail sales per square foot for neighborhood shopping centers. With this information the per capita retail space requirements for shopping center space in the county can be calculated.

$435.22 per capita sales / $142.33 retail sales per sq. ft. = 3.06.

Table 16.4

Demand for Shopping Center Space in the Market Area
(Alternative Ratio Technique)

Year	Space Requirement Per Capita in Sq. Ft.*	Population	Total Retail Space Required in Sq. Ft.	Less Existing Space	Sq. Ft. of Excess Demand
Market Area 1					
1994	3.06	9,774	29,908	00	29,906
1999	3.06	10,812	33,084	00	33,084
Market Area 2					
1994	3.06	20,798	63,642	30,750	32,892
1999	3.06	23,211	71,026	30,750	40,276

* Retail sales were taken from *Reported Gross and Taxable Sales*, provided by the Comptroller of Public Accounts, State of Texas. Categories included were miscellaneous general merchandise; auto & home supply stores; men's and boys' clothing; women's clothing; sporting goods; miscellaneous retail. Denton County population was estimated by North Central Texas Council of Governments (NCTCOG). Retail sales per square foot were derived from information in the Urban Land Institute's *Dollars and Cents of Shopping Centers*. No price index adjustment was used because it is believed that sales have been rather stable or slightly lower due to economic uncertainty in the area.

Step 3.03 Supportable retail space

Multiplying the space requirement of 3.06 square feet by the population in the market area yields an estimate of the amount of shopping center space supported by market area demand. For 1994 the estimate is 29,908 square feet (3.06 x 9,774); for 1999 the estimate is 33,084 square feet (3.06 x 10,812).

Step 4.01 Competitive space

Existing competitive space in the market area must be subtracted from the amount of supportable retail space in the market area. Since there was no existing or anticipated competition in Market Area 1, no adjustment was required. In Market Area 2, there are 30,750 square feet of existing competitive space, which must be subtracted from the estimate of supportable retail space.

Step 5.01 Marginal demand

Marginal demand in the market area is the amount that remains after competitive space is subtracted from supportable retail space. Note that after the adjustment for competitive retail space is made, the estimated marginal demand figures derived from the two data sets are reasonably similar. The difference in the two sets of population estimates reflects the different sizes of the two defined market areas.

Table 16.5 breaks down the supportable retail space in the market area into three categories: supermarket, general retail, and pad site. Table 16.5 shows estimates of the recommended and maximum square foot area to be developed in the defined market area.

Table 16.5
Total New Retail Space Demand in the Defined Market Area

	Retail Space in Square Feet	
Type of Space	Recommended	Maximum
Supermarket	40,000	50,000
General retail	35,000	40,000
Pad site	19,600*	19,600*
Totals	94,600	109,600

* Based on three sites of 26,136 sq. ft. each and a 4:1 land-to-building ratio.

STEP 6 SUBJECT CAPTURE ESTIMATE

Because the subject tract has an excellent location and there is no competition in the immediate market area, it will capture 100% of the marginal demand forecast. If competition existed in the market area or the subject's location was less desirable, the subject's capture rate would have to be estimated. Generally, the test of financial feasibility requires an estimated capture rate for the subject property.

HIGHEST AND BEST USE CONCLUSION

The property's locational attributes indicate a probable retail use, but other attributes suggest alternative uses. For example, the property's physical attributes could support multifamily housing, warehouse/industrial, or office uses. The zoning advantage points to a retail use, as do the complementary properties and land uses found nearby. Finally, the design of the site supports a retail use. Thus, the aggregate of property attributes indicates a retail use, specifically a neighborhood shopping center/supermarket.

The market analysis shows that there is demand for a neighborhood retail facility in the defined market area. It appears that a 40,000-sq.-ft. supermarket can be supported by marginal demand and that another 35,000 to 40,000 square feet of general retail space is also viable.

Threshold testing of the multifamily residential use (Step 7) is presented in the following pages to verify that the use assessment is correct. As mentioned earlier, threshold testing is an analytical procedure commonly employed in feasibility analyses. An alternative use is tested based on especially optimistic forecast data (i.e., marginal demand and capture rate) to give the alternative use every possible chance to succeed. If the threshold testing establishes that the alternative use does not compare favorably with the other financially feasible uses, the use is eliminated from further consideration.

STEP 7 FINANCIAL FEASIBILITY ANALYSIS/ THRESHOLD TESTING

To conclude the highest and best use study, the appraiser conducts a financial feasibility analysis by means of threshold testing. There are several ways to test the viability of a proposed development project. In this case, the client is a developer so financial feasibility is examined from the perspective of a developer. The developer wants assurances that his investment in the project will be justified. This is established once the value of the developed property reaches or exceeds a breakeven point at which project costs are covered. Hence, the developer uses the breakeven point as a risk control measure to ensure the development will have sufficient cash flow to warrant the investment.

Table 16.6 compares the basic financial feasibility of a retail center and a multifamily apartment project. At the top of the table, 13 market-based assumptions for each use are listed. A breakeven model is employed.[1] The retail development appears capable of supporting a land value of $4.41 per square foot on a construction budget of $39.54 per square foot. Both figures are within the parameters set for the project. A multifamily housing use was tested with appropriate variables and the results differed significantly. The land value would be $3.26 per square foot with a supportable construction budget of $28.41 per square foot, 11% below the $32 per square foot it actually costs to construct apartment units in the current market. Thus, the test confirms the appraiser's belief that the site is best suited to retail use.

SPECIFICATION OF HIGHEST AND BEST USE

The highest and best use conclusion for the property is use as a neighborhood shopping center. The timing of this use is current. The market participants specified are the neighborhood residents, who represent the users of the shopping center, and a developer, who would be the likely buyer of the vacant tract.

---

1. James A. Graaskamp, *Fundamentals of Real Estate Development*, Development Component Series (Washington, D.C.: Urban Land Institute, 1981), 21.

Table 16.6
Feasibility Tests: Land under Retail Use versus Land under Multifamily Housing Use

Feasibility Test #1: Retail Breakeven (Default Ratio) Model Market-Based Assumptions

Market-Based Variables

1. Site cost/sq. ft.	$4.13
2. Site size in sq. ft.	435,600
3. Construction budget (direct & indirect) costs/sq. ft.	$38.00
4. Building size in sq. ft.	80,000
5. Equity dividend ratio	3.5%
6. Breakeven ratio (default ratio)	80.0%
Loan	100.00%
Rate	10.50%
Term	25.0 yrs.
7. Debt service constant	11.33%
8. Market rent/sq. ft.	$8.00
9. *EGI* operating expense ratio	31.0%
10. Vacancy rate	8.0%
11. Operating expenses/sq. ft.	$2.48
12. Risk reserve	$0.00
13. Cash replacement reserves	$0.00

Breakeven (Default Ratio) Model Developer's BEP Model Computations

Justified Cash Equity Investment

Potential gross income	$640,000
x (1 – default ratio)	20.0%
= Cash available after operating expenses & debt service	$128,000
– Vacancy & collection loss	$51,200
– Risk reserve	$0.00
= Cash available for investors	$76,800
/ Equity dividend rate	3.5%
= Justified equity cash investment	$2,194,266

Feasibility Test #2: Housing Breakeven (Default Ratio) Model Market-Based Assumptions

Market-Based Variables

1. Site cost/sq. ft.	$4.13
2. Site size in sq. ft.	435,600
3. Construction budget (direct & indirect) costs/sq. ft.	$32.00
4. Building size in sq. ft.	105,000
5. Equity dividend ratio	3.5%
6. Breakeven ratio (default ratio)	75.0%
Loan	100.00%
Rate	10.26%
Term	25.0 yrs.
7. Debt service constant	11.33%
8. Market rent/sq. ft.	$5.76
9. *EGI* operating expense ratio	22.0%
10. Vacancy rate	14.0%
11. Operating expenses/sq. ft.	$1.27
12. Risk reserve	$0.00
13. Cash replacement reserves	$0.00

Breakeven (Default Ratio) Model Developer's BEP Model Computations

Justified Cash Equity Investment

Potential gross income	$604,800
x (1 – default ratio)	25.0%
= Cash available after operating expenses & debt service	$151,200
– Vacancy & collection loss	$84,672
– Risk reserve	$0.00
= Cash available for investors	$66,528
/ Equity dividend rate	3.5%
= Justified equity cash investment	$1,900,800

Table 16.6
Feasibility Tests: Land under Retail Use versus Land under Multifamily Housing Use (Continued)

Justified Mortgage Loan		Justified Mortgage Loan	
Potential gross income	$640,000	Potential gross income	$604,800
x Default ratio	80.0%	x Default ratio	75.0%
= Cash outlays for operating expenses & debt service	$512,000	= Cash outlays for operating expenses & debt service	$453,600
– Operating expenses	$198,400	– Operating expenses	$133,056
– Cash replacements	$0.00	– Cash replacements	$0.00
= Cash available for debt service	$313,600	= Cash available for debt service	$320,544
/ Debt service constant	11.33%	/ Debt service constant	11.13%
= Justified mortgage loan	$2,767,829	= Justified mortgage loan	$2,881,264
Total Justified Investment		**Total Justified Investment**	
Justified equity investment	$2,194,286	Justified equity investment	$1,900,800
+ Justified mortgage loan	$2,767,829	+ Justified mortgage loan	$2,881,264
= Total justified investment	$4,962,115	= Total justified investment	$4,782,064
Justified Construction Budget		**Justified Construction Budget**	
Total justified investment	$4,962,115	Total justified investment	$4,782,064
– Land value	$1,799,028*	– Land value	$1,799,028*
= Construction budget (direct & indirect)	$3,163,087	= Construction budget (direct & indirect)	$2,983,036
/ Square feet in building	80,000	/ Square feet in building	105,000
= Justified budget/sq. ft.	$39.54	= Justified budget/sq. ft.	$28.41
Justified Land Value		**Justified Land Value**	
Total justified investment	$4,962,115	Total justified investment	$4,782,064
– Construction budget	$3,040,000	– Construction budget	$3,360,000
= Justified land value	$1,922,115	= Justified land value	$1,422,064
/ Square feet in land	435,600	/ Square feet in land	435,600
= Justified land value/sq. ft.	$4.41	= Justified land value/sq. ft.	$3.26

* 10 acres x 43,560 sq. ft./acre x $4.13 site cost/sq. ft. = $1,799,028

THE MARKET ANALYSIS PROCESS FOR A VACANT RETAIL CENTER

—⟫•⟪—

- Property productivity analysis
- Market area definition
- Demand analysis
- Competitive supply inventory
- Marginal demand estimate
- Subject capture estimate
- Financial feasibility analysis/threshold testing

CHAPTER SEVENTEEN

---※-◎-※---

Vacant Retail Center

The analysis of highest and best use is most often associated with vacant land, but such an analysis may also be required for an existing improved property. The case study property described in this chapter is a suburban shopping center which was empty at the time of the appraisal. Alternative highest and best use(s) for the property are thoroughly investigated. Sometimes alternative highest and best use(s) must also be examined for occupied structures that may be put to more profitable uses by repositioning them in the market. Enterprising developers and investors are alert to such possibilities.

INTRODUCTION

This chapter presents a Level B market analysis of a recently developed (1991) neighborhood shopping center which remains vacant. The analytical process includes these seven steps:

1. Property productivity analysis. The physical, design/amenity, legal, and locational attributes of the property are examined.
2. Market area definition. The market areas for alternative uses, i.e., retail and office, are identified.
3. Demand analysis. The forecast population and employment are segmented to arrive at the estimated demand for retail and office space.
4. Competitive supply inventory. The supply of competitive retail and office space is investigated.

5. Marginal demand estimate. The demand for retail and office uses is compared to the inventories of retail and office space. An oversupply of both retail and office space over the next decade is indicated.

6. Subject capture estimate. The subject has remained vacant since completion, which suggests that it will not capture a share of the overbuilt retail market. Its prospects under an alternative use as an office building are not promising either because the office market is overbuilt.

7. Financial feasibility analysis/threshold testing. Land residual analyses for office and retail space are conducted to determine which use would result in the highest land value.

STEP 1 PROPERTY PRODUCTIVITY ANALYSIS

The subject shopping center, which has stood empty since its completion, is examined with the understanding that an alternative use might be appropriate.

Step 1.1 Analysis of physical attributes

The retail center occupies 59,000 square feet of a 418,176-sq.-ft. (9.6 acre) tract of land. The typical land-to-building ratio for a one-level shopping centers is about 3:1, but the subject occupies only one-seventh of the area of the site. Much of the remaining acreage is excess land.

The physical features of the site and structure are adequate for a retail center. However, the site has a serious handicap in that it is literally in a hole. Although a roadway adjoins the southern boundary of the site, the site is barely visible from the road. The site slopes sharply downward from the road, which runs along a narrow ridge at the southern boundary of the property. In fact, the shopping center is not visible to traffic until automobiles have passed the site. Moreover, the street rises to a high point at the southwest corner of the site, thereby blocking visibility from the eastern and western approaches. With such abysmal visibility, the site appears suitable only for destination-oriented land uses.

Step 1.2 Analysis of design/amenity attributes

The shopping center structure has a major design flaw. Retail bays in this market are typically 40 to 60 feet deep. Unfortunately, the builder made the bays in the shopping center 80-ft. deep, which obviously added to the construction costs. Even more seriously, rents would have to be high to cover the cost of the extra space. To pay these higher rents, tenants would have to generate higher gross sales than their competitors, or be willing to settle for less profit per square foot. In light of these circumstances, tenants would be reluctant to rent the facilities at existing market rents, even if the center had excellent visibility.

Step 1.3 Analysis of legal/regulatory attributes

No unusual legal or regulatory restrictions encumber the property.

Step 1.4 Analysis of locational attributes

The site's locational attributes are less than desirable. Investigation indicated that the property is in an obviously inferior location. The subject is situated on what will eventually become an important crosstown arterial road, but the present road cannot accommodate the flow of traffic. Unfortunately, the city has decided to delay expansion of the road for a number of years. Congestion is forcing north/south traffic away from the subject to other arterials. Thus, traffic is bypassing the subject and will continue to do so for a number of years. Traffic patterns are expected to be favorable to the site eventually, but not before the late 1990s.

STEP 2 MARKET AREA DEFINITION

The primary market area for the shopping center is the adjacent neighborhood, in which single-family homes are being developed for middle- and upper-middle-income residents. The boundaries of the primary market area are constrained by low-lying land situated in a severe floodplain (see Figure 17.1). Thus, geography permanently limits the size of the primary market area. The only way to

Figure 17.1
Floodplain Map

offset this physical constraint is to increase the density of land use. A change to multifamily construction would increase the population density in the primary market area substantially, but given current trends it will take many years for such a change to come about. The overall metropolitan area can be considered the secondary market area for the shopping center.

In terms of its structure and design, the subject property would be classified as a neighborhood retail center. Problems with the physical site, the design, and the location raise serious questions about the shopping center's ability to succeed. Potential alternative uses include conversion to office space, to flex space that allows for a combination of office and retail uses, or to a service center housing municipal offices. Unfortunately, the city council has recently approved the construction of a large new office building at a superior location.

The following pages describe a market analysis for the empty shopping center under a retail use (Steps 3.1 through 6.1) and a market analysis under an alternative office use (Steps 3.01 through 6.01). Both analyses are based on citywide demand and supply data.

MARKET ANALYSIS FOR RETAIL USE

Step 3.1 Citywide demand for retail space

Population and employment projections for the metropolitan area are shown in Table 17.1. The 1995 data indicate a 4,894 increase in population between 1990 and 1995.

Table 17.1
City Population and Employment, 1970-2000

	1970	1980	1990	1995	2000
Population	10,279	12,602	16,006	20,900	27,300
Total employment	N/A	1,551	2,770	3,762	5,110
Retail employment	N/A	N/A	290	381	500

Step 4.1 Citywide supply of retail space

Table 17.2 is an inventory of existing retail space in the city in 1990. The data in the table indicate that there are 309,979 square feet of occupied space and 215,691 square feet of vacant space. Using the 1990 population of 16,006, there are 19.4 square feet of occupied retail space per person.

Table 17.2

Citywide Retail Center Inventory

	Anchor Space	Multitenant Space	Multitenant Occupancy	Multitenant Leased	Multitenant Vacant
Braewood Shopping Center	0	33,000	88%	29,040	3,960
Coppell Park Plaza	0	33,670	55%	18,519	15,151
Corner @ Coppell	49,053*	64,947	7%	4,000[†]	60,947
Georgetown Plaza	0	59,000	3%	1,600	57,400
Sandy Lake Center	0	21,000	72%	15,120	5,880
Town Oaks Center	42,000	49,000	90%	44,100	4,900
Valley Ranch Center	55,000	37,000	50%	18,600	18,400
Woodside Village	55,000	27,000	100%	27,000	0
Total	201,053	324,617	49.2%	157,979	166,638
Total occupied					309,979 sq. ft.
Total vacant					215,691 sq. ft.

* Vacant   [†] Estimated

Source: Appraiser's survey

Shopping center developers use various rules of thumb to assess the suitability of a given area for retail development. According to one such guideline, a neighborhood shopping center of 30,000 to 100,000 square feet requires a market area with a population of 2,500 to 40,000 people. This demand estimate translates into between 2.5 and 12.0 square feet of retail space per person.[1] Thus, the estimated 19.4 square feet of retail space per person in the subject market is far above the rule of thumb.

Step 5.1 Marginal demand estimate

Assuming that marginal demand is 4,894 in 1995 and that 7.25 square feet of retail space can be supported by one person (i.e., the midpoint between 2.5 and 12.0), about 35,482 square feet of retail space can be absorbed over the five-year period. This indicates annual absorption of 7,096 square feet. At this rate, it will take an astonishing 30 years for the inventory of retail space to lease up (215,691 sq. ft. of vacant space / 7,096 annual absorption = 30.4).

---

1. Urban Land Institute, *Shopping Center Development Handbook* (Washington, D.C.: Urban Land Institute, 1977), 7.

Table 17.1 shows retail employment of 290 in 1995. Thus, the 309,979 square feet of occupied space breaks down to 1,068.9 square feet of space per employee. The data indicate an increase of 91 retail employees between 1990 and 1995. This suggests a more rapid absorption of space—i.e., 97,270 square feet over five years (91 new employees x 1,068.9 sq. ft. per employee), or 19,454 square feet per year. Even at this rate, however, it would take more than 11 years for the current supply of retail space to be absorbed.

Step 6.1 Subject capture estimate

Given the design and location problems of the shopping center, the subject appears to be one of the least attractive retail properties in the city and will be one of the last to lease up.

MARKET ANALYSIS FOR OFFICE USE

Step 3.01 Office space demand

Office building developers estimate the demand for office space from forecasts of the number of employees in service industries. Table 17.3 provides forecast employment figures for the subject city. The data indicate that, between 1990 and 2000, an additional 760 service industry employees are expected in the citywide market area.

Table 17.3
City Employment Forecast

	1990	2000	2010
Basic employment	1,840	3,200	3,670
Retail employment	290	500	810
Service employment	640	1,400	2,370
Total employment	2,770	5,100	6,850

Source: North Central Texas Council of Governments, *Dallas-Fort Worth Economic Outlook* (Arlington, Texas: Regional Data Center).

Step 4.01 Office space supply

The high number of vacancies in the city suggests a serious oversupply of office space (see Table 17.4).

Table 17.4
Citywide Office Space Inventory

	Multitenant Space	Multitenant Occupancy	Multitenant Leased	Multitenant Vacant
Shady Shore Office	38,200	72%	27,504	10,696
Comers Office Plaza	18,347	62%	11,375	6,971
Valley View Office	52,400	44%	23,056	29,344
Forest Ridge Office	16,900	92%	15,548	1,352
Oak Lane Plaza Office	24,600	18%	4,428	20,172
Town Oaks Office	42,000	62%	26,040	15,960
Post Oak Office	28,300	47%	13,301	14,999
Woodsong Office	24,300	88%	21,384	2,916
Total	245,047	58%	142,636	102,410

Source: Appraiser's survey

Step 5.01 Marginal demand estimate

An allocation of 202 square feet of office space per employee is the national average;[2] estimates for the local metropolitan area put the figure at 286 square feet per employee.[3] The inventory of supply in Table 17.4 indicates 245,047 square feet of office space in the city. Table 17.3 shows 640 service industry employees in 1990. These figures suggest 383 square feet of space per employee, which is 1.9 times the national average and 1.34 times the local average. These data reflect a seriously overbuilt market.

With 640 service industry employees and 142,636 square feet of occupied space in the citywide market area, the actual allocation is 223 square feet per employee. Between 1990 and 2000, service employment is expected to increase by 760 people, an extra 76 per year. Given the current space allocation per employee, there will be demand for an additional 169,480 square feet of office space over 10 years, or 16,948 square feet annually. At this rate, it will take six years for the current excess supply of office space (102,411 square feet) to be absorbed. If the national average of 202 square feet per employee is used, the current excess supply will be absorbed in 6.67 years. Thus, the market will likely be oversupplied with office space for another 6.0 to 6.67 years.

2. Urban Land Institute, *Office Development Handbook* (Washington, D.C.: Urban Land Institute, 1982), 16.
3. *Office Building Survey* published by a local brokerage company, 1989.

Step 6.01 Subject capture

The poor visibility of the site and the atypical size of the retail bays might not impact the office building use as adversely as the retail use. However, the site's location along a traffic-congested, crosstown arterial represents a serious disadvantage in an overbuilt office market. Again it seems that the subject is one of the least attractive properties on the market and will be one of the last to lease up.

HIGHEST AND BEST USE CONCLUSION

The property productivity analysis for the subject indicated that it could be used for several purposes—i.e., retail, office, or perhaps an office/retail combination of flex space. For any of these uses the physical features of the site, the design of the structure, and the location all represent serious deficiencies.

The market analyses suggest that there is a significant oversupply of both retail and office space. The oversupply of retail space is perhaps more severe than the excess space in the office market.

STEP 7 FINANCIAL FEASIBILITY ANALYSIS/ THRESHOLD TESTING

To determine the highest and best use of the property, the financial feasibility of the two possible uses is explored by means of land residual analyses and threshold testing. The financial feasibility of each use is tested using especially optimistic forecast data. In the two examples, accelerated absorption rates are postulated for both land uses.

In the land residual analyses, it is assumed that the operating costs of the property would be the same under the retail and office uses. The existing structure is in very good condition, requiring only interior finishing to bring it to an operational state. This type of structure can be finished reasonably well for $10.00 per square foot. The analyst assumes that the construction costs are a *sunk cost*, i.e., an expenditure made in the past with no relevance for current decision making. Thus, the marginal cost to make the property operational is the finish-out cost only. If the property can generate enough revenue to cover fixed costs including property taxes, it should be put to an appropriate use.

The findings of the residual analyses, which are shown in Tables 17.5 and 17.6, indicate that neither retail use nor office use is viable because the land value under both uses is negative. The value of the land under the retail use is −$353,000, even worse than the land value under the office use, which is −$122,000. Thus threshold testing reveals that neither land use is financially feasible. The improvement should be closed up and the property held as a speculative investment until market demand warrants putting the property to use.

HIGHEST AND BEST USE SPECIFICATION

The highest and best use conclusion for the property is use as a speculative hold-ing. The timing of a future retail or office use is five to 15 years out. The market participants specified are speculative investors, the most likely buyers of the prop-erty. The neighborhood residents represent the primary users of a future shopping center; the users of future office space would be drawn from the citywide popu-lation.

Tables 17.5 and 17.6 are presented on the pages that follow.

Table 17.5
Land Residual Analysis to Test Financial Feasibility under Retail Use

		Year 1	Year 2	Year 3	Year 4	Year 5	Year 6	Year 7	Year 8	Year 9
Vacancy & collection loss (%)					50.00%	40.00%	30.00%	20.00%	10.00%	5.00%
Potential gross income										
Potential rental income	$6.25	0	0	0	368,750	368,750	368,750	368,750	368,750	368,750
Less vacancy & collection loss		0	0	0	184,375	147,500	110,625	73,750	36,875	18,438
Effective gross income		0	0	0	184,375	221,250	258,125	295,000	331,875	350,312
Operating expenses										
Variable					29,500	29,500	29,500	29,500	29,500	29,500
Management	4.0%				7,375	8,850	10,325	11,800	13,275	14,013
Property insurance					6,641	6,641	6,807	6,977	7,152	7,330
Real estate taxes	1.56%	9,204	9,204	9,204	157,571	157,571	162,298	167,167	172,182	177,348
Replacement allowance					34,741	34,741	51,554	60,356	63,223	66,226
Holding costs	1.00%	5,900	5,900	5,900	5,900					
Total operating expenses		(15,104)	(15,104)	(15,104)	(241,728)	(237,303)	(260,484)	(275,800)	(285,332)	(294,417)
Net operating income		(15,104)	(15,104)	(15,014)	(57,353)	(16,053)	(2,359)	19,200	46,543	55,895
Sq. ft. in building	59,000									
Less development cost/sq. ft.										
(finish only)	10.00				(590,000)					
Plus reversion									10,471	
Less cost of sales	2.0%								209	
Net reversion									10,262	
Total property cash flow		(15,104)	(15,104)	(15,104)	(647,353)	(16,053)	(2,359)	19,200	56,806	
PV factor @ 18.0%		.8475	.7182	.6086	.5158	.4371	.3704	.3139	.2660	
Present value of cash flows @	18.00%	(12,800)	(10,847)	(9,193)	(333,897)	(7,017)	(874)	6,027	15,113	

414

Table 17.5
Land Residual Analysis to Test Financial Feasibility under Retail Use (Continued)

	Year 1	Year 2	Year 3	Year 4	Year 5	Year 6	Year 7	Year 8	Year 9
Cumulative value (check)	(12,800)	(23,647)	(32,840)	(366,738)	(373,755)	(374,628)	(368,601)	(353,489)	(353,489)
Sum of present values	(353,489)								
Net present value	(353,489)								
Residual to the land (rounded)	(353,000)								
Land square footage	418,176								
Land value per sq. ft.	(0.84)								

Yield	Total Cost (Land plus Const. Cost)	Cost to Construct	Land Value	Land Value per Sq. Ft.
14.00%	189,824	590,000	(400,176)	(0.96)
16.00%	214,060	590,000	(375,940)	(0.90)
18.00%	236,511	590,000	(353,489)	(0.85)
20.00%	257,324	590,000	(332,676)	(0.80)
22.00%	276,632	590,000	(313,368)	(0.75)
24.00%	294,559	590,000	(295,441)	(0.71)
26.00%	311,216	590,000	(278,784)	(0.67)
28.00%	326,707	590,000	(263,293)	(0.63)

Table 17.6

Land Residual Analysis to Test Financial Feasibility under Office Use

	Input	Year 1	Year 2	Year 3	Year 4	Year 5	Year 6	Year 7	Year 8	Year 9
Vacancy & collection loss (%)				30.00%	15.00%	10.00%	5.00%	5.00%	5.00%	5.00%
Potential gross income										
Potential rental income	$7.00	0	0	413,000	413,000	413,000	413,000	413,000	413,000	413,000
Less vacancy & collection loss		0	0	123,900	61,950	41,300	20,650	20,650	20,650	20,650
Effective gross income		0	0	289,100	351,050	371,700	392,350	392,350	392,350	392,350
Operating expenses										
Variable				29,500	29,500	29,500	29,500	29,500	29,500	29,500
Management	4.0%			11,564	14,042	14,868	15,694	15,694	15,694	15,694
Property insurance				6,641	6,641	6,807	6,977	7,152	7,330	7,514
Real estate taxes	1.56%	9,204	9,204	157,571	157,571	157,571	162,298	167,167	172,182	177,348
Replacement allowance				34,741	34,741	34,741	51,554	60,356	63,223	66,226
Holding costs	1.00%	5,900	5,900							
Total operating expenses		(15,104)	(15,104)	(240,017)	(242,495)	(243,487)	(266,023)	(279,869)	(287,929)	(296,282)
Net operating income		(15,104)	(15,104)	49,083	108,555	128,213	126,327	112,481	104,421	96,068
Sq. ft. in building	59,000									
Less development cost/sq. ft. (finish only)	10.00			(590,000)						
Plus reversion									15,998	
Less cost of sales	2.0%								320	
Net reversion									15,678	
Total property cash flow		(15,104)	(15,104)	(540,917)	108,555	128,213	126,327	112,481	120,099	
PV factor @ 16.0%		.8621	.7432	.6407	.5523	.4761	.4104	.3538	.3050	
Present value of cash flows @	16.00%	(13,021)	(11,225)	(346,543)	59,954	61,044	51,850	39,799	36,633	

Table 17.6
Land Residual Analysis to Test Financial Feasibility under Office Use (Continued)

	Year 1	Year 2	Year 3	Year 4	Year 5	Year 6	Year 7	Year 8	Year 9
Cumulative value (check)	(13,021)	(24,245)	(370,788)	(310,834)	(249,790)	(197,940)	(158,141)	(121,508)	
Sum of present values	(121,508)								
Net present value	(121,508)								
Residual to the land (rounded)	(122,000)								
Land square footage	418,176								
Land value per sq. ft.	(0.29)								

Yield	Total Cost (Land plus Const. Cost)	Cost to Construct	Land Value	Land Value per Sq. Ft.
12.00%	484,587	590,000	(105,413)	(0.25)
14.00%	475,495	590,000	(114,505)	(0.27)
16.00%	468,492	590,000	(121,508)	(0.29)
18.00%	463,225	590,000	(126,775)	(0.30)
20.00%	459,400	590,000	(130,600)	(0.31)
22.00%	456,771	590,000	(133,229)	(0.32)
24.00%	455,133	590,000	(134,867)	(0.32)
26.00%	454,317	590,000	(135,683)	(0.32)

EPILOGUE

━━━◆━━━

Application of Market Analysis
Concepts in the Approaches to Value

This chapter describes how market analysis relates to property value—"the bottom line" of most appraisals. Market analysis provides the underpinnings for determining property value, which is estimated with the valuation approaches. In other words, incorporating the findings of market analysis into the three approaches and the reconciliation of value brings the market analysis to its logical conclusion. The specific uses of market analysis in the three approaches to value are outlined below.

THE APPRAISAL OF VACANT LAND

Market Conditions Adjustment

The highest and best use analysis of vacant land provides information used to estimate an adjustment for changes in market conditions. Comparable tracts of vacant land may have been sold to users or investors, and market expectations at the time of sale, occurring one to two years earlier, may have been different from market expectations on the date of the appraisal. The best sales data available are often historical sales to purchasers who bought the land with a specific use in mind. These sales provide an indication of the anticipated land value under the specific use. A study of marginal demand can establish the time horizon for development of the subject, and the prospective values of the subject under the specific use plan can be estimated. Discounting the prospective value yields an estimate of the present value of the subject land, which can be compared to the values indicated by past sales.

Financial Feasibility/Development Approach

The appraiser must investigate the financial feasibility of the use of the real estate. Industry guidelines require the appraiser to identify the motives behind sales transactions because the financial feasibility of a parcel of real estate under a specific use does not always explain market transactions. Factors such as liberal lending practices, investment in land as a hedge against hyperinflation, insolvency that results in the liquidation of holdings, and even misinformation help account for sales and purchases of real estate. To test value estimates derived from comparable sales and to determine whether the intended use of a property is indeed financially feasible, the development approach is often applied. A forecast of marginal demand allows an appraiser to draw up a land use concept plan, on which the application of the development approach depends. Furthermore, a Level C market analysis generates the specific information on use and timing required in the development approach.

Identification of Appropriate Comparables

The valuation section of an appraisal represents a detailed financial analysis of the property under the highest and best use specified in the market analysis. For a vacant tract with strong mixed-use potential, identifying reliable comparable tracts can be especially challenging. In Chapter 15, the subject tract was zoned for retail and garden office uses and was located near sites developed under retail and garden office uses. These sites would have seemed to be appropriate comparables, but the highest and best use concluded for the tract was a mix of office (9 acres), retail (12 acres), and multifamily apartment (36 acres) uses. Although the land value under this mix was slightly lower than the value under a mix with more land devoted to office use (21 acres) and less to mulifamily apartment use (24 acres), the projection period was shorter and, consequently, the project was less risky. Because marginal demand and the development horizon for each potential use were identified in the Level C market analysis, it was possible to determine the best allocation of land uses.

THE APPRAISAL OF IMPROVED PROPERTIES

Sales Comparison Approach

When sufficient sales data are available to support the application of the sales comparison approach, the appraiser's market analysis can provide information about the attributes of comparable improved properties. This information is the basis for the adjustments made to the sale prices of comparable properties for changes in market conditions and differences in physical and locational attributes. Market analysis can also provide insights into other property characteristics such as the quality of management, the profile of the tenancy, and the nature of special lease provisions, which have special relevance to income-producing properties. These characteristics are considered in analyzing the income the subject and comparables produce and the potential income they are capable of generating. Information on these characteristics provides the basis for adjustments made on the market data grid.

Market analysis may also shed light on the reasonableness or appropriateness of an overall cap rate (R_O). Overall cap rates are used in direct capitalization to convert a single year's income expectancy (NOI) into an indication of property value. An overall cap rate is derived by analyzing actual market data on the sale prices and net operating incomes of comparable properties. The overall capitalization rate also serves as a unit of comparison.

Cost Approach

The knowledge of market conditions derived from market analysis is essential to the application of the cost approach. The appraiser uses this information to determine whether the property has incurred external obsolescence or has an economic advantage. The cost approach is based on the premise that the depreciated cost of the improvement(s) plus the value of the land will tend to equal market value when supply and demand are in balance. The cost approach also recognizes that properties can gain or lose value because of external market conditions such as an economic upswing or an economic recession. In a down market, the appraiser considers the loss in rent for the anticipated period as a charge for external obsolescence, which is deducted from the depreciated cost of the subject improvement.

Income Capitalization Approach

Selection of R_O in Direct Capitalization

Overall capitalization rates derived from historical data reflect past conditions, but the overall rates applied in direct capitalization must be responsive to changes taking place in the market. If the demand forecast developed in market analysis does not seem likely to sustain the income expectations reflected in the overall rates derived from historical sales data, current values may no longer be supportable and a decline in the market will be indicated. In such a case, a higher overall capitalization rate might be selected because an inverse relationship exists between R_O and value. If the demand forecast seems to support development, property values are likely to increase. In a developing market, a lower overall capitalization rate might be selected.

DCF Modeling

To perform a discounted cash flow (DCF) analysis for a property, an appraiser prepares a reconstructed operating statement forecast (pro forma) based on data pertaining to the property's current and forecast occupancy levels, rents, and operating expenses. The estimates of net operating income developed for each year of the projection period are supported by the conclusions of the market analysis.

In the DCF model, the projected cash flows are further refined to reflect all factors that affect net operating income. These factors reflect property performance and include gross potential income, vacancy and collection losses, fixed and variable operating expenses, and debt service. The supply and demand forecasts made in the market analysis establish the ranges in property value, and the pro forma statement reflects future market expectations. The information gathered in market analysis enables the appraiser to test the reasonableness of each element forecast in the DCF model. Will the rents and occupancy levels in the market continue to rise or will they fall? Will rents and occupancy levels increase initially, but then head downward over the forecast period?

The income streams estimated in the reconstructed operating statement are discounted using a rate derived from analyzing the relationship between demand and competitive supply. A discount rate is a rate of return on capital which is used to convert future payments into present value. As such, it reflects the measure of risk associated with an investment. If the market forecast indicates a strong market for the subject, the investment risk and discount rate will probably be lower. If the market forecast indicates a weak market, the investment risk and discount rate will be higher. The findings of the market analysis help set the range for the discount rate.

The choice of a discount rate also depends on the appraiser's confidence level in the absorption/capture forecast. The level of detail found in the market analysis must be considered. A low level of confidence will be associated with a general market study, which offers little support for the absorption forecast. The cash flows projected on the basis of such a forecast are riskier, and thus the selection of a higher discount rate is warranted. On the other hand, a high confidence level is associated with a detailed market study, which offers persuasive support for the capture forecast, and thereby narrows the range of upside and downside possibilities. The cash flows projected on the basis of such a forecast are more secure, and the choice of a lower discount rate would be justified.

BIBLIOGRAPHY

General surveys and anthologies

Appraisal Institute. "Real Estate Cycles: Trends and Analysis." Technical report from the 1993 Annual Research Symposium, Chicago.

___. *Real Estate Market Analysis and Appraisal*. Research Report 3. Chicago: American Institute of Real Estate Appraisers, 1988.

___. *Real Estate Market Analysis: Supply and Demand Factors.*[1] Technical report from the 1992 Annual Research Symposium. Chicago: Appraisal Institute, 1993.

Carn, Neil, Joseph Rabianski, Ronald Racster, and Maury Seldin. *Real Estate Market Analysis.*[2] Englewood Cliffs, N.J.: Prentice-Hall, 1988.

Clapp, John M. *Handbook for Real Estate Market Analysis.*[3] Englewood Cliffs, N.J.: Prentice-Hall, 1987.

DeLisle, James R. and J. Sa-Aadu, eds. *Appraisal, Market Analysis and Public Policy in Real Estate: Essays in Honor of James A. Graaskamp*. American Real Estate Society. Norwell, Mass.: Kluwer Academic Publishers, 1994.

Fanning, Stephen F. and Jody Winslow. "Guidelines for Defining the Scope of Market Analysis in Appraisals." *The Appraisal Journal* (October 1988).

Ratcliff, Richard U. *Real Estate Analysis*. New York: McGraw-Hill Book Company, Inc., 1961.

Vernor, James D., ed. *Readings in Market Analysis for Real Estate*. Chicago: American Institute of Real Estate Appraisers, 1985.

---

1. A useful collection of articles on forecasting with census data, delineation of retail areas, analysis of supply and demand for subdivisions, and urban land use mix in general equilibrium theory.

2. Contains excellent bibliography on data sources and data services available for market analysis.

3. See note 2 above.

Economic base analysis, census data, location theory, city planning, real estate trends, and finance/investment

Alonso, W. and J. Friedmann. *Regional Development and Planning*. Cambridge, Mass.: MIT Press, 1964.

Andrews, Richard B. *Urban Land Economics and Public Policy*. New York: The Free Press, 1971.

___. "Situs: Variables of Urban Land Use Location," *Urban Land Economics and Public Policy*. New York: The Free Press, 1971.

Christaller, Walter. *Central Places in Southern Germany*. Englewood Cliffs, N.J.: Prentice-Hall, 1966.

Crispell, Diane. *Demographic Know-How: Everything You Need to Find, Analyze, and Use Information About Your Customers*. 3d ed. Ithaca, N.Y.: American Demographic Books, 1993.

Etter, Wayne E. "Putting a Leash on Risk: Toward Evaluating Commercial Properties." *Tierra Grande: Journal of the Real Estate Center at Texas A&M University* (Spring 1994).

Feagin, J.R. *The Urban Real Estate Game*. Englewood Cliffs, N.J.: Prentice Hall, 1983.

Greer, Gaylon E. and Michael D. Farrell. *Investment Analysis for Real Estate Decisions*. 2d ed. Chicago: Dearborn Financial Publishers, 1988.

Heilbrun, James. *Urban Economics and Public Policy*. 2d ed. New York: St. Martin's Press, 1981.

Isard, Walter. *Methods of Regional Analysis*. Cambridge, Mass.: MIT Press, 1960.

Jackson, John Brinckerhoff. *A Sense of Place, a Sense of Time*. New Haven, Conn.: Yale University Press, 1994.

Kostof, Spiro. *The City Shaped: Urban Patterns and Meanings Through History*. New York: Little, Brown, 1991.

Kostof, Spiro with the collaboration of Greg Castillo, *The City Assembled: The Elements of Urban Form Through History*. New York: Little, Brown, 1992.

Kunstler, James Howard. *The Geography of Nowhere: The Rise and Fall of America's Man-Made Landscape*. New York: Simon and Schuster, 1993.

Lessinger, Jack. *The Crash of Suburbia: The Coming Boom of Small Towns*. Seattle: Socioeconomics, 1990.

___. *Penturbia: Where Real Estate Will Boom After the Crash of Suburbia*. Seattle: Socioeconomics, 1991.

___. *Regions of Opportunity: A Bold Strategy for Real Estate Investment with Forecasts to the Year 2010.* Seattle: Socioeconomics, 1986.

Lösch, August. *Economics of Location.* New Haven, Conn.: Yale University Press, 1954.

Malkiel, Burton G. *A Random Walk Down Wall Street.* 5th ed. New York: Norton, 1990.

Martin, W.B. "How to Predict Urban Growth Patterns." *The Appraisal Journal* (April 1984).

McShane, Clay. *Down the Asphalt Path: The Automobile and the American City.* New York: Columbia University Press, 1994.

Myers, Dowell. *Analysis with Local Census Data: Portraits of Change.* San Diego: Academic Press, Inc., a subsidiary of Harcourt Brace Jovanovich, 1992.

___. "Ransacking the Federal Census." A paper delivered at the annual meeting of the American Real Estate Society, 1992.

Pfouts, R.W., ed. *The Techniques of Urban Economic Analysis.* West Trenton, N.J.: Chandler Davis Publishing Co., 1960.

Rabianski, Joseph. "The Accuracy of Economic/Demographic Projections Made by Private Vendors of Secondary Data." *The Appraisal Journal* (April 1992).

Tiebout, Charles M. *The Community Economic Base Study.* Supplementary Paper No. 1. New York: Committee for Economic Development, December 1962.

Whyte, William Hollingsworth. *City: Rediscovering Its Center.* New York: Doubleday, 1989.

Zeckendorf, William. *Zeckendorf: The Autobiography of William Zeckendorf.* New York: Holt, 1970.

Appraisal literature

Clapp, John. *Real Estate Absorption for Appraisal, Investment, and Lending.* Conn.: Land Publications.

Graaskamp, James A. *The Appraisal of 25 N. Pinckney: A Demonstration Case for Contemporary Appraisal Methods.* Madison, Wis.: Landmark Research, Inc., 1977.

___. *Fundamentals of Real Estate Development.* Development Component Series. Washington, D.C.: Urban Land Institute, 1981.

Mitchell, John S. "What Is Land Worth?" *Urban Land* (June 1988).

Monographs and articles about specific property types

Office Buildings

Alexander, Ian. *Office Location and Public Policy*. New York: Chancer Press, 1979.

Building Owners and Managers Association. *Downtown and Suburban Office Building Experience Exchange Report*. Washington, D.C.: BOMA.

Garreau, Joel. *Edge City: Life on the New Frontier*. New York: Doubleday, 1991.

Gordon, Edmond S. *How to Market Space in an Office Building*. Boston: Warren, Gorham, and Lamont, Inc., 1976.

Kimball, J.R., and Barbara S. Bloomberg. "Office Space Demand Analysis." *The Appraisal Journal* (October 1987).

Urban Land Institute. *Office Development Handbook*. Washington, D.C.: ULI, 1982.

White, John R., ed. *The Office Building From Concept to Investment Reality*. A joint publication of the Appraisal Institute, American Society of Real Estate Counselors, and Society of Industrial and Office Realtors.® Chicago, 1993.

Residential

Kimball, J.R., and Barbara S. Bloomberg. "The Demographics of Subdivision Analysis." *The Appraisal Journal* (October 1986).

Myers, Dowell. *Housing Demography: Linking Demographic Structure and Housing Markets*. Madison: University of Wisconsin Press, 1991.

___. "Housing Market Research: A Time for Change." *Urban Land* (October 1988).

Urban Land Institute. *Residential Development Handbook*. Washington, D.C.: ULI, 1978.

U.S. Department of Commerce, Bureau of the Census. *Construction Reports*. Washington, D.C.: U.S. Government Printing Office.

Shopping Centers

American Planning Association. "Changing Retail Trends." *Planning* (January 1991).

Berry, Brian L.J. "Spatial Theories of Marketing Systems, Abstract and Operational" in Robert L. King, ed. *Marketing and the New Science of Planning*. Chicago: American Marketing Association, 1968.

Berry, Brian and J.B. Parr. *Market Centers and Retail Location: Theory and Applications*. Englewood Cliffs, N.J.: Prentice-Hall, Inc., 1988.

Clapp, John. *Acorn Hill Mall: A Case Study for Retail Market Analysis*. Conn.: Land Publications.

___. *Retail Gravitation Analysis*. Conn.: Land Publications.

Nelson, Richard L. *The Selection of Retail Locations*. New York: F.W. Dodge, 1958.

Rabianski, Joseph, and James D. Vernor. *Shopping Center Appraisal and Analysis*. Chicago: Appraisal Institute, 1993.

Reilly, William J. *Methods for the Study of Retail Relationships*. Austin: Bureau of Business Research, University of Texas, 1929. Reprinted in Austin in 1959.

Rocca, Ruben A., ed. *Market Research for Shopping Centers*. New York: International Council of Shopping Centers, 1985.

Urban Land Institute. *Dollars and Cents of Shopping Centers*. Published triennially. Washington, D.C.: ULI.

Urban Land Institute. *Parking Requirements for Shopping Centers*. Summary Recommendations and Research Summary Report. Washington, D.C.: ULI, 1986.

Urban Land Institute. *Shopping Center Development Handbook*. 2d ed. Community Builders Handbook series. Washington, D.C.: ULI, 1985.

Vacant Land and Proposed Development (Mixed-Use Developments)

McMahan, John. *Property Development: Effective Decision Making in Uncertain Times*. New York: McGraw-Hill, 1976.

Peisner, Richard B. "Optimizing Profits from Land Use Planning." *Urban Land* (September 1982).

Reports and forecasts on real estate market trends

Compiled by David A. Mulvihill and published in *Urban Land* (August 1994.)[4]

Baring Consensus Forecast
Baring Advisors
2 Grand Central Tower, Suite 4000
140 East 45th Street
New York, NY 10017-3144
212-697-3340
March issue of firm's *U.S. Property Report*. Ranking of top investment markets based on analysis of more than 30 separate forecasts.

---

4. Courtesy of the Urban Land Institute

Commercial Property Trends
Oncor International
3040 Post Oak Boulevard, Suite 500
Houston, TX 77056
713-961-0600
Annual. Information on commercial property and economic trends in 55 markets
in the United States, Canada, and Europe.

Dodge/Sweet's Construction Outlook
McGraw-Hill, Inc.
1221 Avenue of the Americas
New York, NY 10020
212-512-3853
Annual. Forecast of construction activity in the residential, commercial, public
works, and manufacturing sectors.

Emerging Trends in Real Estate
RERC Real Estate Research Corporation and Equitable Real Estate
Investment Management, Inc.
RERC Real Estate Research Corporation
2 North LaSalle Street, Suite 400
Chicago, Illinois 60602
312-346-5885
Annual. Information on general economic trends, investment trends, capital
sources, specific markets, and property types.

Hospitality Directions
Coopers & Lybrand
1301 Avenue of the Americas
New York, NY 10019-6013
212-259-2620
December issue of quarterly journal. Twelve-quarter forecast of average hotel
occupancy rates, room rates, total receipts, room supply, and construction.

The Host Report
Arthur Anderson & Co., SC
The Arthur Anderson Real Estate Services Group
633 West Fifth Street
Los Angeles, CA 90071
800-959-1059
Annual. Operating statistics and supply and demand information for U.S. full-ser-
vice, limited-service, and all-suite hotels based on information from Smith Travel Research, with specific information on 21 major markets.

Market Trends
Julien J. Studley, Inc.
300 Park Avenue
New York, NY 10022
212-326-1000
Annual. Overall U.S. and international real estate market trends and specific commercial property market information for a limited number of major markets.

Property Report
The Yarmouth Group
Swiss Bank Tower
10 East 50th Street
New York, NY 10022
212-355-4810
Annual. General economic and real estate trend information for office, retail, industrial, and lodging markets in 18 U.S. and European markets.

Real Estate Market Forecast
Landauer Real Estate Counselors
335 Madison Avenue
New York, NY 10017
212-687-2323
Annual. U.S. economic information as well as specific performance information for the office, retail, industrial, residential, and hotel sectors and for two dozen U.S. metro areas.

Real Estate Value Trends
Valuation Network, Inc.
608 2nd Avenue South
Northstar East, Suite 700
Minneapolis, MN 55402
800-345-1277
Annual. List of economic and demographic growth markets and top investment markets for the office, industrial, retail, and apartment sectors.

Top Construction Markets
Cahners Economics
Cahners Publishing Company
275 Washington Street
Newton, MA 02158
617-964-3030
Annual. U.S. economic, demographic, and employment information and predictions for the top 50 construction markets for each upcoming year in both residential and nonresidential sectors.

Trends in the Hotel Industry
PKF Consulting
PKF Consulting Headquarters
425 California Street, Suite 1650
San Francisco, CA 94104
415-421-5378
Annual. National and regional operating and financial data for U.S. hotels and motels as well as overall demographic and economic information pertinent to the lodging industry.

A P P E N D I X

————➤◄————

NCREIF Suggested
Market Analysis Guidelines[1]

Purpose and Scope

*Recognizing the importance of market analysis in an appraisal, the Valuation
and Research Committees of NCREIF [National Council of Real Estate Investment Fiduciaries] conducted a careful study of the issues with the objective of
providing practical guidelines to the appraisal industry. The result is the following outline, which contains suggested elements of a complete market analysis for
appraisals of investment-grade real estate. However, the level of detail and analysis in each appraisal is dictated by the nature of the assignment, time and expense constraints, and other specific considerations of the particular assignment.*

*This document is the first attempt at consolidating the thoughts of the mem-
bers of NCREIF on this issue. Because of the dynamic nature of the subject matter, the market analysis guidelines will likely be updated from time to time. We
encourage industry input on this subject. Please contact any of the NCREIF committee members or the committee cochairs.*

Market Area Delineation

1. Define and describe the metropolitan area.
   a. Identify the economic base industries of the metropolitan area, with
      emphasis on activities that influence the quantity, quality (risk), and
      duration of the specific space market.
   b. Identify possible and expected changes in the economic base.

---

1. Courtesy of the National Council of Real Estate Investment Fiduciaries, D. Richard Wincott, MAI, and
   Glenn R. Mueller, PhD.

2. Delineate market study area(s). The market study area encompasses the competitive demand for and supply of space that is similar to the subject property. It is the subject's competitive market in terms of geographical area, product type, and price.

3. Demarcate the boundaries of the market on a market area map.

4. Explain reasons for selecting the boundaries of the market area.

Demand Analysis

The purpose of demand analysis is to show the development of historical relationships as a basis for forecasting future demand. However, merely extending the historic trend beyond the present to project future demand is not acceptable. It is necessary to identify changes in relationships and patterns that may affect trends and influence expectations and to explain the assumptions that underlie these projected changes and their implications.

The submarket area strength conclusion in the population, demographic, and economic analysis serves as a background to and frame of reference for the submarket demand analysis. Link these conclusions to the metropolitan economic base analysis and expected changes.

The suggested procedure for demand analysis is as follows:

1. Determine the major market demand factors (e.g., employment, population, shipping, trade, income) that affect the specific property type.

2. Define the unit of demand for the property type (e.g., households, retail sales, office employment, per capita occupancies for the property type).

3. Present historic and projected demand data for the metropolitan area and the specified market study area. It is important to use a reliable service for population, employment, and other demographic projections.

4. Relate the effect of total market demand on submarket demand (i.e., historic and prospective market share analysis for each submarket).

5. Relate the effects of U.S. macroeconomic demand factors to local market demand to the extent that the local market is influenced by macroeconomic factors.

   a. GDP growth projections
   b. U.S. consumption trends
   c. Employment trends
   d. Federal trade policies
   e. Currency fluctuations
   f. Interstate commerce policies
   g. Changing technologies
   h. Cost of capital
   i. Capacity utilization levels
   j. Political influences
   k. Other

APPENDIX

Demand Analysis by Property Type

Office Demand Analysis

1. Determine appropriate demand factors.
   a. Office-using employment such as FIRE, service, professional, technical, and sales. If aggregating employment data according to Standard Industrial Classification (SIC) codes, four-digit codes provide the appropriate level of specificity for office-using industries.
2. Develop use ratio (i.e., percent of total employment that is office-using).
3. Calculate total office employment demand.
4. Present historical use ratios and forecast changes in future use ratios.
5. Present historical demand and forecast changes in future demand.
   a. Marginal demand (i.e., increase over base)
   b. Migrational demand (i.e., intra-urban or office class migration)
6. Develop demand factor ratio (i.e., space per employee).
7. Calculate average annual demand for all office space, both owner-occupied and multitenant.
8. Calculate total forecast demand.

Industrial Demand Analysis

The procedure used for industrial demand analysis is the same as for office demand analysis. However, in addition to employment in manufacturing, wholesale, retail, transportation, communications, and public utilities (two- to four-digit SIC codes), demand factors may also include U.S. and regional economic growth that affects local demand; population growth; overall employment growth; household growth; retail sales (applicable in market analysis for retail storage and wholesale distribution properties); and cargo flows by transport type (e.g., truck, rail, water, air) and product type (e.g., high or low bulk). Some of these factors may also be used in office demand analysis.

Multifamily Residential Demand Analysis

1. Determine appropriate demand factors.
   a. Demographics by income, age, and family size
   b. Employment (e.g., labor force trends, future growth by industry segments)
   c. Population growth/decline
   d. Household formation and household size forecasts
   e. Migration trends
2. Perform internal mobility analysis (i.e., demand for units due to change in households, upgrades, demolition). Segment rental markets and owner markets according to percent of demand.

3. Conduct rent vs. buy analysis (i.e., calculate percent of population that can afford to buy units at the price they can afford to buy) to segregate effective demand from total demand.

4. Develop ability-to-pay model (from housing cost to finance payment [debt service] to debt service, to loan amount [loan-to-value ratio], to housing price, to required income, to submarket by income groups).

5. Present total demand.

6. Apply appropriate demand factor (e.g., units per population).

7. Profile appropriate tenants (e.g., single professionals, families, retirees).

8. Calculate average annual demand.

9. Forecast future demand.

Retail Demand Analysis

1. Determine appropriate demand factors.
   a. Population/employment growth.
   b. Households and household size breakdown.
   c. Average household income and disposable income.
   d. Trade area disposable income.

2. Project level of retail sales based on trends in population, household patterns, personal income, consumer purchasing habits, historical retail sales, and shopping center sales.

3. Calculate disposable income factor (i.e., money remaining after taxes).

4. Present total disposable income, both historical and forecast.

5. Apply retail sales factor (i.e., retail sales as a percent of disposable income).

6. Calculate total retail sales.

7. Apply shopping center sales factor (i.e., general merchandise, apparel, home furnishings, and other merchandise normally sold in malls [GAFO] or department store-type merchandise [DSTM]).

8. Calculate total shopping center sales.

9. Calculate total shopping center sales per household.

10. Calculate total shopping center sales for trade area.

11. Calculate sales per square foot, broken down by retail store type.

Supply Analysis

Supply analysis begins with a review of the historical relationships between demand growth and supply growth. It includes defining the generally accepted attributes for specific building types (e.g., Class A, B, and C office; regional vs. neighborhood retail), relating these to the specific tenant profile and the current market capacity to satisfy that specific demand. The total space inventory is described by both quantity and quality. It is described by location, quality (e.g., premier regional mall, Class A office building, luxury multifamily), type (e.g., owner-occupied, rental), size, age, and other classifications related to property type (e.g., shopping center classification, unit types for multifamily).

The items covered in supply analysis include existing inventory (e.g., total square feet, number of properties, building area); existing available space; historical construction trends (e.g., total square feet, number of properties, average building area); inventory under construction, expansion, or revision; cost-feasible rent level necessary for new construction; and inventory proposed and the probability of completion.

The suggested procedure for supply analysis is as follows.

1. Present an inventory of competitive supply in the market and submarket.
2. Analyze the salient characteristics of this supply.
3. Show historic supply trends in the market and submarket.
4. Explain the reasons for past supply growth (as a reaction to increased demand, overbuilding without regard for demand, and special circumstances).
5. Define where the market is in the current supply cycle.
6. Identify the factors that will affect new supply in the future as a basis for forecasting future supply (i.e., relationships and patterns as they relate to the trends identified in the demand analysis). Link conclusions to the metropolitan economic base analysis.
7. Forecast near-term supply in square feet or units per year, using construction starts, permitted starts, planned starts, and dates of completion.
8. Forecast long-term supply, using potential future inventory based on a balanced market demand-supply model. Correlate with land availability in the subject area. Link analysis to the metropolitan analysis with respect to direction and potential growth.
9. Review specific constraints to future supply, such as financing availability, regulatory climate, and infrastructure capacity.
10. Relate the effect of metromarket on submarket supply. Relate statistics to historical and present market conditions.

Absorption Analysis

The suggested procedure for absorption analysis is as follows:

1. Describe historical absorption patterns (e.g., amount of space absorbed, rate of absorption) in the macromarket and the submarket. Relate the effect of macromarket demand on submarket demand and the components of demand and prevailing market conditions. This may be accomplished by a fair-share analysis and penetration analysis by submarket. Historic demand and supply statistics should correlate to historic ab-

sorption patterns. If not, reconcile and explain differences.

2. Use forecast demand trends to relate to market conditions (e.g., evidence of potential national, regional, or local changes that would alter demand). Make adjustments for unique considerations in the submarket.
   a. Present historic total demand factor.
   b. Calculate historic growth rate.
   c. Forecast future growth rate.
   d. Calculate property-type use ratio.
   e. Apply property-type demand factor.
   f. Calculate annual space demand.
   g. Calculate total forecast space demand.
   h. Calculate future annual forecast demand.

3. Analyze available space and, to the extent possible, "hidden" space (e.g., sublet space) and calculate amount of time needed to absorb all available space and space under construction (known as "years to absorb"). Distinguish between owner-occupied and multitenant space.
   a. Present total inventory.
   b. Calculate availability rate.
   c. Present amount of occupied space.
   d. Calculate net absorption per year. Net absorption is defined as the change in total occupied square feet from period to period.

4. Analyze cost-feasible rent levels for the type and class of property being analyzed and how they relate to current and historical rental rates. This provides a benchmark similar to the supply aspect of the space analysis. Correlation of cost-feasible rental rates to market rental rates can provide inference to future absorption rates and probable real rental rate increases in the future.

Vacancy Analysis

The suggested procedure for vacancy analysis is as follows:

1. Present historical, current, and forecast vacancy and occupancy trends. Relate to market conditions. Link absorption estimates to occupancy levels.

2. Develop an equation from historic supply, demand, and absorption statistics to explain historic vacancy rates and discuss changes that would modify the equation.

3. Use the equation and the forecast inputs from the supply, demand, and absorption work to forecast future vacancy rates.

It is important to correlate assumptions of structural or stabilized vacancy rates with the assumptions in the discounted cash flow analysis (e.g., tenant attrition rate, down time between leases, credit loss).

Market Rental Rate Analysis

The suggested procedure for rental rate analysis is as follows:

1. Describe typical lease terms, including free rent and other concessions. Effective rent is a key consideration. For example, flat face rental rates accompanied by a reduction in rental concessions equate to an increase in effective rental rates.
2. Present historic rental rate trends. Relate to absorption and vacancy trends and market conditions.
3. Differentiate rental rates by building quality class (e.g., Class A vs. Class B office; warehouse vs. R&D [research and development] space; regional mall vs. community retail space; high-rise vs. garden apartments). Address rental rate differentials resulting from building age.

It is important to link rental rate growth assumptions to demand indicators in the attempt to ascertain the users' ability to pay (e.g., occupancy cost as a percent of retail sales in shopping centers, household income growth and the percent applicable to housing for multifamily properties, increases in service revenues for office tenants). Supply constraints may not be the sole determinant of upward movement in rental rates. Rental rate changes can be correlated to inflation and expense growth assumptions to make clear the real rental rate growth assumptions.

INDEX

—⇒‣0‣⇐—

This index uses two types of cross-references. *See* references refer the reader from one term to another term—often the more common usage—under which page numbers are listed. *See also* references refer the reader from one term, under which page numbers are listed, to a second, related term, under which more information can be found.

wages. *See* income
warranty deeds, 42
wind direction, 64
working women
    and housing preferences, 301

yield capitalization models, 102

Zeckendorf, William
    and "Hawaiian technique," 41

zones of conflux, 61
zoning, 46-47
    and highest and best use, 342
    policies in Texas, 43-44
    and shopping centers, 203, 206, 248
    and vacant land, 357, 359
    See also government regulations; legal
      constraints